BRITTLE WITH RELICS

BRITTLE
WITH
RELICS
A HISTORY
OF WALES
1962–1997
RICHARD
KING

faber

First published in 2022
by Faber & Faber Limited
Bloomsbury House
74–77 Great Russell Street
London WC1B 3DA

Typeset by Donald Sommerville
Printed and bound by CPI Group (UK) Ltd, Croydon, CR0 4YY

A CIP record for this book
is available from the British Library

ISBN 978-0-571-29564-7

2 4 6 8 10 9 7 5 3

Dedicated to Sarah Chilvers and Elijah Aneurin King

There is no present in Wales,
And no future;
There is only the past,
Brittle with relics

From 'Welsh Landscape', R. S. Thomas

CYNNWYS / CONTENTS

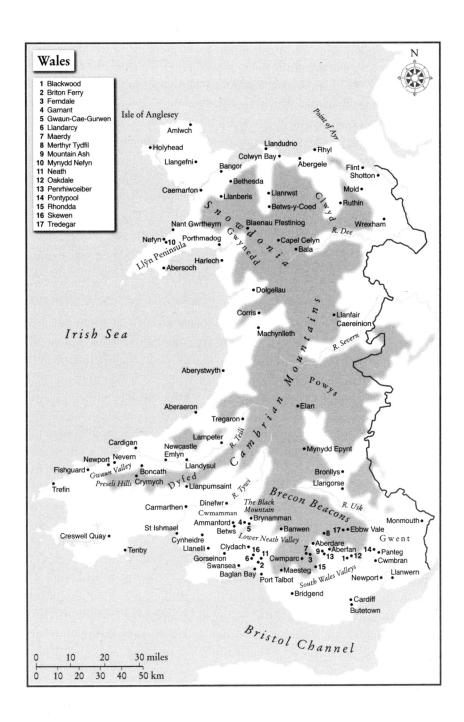

Wales

1 Blackwood
2 Briton Ferry
3 Ferndale
4 Garnant
5 Gwaun-Cae-Gurwen
6 Llandarcy
7 Maerdy
8 Merthyr Tydfil
9 Mountain Ash
10 Mynydd Nefyn
11 Neath
12 Oakdale
13 Penrhiwceiber
14 Pontypool
15 Rhondda
16 Skewen
17 Tredegar

N

Isle of Anglesey

Amlwch

Holyhead

Llandudno

Rhyl

Point of Ayr

Colwyn Bay

Abergele

Llangefni

Bangor

Flint

Shotton

Bethesda

Mold

Caernarfon

Llanberis

Llanrwst

Ruthin

Betws-y-Coed

Clwyd

Nant Gwrtheyrn

Blaenau Ffestiniog

Wrexham

R. Dee

Snowdonia

Nefyn •10 Porthmadog

Capel Celyn

Bala

Llŷn Peninsula

Harlech

Abersoch

Gwynedd

Dolgellau

Irish Sea

Corris

Llanfair Caereinion

Machynlleth

R. Severn

Cambrian Mountains

Aberystwyth

Powys

Aberaeron

Elan

Tregaron

Lampeter

Cardigan

Newcastle Emlyn

Mynydd Epynt

Newport Nevern

Fishguard

Gwaun Valley

Boncath

Llandysul

R. Teifi

Preseli Hills Crymych

Llanpumsaint

Bronllys

Llangorse

Dyfed

Trefin

R. Tywi

Brecon Beacons

R. Usk

Carmarthen

Dinefwr

The Black Mountain

Cwmamman

Monmouth

Creswell Quay

Ammanford •4 • Brynamman

Betws •5 • Banwen

•8 17 • Ebbw Vale

St Ishmael

Lower Neath Valley

Gwent

Cynheidre

Aberdare

Llanelli

Clydach •16

•9 • Aberfan 14 • Panteg

Tenby

Gorseinon

6 •11

7 • Cwmbran

Swansea• •2

13 •1 •12

Baglan Bay

Cwmparc •3

Maesteg •15

Llanwern

Port Talbot

South Wales Valleys

Newport

Bridgend

Cardiff

Butetown

Bristol Channel

0   10   20   30 miles

0   10   20   30   40   50 km

There are many words in Cymraeg, the Welsh language, that have more than one possible translation or that have no directly equivalent meaning in English, making accurate translation difficult. The translations in this book are, therefore, offered only as a guide to the casual reader.

LLEISIAU / VOICES

Sir Mansel Aylward, medical student at Aberfan, Chair of Public Health Wales

Iwan Bala, artist

Nici Beech, concert promoter, Welsh-language activist, former member of Cymdeithas yr Iaith Gymraeg

Hanif Bhamjee, lawyer, former chair of Anti-Apartheid Wales

Kirsti Bohata, Professor at the Centre for Research into the English Literature and Language of Wales, Swansea University

Dewi 'Mav' Bowen, antiquarian and folklorist

James Dean Bradfield, member of Manic Street Preachers

Marilyn Brown, Aberfan resident

Jane Bryant, former member of staff at the Centre for Alternative Technology, Machynlleth

Rosemary Butler, former Labour Member of the Assembly (now Senedd) for Newport West

Cian Ciarán, member of Super Furry Animals, son of **Carl Iwan Clowes**

Carl Iwan Clowes, founder of Nant Gwrtheyrn (National Welsh Language and Heritage Centre), GP, former member of Cymdeithas yr Iaith Gymraeg, former chair of Public Health Wales, father of **Cian Ciarán**

Ian Courtney, former member of staff, Welsh Development Agency, former government advisor

Bob Croydon, former property consultant

Phil Cullen, former NUM chairman at Cynheidre Colliery Lodge

Cynog Dafis, Welsh-language activist, former Plaid Cymru and Green Member of Parliament for Ceredigion, former chair Cymdeithas yr Iaith Gymraeg

Jane Davidson, former Minister for Environment, Sustainability and Housing, former Labour Member of the Assembly (now Senedd) for Pontypridd

Andrew Davies, former Minister for Economic Development, former Labour Member of the Assembly (now Senedd) for Swansea West

Philippa Davies, author and poet

Ron Davies, former Secretary of State for Wales, former Labour Member of Parliament for Caerphilly, former Member of the Assembly (now Senedd) for Caerphilly

Nigel Dudley, environmentalist, former member of staff at the Centre for Alternative Technology, Machynlleth

Steve Eaves, singer, songwriter, academic, former member of Cymdeithas yr Iaith Gymraeg

David R. Edwards (1964–2021), poet, author, founder of Datblygu

Jeff Edwards, schoolchild, Aberfan

Menna Elfyn, poet, Welsh-language activist, former member of Cymdeithas yr Iaith Gymraeg

Arfon Evans, former NUM Chairman, Maerdy Colliery Lodge

Ffred Ffransis, Welsh-language activist, former chair of Cymdeithas yr Iaith Gymraeg, husband of **Meinir Ffransis**

Meinir Ffransis, Welsh-language activist, former member of Cymdeithas yr Iaith Gymraeg, daughter of Gwynfor Evans, wife of **Ffred Ffransis**

Richard Frame, local historian, author, mental health campaigner

Bob Griffiths, member of the Mines Rescue Service, Aberfan

Gethin ap Gruffydd, Welsh-language activist, former member of Free Wales Army and Mudiad Amddiffyn Cymru (Movement for the Defence of Wales)

Len Haggett, fireman and rescuer, Aberfan

Peter Hain, Lord Hain, former Secretary of State for Wales, former Labour Member of Parliament for Neath

Nick Hand, letterpress printer, former member of staff at the Centre for Alternative Technology, Machynlleth

Edwina Hart, former Minister for Economic Development, former Labour Member of the Assembly (now Senedd) for Swansea

Calvin Hodgkinson, schoolchild, Aberfan

Kim Howells, former Labour Member of Parliament for Pontypridd

David Hurn, photographer, member of Magnum, founder of the School of Documentary Photography, Newport

Meri Huws, Welsh-language activist, president of National Library of Wales, former chair of Cymdeithas yr Iaith Gymraeg

Rhys Ifans, actor, Welsh-language activist, former member of Cymdeithas yr Iaith Gymraeg

Dafydd Iwan, folk singer, Welsh-language activist, former president of Plaid Cymru, former chair of Cymdeithas yr Iaith Gymraeg

Mari James, academic, former vice-chair of Yes for Wales

Siân James, community activist during the 1984–85 Miners' Strike, former Labour Member of Parliament for Swansea East

John Barnard Jenkins, 1933–2020, Welsh nationalist, leader of Mudiad Amddiffyn Cymru (Movement for the Defence of Wales)

Siôn Jobbins, Welsh-language activist, former chair of Yes Cymru

Adrian Jones, town planner

Patrick Jones, poet, playwright, lyricist

Tecwyn Vaughan Jones, former member of Cymdeithas yr Iaith Gymraeg, academic and historian

Neil Kinnock, Lord Kinnock, Leader of the Labour Party, Leader of the Opposition 1983–92

Ben Lake, Plaid Cymru Member of Parliament for Ceredigion

Gaynor Legall, Labour councillor, Cardiff City Council

Sue Lent, Labour councillor, Cardiff City Council

Alun Llwyd, founder of Ankst records, PYST Distribution and AM Platform, former manager of Gorky's Zygotic Mynci and Super Furry Animals, former chair of Cymdeithas yr Iaith Gymraeg

Tom Marston, community activist during the 1984–85 Miners' Strike

Mary Millington, peace campaigner and social activist

Eluned Morgan, Baroness Morgan of Ely, Labour Member of the Senedd for International Relations and the Welsh Language

Kevin Morgan, academic, former chair of Yes for Wales

Pat Morgan, member of Datblygu

Rhys Mwyn, archaeologist, broadcaster, author, founder of Anhrefn

Branwen Niclas, Welsh-language activist, former chair of Cymdeithas yr Iaith Gymraeg

Julian Orbach, archaeologist, co-founder of Brithdir Mawr eco-community

Gorwel Owen, musician, record producer

Richard Parfitt, author, academic, member of 60 Ft. Dolls

Max Perkins, former Political Editor of HTV Wales

Ann Pettitt, smallholder, founder of Women for Life on Earth

Christine Powell, trade unionist, community activist during 1984–85 Miners' Strike

Adam Price, Leader of Plaid Cymru 2018–present, Member of the Senedd for Carmarthen East and Dinefwr, former Member of Parliament for Carmarthen East and Dinefwr

Helen Prosser, Welsh-language activist, former chair of Cymdeithas yr Iaith Gymraeg

Guto Pryce, member of Super Furry Animals

Dewi Prysor (Dewi Prysor Williams), stonemason, poet, author, former Welsh-language activist

Gruff Rhys, singer-songwriter, former member of Ffa Coffi Pawb, member of Super Furry Animals

Mark Roberts, member of Y Cyrff

Gwenno Saunders, musician, composer

Michael Sheen, actor, social activist and campaigner

Davinder Singh, writer and broadcaster

Ken Smith, community activist during the 1984–85 Miners' Strike

Lesley Smith, community activist during the 1984–85 Miners' Strike

Huw Stephens, DJ and broadcaster, son of **Ruth Stephens**

Ruth Stephens, Welsh-language activist, wife of Meic Stephens

Terry Stevens, academic, international tourism consultant to governments and development agencies

Hettie Taylor, teacher, Aberfan

Alan Thomas, schoolchild, Aberfan

Bernard Thomas, schoolchild, Aberfan

Karen Thomas, schoolchild, Aberfan

Karmen Thomas, academic, trade unionist, activist during the 1984–85 Miners' Strike, founder of Women for Life on Earth

Ned Thomas, publisher, academic, author, Welsh-language activist, former member of Cymdeithas yr Iaith Gymraeg, editor of *Planet: The Welsh Internationalist*

Angharad Tomos, author and Welsh-language activist, former chair of Cymdeithas yr Iaith Gymraeg

Rachel Trezise, author, playwright

Bedwyr Williams, artist

Phil White, NUM Compensation and Welfare Secretary, St John's, Maesteg, Colliery Lodge

Charlotte Williams, writer and academic

Rowan Williams, Welsh Anglican bishop, theologian and poet, 104th Archbishop of Canterbury

Mary Winter, trade unionist, community activist during the 1984–85 Miners' Strike

Tony Winter, community activist during the 1984–85 Miners' Strike

Nicky Wire, member of Manic Street Preachers

Leanne Wood, former Leader of Plaid Cymru, former Member of the Senedd for Rhondda

David Wrench, record producer and musician

CYFLWYNIAD / INTRODUCTION

In the West Wales Chapel tradition Sul y Blodau, 'flowering Sunday', falls on the day more popularly known as Palm Sunday and is the occasion relatives dedicate to tidying the ground and foliage around the gravestones of the departed, before supplying the monuments with fresh flowers. As Easter is a movable feast and Palm Sunday is celebrated a week before Easter Day, Sul y Blodau may take place on any date in spring between the sharp winds of March and the lengthening daylight of mid-April. Although named as a Sunday, this is an activity that more usually takes place on a Saturday.

The journey I make to carry out duties on Sul y Blodau takes me from my home in Powys, in the middle of mid-Wales, to the lower reaches of Y Mynydd Du, the Black Mountain, a series of peaks in Carmarthenshire typical of the Welsh hinterland. It then leads me to the churchyard of Hen Fethel, the cemetery where the extended family on my mother's side are buried, which stands alone on a hillside above the village of Garnant in the Amman Valley.

Hen Fethel consists of a graveyard, a long-shuttered chapel or tŷ cwrdd (a 'meeting house'), and a derelict stables. A sign on the front of the chapel wall bears an inscription notable for being written in English rather than in the Welsh language, Cymraeg: 'This Bethel was built in 1773.' Looking up towards Y Mynydd Du and its unencumbered expanses free of telegraph poles or any other signifier of modern activity, it is possible to imagine the life of the chapel in previous centuries. Hen Fethel is the oldest chapel in the Amman Valley and was a place of worship for the branch of Welsh Nonconformity that

1

took hold with great vigour during the late eighteenth century in both rural and urban areas of the country. Where country families would have previously congregated in farmhouses, this isolated meeting house provided a venue for communal services. The atmosphere of the rural graveyard and its now abandoned buildings bestows a numinous charge familiar to all who regularly visit. As is the case for many, if not all, graveyards, there is an eeriness to the place. Local folk tales speak of a top-hatted figure who stands watch at the chapel gate; of spirits that process up and down the narrow, winding country road that leads to the churchyard; of ghosts that have not yet been laid to rest; and of organ music being played in the chapel at night, music that is audible despite the fact the chapel has never contained such an instrument.

To imagine the view downwards from Hen Fethel towards Garnant a century ago is more demanding. During these years, when the Amman Valley lay at the centre of the anthracite mining industry, its built environment included the chimney stacks and winding towers of collieries, their pitheads and washeries, which stood adjacent to fields of livestock grazing in the shadows of the precarious spoil tips that were raised in piles and took the form of new, black tumuli in the landscape. The geology of the valley was rich in a coal prized for its lack of impurities, high carbon content and energy density, so collieries were established accordingly along the Amman Valley in the 1870s. These characteristics ensured anthracite, the black diamond, was the most valued form of coal and led the industrial communities at the western edge of the South Wales coalfield to boast, with justification, that they mined the finest coal in the world.

Garnant, Pontamman, Gwaun-Cae-Gurwen, Brynamman and Rhosamman, the villages of the Amman Valley that grew next to one another along the anthracite seam, all contained a substantial number of collieries. According to the 1921 Census, the immediate area surrounding Garnant, the village in which my family lived, contained a workforce sufficient for twenty mines. The Amman river, which flows from its source among the cold peaks of Y Mynydd Du, was blackened by coal dust as its water ran through the anthracite villages towards the town of Ammanford. In the foothills above the villages remnants of open pits are still visible. There are holes in the fields that initially suggest badger setts or rabbit warrens but are too substantial for animals. On closer inspection they are revealed to be the grassed-over sites of former ventilation shafts, or the soft edges of what were once tunnel entrances.

Many small mining communities suffered the tragedy of industrial disasters. In Garnant, in 1884, seven men and three fourteen-year-old boys fell to their deaths in the main local pit known as Pwll Perkins. The winch rope holding the cage that transported the miners during their descent to the coalface snapped. The cage and its ten occupants were sent plummeting seventy metres to the bottom of the mine shaft; the families of the men and children were left without any compensation.

In each of the anthracite mining villages the neat terraces built to house the labour force remain. Other buildings also provide an echo of the ethos of these communities in their industrial heyday. Though barely a mile apart, every village is represented by a rugby club and is home to a significant number of chapels and churches. But the buildings most laden with history are the now largely deserted miners' institutes and workmen's halls. These proud spaces were the physical manifestation of the urge for communal self-improvement and the egalitarian spirit of working towards the shared purpose of better conditions and livelihoods characteristic of the mining industry. This impetus thrived until the middle of the twentieth century and endured still, in the decades that followed.

Such places were also a locus of an altruism that ensured families affected by industrial accidents would not be abandoned without support and resources. In addition the halls and institutes provided every member of the community with access to a library and, through initiatives such as the Workers' Educational Association, founded in 1903, an opportunity to learn, study and discuss. Although easily romanticised, the epoch of the miners' institutes achieved an accumulation of knowledge and sustained a mutual philanthropy that was unparalleled in Wales during the twentieth century. This shared educational wealth produced communities of autodidacts who practised an avowed collectivism. It was a social contract that prospered equally below ground, in the frequently challenging conditions of the coalface, and in daily life above the surface.

In Garnant, the Workmen's Hall and Institute remains one of the most prominent buildings in the village. Long encased in barriers and perpetually For Sale, it once served as a meeting room; a venue with the capacity for an audience of almost a thousand; a cinema and a community hall. This last function was reflected in its nickname: Hall y Cwm, the valley hall.

The hall was opened in 1927, the year following the General Strike, at a ceremony held on 19 February. My grandfather, himself a miner, was among the audience. Until its closure almost fifty years later in 1972 the hall staged operas, operettas and musicals and hosted meetings of societies and organisations including the Young Farmers' Club, the Urdd, the Cwmamman Silver Band, the local branch of the Red Cross Society, the Association for the Blind, the Old Age Pensioners' Society, Amman United Football Club, the Carnival Committee, the Cwmamman Peace Committee, numerous political parties, trade unions and various Chapel denominations. In 1960 my parents spent a terrified hour and a half there watching the newly released *Psycho*.

Almost four decades after its closure, a period in which the building struggled to find a purpose, a significant cannabis harvest was discovered during a police raid in 2009; a secular temple to community culture and social energy had been secretly redeveloped for the black economy.

During the hour or so I spend at the Hen Fethel cemetery each year there is a steady stream of people, all going about the same business of cutting back grass and ivy, emptying flower-holders of their remnants and replacing them with new blooms. The procession of visitors to and from the tap in the corner of the churchyard is distinguished by the stoic looks on their faces, as the winds suddenly swell around this lower mountainside and ice-cold water flows over their hands from the newly watered vases and containers. It is rare not to be engaged by strangers in warm, if occasionally vague, conversations regarding ancestry, local connections and historical neighbourly relations.

Nearly all of the activity at Hen Fethel is conducted in Cymraeg. The same was true of the conversations my grandparents had with their friends and neighbours while participating in events held at Hall y Cwm and of the funeral of my grandmother. This was the first occasion when I visited Hen Fethel. My mother was one of only a scant handful of women present at the graveside as Chapel tradition meant that men alone normally attended the burial. It was a ceremony without any order of service or sense of formal structure, beginning at the house of my great aunt. My grandmother's coffin was placed in the dining room as the parlour filled with mourners and a crowd spilled from the doorway down into the street. A minister from the Nonconformist tradition proclaimed and declaimed for twenty minutes in a rich and vivid Cymraeg. The majority of what he said was lost to my very basic Welsh. The language was one I was never taught, as it was considered irrelevant in the South Wales of my childhood. Newport, Gwent, the town in which I was born and brought up, was one in which a certain section of the population seemed incapable of accepting it was located in Wales. Other than in my home, the only Cymraeg I heard spoken in Newport was by a neighbour, who commuted for an hour every day to attend the nearest Welsh-speaking school twenty miles away.

———

During the final four decades of the twentieth century Wales witnessed the simultaneous effects of deindustrialisation and a struggle for its language and identity. The country's voice fought to be heard outside its frequently tempestuous borders and was argued over within them, as the people of Wales underwent some of the nation's most traumatic and volatile episodes: the disaster at Aberfan; the inundation of Capel Celyn in the Tryweryn valley to create a reservoir for Liverpool; the rise of the Welsh-language movement and its policy of direct action; the Miners' Strike and its aftermath; and the vote in favour of partial but significant devolution.

This history of Wales begins in 1962, with a radio speech delivered as a warning that Cymraeg, and the identity and way of life it represented, faced extinction. Titled 'Tynged yr Iaith' ('The Fate of the Language'), the speech was given in the form of a radio broadcast by its author, Saunders Lewis, the former leader of Plaid Cymru. The impact and influence of the speech have long been debated; what is certain is that Lewis' polemic contributed to a renewed sense of purpose among those resistant to the language's increasing marginalisation.

Over the subsequent three decades the case for Cymraeg would be campaigned and argued for with an applied fervour. In 1990 Welsh became a compulsory subject for all pupils in state schools in Wales up to the age of fourteen. Three years later the Westminster government passed a Welsh Language Act, which formally recognised that 'in the course of public business and the administration of justice, so far as is reasonably practicable, the Welsh and English languages are to be treated on the basis of equality'.

As the decline in the language was gradually halted, the industrial centre of South Wales – the area in which over half of the country's population lived and worked and where the Welsh language was heard less frequently than English – entered into a moderate then accelerated decline of its own. The heavy industries of steel, oil and mining were all significant employers in the region; the centre of the last of these was the South Wales Coalfield, home to the historic communitarian radicalism fathered by the Miners' Federation and its welfare institutes and libraries. The libraries, the Manic Street Preachers would sing, 'gave us power'. In the year of Saunders Lewis' radio lecture, a job in heavy industry offered above-average terms and wages in a form of employment that had strong links with the area in which the work was based. As well as payment in exchange for labour, the work provided social capital. In these close-knit communities, employment was ingrained with identity, an attribute that grew in significance during the increasing secularisation of Wales that had gained momentum by the 1960s.

Wales consequently experienced a period lasting almost forty years in which two distinct energies animated the country. The first derived from an often youthful, determined movement dedicated to the survival and revival of Cymraeg; the second energy came out of a crisis, one not limited in this period to Wales nor any of its regions, but one the country, due to its reliance on heavy and light industry, experienced acutely: an initially gradual then substantial reduction in remunerative long-term employment opportunities.

The country's political and legislative authority, such as it was, was held in the Labour stronghold of the South, a part of Wales that often considered itself to be as British as it was Welsh. Here, in the offices of MPs and powerful, usually male-dominated council chambers, concerns for the fate of the language and the ideas of Welsh independence proposed by Plaid Cymru in the west and north-west of the country were marginal issues. Such concerns were at best dismissed as student politics. For much of this period, in the eyes of South Wales Labourism, a self-governing Wales was a cause proposed by dangerous nationalists, or 'Nats'. The country was accordingly often forced to navigate its way through a period of great change in a state of internal contradiction and frequent animosity.

This history concludes with the vote for Welsh devolution in September 1997, held five months after the Labour Party had been returned to government in the UK for the first time in eighteen years. The vote was carried by a majority of 6,721, or 50.3 per cent of the vote, among the narrowest of margins in British electoral history. The country nevertheless voted for the limited form of self-determination represented by the creation of a National Assembly for Wales.

———

In order that the participants in this history are heard on their own terms and by their own authority, this book is an oral history, a form that favours the grain of the voice and the grain of the Welsh voice in particular. The voices in this book bear witness to the struggle Wales endured during the period and frequently belong to people determined to rectify the damage left in that struggle's wake.

A great number of these voices will be familiar to the reader; others may not be. Many of those present are speaking in their second language. And there are voices missing from this history that belong to people now departed, or to people who, despite their willingness to share them, no longer trust in the accuracy or function of their memories. The history of the relationship between Cymru and Cymraeg, between Wales and its language, has most usually been told in the mother tongue. To present the history of the Welsh language during the period covered in this book in English is an act of faith: it is one not entered into lightly.

This is a history of a nation determined to survive during crisis, while maintaining the enduring hope that Wales will one day thrive on its own terms.

ONE

YR IAITH GYMRAEG / THE WELSH LANGUAGE

Voices

Iwan Bala

Carl Iwan Clowes

Cynog Dafis

Philippa Davies

Ffred Ffransis

David Hurn

Meri Huws

Dafydd Iwan

Siôn Jobbins

Tecwyn Vaughan Jones

Ruth Stephens

Ned Thomas

Rowan Williams

———

On 8 September 1936, the author, playwright and university lecturer Saunders Lewis set fire to a partially built RAF base at Penyberth farmhouse near Pwllheli, Gwynedd, in north-west Wales. Lewis was joined in the action by two accomplices, the Reverend Lewis Valentine, a Baptist minister, and a schoolteacher and writer, D. J. Williams. Once the premises had been set ablaze, the three men reported themselves to the local police station and handed the duty officer a letter in which they claimed responsibility for the arson attack. The base was to serve a newly constructed bombing school, RAF Penrhos. The Air Ministry's plans had met with considerable opposition on anti-militaristic, linguistic and environmental grounds from Plaid Cymru, the National Party of Wales, which Saunders Lewis had founded and led from 1926 to 1939.

At the trial of Lewis, Valentine and Williams the jury could not agree a verdict; a subsequent retrial was moved from North Wales to the Old Bailey, where the three men were found guilty and

9

sentenced to nine months' imprisonment. On their release, at a rally in Caernarfon, The Three, as they became known in Welsh folklore, were given a heroes' welcome by a crowd of over fifteen thousand whose members regarded the burning of the RAF station as an act of defiance and an assertion of the relationship between Welsh identity, Cymraeg and patriotism.

Despite the three men's protest, the appropriation of rural Wales for military purposes continued. During the Second World War the War Office seized 30,000 acres of land surrounding the Epynt Mountain in mid-Wales for infantry and artillery training, which resulted in the forced displacement of the area's Welsh-speaking inhabitants.

In 1962 Saunders Lewis, by now a more marginal figure in Welsh public life, broadcast his 'Tynged yr Iaith' lecture on BBC Wales Radio. Lewis was inspired to speak publicly by the results of the census of the previous year, which showed a decrease in the number of Welsh-speakers from 36 per cent in 1931 to 26 per cent in 1961.

In his speech Lewis predicted the extinction of the Welsh language and declared that Cymraeg would wither and die unless revolutionary methods were used to defend it. Lewis reversed his earlier position that achieving self-governance should be the priority for Wales, and identified instead direct action and civil disobedience as the means by which to achieve official recognition for the language. Lewis was trenchant in his conclusions, stating: 'Success is only possible through revolutionary methods.'

David Hurn: I was born at the time of the real Depression of 1934. It was difficult to find employment and my father had gone up to London to work for London Transport as an engineer or something, I don't know. And Mum had gone up to London to see him from our home in Cardiff and I was born prematurely, in Redhill, which is near Guildford, much to their horror. And Wales is one of those countries which I think feels a little bit insecure, and therefore you sense that there's groupings in the country who really make incredible issues out of where you were born and all that sort of stuff, which is most peculiar. It's a strange country, because three sides of it are an island, almost, and then, suddenly, the other side is totally tacked on to England and the problem with Wales being tacked on to England so closely is that it's incredibly difficult to have an identity of its own, particularly now.

If you go to New Zealand, which is roughly the same population as Wales, you don't think it unusual that New Zealanders once had *Vogue New Zealand* magazine. Now, the idea of there being a Welsh *Vogue* magazine is to say the least slightly preposterous. Why? Well, one of the reasons, obviously, is that British *Vogue* and French *Vogue* and Italian *Vogue* are put on the train and they're down in Cardiff the next morning, so why try to pretend you can have a *Vogue* magazine? And it's the same with the newspapers: the *Western Mail* can never be a major paper, because when you go down to buy it in the morning, you've got the *Times* and the *Telegraph* and the *Guardian* there. I think that has always been a major problem for Wales – it's very difficult for it to have its own identity. Small countries tend to build identities on myths and fantasies; you get the whole thing to do with druids and you think, 'Hang on, what's that all about?' It's nearly all myth and fantasy, even things like the Welsh national dress, so you have that problem. One of the things that Wales has, which it can cling on to, is the language, obviously.

Ned Thomas: My maternal grandparents were farmers, originally from Porthmadog, but they moved to just outside Bangor. They were, I wouldn't say completely, monolingual Welsh. My grandfather could write a cheque in English when he needed to use one, but basically his life was lived in Welsh, even on the outskirts of Bangor. He sold milk around the houses and during the war my visits there to that part of Wales, what is Gwynedd today, were sometimes for months on end. I think in Welsh-language culture, in those days, there was a tendency to perceive English-speaking Wales as the lost lands; they had lost Welsh and become, not fully English, but were on the way there.

Ruth Stephens: I had uncles who used to go to sell their cattle over in Oswestry. They were good farmers, their cattle would fetch a good price and they must have had a bit of English just to get on with these people that they were working with over the border. They used to travel and use the English language to help them; they used it a bit.

Dafydd Iwan: My grandfather was one of the founding members of Plaid Cymru and my father and mother were what I would call natural supporters of Plaid Cymru, and I grew up with the notion of nationalism as a very natural form of patriotism, translated into politics, just as I supported the Welsh rugby team. The unfortunate connotations of nationalism only came in much later, when I heard about Nazism and so on. I grew up knowing about things like the bombing school as one of the outstanding events of the growth of Plaid Cymru. The Three, as we call them, D. J. Williams, Saunders Lewis and Lewis Valentine, were heroes, and gradually I came to know of them as men of letters more than anything and Saunders as a dramatist.

Carl Iwan Clowes: My mother was from Llanberis. I used to go and stay with Nain [Grandma] in Llanberis every year at some point, from say six, seven on, by myself, and then my parents would go down fairly regularly with me as well. I remember being with Nain and learning the language. The sounds of the language were in the family, but the language was something in my head; it was around me, but not as a spoken language. Then I would go down to Llanberis and I would learn to count to ten and then to a hundred and then the odd verse or the odd proverb.

My mother was one of seven children, only two of whom survived into adulthood; those are the kind of statistics you would barely find in the developing world today. I've done a lot of work in Lesotho in southern Africa, and I've seen maternal mortality at its height. Two out of seven children survived into adulthood, that's the backcloth, that's what made my mother feel that there had to be something better for me and made me appreciate the importance of the environment for health. For my mother's generation, a family living in the quarries in Dinorwig and Llanberis, there was that mantra even then in the 1950s when I was young: 'Education, education, education.' It was very much part of her thinking, because the last thing she wanted me to do was to do something menial, having seen the consequences of it within her own family.

Cynog Dafis: There was a sense that the Welsh language was facing a crisis. What Saunders Lewis said about the language facing its demise within a generation or two, there was that, certainly. And the other thing that was in the background was the territorial integrity of Y Fro Gymraeg [the Welsh-speaking heartlands], which was under threat, or was in the process of being eroded through what we can politely call demographic change, and more impolitely call in-migration or immigration of English families. There was quite a startling change in the composition of primary schools that you could observe in the 1960s, with increasing numbers of English-speaking children becoming pupils in those schools, and teachers and head teachers not able to cope with it. The schools were being anglicised, before our very eyes.

Meri Huws: I came from what was quite a traditional Welsh family. My father went to war in the forties, came back, went into the bank. My mother during that period was unusual, in that she went to Aberystwyth University, graduated, and became a civil servant. I was brought up in a household where, in my early years, they spoke English to each other, because that's what young people did in the 1950s, post-war, even in places like Llandysul. Dad was very definitely Chapel; he was a deacon, sat in the sêt fawr [elders' pew] all his life. My mother had been brought up in the church but was atheist by the time I came along. She worked in the Ministry of Agriculture and was perceived to be educated, well-off and, as a consequence, became quite bloody-minded as she got older.

It was a family that reflected the sixties in Wales, slowly becoming middle class. I went to a Welsh-medium primary school in Llandeilo in 1966, a school which probably had at that stage twenty pupils. We met in the local drill hall, and at a shed out the back.

Then I went through schooling in Fishguard, educated entirely through the medium of English, and then went to Aberystwyth. It was during that period in Fishguard that I became very, very aware of Welsh-language politics, because of the attitudes around me in Pembrokeshire.

Siôn Jobbins: In Pembrokeshire you still had a sense that, if you chose to speak Welsh, you would be being nasty to English people. There was also almost a Victorian hangover lingering on into the 1970s, where there was a preference, especially in the older generation, for speaking English, which almost by definition made you seem more intelligent. In that sense the Welsh language wasn't a strong language.

In Dyfed, in the 1970s, with the exception of South Pembrokeshire, you could have made every school a Welsh-medium school. It could have been done sensitively, over four or five years, and it wasn't. Part of that was still this residual cultural feeling among Welsh-speaking councillors that they didn't want to push it, that it would be an affront to make English-speaking kids of five years old learn Welsh as well.

Carl Iwan Clowes: I got a scholarship to go to a grant-aided school and I got an entrance to university. There was no history of medicine in the family. Mum said, 'Medicine, why not?' and I wasn't in a position to argue, so I drifted into medicine, and became more and more aware, as the years went by, that there was scorn, disdain, certainly a lack of understanding, about Wales and its culture and its language. And like so many people that go away, that reinforced my awareness and I thought this was something I began to feel. It made me more passionate, more of a nationalist, than I ever thought to be when I went to university. I met my wife-to-be, Dorothi, in my first year at medical school. Northern Irish in background, she came to Llanberis for the first time at eighteen and had never heard the Welsh language, didn't really understand it existed and was so taken aback by it. That probably reinforced my awareness of it as well.

I did the usual house jobs in Manchester Royal Infirmary, and then hospital in Saltwood and then an SHO, senior house officer, job in Llangwyfan Hospital, which was at the end of a generation: it was the old chest hospital for North Wales, where the quarrymen used to go with their TB and pneumoconiosis. I was at a bit of a crossroads, because I went to do post-grad; I started off at Christie Hospital in Manchester, but clearly it was in my head to return to Wales. Saturday morning in the hospital mess, my wife upstairs in the flat with a little one, one year of age, I picked up the *BMJ*: 'Single-handed dispensing medical practice at Llanaelhaearn in Llŷn'.

I was on a trajectory to hold a consultant post in this brilliant hospital, in a discipline I enjoyed, but somehow that advert won the day. Llanaelhaearn was emphatically Welsh-speaking, 90 per cent of the population were Welsh-speaking in the 1971 Census, and I was thrown in at the deep end clinically, and culturally as well. It was literally twenty-four hours a day, seven days a week, fifty-two weeks a year. There was no escape unless I arranged a locum. One of the obvious advantages of that was that I inevitably was very much involved in everything that went on in the community. I got to know everybody, I knew everybody's work, I knew everybody's family connections, and that is hugely important in medicine.

Cynog Dafis: I remember working out that 90 per cent of the children who were in the same class as I was in school in Aberaeron left Wales. Some of them came back in dribs and drabs but, by and large, that generation, and a whole series of generations of very clever, very talented and well-educated people, left Wales, because there was no concept of Wales – a familiar term – as a nation. The Welsh were a tribe, and they were highly motivated and organised as a tribe. In London, for example, they worked together and they helped each other and they promoted each other, no doubt, in all sorts of ways, but essentially, that was what it was about. That's what the philosopher J. R. Jones had in mind when he said that the Welsh were a people, not a nation, but our big mission in Plaid was nationhood of course.

Carl Iwan Clowes: I was twenty-six when I went into practice, and within two weeks the village school was threatened with closure. There was a public meeting, I'll never forget it, this coke stove in the corner, crowded, everybody as one – I could say on fire – for the cause: this school must be saved. And I was with them. I didn't want the school to close; it's still under threat, even now, but so is much of rural Wales.

The school was reprieved. It was the Welsh Office, as it was, that intervened, and said, 'Give them a break.' There was the Gittins Report of 1967, which suggested that every school with fewer than fifty pupils and three teachers should close, so Caernarvonshire, as it was then, was only implementing what was government policy. A third of the population had disappeared post-war: the parish had gone down from 1,500 to 1,000, and that had a big impact on the morale – but clearly, if you had any belief in the future of that community, something had to be done about that. Immobility was very, very high, [with] one of the highest levels of hypertension, high blood pressure, you'd probably find anywhere at that period; there were high levels of diabetes, high levels of depression – these are all related to a community in decline.

In his radio speech 'Tynged yr Iaith', Saunders Lewis referred to Brad y Llyfrau Gleision ('The Treachery of the Blue Books'), an incident named after a report submitted to a parliamentary inquiry commissioned in 1847 to assess the state of education in Wales. The report's findings were bound together in three volumes whose covers, following parliamentary convention of the day, were blue. The inquiry was conducted by three commissioners, none of them professional educationalists, who had undertaken a tour of Wales and made an examination of its education system. The terms of their investigation had been expanded, however, to include an evaluation of the 'morals and behaviour' of the Welsh people.

The report contained remarks that many in Wales considered ignorant and pejorative. The commissioners concluded that the country's people were lazy, dim-witted and immoral; of further concern to the commissioners was the emphasis placed on Cymraeg and Nonconformity, the form of religion most popular in Wales, to which the commissioners attributed the country's supposed moral failure. That such conclusions had been reached by three Anglican, non-Welsh-speaking, gentlemen amateur commissioners, who had sought the advice and expertise of prejudiced members of their own minority faith, was met with indignation and anger.

One response was the amalgamation of the Calvinistic Methodists with Wales's older Nonconformist denominations; both groups united against what was now perceived to be their mutual enemy of Anglicanism.

The development of Welsh Nationalist aspirations later in the century unified around this new, self-consciously Welsh Nonconformist identity, identified as Chapel, which revived religious education and contributed to the politics of Wales with a newfound vigour.

The influence of Chapel reached beyond the places of worship into every sphere of life. The Nonconformists' opposition to intoxicating liquor gave rise to an influential teetotal and temperance movement that resulted in the Welsh Sunday Closing Act of 1881. As democratic organisations, the chapels encouraged a sense of participatory debate and ownership from which their members were excluded in the workplace, and regularly staged eisteddfodau and other entertainments, including dramatic productions and choir concerts.

An Anglican revival in the 1910s ensured their Church was stronger in relation to Nonconformity than it had been in 1851. Yet the dominance of the Nonconformists in Wales was obvious. Chapels remained at the centre of most communal activities; Nonconformism was synonymous with Welsh identity and an unwavering source of strength for Cymraeg. The presence of Nonconformity in many communities made palpable the ancient idea of Wales as 'y werin bobl', a classless, cultured, respectable society of 'folk people'. The convergence of Cymraeg and Nonconformity also engendered the sense that those participating in this form of worship were 'parchus' (respectable) and had consequently achieved a societal position and set of values from which they would be disinclined to deviate. For later generations 'parchus' would signify a behavioural rigidity from which Wales and its language needed to be liberated. Despite the effects of the Great War on both population numbers and society's faith in religion, there were over 400,000 Chapel members in Wales during the 1920s, about a quarter of the adult population. Four decades later, at the time of Lewis' speech, attendance figures of all denominations had dramatically decreased in Wales.

Saunders Lewis, a practising Roman Catholic, maintained that the Blue Books were 'the most important nineteenth-century historical documents we possess'. In referring to them he linked the survival of the language with the fight for Welsh identity and the perpetual need to resist attitudes of condescension and arrogance.

Rowan Williams: I was brought up in one of those typical post-war Welsh-speaking families where Welsh wasn't spoken to the younger generation. We had a Welsh Bible, obviously, in the house, and a Welsh translation of *The Pilgrim's Progress*, but I don't think the family read the Welsh-language press at all or connected very much in that way. That's partly because we'd moved from Ystradgynlais to Cardiff when I was about five, and spent a few years there before going back to Swansea, and the environment we were in in Cardiff, the work and school environment, was not particularly Welsh. I think there was this feeling that Welsh was the language of the culture you were climbing away from. There was not much sense that Welsh continued to be a language being used for creative work, or intellectual work, or whatever. My grandmother went to a Welsh-language chapel on Sunday evenings in Cardiff; she went to Crwys Road, that great mecca of Presbyterian orthodoxy, but it was a grandparents' thing.

Ffred Ffransis: From the late 1960s, not that it affected everybody, there was a strong Christian element within the Welsh-language movement, which dovetailed with non-violence and with the peace movement as well. It was very much the Nonconformist element of Christianity, part of what was perceived and romanticised by liberals and by Plaid Cymru as the radical tradition in Wales, which grew out of Nonconformity and so on. And there's lots of truth to that.

Rowan Williams: It's such a cliché when people say that socialism in Wales owes more to Methodism than Marxism, and yet there is something in that. I don't think it's the whole truth, because I think you'd have to recognise there is a strong secular element in Welsh radicalism as well, but what you see is what I call the pitch being rolled for a hundred years beforehand, so that the notion of the small local discussion group, the high expectations of literacy and critical exchange, really do make the particular culture of the working men's institute, the miners' library, all these things, intelligible.

Iwan Bala: The Chapel was a hierarchical system. I was brought up in Chapel and my mother was an organist, my father was a layman deacon. In Gwyddelwern there were two chapels, the Wesleyan and the Methodist, and a Church in Wales church, with a wonderful spire that I thought was amazing – I thought it was the tallest in the world. We only went to the top chapel, the Methodist chapel; we never would go into the Wesleyan and the Wesleyans would never go into the Methodist chapel. You knew who was who by looking at them. You knew who were Church people, who was a Wesleyan and who was a Methodist. The problem with the chapels is that as the congregations diminished, they still wouldn't join. They kept maintaining these old chapels with only three or four people in them, instead of joining together.

In South Wales, in the mining communities, you look at the huge chapels and the male voice choirs that they had and the eisteddfodau that they hosted in these chapels. Chapel was also seen as a bastion against drunkenness amongst the miners. I think when chapels were very strong, they were just as strong, if not stronger, in the Valleys.

Rowan Williams: My closest friend at school was someone who came from a very Welsh-speaking, Nonconformist background, living a bit further up the Swansea Valley – we lived in the very Anglophone west side of Swansea, my friend lived in Morriston. We spent a lot of time together, so I used to go to social events in Morriston with his family quite often, which would often rotate around Tabernacle or the parish church, which had a very active Gilbert and Sullivan Society, but that was, I suppose, how in my teens I was most conscious about that, and visits back to the family in Ystradgynlais, still feeling to be part of all that. And I remember, I think it was in 1967, that quite famous pamphlet published, *Gwerth Cristionogol yr Iaith Gymraeg*, 'The Christian Value of the Welsh Language', by Pennar Davies and Gwynfor Evans and that was a statement for all the sixties' Welsh communitarian values enshrined in the language itself; the language had a real moral timbre to it.

Philippa Davies: My parents were both from quite poor backgrounds. My father had a couple of sisters, and his mother was called Nell Peg, because she'd had polio, but everybody knew her in Carmarthen as Nell Peg. She had a pronounced limp, and she was a second-hand-clothes dealer on Carmarthen Market. From the age of about three, I used to help her with the second-hand clothes and jewellery and things like that. She was quite a renowned black marketeer during the war. My grandfather's job had been playing the violin in the pubs, and he died in his early forties, so she was a widow, but she was quite a character. She knew Lloyd George; she knew Dylan Thomas; she was a really feisty woman. She lived until her late eighties, even though she was quite a heavy smoker and drinker, and she always had minks around her neck and a fag and lipstick. She was a huge role model to me, my grandmother.

And my other grandmother had what's called puerperal psychosis, which is now treatable by antibiotics and things; it's also called postpartum psychosis. She was in St David's asylum, which was called St David's Hospital but was actually an asylum, when my mother was about eight. Then they did a lobotomy, but they did the wrong side of her head, so she was there for good. My mother brought up her family, even though she didn't know where her own mother was between eight and fourteen. An awful lot of my mother's family had psychiatric problems because her dad had got this Victorian housekeeper who was terribly cruel and beat them, so they all had a lot of issues.

My mother and father met in what was called the Young People's Fellowship in the chapel, where chapels used to intermingle. My father came from Penuel Chapel and my mother came from the Upper Chapel, both in Carmarthen, and that's how they met.

They spoke equal amounts of Welsh and English, but both the chapels were all-Welsh. And my mother was a Communist. She used to get *Soviet Woman* sent over. She was friends with the chap who was the mayor of Carmarthen for quite a long time, called Ifor Morris, who was an official in the Railway Union and known across Carmarthen as Stalin. He and his wife, Mattie, and their daughter, Joan, used to go to Moscow for their holidays, which was then quite a bold thing to do. But my mother was in the Labour Party and a big activist, and my brother and I, from as young as we can remember, would spend the lead-up to elections making rosettes. My mother had heard from Jehovah's Witnesses it was always good to take children with you

– we'd be dragged around all these housing estates campaigning for Labour.

Rowan Williams: You can't really come at the role of Chapel without some sense of what it meant for the Welsh to be a subaltern people, a subaltern culture. Now, typically, colonised subaltern cultures find ways round, find ways of navigating or negotiating the system to make sure that their identity isn't swallowed up by what happens to be dominant.

In Wales, Chapel life, especially outside the cities, had been so much a focus for every kind of social activity. I can remember the last glow of that in the fifties and sixties. Back in Swansea in the sixties, a place like Tabernacl Treforys, which was another of the great cathedrals of Presbyterianism, was still providing quite a lot in the way of concerts and social evenings and drama. Wales was never feudal, and I think that is an important difference with England. It certainly helps to explain that particular pressure for mass literacy; it's not just about keeping the masses in their place, because that's not an issue. It is, I think, wanting to create a self-reliant rural community which can cope with the Prayer Book and the Bible in Welsh, which has an ethical perspective.

I think of my mother's cousin, who was a secondary school teacher in Mountain Ash, taught Latin and History, and the idea that you could have somebody teaching Latin in the Valleys, that was part of the Welsh middle-class self-image too. And there was employment. [But] when I think of Ebbw Vale in my time as the local bishop many years later, healthy, happy families wasn't the first phrase that would come to mind.

Tecwyn Vaughan Jones: The Sunday School trip in the early sixties was one of the few opportunities that kids that I knew had of leaving the community and visiting somewhere else, without having to walk to surrounding villages. They would have a trip on the train to places like Rhyl and Llandudno; the women would prepare all the food. All the food was put on the train, this one train for everybody, going from Blaenau Ffestiniog to the coast, and then we'd eat in the vestry at a sister chapel up in Llandudno. We had a fantastic time. This was so important to us because you didn't have to pay for it. It was free, the chapel paid for all this.

I didn't think of it then. I thought that was the way things were done; it's only when I lived away that I thought, 'Goodness me, that was the case,' and it made me so much prouder of where I come from and my roots in that community.

We were Chapel-goers, three times a day in the 1960s. It was becoming less and less popular. Most of the people that I was at school with went to Chapel and went to Sunday School, and I remember being asked in Cardiff, 'Wasn't it a big burden for you to go to church and Chapel and being gay in a community like that?' and I thought, 'I never, ever thought of that.'

When I was in school, we were encouraged to go to adult classes, which I did from about the age of thirteen or fourteen. When I was in the sixth form, I was studying geography, English and Welsh, and the Welsh teacher would enrol us into two night-school classes that were being taught by professors from Bangor University and we had to go to them as part of our schoolwork. We'd be there from seven till nine in these classes. All of us went.

Dafydd Iwan: Many of the people I saw, going with my parents to the Plaid conference or Ysgol Haf ['Summer School'] as it was known, many of the people there were men of letters or women of letters. The link with the creative arts, especially literature and poetry, was very strong and also with academia and religious leaders. Pennar Davies and Gwynfor Evans were both from the Annibynwyr Cymraeg, the Congregationalists, and were recognised as religious thinkers as well as political thinkers.

Rowan Williams: Pennar Davies is a very interesting figure in all this, and I vaguely remember him as a presence in Swansea in my youth, being referred to from time to time, you would see him at events – one of his sons was at the same school as I was, a very Welsh kind of connection. But the sense [was] that here was somebody who was a public intellectual, who had made a very conscious commitment to the language, writing almost exclusively in the language, along with Gwynfor Evans.

Dafydd Iwan: My father was a minister in Brynamman but a very socially minded preacher. It was listening to his sermons that I first heard of the anti-apartheid struggle in South Africa, and of Trevor Huddleston, and so through Christianity, through the Chapel, I heard of things like the protest marches against the nuclear bomb.

Rowan Williams: When we were living in Cardiff, we worshipped at an English-language Welsh Presbyterian church, Park End, near Roath Park, which was an enormously successful, flourishing church with quite a few Welsh-speaking people around in it, especially the minister, who was part of the great Nantlais Williams dynasty, so that still felt a bit like whatever there was of a religious establishment in Wales. I think that was really the last glow before night fell, in a sense: in the sixties, I think membership and attendance in a lot of the Nonconformist churches fell off a cliff.

Carl Iwan Clowes: There's a proverb, in Welsh, 'cenedl heb iaith, cenedl heb galon', 'a nation without a language is a nation without a heart'. Politicians, including Plaid, might find it hard to say that. There's a suggestion that you're going to alienate people who don't speak the language, but there's a lot of truth in that, I think. It's such a strong identity: if you hear somebody speaking Welsh outside of your area it becomes something to notice. You go overseas and you hear somebody speaking Welsh, it's almost inevitable that you sidle over to them and say, 'O ble wyt ti'n dod?' – 'Where are you from?'

It was said to me years ago, and I'm sure it's true, that when you're outside of your patch, or your continent, Africa, wherever you may be, and you see somebody who is obviously a Brit, and you start talking to them, the first thing they will say if they're from England, is, 'What do you do, then?' 'I'm a joiner, I'm a carpenter, I'm a doctor.' Welsh people, the first thing they say is, 'O ble wyt ti?' The relationship between a language and the confidence of the people in that language and the confidence in themselves, in the environment that they've got, all contribute to the picture of health.

The direct-action pressure group Cymdeithas yr Iaith Gymraeg, the Welsh Language Society, was founded in 1962 within a few months of Saunders Lewis' radio speech. 'Welsh Language Society' is an imperfect translation and fails to capture the essence of the organisation. The methods of direct action that the society adapted had been pioneered in the 1950s by Eileen and Trefor Beasley of Llangennech near Llanelli. The couple, a schoolteacher and her miner husband, had enacted a campaign of civil disobedience against the local authority, the Inland Revenue, the Westminster government and other public bodies, which had continually refused their requests to communicate with them in the medium of Cymraeg.

The Beasleys consequently refused to pay taxes, and after numerous court appearances succeeded in forcing Llanelli council to issue its summonses to them in Welsh. In his radio speech Saunders Lewis hailed the Beasleys as inspirational figures, claiming: 'Their trouble became the subject of the country's attention.' In an immediate echo of the couple's activities Cymdeithas yr Iaith's first campaign was to establish the right to receive court summonses in Welsh. The society commenced its activities in February 1963 with a sit-down occupation of the Trefechan Bridge that prevented traffic from entering Aberystwyth, although no summonses were issued in response to the

protest. Cymdeithas yr Iaith Gymraeg was forced to wait until 1966
before one of its members was finally arrested as a consequence of
direct action. The offence in question was the refusal to display the
appropriate tax disc in a vehicle, because the disc was written, like all
official documents in Wales, in English.

Cynog Dafis: There were two functions in Saunders Lewis' speech
that ran together: the one was a response to the Tryweryn issue and the
frustration at Plaid Cymru's continuing electoral failure, and of course
direct action was in the air, and there is more to that than I can tell you.
All kinds of direct action. And that eventually expressed itself later in
the bombing campaign around the Investiture [of the Prince of Wales].
What Saunders Lewis' lecture did was offer an alternative route for
the frustration and for the wish to get involved in direct action. And
of course, Saunders Lewis based his suggestions on the campaigns of
Trefor and Eileen Beasley. The whole question of official status for the
Welsh language following the radio lecture made it possible for one to
devise a law-breaking direct-action-type campaign on that issue.

Ffred Ffransis: When Saunders Lewis made his speech, 'The Fate of the
Language', which, looking back, seems like a very tame speech in 1962
but there we are, it was said – I don't know if it's true – that primarily
this was aimed at Plaid Cymru, to suggest to Plaid Cymru that they
should build up something which was not just a political party, but
was a social and cultural movement as well, in the same way that Sinn
Féin would be in the six counties of the north of Ireland. That was one
potential route, and the other route was no, we are a constitutional
political party and that's for others.

Cynog Dafis: There was that sense of threat and Saunders Lewis
articulated that. Saunders Lewis also said that the only way out of this
involved revolution – yes, he used the term 'revolution' – and only
revolutionary methods could tackle this whole issue. It was those two

26

things combined. And I remember when I was chair of Cymdeithas yr Iaith, I led a little delegation to meet Saunders Lewis. There was this debate about Plaid adopting a direct-action strategy and somebody said to Saunders Lewis, 'But Gwynfor Evans says that he doesn't understand what it would mean to use the Welsh language as a political instrument.' And Saunders Lewis said – I remember him very clearly saying – 'Well, in that case, Gwynfor Evans doesn't understand politics,' because it was quite evident to him that using the Welsh language as an instrument for creating a revolutionary climate could then change Wales.

Dafydd Iwan: My father met the three of them – Saunders Lewis, Lewis Valentine, D. J. Williams – and I met the three of them in time. They were very important figures in my upbringing, because of their writing, because of their Christianity and because they were nationalists, with high ideals, for Wales and the language. They were my heroes, notwithstanding the burning of the bombing school. But that has become a very important symbol; like Tryweryn, it has a very special place in our consciousness as Welsh people. The lecture Saunders Lewis gave in 1962 was certainly a pointer and was very relevant, but I think Cymdeithas yr Iaith would have happened even without the lecture. Obviously with time the two things have become seen as a cause and effect, because Saunders said that we need a movement dedicated to the resurrection of the language.

Cynog Dafis: What Saunders Lewis said in that lecture is that the language is more important than self-government. And people were taken aback by that at the time, and I never gave up on the idea that these two things had to be seen together: that we wouldn't get the language moving unless we had self-government. But it's unquestionably the case that the radicalisation, the awareness and the energy that was released by the language movement played a huge part, a huge part, in the political transformation that occurred.

Ffred Ffransis: The first time I became politically aware of anything, really, was 1963 or '64, during the build-up to the UK general election. In the old grammar school that we had in Rhyl there were always mock elections and so on, and together with that and the local Plaid Cymru office opening in Rhyl, that's when I became interested in politics. It was Tryweryn for the generation before me. For me, it was what became known as the Brewer Spinks episode, whereby a guy, presumably, from his name, not indigenous to Wales, opened up a factory in Blaenau Ffestiniog. I would suspect he [hoped to] find a fairly cheap pool of labour, people who might be unemployed, and he banned them from speaking Welsh in the workplace, even though 100 per cent of the workforce would be Welsh-speaking, it would be their natural language. Now that was something which enraged people, and not just me, but in that area of Wales, in Rhyl, the vast majority of people who'd grown up in the area, they would identify with the Welsh language, even though they didn't speak it themselves. They'd think of it as a language which in some form or another, to various degrees, belonged to them, and they would take it as a personal insult if the language was denigrated.

I was determined. I was going to take a train to get down to Blaenau Ffestiniog – actually, that railway line is the one branch line in Wales which is still open – to take part in the protests. Before I was able to do so, the thing was resolved very quickly: he backed down. But it was enough for me to notice an advert in *Y Cymro*, the weekly Welsh-language paper. I was studying Welsh at school, as a modern foreign language, the way in which most of the second-language Welsh was taught in those days to non-Welsh-speaking children. I wouldn't normally have taken Welsh as my main subject in sixth form at college – I wasn't all that interested in literature, but it was the only way really of becoming fluent in the language, so I was doing that. To help that, I received every week the Welsh-language weekly newspaper *Y Cymro*. There was an advert to join Cymdeithas, the Welsh Language Society, I filled it in, I sent it away, and I joined.

28

And a year later, when I arrived at Aberystwyth University, I went straight to registration on freshers' day to the desk of Cymdeithas yr Iaith. I joined the local branch and the following Saturday there was going to be a protest outside Swansea Prison for one of the main founder members who had been imprisoned for refusing to pay a fine because he refused to show a tax disc because it was English-only. Not only did I do that, but within a few weeks I'd passed my driving test – I couldn't drive properly, there'd never been a car in the family – but I invested £5 of my student grant in buying a 1951 Ford Anglia, which couldn't go out of Aberystwyth because it couldn't go up any hills. I parked it on the side of the road with a note on the windscreen to the police, saying this wasn't being taxed because the tax discs were in English only, and went away to my student flat and waited for the police to arrive. I was still waiting four weeks later – they didn't think it was the number one priority in Aberystwyth to come after me.

TWO

COFIWCH DRYWERYN /
REMEMBER TRYWERYN

Voices

Dewi 'Mav' Bowen	Dafydd Iwan	Rhys Mwyn
Cynog Dafis	John Barnard Jenkins	Dewi Prysor
Philippa Davies	Tecwyn Vaughan	Huw Stephens
Ffred Ffransis	Jones	Ruth Stephens
Meinir Ffransis	Ben Lake	Ned Thomas
Gethin ap Gruffydd		Rowan Williams

———

The urgency of the founding of Cymdeithas yr Iaith Gymraeg was demonstrated not only by Saunders Lewis' speech, but by the need to respond to a series of political interventions undertaken by the Westminster government in rural Wales. Most notably, impetus for the creation of Cymdeithas yr Iaith Gymraeg in 1962 was provided by the proposed imminent drowning of the village of Capel Celyn in Tryweryn, North Wales, for the building of a reservoir to pump water to the city of Liverpool. Despite the objection of every MP representing a constituency in Wales, apart from one Conservative, who abstained, Liverpool City Council was able to bypass planning legislation by obtaining an Act of Parliament in 1965 and the swift clearance of Capel Celyn was approved for the construction of the dam. The following year Gwynfor Evans, the leader of Plaid Cymru, would become the party's first elected Member of Parliament, representing the constituency of Carmarthen. His election represented a watershed

moment for both parties and was regarded as a demonstration of
the strength of feeling at large in Welsh nationalism. This sense of
insurgency would be further asserted during the preparations for
the investiture of Charles Windsor as Prince of Wales at Caernarfon
Castle in 1969.

Dafydd Iwan: I went to Aberystwyth University for a year, and that
was the year leading up to the founding of Cymdeithas yr Iaith, so it
was very much at Aberystwyth University that the whole thing was
coming up to the boil, and then I went to do the architecture course in
Cardiff, and during that summer, I think it was during the Plaid Cymru
summer school, the society was set up.

Meinir Ffransis: I think it was decided to found Cymdeithas yr Iaith
in the summer school in Pontarddulais by Tedi Millward and John
Davies, but it was done under Plaid Cymru. Wherever you went,
people said, 'Oh, Plaid is only for Welsh-speakers,' and this kind of
thing, and Saunders had made this plea in his radio lecture 'Tynged
yr Iaith' and it was decided there should be a movement explicitly
to focus on the language, and it was decided that non-violent illegal
actions could be undertaken. Saunders Lewis, Lewis Valentine and
D.J. took their action of course, against the RAF bombing school, but
because of the danger somebody could be hurt, we never, ever used
that method.

Cynog Dafis: If I were to be asked, 'What was the main motivation at
that meeting in the classroom in the school in Pontarddulais at the time
of the Plaid Cymru conference?' I think it was frustration and wanting
to start using direct action: I think that was it.

Ruth Stephens: Cymdeithas was constituted in my parents' house in
Aberystwyth, 51 North Parade.

Meinir Ffransis: Yes, it was in Uncle John and Aunty Bessie's house.

Ruth Stephens: That was where they had the first meeting. I don't know if they signed the official bits there, but that's where they first met: Tedi Millward, John Bwlchllan, people like that came together to set up Cymdeithas in 51 North Parade, Aberystwyth. As for Cymdeithas, well, it started off with students, in the universities, and the demonstrations against road signs. Meic did a lot of that with John Bwlchllan, the historian, they used to go round changing the Post Office signs in Dinas Mawddwy; he asked them to change the signs there, and at Trefin, down in Pembrokeshire, they changed the signs, and then they took up all these ideas and made them work on a massive scale.

They'd shown we don't want to harm people, we don't want to kill anyone, but we're desperate for a way of showing how we feel, and we'll do amazing things to show the strength of the feeling that we've got against what is being done to us.

We had to demonstrate with as strong a voice as possible how we felt, and as young people. One of the first acts of protest was to bicycle up and down the promenade at Aberystwyth in front of the police station with someone sitting on the handlebars, which was illegal. They went up and down all day, but they had better things to do than arrest them.

Meinir Ffransis: For my father [Gwynfor Evans], first and foremost, it was a matter of his heart and what was right and coming to the realisation that Wales was a nation. His Welsh teacher was a great influence on him. He was very lucky when he was in the sixth form – there were only two of them studying Welsh, and Gwyn ap Jones was his teacher and he was almost the same age as them, fresh from college. David Williams, the historian, was his history teacher, so David Williams urged him to read history books like *Religion and the Rise of Capitalism* by R. H. Tawney, who was on the left of the spectrum as regards economics. He went to a few lectures by R. H. Tawney,

32

when he was in Oxford, and he was a member of the Left Book Club and his friend in school was a member as well. He became a great admirer of Keir Hardie and his parents were Liberals who idolised Lloyd George, but my mother's parents, her father in particular, was a strong Independent Labour Party man in Liverpool – my mother was brought up in Liverpool – and very friendly with George Lansbury. He organised meetings in Liverpool and he was working in the bank and he was very, very active with forming unions for the bank workers. I remember Ffred and me going to meet some bank managers when there was a campaign for equal status for Welsh. There were about ten of them and it was at dinner, and they'd all heard of my grandfather and his work with the banking unions and that he was a member of the ILP. Of course, he became a little bit disillusioned with the Labour Party, as did Keir Hardie, with the attitude towards war.

Dafydd Iwan: I knew Gwynfor, and my father knew him and thought very highly of him, because of this mix of being a Christian, a pacifist and a politician of great integrity. His strength in the end was this sticking to his principles for a long time and not allowing himself to become a great orator or a passionate campaigner: he was just a steady constant in the campaign for Wales. A lot of people thought he was too quiet and too much of a pacifist and a Christian, and that that stood in the way, but in the end that was his strength.

Ruth Stephens: Gwynfor's wife was my mother's first cousin, and we lived in Aberystwyth. My father was a minister in Aberystwyth, and it was quite central for Wales, so Gwynfor used to call on us often. Because he farmed tomatoes in his greenhouse down in Llangadog and he looked after the greenhouse himself, he wanted to get home every night. Wherever he was travelling from, he'd want to get home to Llangadog.

Dafydd Iwan: Gwynfor in many ways was ahead of his time. He set himself up as a tomato-grower, which was often ridiculed by the Labour Party, but he went from Barry to live in a rural village and set up a business which allowed him time to trek around Wales campaigning.

Ruth Stephens: He was so principled, and very genuine, and it took a long time for people to get to know him, but it was his personality that got him to where he was. Small countries, that was his big thing then.

Rowan Williams: Plaid Cymru, at that time, I think especially under Gwynfor Evans' leadership, was very much the political organ of all that. It was the time when Plaid Cymru really had left Saunders Lewis a long way behind, and, clearly, Saunders Lewis was not very happy about the direction taken by Plaid in the fifties and sixties, because Plaid was happily drifting leftwards in his view. His image of Plaid Cymru had been of Action Française in Wales, but the uncomfortable fascist resonances of those early days had been, I think, very successfully buried by the sixties.

Meinir Ffransis: My father was for workers' control and workers profiting from businesses where they worked. In the colliery near Pentremawr the workers were very, very keen to form a confederation where they would own the colliery and my father supported them, but the local Labour Party was strongly opposed to it, because they wanted, of course, to centralise everything. The National Coal Board was so opposed to it that it didn't come to fruition. My father took the *New Statesman*, which Saunders Lewis didn't approve of at all. He was a bit different in his standpoint to economics from Saunders Lewis. My father was also a strong pacifist, and Saunders wasn't.

Dafydd Iwan: I went to school on a train from Llanuwchllyn to Bala and saw the preparations for the dam at Tryweryn before they even mentioned drowning the valley; they were preparing where the two rivers, the Tryweryn and the Dee, come together. They had to control the flow from the lake down the Dee, and from the new Tryweryn Dam, as it was going to be. They were saying that they were doing it to stop flooding in Bala. There must have been collusion between the local authority and probably the politicians before they recognised openly that, in fact, they were part of preparations for a dam.

Gwynfor did more than most of his detractors in campaigning against the flooding of Tryweryn. He marched with the residents of Tryweryn in Liverpool, he spoke in their council chamber – my father also went on a lot of the protest marches regarding Tryweryn. The inference has grown that Plaid Cymru sat back and did nothing, which wasn't true. I lived in the area during the 1960s, so I knew that Plaid Cymru was very much involved with the campaign to try and save Tryweryn, but of course we failed. Those who did use explosive devices there were seen, not as enemies of Plaid Cymru, but outside the ranks of Plaid Cymru – they had come up from South Wales. But again, Gwynfor went to Bala during one of their trials to shake hands with two of the people charged, which was quite a risk for him.

During the Tryweryn protests period there was quite a vociferous minority in Plaid Cymru who believed that, as the national party of Wales, we should not just condone but use direct methods, even if it meant using bombs – they never said that, but that was the gist of it, and Gwynfor Evans, as the long-time president of the period, was getting a lot of flak from a minority of Plaid members because he was so very much in favour of non-violent campaigning.

Gethin ap Gruffydd: Saunders Lewis had told Mudiad Amddiffyn Cymru not to bother with Tryweryn, but what never happened at Tryweryn was an occupation. They could have occupied the whole village like the Native Americans occupied Wounded Knee; they could have occupied the village and stopped it being knocked down; they just occupied a bloody bridge instead. Cymdeithas would pull signposts down and all the rest of it, anything more serious, no way.

Ffred Ffransis: That's the debate that came to a head with Tryweryn; that's the significance of Tryweryn. Plaid Cymru members and Gwynfor himself were involved in a number of direct protests against the construction of the dam, and taking the campaign to the streets of Liverpool, but in the end it failed, and whenever anything fails there are always two possible interpretations. One that that isn't the way, and the other, that that is the way, but we didn't go far enough along that way. So that was the schism, that Plaid Cymru said, 'Well, this is never going to work; this is only going to work when we become a serious political constitutional force and we get members of parliament and so on,' whereas those who formed Cymdeithas yr Iaith, practically all of them members of Plaid Cymru, said, 'Right, what we have to do, then, is form a separate movement which will be involved in direct action and constitutional actions. The two movements might well have an understanding, but they'll be two separate movements.'

And that was the main schism.

Cynog Dafis: On the Tryweryn issue, Gwynfor was in favour of direct action. It wasn't Gwynfor that opposed it; it was the local Plaid Cymru party that had by that time managed to gain a toehold of political credibility and influence, even power, locally. He was in favour of that and then, of course, when the party decided not to act, he was the one – poor fellow – who had to carry all the opprobrium. There was a kind of stoical heroism about people: they just took it.

Dafydd Iwan: It was quite nasty at the time, because of this feeling of frustration, and they took it out on Gwynfor. At the time there was this feeling of frustration and inability– you know, every MP bar one voted against the bill – but it made no difference whatsoever, and that was a pretty strong message and a lesson, which Plaid Cymru obviously used, and has grown again in meaning over the years. Other people now throw it back – not throw it back but use it as an argument: fancy them drowning that village. It's taken a time, but on the other hand, to my generation and to young members of Plaid and Cymdeithas yr Iaith, Tryweryn was certainly very potent.

Ffred Ffransis: Tryweryn was a massive issue. I remember the very early 1960s when I'd just moved to secondary school and people talking about it at school. It was portrayed at the time that one was depriving the people of Liverpool of any drinking water at all, which wasn't the case, and so on.

Dafydd Iwan: Tryweryn has grown over the years as a symbol of the inability of Wales to stand up for itself and take care of its own resources. It's a very potent symbol.

Ffred Ffransis: The negative news which awoke me was the way in which we were being treated in Wales: the fact that we had no control of our own future, the fact this was shown in unemployment rates and the fact that our language had no official status at all, and the decline of our communities, and so on and so on. It was the sort of thing which kept me awake at night. Now, over the years, over the decades – and it's not as if it's the most recent thing, because it began to happen way back – back in the 1960s, we began to be aware that what we were doing in Wales was part of an international movement. Paris 1968 had effects on us all, the Vietnam War of course, then over into the 1980s, the Cold War, Greenham Common and so on. And anyway, more and more so, the concept of freedom for Wales turned from being something negative that we couldn't stand the oppression, the way we were being treated: it used to keep me awake till the early hours every night as a sixth-former at school; I just couldn't sleep, thinking about that, I had to be out, doing something about it. It gradually moved over to a positive idea of, right then, why can't we have the freedom to build up a model society here in Wales, something which would be different from the injustices all around the world, where we can show people what social justice and brotherhood and sisterhood would really look like? We can have a voice in the world community, be accepted as a member of the family of nations – it's so perverse to think of nationalism and national liberation as cutting oneself off: it's the very opposite. It means joining the international community. So those were upon my awakening, but the initial awakening was in those negative terms, and there were a few things which did illustrate the way in which Wales was being treated, not just the fact that we didn't have control over our own affairs and we weren't able to use our own language, but the fact that we were being treated badly as well.

Meinir Ffransis: They had used violent methods in Penyberth at the bombing school and there was great pressure on my father to do the same at Tryweryn, so it wasn't out of the question, but obviously it would be a very exceptional thing for the political party of Wales to be involved in.

I know that hundreds of young people from all over Wales, especially south-east Wales, became involved in nationalist politics and then Plaid Cymru because of Tryweryn.

Things can kick people and make them sit up and take notice, and Tryweryn was one of those. Other valleys had been drowned previous to Tryweryn, like Elan and Clywedog, but it was because there was a community which was so cultured living in Tryweryn and it was such a blatant colonialist action – some valley in the north of England somewhere had been saved because of a flower or something, it was all so blatant. The people who lived in Tryweryn didn't hear of their fate first-hand, they only read it in the papers. Nobody spoke to them before the decision was made. It was such an imperialistic way of doing things.

Ruth Stephens: I remember my younger brother, he was fifteen at the time, hitch-hiking to be part of the protest in Liverpool. We felt strongly about what was going on in Tryweryn, because they had no right, and all the Welsh MPs were against it. It didn't make sense at all to us. We had family living in Frongoch Farm. My mother's sister lived in the next farm down the valley from where the lake is, my Aunty Gret. We were all, 'You can't drown the valley up the road.' It was very real to us, what was happening. They said they wanted the water for poor little people without water to drink in Liverpool, but it wasn't for that, it was for industry and jobs for people outside Wales. The government did nothing to help us in Wales, to set up work for people: they wanted people to move to where the work was with no plans at all. There were no plans with Thatcher, with what they did in the Valleys years later; they just closed everything down and left. Barbarous.

It was part of our identity that we were losing as well. You understand what Welsh was about, you understand life better. If you're going to live in Wales, it's a huge step to understand what you're going into if you can speak some Welsh. When people move out of a district like from Capel Celyn that's dispersed, we've all lost something, and it illustrated that perfectly, drowning a valley and a community, a village, and moving people out and some of them probably ended up on the border and across in England, looking for work again. They were content where they were, and they should have had more help to develop where they were already living than to be moved somewhere else to try to make a go of it again.

Prior to the dam's completion a graffito was painted on the stone wall of a ruined cottage near Llanrhystud, Aberystwyth, bearing the message 'Cofiwch Dryweryn' ('Remember Tryweryn'). The image was the work of a young author and journalist, Meic Stephens. In subsequent decades the phrase developed into a prominent political slogan, used to assert the cause of Welsh nationalism and the need for a more assertive approach to Welsh identity. The cause was provided with momentum in 1966, the year following the drowning of Capel Celyn, when Gwynfor Evans was elected in Carmarthen as Plaid Cymru's first Westminster MP.

Huw Stephens: I didn't realise until I made a programme about it that my father painted the Cofiwch Dryweryn stone before Tryweryn was actually drowned. He was ready to go, with some friends. It was the fact that every Welsh MP in Westminster voted against the drowning of the valley and the political decision was made for it to go ahead. The actual drowning and the protests of the Welsh going to Liverpool to protest and the grand opening ceremony of the reservoir which turned into a farce, it was before all of that. And the fact it's been there since is incredible.

He'd graduated from Aberystwyth and he lived in the commune in Merthyr Tydfil with the poet Harri Webb and other politically interested people. It was a house where, if people needed to stay, they could. They had a pirate radio station broadcasting Welsh thoughts to a Welsh audience, called Ceiliog, 'Cockerel'.

The stone wasn't red and white in the first place, the red came after, and my dad, because he was a Welsh learner, hadn't mastered mutations, so his original said 'Cofiwch Tryweryn', and somebody then corrected it to 'Cofiwch Dryweryn', which is one of the most Welsh things ever. And years later, somebody wrote 'Sorry, Miss' next to it as well, which is brilliant.

It was only in later years my dad spoke about it publicly and admitted that he had painted it. In his autobiography it's a paragraph where it could be a chapter – it could have been a book. My dad edited 150 more books, but he says those two words were his most important, because of the weight of what happened to that valley and what it meant to Wales as a country.

Obviously, there's a lot of confusion over Tryweryn, for people who know the story, even: was anyone hurt when the valley was drowned, did anybody die? Did anyone drown? No. Was it in Aberystwyth? Well, no, that's where the wall was. Where is Tryweryn?

It was in a time of political excitement in Wales, lots of painting of slogans. Cofiwch Dryweryn was a lot of things; it was everything. It was the language, in that a naturally Welsh-speaking community was forced to move and everything was destroyed; I've interviewed a lady called Eurgain Prysor Jones who was one of the children there, and we were sat on the dam in Tryweryn, and the dam is made of the wood and the bricks from the chapel and from the school in the valley. It was moved and it was moved to build the dam.

My dad dedicated his life to promoting the literature of Wales, the political side of Cofiwch Dryweryn and being a young student and being a young man who painted slogans, and standing as a Plaid Cymru candidate was a very short window of his life. He got a job at the Arts Council of Wales; he was the literature man, and he was there for about thirty years, promoting Welsh literature. His passion was literature from Wales in English, and bridging the gap between the Welsh-language world and the English-language world, and that's why *Planet: The Welsh Internationalist* and *Poetry Wales* and all of those things, the Rhys Davies Trust later on, were so close to his heart.

Tecwyn Vaughan Jones: My political stance was crystallised by my parents. My father was from a strong Labour background, having been brought up and lived in Blaenau Ffestiniog, but his experiences during the war had made him into a Welsh nationalist, a Plaid Cymru supporter. I have a vague recollection of the 1959 election, when he was canvassing for Gwynfor Evans, who stood in the Merioneth constituency then. The biggest deal was 1966, when Gwynfor Evans won Carmarthen: that was a big deal in our house. It was a big news item, of course, and I remember my mother – I was home from school at the time – sending me to his workplace to tell him: 'Just tell him that Gwynfor has won.' And then he walked back home with me to see the television news. I thought, 'Well, this is really, really important.' I was fourteen years old then.

Huw Stephens: There's a picture of my dad carrying Gwynfor on his shoulders on the day he was elected the first Plaid Cymru MP at the big celebration of him going to Westminster.

Ruth Stephens: Gwynfor got in in Carmarthen, in his home town. He was fantastic, it was the best place for him to stand.

Meinir Ffransis: When he went to Parliament, as an MP, Emrys Hughes was showing him round and said, 'Don't sit on the Welsh table,' where they were almost all Labour, 'Your name is mud there,' he said. But he did have a friend in Elystan Morgan, who was the Cardigan Labour MP, and I think Cledwyn Hughes from Anglesey was quite kind, but nobody else.

Dafydd Iwan: Gwynfor became a figure much hated by the Labour Party, and he wasn't afraid of saying it as it was, in the chamber.

Philippa Davies: The evening Gwynfor Evans got in my mother took me down because she was so incensed about it. My mother was booing and hissing with a load of her Russian friends and I was taken along as well. I can remember it clearly. They thought it was an absolute catastrophe. A catastrophe. Mattie Morris, Joan Ifor and my mother who were pro-Russia, were there absolutely stamping about it. They would have regarded Plaid as a bit right-wing then.

Dafydd Iwan: If you go back to the time of S. L. Davies or Jim Griffiths, or Keir Hardie before them, the ideas of self-government for Wales, and indeed full status for the Welsh language, were accepted as a part of the whole socialist agenda that Labour had. Gradually, with the growth of Plaid Cymru, the Labour Party grew more antagonistic to the Welsh language, because they saw it as a threat. Having been a party motivated by good intentions for the working class and the workers, the Labour Party became very entrenched in its power base and jealous of any threat and saw Plaid Cymru and the growth of Welsh nationalism as a threat, and therefore they became an anti-Welsh-language party. This was not true of all Labour MPs, but it was certainly true of the main thrust of things. They thought that the Labour Party had the divine right to run Wales, and they perhaps knew and still know that if anybody's going to break their hegemony – is that the word? – it's going to be Plaid Cymru.

Meinir Ffransis: My father hated being an MP. It made him so ill. I remember well, he had terrible, terrible nightmares, and he'd wake himself up, shouting. My mother said she had to move to a different room, because he was shouting so – 'I protest!' It did have a massive effect on him, and he knew that that's what was in front of him when he went in 1966 – he would be all on his own. Everybody was so happy and it was only he himself who was very, very apprehensive. They were so horribly nasty. The old gentlemanly Tories, like Whitelaw, he much preferred them personally, because of the nastiness. He liked Michael Foot a lot, as well. Michael Foot seemed to be a different type of man. I think he had some admiration for Tony Benn, but Tony Benn didn't have anything to say to Welsh nationalism or Scottish nationalism. No, quite the opposite.

But he became so ill and my sister went to see him in hospital, and she had to walk out of the room and broke down, because he looked so terrible. In Carmarthenshire the Labour Party were spreading the rumour that he didn't have long to live and this kind of thing.

The leading Welsh Labour politician George Thomas, Secretary of State for Wales 1968–70, regarded these developments, such as the Tryweryn protests and the election of Gwynfor Evans, with a marked sense of unease that included a disdain for Cymdeithas yr Iaith Gymraeg and the coalition of activism in favour of the Welsh language. Thomas, originally from Port Talbot in South Wales, held the royal family in pronounced esteem and took personal charge over the forthcoming investiture of the Prince of Wales at Caernarfon Castle in 1969. The investiture, a ceremony that is a theatrical formality rather than an official requirement for the appointment of a Prince of Wales, had only been revived in 1911 and was interpreted by many within the movement as an attempt by the Westminster establishment to nullify interest in Welsh nationalism by staging a display of royal theatre. As a production the investiture proved successful.

This was despite the fact the event had been targeted as part of a bombing campaign initiated three years earlier by Mudiad Amddiffyn Cymru. Mudiad Amddiffyn Cymru had been founded by Owain Williams, Emyr Llywelyn and John Albert Jones, in order to prevent the construction of the Tryweryn reservoir. In 1963 the three had planted a five-pound bomb on an electricity transformer that supplied power for machinery used at the site. Other targets of Mudiad Amddiffyn Cymru's bombing campaign had included a water pipeline in Llanrhaeadr-ym-Mochnant, which was responsible for transporting water seventy miles from a reservoir near the River Vyrnwy to Liverpool, and the Temple of Peace in Cardiff, which was adjacent to a venue used by the Investiture Organising Committee. Some twenty explosions were estimated to have occurred over a two-year period. By 1969 Mudiad Amddiffyn Cymru was led by John Jenkins, a former non-commissioned officer in the British Army Dental Corps.

Whilst the Mudiad Amddiffyn Cymru membership remained secretive, another separate organisation, the Free Wales Army, founded by the flamboyant Julian Cayo-Evans, claimed affinity with the Mudiad Amddiffyn Cymru bomb attacks to a point that suggested responsibility. In the lead-up to the investiture more explosives were detonated, including one in George Thomas' Cardiff office. Thomas, who would be the sole passenger to accompany Prince Charles in his carriage on the day of the investiture, was emotionally devoted to the success of the occasion and gave public assurances that the bombing campaign had been extinguished.

Around 2,000 members of Special Branch were deployed across Wales in the months before the royal event. Many of the Welsh nationalists whose names were mentioned on police records, including the three founding members of Mudiad Amddiffyn Cymru, were placed under surveillance or intimidated. The explosions continued across Wales, however, and several devices that failed to detonate remained undetected. Nine members of the Free Wales Army were arrested and charged with public order offences. The nature of the arrests suggested the authorities were attempting to curtail the braggadocio of the Free Wales Army, which was sustained by regular media interest, rather than award the organisation any credit for arranging the explosions campaign. The trial of the nine was held in Swansea, lasted fifty-three days and concluded on the day of the investiture. The prosecution's case largely rested on evidence from journalists' interviews with Cayo-Evans. He, his second-in-command Dennis Coslett, and four other members were convicted; Cayo-Evans and Coslett were imprisoned for fifteen months.

Gethin ap Gruffydd: There were very many similarities between Wales and Algeria. After the Second World War, [in opposition to] French colonialism, a lot of Algerian soldiers had gone home and started the National Liberation Front. People like Cayo-Evans, Tony, Glyn and Cofyd of the Free Wales Army had all been in the British Army and they came home and had a totally different attitude to fighting for Welsh freedom to the one Cymdeithas and Plaid had. My brother went on a training course to learn how to silk screen so we could put posters up. It was a government-funded course but nearly everybody on it was a revolutionary, from Welsh nationalists to Irish nationalists to Black Panthers. We learned how to silk screen, then print them in the garage at night, and the next morning we'd go and stick them up. Our biggest problem in Wales is we have never had a *Private Eye* or an investigative press; the Welsh-speaking working class in Wales has never been represented.

I met John Jenkins at the Plaid Cymru summer school of 1965 or 1966. Neither of us were members of Cymdeithas; as far as we were concerned they were opportunists. We had a public meeting about the investiture of Prince Charles, and Cymdeithas saw this and immediately jumped on the anti-investiture campaign and used it as a platform for Dafydd Iwan's songs; I think of them as the crachach newydd, the *nouveaux riche*.

John Barnard Jenkins: I do not personify our country [old Mother Wales] because of a sentimental streak, although I am not glacial and iron-hard normally, but because it is the best way to describe her in relation to my personal feelings.

She is not a beautiful young girl after whom I lust, or an old duchess whose money and status I desire; she is old, well past her best, decrepit, boozy, and has taken strange bedfellows without the saving grace of desperation . . .

I owe her my love and my loyalty: she is my mother. She may be a liability but is the sort of liability that a crippled child is, in the eyes of its parents. If I ignore her in her hour of need no one will ever know or condemn, except myself, and I have the sort of conscience that stops functioning the moment I stop breathing.

I 'took up arms' because with many other people, I could feel instinctively that our national identity, our sacred soul, our everything, was not only being threatened but was in the last stages of survival. My aim was to create a state of mind, so that people would not accept all that the English government said and did as Moses on the Mount, to make them realise that all actions are acceptable when performed in the national interest.

Dafydd Iwan: The things that happened in Wales with John Jenkins planting bombs at the investiture of Prince Charles, I was ambivalent, in the sense that a lot of us thought, 'Well, somebody's doing something quite directly to show opposition to these things.' You couldn't condemn them for that, but I still said openly that I don't agree that that is the way we should go, but it's happening, and it's happening for reasons I fully understand. I met John Jenkins when he came out of prison, and he was obviously a man of strong convictions who had thought very deeply about these things. I also knew several members of the Free Wales Army, but that was more of a drinking club or a joke. Cayo was a character, and I met him in prison, when I was in there for Cymdeithas yr Iaith activities and he was in there after the investiture.

Ben Lake: My grandfather, my father's father, was a country policeman for the Tregaron area for thirty, forty years, and Silian, where Cayo lived, was between Lampeter and Tregaron, so my grandfather knew him very well. Much was made at the time of the trial that Cayo had the mental age of a twelve-year-old; there were a lot of quite vicious attacks on him. My grandfather was a typical old-school policeman to the end. I don't think you'd ever find him condoning some of the actions – but he always spoke against that characterisation of Cayo as a simpleton, always. Cayo passed away in '97, so he would have known Cayo through the eighties to the early nineties, both in uniform and as a local youngster – and the same is true of my father; he says it was unfair of the prosecution to characterise Cayo like that.

Dewi 'Mav' Bowen: The first time I met Cayo, I went to a Plaid Cymru meeting and I was about fifteen. Gwynfor Evans' daughters, who were very beautiful, were there. I got away with drinking beer at fifteen, because I was with mature company, Gwynfor Evans and the daughters were buying me beer, and they said, 'Where does he put it all?' I think it was the first time I'd really had a proper drink, and I found I was very good at it straight away. Then Cayo came in with all the uniform on. I said to him, and I'd had a couple of drinks, 'Who the fuck do you think you are, coming in here, spoiling our day?' With that, he gave me a clip around the ear and I went over the wall: bang. And everybody had a go at Cayo, 'Hitting a boy like that, what's the matter with you?' He said, 'Yeah, gobby little fucker, he should have shut up.' And then after that I hung about near the university in Lampeter, and of course Cayo was the big boy up in Lampeter and I reminded him of that incident with Gwynfor and his daughters and we got on famously. I told him that I was a wannabe Free Wales Army type of kid, I was still only sixteen, but I painted the railway station with the Snowdon Eagle and had been involved in activities at Tonypandy. Cayo said, 'I'm going to have you on manoeuvres.'

A couple of weeks later he took me up to Glendennis where there was this copper who'd upset him and he knew his car was in the rugby club in Lampeter, which is out in the woods. He gave me the balaclava and some clutch fluid, and I was to tip clutch fluid all over this car – I had the number plate – and then walk down towards town, and then there I was, in the Black Lion in Lampeter, a meal had been ordered, and of course according to everyone present I'd been there all night with Cayo. The copper was called Inspector Fisher, and his son was an actor in *Pobol y Cwm* – I met him later on. In one of Cayo's famous court cases, he said, 'The trouble is, this police officer has got an extreme prejudice against my personal self, because I was seeing his missus,' and that's the kind of bloke Cayo was. He had a very sad end: he started taking tranquillisers and things like that, and I think he lost the plot, poor boy. We were a strange bunch altogether, really. I didn't see a lot of extreme nastiness in the Free Wales Army, in the kind of way I'd seen it elsewhere, in Ireland for instance.

Rhys Mwyn: We had a family in our school in Llanfair, they were three brothers, the sons of Glyn Rowlands from the Free Wales Army. Glyn was known as the lone bull of Corris: he lived in Corris and was a forester. His boys were in school with us, and a cache of rifles was found underneath his stairs, so he went to prison, and because the boys were in school with us, Glyn Rowlands became this hero, so we were aware of the Free Wales Army through the boys.

I met Glyn over the years, on various occasions, and we always had that bond, because he knew we were friends with the boys, and Glyn was hardcore; he had no regrets. You get it in the north of Ireland as well, some of these characters – they have no regrets, they do their time and not for one second do they regret what they did. I always liked Glyn. He knew that I differed politically, because we went on a rally once, and I was with Glyn, and we were talking about the boys, and at this rally they all toasted Owain Glyndŵr, and I didn't, and I remember saying to Glyn, 'I don't do Glyndŵr.' For me, if it was class war, he's landed gentry, and I would always joke with him: 'What's the Marxist view of Glyndŵr?' and he'd never have an answer, I would always throw that in. 'What would Aneurin Bevan make of Glyndŵr?' You can see the nationalists stumble, because it's too easy a narrative: Glyndŵr, national hero, but what if it's class war? And they're stuck.

The Free Wales Army was Cayo-Evans and his mates. They were extremely, some of them, to the right. I went down to Cayo's home and I recorded him. Cayo played accordion, and he rambled on. When I went down to do that, one of his entourage had a, well, I'm not sure what it was, it was a German t-shirt, and I thought there was a sub-text there that some of them were probably out to lunch politically.

Dewi Prysor: By the time I got to secondary school there were Free Wales Army slogans everywhere. This is working-class children now, with parents in industrial backgrounds, they turned into nationalists. On the desks would be painted the Snowdonia Eagle; there was a massive Free Wales Army slogan on the wall of the gym, which everyone who walked past could see.

Dafydd Iwan: There were very few members of the Free Wales Army. I think most of them were imprisoned on 1 July, the day of the investiture, and it's quite tragic, because most of them have died fairly young, in difficult circumstances, but they were all characters, eccentric characters in a sense, and Cayo was not making a secret of the fact that he was on a PR exercise, but it was a pretty ineffective PR exercise. When they appeared on the David Frost show *That Was the Week That Was*, it looked like a pantomime farce: they were all shapes and sizes and their costumes were hopeless.

49

Dewi 'Mav' Bowen: I think a reporter from something like the *Daily Sketch* went up to the Ram in Lampeter and he'd seen old Hywel the farmer. Hywel was a character up around there in Lampeter and the Ram is where they all hung out. And the reporter asks, 'How many of the Free Wales Army are there then?' and Hywel said, 'I'd say about twelve, or thirteen if you count Cayo's dog, Queenie. And really you ought to, because she's brighter than the rest of them put together.' And that was his opinion, as a canny hill farmer.

Ned Thomas: John Jenkins was imprisoned and then released. He was arrested a second time on some trumped-up charges because they couldn't find who was responsible for things. He was an intelligent, thoughtful man, different to Cayo-Evans' type.

Dafydd Iwan: Tedi Millward, who taught Welsh to Prince Charles, made a very outspoken attack on the Free Wales Army as paper tigers who do our movement so much harm. I never really saw the need to attack them in that sense, but I never really took them seriously, and yet, knowing them personally, I knew they were genuine in the sense that they were nationalists.

On 30 June 1969, the day before the investiture, two members of the Mudiad Amddiffyn Cymru, Alwyn Jones and George Taylor, were killed when a device intended for government offices in Abergele exploded prematurely in their hands. At 2.15 p.m., mere minutes before the scheduled firing of a twenty-one-gun salute to welcome the royal family, a bomb was detonated in the garden of the Chief Constable of Gwynedd.

Another device planted at Caernarfon went undetonated until its discovery five days after the investiture by Ian Cox, an eleven-year-old boy holidaying in the area, who, mistaking the explosive for a football, triggered its detonation and tragically lost his right leg.

The arbitrary nature of Mudiad Amddiffyn Cymru's policy of
utilising bombs to create disruption rather than cause physical harm
was placed in relief by the maiming of a child of eleven, who was
understandably the beneficiary of a great deal of public sympathy.

A final bomb placed beneath Llandudno Pier to prevent the royal
yacht Britannia *from being able to berth also failed to detonate and*
lay undetected, until Jenkins revealed its existence under questioning
following his eventual arrest on 2 November. Jenkins was consequently
given a ten-year sentence. His prison letters were published in
book form in 1978. Jenkins' correspondents included the Cymraeg
intelligentsia of the day and the letters reveal a thoughtful individual,
whose resolute convictions were maintained by historical analysis,
rather than impulsive or delusional perceptions of nationhood.

Dewi 'Mav' Bowen: During the investiture, I went up to Caernarfon –
psychedelic drugs were involved in this, because we took some acid. We
realised that we were being monitored by Special Branch. I remember
going for a long walk and this guy following me, and I said, 'What
the fuck are you up to? What have I done?' and he said, 'Well, it's the
people you hang out with, isn't it?' I said, 'Oh, fair enough.' He said,
'I'll get off your case. Do you mind if I look in your pockets?' and I
knew I didn't have any drugs on me so I said, 'Carry on.' And he was
looking for weapons. But it was a strange experience.

Gethin ap Gruffydd: At the investiture a few people went to protest,
a few were arrested, but a hell of a lot more ducked out and buggered
off to Ireland. There was intimidation by the authorities – people had
had police guards stationed at their houses so they couldn't go out.
They arrested nine of us, most of us leaders of the campaign, so the
campaign fell apart. I used to work in Somerset in the early sixties and
I read all this stuff about Tryweryn, all this stuff about Welsh princes,
and I came home to fight. I hitched to Cardiff to see Pedr Lewis and
the first thing he showed me in the Plaid Cymru offices was a map of

Wales with all the water pipes in it. Pedr had gone to jail for supplying detonators for the first bomb attack on the Elan Valley, and that was me, I was well into it. I met Tony Lewis and we formed the Patriotic Front and we got going, but by the time of the investiture we were in jail, then I was on trial.

During the trial I went into the witness box as John Jenkins had done. I saw Inspector Vivian Fisher giving notes to Tasker Watkins, QC, and I thought what are these buggers going to come up with? Years later I lived in Ireland and the Irish Special Branch came to see me – they'd been sent by Inspector Fisher, who had always been after the Free Wales Army. They said we won't do anything the English police want us to do, just stay out of Irish politics, which I did, which was sad because a lot of Irish people had helped me. I had to stay out of everything. I thought Plaid and Cymdeithas did little at the investiture other than turn it into promotion for Dafydd Iwan's song 'Carlo'.

Tecwyn Vaughan Jones: The investiture in 1969 is where my political activity was formed, as I was very much opposed to the investiture. I used to do things to rile people more than anything: I knew about the Welsh Language Society, I hadn't taken part in any Welsh Language Society activities then, but I put a banner outside the window: 'Carlo Cer Adref!' ('Charles Go Home!') We lived in a terraced house and in the summer when the investiture happened, on my Dansette I would play the song 'Carlo' with the windows open, just to upset people in the street that were passing by. In the end, they came knocking on the door and asked my father to take the banner down, which I had to do.

Carlo

by Dafydd Iwan

[*1st verse*]

Mae gen i ffrind bach yn byw ym Muckingham Palas,
A Carlo Windsor yw ei enw ef.
Tro dwethaf es i gnocio ar ei ddrws ei dy,
Daeth ei Fam i'r drws a medde hi wrthof i ...

[*Chorus*]

O, Carlo, Carlo,
Carlo'n warae polo heddi, heddi
Carlo, Carlo,
Carlo'n warae polo gyda Dadi, Dadi.

[I've a little friend who lives in Buckingham Palace,
And Charles Windsor is his name.
Last time I went to knock on his door,
His Mother answered and she told me ...

O, Charles, Charles,
Charles is playing polo today, today,
Charles, Charles,
Charles is playing polo with Daddy, Daddy.]

John Barnard Jenkins: On Christmas Eve 1972 I underwent one of the most emotional and intense experiences in my entire life, which convinced me finally of the existence of race memory, instinct and the strong compelling ties between those who unite in love of country and people. I was sitting down in my little cell, after looking out the bars at the moon shining. The moonlight outside sparkled on the frosty walls and glinted on the menacing tinsel of the barbed wire above them, but I was happy for I was not alone. There were others looking at the same moon who were, like me, in prison for Cymru Rydd Gymraeg [A Free

Welsh-Speaking Wales] and others fasting for Christmas, and I was linked to them all in a way unaffected by walls and wire. At that instant, as I became aware of this, it was as though my thought had completed a circuit which channelled and directed our united love and energy, for I felt a tangible wave of warmth and love flood over and into me. I was completely transformed, my blood was thrilled and singing, and I was possessed by a compelling ecstasy which was pure love for my country and people. I *knew* beyond doubt at that moment, the terrible power of the love which had motivated our fighting ancestors such as Caradoc, Buddug, Arthur, Glyndŵr, Llywelyn; my blood was singing to me of a long race memory of dungeons and death for the cause, and I was so submerged in the compelling ecstasy of sacrifice that I would have welcomed pain with joy. The intensity lasted for perhaps fifteen minutes, and finally receded slowly, leaving me drained but happy and filled with pity for those inadequates who have to resort to drugs for this experience. I knew that I had not been alone, and I knew that we were not going to lose this fight, *because* I had not been alone. All of Wales had been with me in spirit.

THREE

GWEITHREDU UNIONGYRCHOL / DIRECT ACTION

Voices

Philippa Davies

Steve Eaves

Menna Elfyn

Ffred Ffransis

Meinir Ffransis

Meri Huws

Dafydd Iwan

Tecwyn Vaughan Jones

Neil Kinnock

Rhys Mwyn

Helen Prosser

Dewi Prysor

Huw Stephens

Ned Thomas

Angharad Tomos

Charlotte Williams

Rowan Williams

———

At the beginning of the 1970s Cymdeithas yr Iaith developed its policy of direct action to include a set of protesting strategies that would regularly result in prison terms for those participating. As a youthful organisation, Cymdeithas embraced many of the energies abroad in the wider, international culture as the 1960s begat the 1970s. The publishing house Y Lolfa was established in Tal-y-bont, Ceredigion, in 1967 and printed much of Cymdeithas yr Iaith's literature, as well as publishing material by Cymraeg authors and poets, including irreverent broadsides, and texts and memoirs by many involved in the struggle for the language.

Other Cymraeg media companies founded in the era included Recordiau Sain, a record company established in 1969 by Dafydd Iwan, who from 1968 to 1971 was chairman of Cymdeithas, and the singer-songwriter Huw Jones. The debut Sain release was Jones' 'Dŵr', a song whose subject was the drowning of Tryweryn. By 1975 Sain had grown in scale and owned a recording studio near Llandwrog. Many of the songs Iwan released on the label and performed on a now energetic Cymraeg live-music circuit either drew on the history of Welsh protest or encouraged its proliferation. His song 'Peintio'r Byd yn Wyrdd' ('Painting the World Green') was written at the height of a Cymdeithas campaign that saw English-only road signs disfigured and daubed in green paint by activists. It was written in an idiom Iwan termed 'battle hymn'. The opening lines of another such song, 'Ffarwél i blygu glin / A llyfu tin y Sais', may be translated as:

> *'Farewell to bending the knee*
> *And licking the arse of the English.'*

Iwan himself had received jail sentences, and his willingness to do so helped to inspire many of the younger activists drawn to Cymdeithas. Also inspirational was his holistic approach to promoting the Welsh language – performing songs detailing its historic struggle, placing this struggle in a contemporary context and encouraging others to participate in direct action.

Ffred Ffransis: Direct action, to my understanding, was the whole raison d'être of Cymdeithas yr Iaith. It was fairly unique amongst movements in that it was formed, not because of a specific or unique aim, but because of unique forms of action; that's the whole reason it was set up, in support of the idea of direct action.

In 1967 or 1966, at the annual general meeting of Cymdeithas yr Iaith at the Marine Hotel, there was a big debate, the first big debate about non-violent direct action, and in 1970 there was a further debate about taking responsibility for our actions. In 1967, I think I probably contributed something from the floor, but I was more or less an onlooker. I wasn't an activist; I wasn't within any of the circles of people that made the decisions in Cymdeithas yr Iaith. There was an argument between two former chairs, Neil ap Jenkin and Emyr Llywelyn.

Both the life and works of Gandhi and of Martin Luther King were translated into Welsh between 1967 and 1969, and they had a substantial influence on the movement: Martin Luther King because he was nearer to our time and Gandhi because it was a national liberation movement, whereas Martin Luther King's was purely civil rights within a nation. And Emyr Llywelyn proposed a motion which any other society would see as a strange motion, that Cymdeithas yr Iaith would refrain from and reject the violence of the fist, the violence of the tongue and, more controversially, the violence of the heart. 'How's this going to be enforced then?' I was thinking. Emyr Llywelyn made an emotional speech, a personal speech, and he carried the day.

Charlotte Williams: I was ten in 1964 and during the decade grew very aware of African independence movements in different countries. I come from a mixed-heritage family; my mother said she was more black than my dad in her attitude because of her Welshness. She translated Welshness as resistance, as questioning, as being a critical advocate; and my father was a subject of colonial Britain in Guyana, and in our family there was an understanding of Welshness as being disadvantaged and racialised. But Welshness couldn't be assumed for a person of colour like myself, despite having been brought up in Wales, having received my entire education in Wales, having a Welsh-speaking mother. It was something as a family we always knew was our right, but it was not assumed, you couldn't assume it, and we had to claim our Welsh identities. My claim to Welshness was through the fact that my mother demanded it for us. Her fight was against the parochialism of Welshness, those traditional ideas: 'land, language, lineage' and how important those are in the DNA of Welshness. My mother told me: 'I had to climb out of a pile of slates,' and she had to climb out of that pile, married a black man, travelled the world.

Menna Elfyn: We saw ourselves emulating the civil rights movement in America. One of my first poems in my first book, *Mwyara*

['Blackberrying'], was about George Jackson, about the Black Panthers, Angela Davis. These were on my radar as much as Tryweryn was and Cymdeithas yr Iaith; not Plaid Cymru, because there was a bit of a divide there. We thought they were a bit meek but they were a political party – you could understand looking back why they couldn't go into activism and were always a non-violent organisation. Cymdeithas yr Iaith were adopting the same kind of principles as Martin Luther King and Gandhi. These were our heroes, prisoners of hope, and when I went to the university in Swansea, I was a member of the Socialist Society there, and we'd march for the anti-apartheid movement. We'd march in London and shout, 'Kiss, Kiss, Kissinger, how many kids have you killed today?'

Charlotte Williams: Race in the sixties as I was growing up was happening somewhere else. It was seen as an American civil rights issue: somewhere, elsewhere, is where this was all happening. I knew what colonialism was from a very young age, because my parents talked about African independence. We were in Llandudno, this funny little seaside town, where people from Liverpool or Manchester would come on holiday; it was very, very white.

Rowan Williams: It was an interesting thing, the direct action element, apart from some of the outlying oddities – the bomb around the time of the investiture possibly – but direct action in terms of defacing signs, that's very much within Gandhian pacifist direct action, the non-violent direct action tradition, which is part of that leftward shift.

Menna Elfyn: During the road signs campaign – I don't like to say the first, because it doesn't mean much, our being arrested for pulling down road signs – but my husband, Wynfford James, Ieuan Ross and another person, Maria Walsh, and I pulled down road signs in Briton Ferry and got arrested. That was a big court case and it was one of the first, along with some in North Wales as well. And we were fined. In those days, being fined meant that you never got to prison, because you would get sympathisers paying your fine before you could say in court, 'I'm ready to go to prison,' but it never happened in those early days.

Dafydd Iwan: I felt out of things a bit at university in Cardiff and I missed the first protest at Trefechan Bridge, and I said, 'Right, no more of this: I'm going to be a part of whatever's happening,' and so I joined Cymdeithas yr Iaith during that first year, and never missed a thing for about ten years and became Chair in '68. It's interesting because a crowd of us from young Plaid Cymru went over to the '66 celebrations of the Rising in Ireland and I must confess that . . . the Easter Rising was something which gave us, what shall I say? It was exciting and an inspiration. I mention it in one or two of my songs. And I remember a prominent member of Plaid Cymru said, 'That's the only bit of your song which I don't agree with.' He'd been living in Ireland and he was afraid that that would catch on in Wales, so he said, 'You talk about the martyrs of the '16 rebellion. I don't believe that that is the correct way to do it.' I was doing it as a historical reference, which was a reality and which you could see in Ireland had the desired results. I suppose that is an example of a kind of difficulty we had, in having a strict non-violent belief in our campaigns in Wales, while still applauding the people who had fought for a free Ireland. This was always brought up, or very often brought up, in discussions and in interviews: 'But you think that was a good thing?' 'Well, we face the reality, but we don't think that is the way for us to go.' And I was quite certain of that as the principle.

Menna Elfyn: My father was a minister. He was a pacifist, but also a member of Plaid Cymru at that time. He spoke a lot about Tryweryn, and I suppose it seeped into my consciousness of the injustice of it all. But always side by side with Wales, I tended to have an outlook on the world, and in the same way as Auden writes about Yeats being hurt into poetry, I was hurt into poetry through the Vietnam War, because I could see the parallel of a small nation. Vietnam, alongside Tryweryn, made me realise about the big powers that be. We had England, and there was America in Vietnam, and I could see a parallel there. I became conscious of that, of the injustice that allowed those things to happen.

Angharad Tomos: I didn't realise Cymraeg was in danger until I went to university, but I took an interest when I was about thirteen, fourteen, because Cymdeithas was all prevalent and exciting. I think it was through the music. I was a Welsh nationalist because of my parents, and people tended to look at that as something old-fashioned, but once we had a lively pop scene it became more acceptable. I remember thinking, 'Oh, Welsh can be cool.' Dafydd Iwan was such a prominent part of that, and his political message touched me.

Huw Stephens: My parents were avid supporters of Welsh culture. They'd have bought the records, and Sain Records were selling tens of thousands of singles and albums. I grew up in a house full of music like that. I've got three sisters, who are about fifteen years older than me, and they were into what was popular when they were in university, so I got to know about Geraint Jarman and Steve Eaves and Bryn Fôn, and people like that who were very popular singing in Wales.

Steve Eaves: My father and his father and me after him, we were all itinerant labourers. Before I had any education I just did what they did; I worked all around North Wales and the Welsh language was part of that, wherever I worked. For a long time I was illiterate in Welsh. Although I spoke Welsh on the building site and in the factory, I wasn't literate until I went to college. I didn't really know any middle-class people. I didn't know anybody whose father was a teacher. I didn't know any people who owned their own houses. I didn't know anybody like that. I became aware of Cymdeithas yr Iaith when I was working in Butlin's in Pwllheli in the kitchens, and next to the kitchens there was a huge boiler and there were these local guys from Pwllheli, Welsh-speakers, and they would talk about what was happening. This was the late sixties, and I was hearing their views on it and I was reading about it. Looking back, I realise I was hungry for education. I was really into poetry and it was a time when Dafydd Iwan was putting an intellectual approach to popular music along with a poetic sensibility, and using a medium which was basically a juvenile medium. Dafydd was using it to express emotions which hadn't been expressed before.

Dafydd Iwan: Plaid Cymru had to move from that image of intellectuals and preachers and teachers and literary figures, because it was far too easy a target for Labour to knock, and it was a disadvantage for a long time: 'Oh, you're just a party of teachers and preachers, and you don't know anything about the working class.' It was far too easy.

The process has been a gradual one to accept that Plaid Cymru is as diverse as any other party, but we can't ever say that we grew out of the working-class struggle. Cymdeithas yr Iaith helped, in the sense that although they were, and still are, criticised for being a bunch of students, at its peak in the late sixties and early seventies, we had wide support from young people of all backgrounds. At the same time as Cymdeithas yr Iaith was gaining ground, we were setting up things like Sain, the record company.

Ffred Ffransis: The Welsh music scene, Dafydd Iwan and Huw Jones, came out of Cymdeithas yr Iaith, and Cymdeithas yr Iaith activists set up all the Welsh book and record shops; they travelled Wales and set up companies.

Dafydd Iwan: Part of the drive to set up Sain was the realisation that, technically, the Welsh recording industry had to move with the times. It was partly that, but it was also a critical thing which chimed with what Cymdeithas yr Iaith was saying: 'We have to do things ourselves. It's no use complaining about people moving from rural areas; we have to move there or stay there and start businesses there.' It was a very strong part of our argument. We set up record companies, publishing houses, printing presses and shops ourselves, a lot of people in my generation – in the case of Sain, borrowing £500 from a friend of ours, Brian Morgan Edwards. He was an interesting character, he was Young Tory of the Year, and had lived in England, from a Welsh family, very English-sounding boy. He came back to Wales and went, 'Right, I'm going in with Plaid Cymru and I'm going to help you win self-government,' and he came in with great ideas. He was a character, and of course we tried to keep him in the background, because his accent and his whole demeanour was so English, and his whole background was Conservative: he was a strange bedfellow. But he played an important part in setting up Sain and also changing Plaid's attitude to campaigning. He brought in ephemera and badges and banners and loudspeakers. He really transformed the way we were campaigning. And he gave us £500 to start Sain, and said, 'All you have to do is buy a company off-the-peg' – we knew nothing about this kind of thing, and he said, 'I'll get you a company and you can use my friend as a guarantor' – he was really a great catalyst. We were supporting ourselves by singing and whatever else we could do. And the company grew from one record to the next. Meic Stevens came to us quite early on, and he was one of the best artists. The seventies became a very, very active period, very creative, and there were a lot of good sellers in the pop field: pop folk, folk rock, Hergest, Mynediad am Ddim, Tecwyn Ifan, Heather Jones. But the best-sellers, looking back, were the middle-of-the-road singers like Trebor Edwards and Hogia'r Wyddfa. Those were the ones who really brought the money in. Radio Cymru started up again during the seventies, and television then gradually began to play a part.

During the late 1960s and 1970s the major area of campaigning undertaken by Cymdeithas was for bilingual road signs. The standard English-only signs of the day were initially painted green, before the signs, in an escalation of the campaign, were removed or dismantled.

This was a form of direct action that ensured many members of the society were arrested.

The road sign campaign ran in parallel to a campaign for a Welsh-language television channel that saw members of the society take action such as climbing broadcasting masts and occupying television stations. The authorities responded by charging the protestors with offences such as criminal damage and conspiracy to trespass. Both were crimes that potentially carried lengthy prison sentences. Conspiracy charges in particular were seen by activists as a means by which the government could use draconian measures to undermine activities it associated with Welsh nationalism.

Ffred Ffransis: In Cymdeithas we had to work out the principle of direct action, but direct action for a purpose, not merely because we had the power, as a violent army would have, to destroy the system and to force our will that way, but to take enough action so that the authorities would have to prosecute us and that there would be a trial where we could argue our case and their response was in full view, as a forum.

Steve Eaves: Even before I went to university I never thought of Cymdeithas yr Iaith as just an intelligentsia, I saw it as part of a radical upheaval. At university I was more mature than the other students, at least in age. There were one or two people there who had come to university via the college in Harlech; my best friend was sponsored by his union, he was a railway worker. Lampeter was a small college. The other students who were interested in Cymdeithas yr Iaith were from a more traditional rural, cultural nationalist kind of background, but my friends and I started energising the system of cellau, the cells. There was a cell in the college, and it was a bit dormant, only putting Welsh language stickers on doorways and things like that. We joined in with the road signs campaign: we organised things to take down and smash up the road signs, and then, later, when the TV campaign kicked in, we organised squads to go and smash transmitters.

Angharad Tomos: My parents were strong nationalists, but I couldn't see my part in Plaid Cymru: there was no role for me to play. My mother's family was Liberal, my grandfather was very prominent with the Labour Party, but my mother changed to Plaid Cymru and convinced my father, so my father became later a councillor with Plaid. My mother always went to the local meetings of Plaid, so they were very political. Through Dafydd Iwan's songs, talking about the Beasleys and the Penyberth fire, I was asking my parents, 'What's this about?' and, for me, the fact that it wasn't an official history made it more exciting. It was all undercover and I just wanted to learn. I'm very, very interested in Welsh history, but in school we didn't have much Welsh history and it was boring: it was about the Methodist revival – there was nothing current.

Dafydd Iwan: I suppose songs are very handy like that. I was deliberately referencing things like the Beasleys' campaign and the burning of the bombing school and individuals like Saunders Lewis, Lewis Valentine and D. J. Williams. I brought them into my songs, partly to tell people about them, to educate in that sense, and it makes people think, as well.

Angharad Tomos: I think the sense of injustice of hearing those songs and learning about Tryweryn made me very interested in it. One of the first books I'd read was *The Welsh Extremist* by Ned Thomas. I had the badge 'Extremist' on my school uniform, and remember the schoolteacher saying, 'Oh, you'll be in jail and in over your head,' but Cymdeithas used it as a tongue-in-cheek badge.

Meri Huws: I became involved in Cymdeithas on a non-active basis when I was in school. I went to Aberystwyth in '75, so I'd become aware of the politics of Cymdeithas, the music of the time, Dafydd Iwan, in the very early seventies, probably also triggered by '69 and the investiture. I remember standing at the side of a road, watching a car drive past very fast, with a young man sitting in the back who was obviously wearing make-up, whom I was told was this man who was to be invested as the Prince of Wales. That was part of that growing awareness. I went to Aberystwyth and then became more involved, was arrested and freed before my first Christmas at home, which wasn't the jolliest Christmas we ever had, I was arrested at various points, occupying holiday homes, occupying council chambers.

Dafydd Iwan: Court cases and even imprisonment were becoming almost a regular occurrence, because we realised that having chosen that path of campaigning, any fine which resulted from the campaigns would not be paid, and not paying a fine usually meant imprisonment. Later, there were actions which were extreme enough to lead to direct imprisonment, but during the sixties and early seventies it was mostly non-payment of fines or contempt of court which led to imprisonment. There was a great deal of difference between some courts and others: some magistrates and juries wanted to show support for the campaign by imprisoning for a single day or insisting on a very small fine. In my case, magistrates came together from many parts of Wales to pay my fine and to show support for the cause.

Ffred Ffransis: By the time we got on to the 1970s, that's when the big argument happened within Cymdeithas yr Iaith. Are we about the official status of the language, purely – there are unfortunate connotations of the word 'pure' – a language movement? Or do we recognise that all socio-economic changes, decisions and political power affect the status of the language, especially in our counties which are Welsh-speaking? Which is the route that Cymdeithas yr Iaith took. But it didn't take that route until the 1970s, over a decade after its inception. Cymdeithas did not take that particular line in the 1960s; we did confine ourselves very much to campaigning on the official status of the language, which moved on to the very beginning of the campaign for Welsh-language broadcast television and radio channels.

Tecwyn Vaughan Jones: I had to go and work when I was in the sixth form during the holidays, and I worked in a hotel in Llandudno. I met a guy who was a PhD student at Bangor University, where I'd been accepted, and I ended up having a relationship at the age of eighteen with this person. He introduced me to all his gay friends at the university, and I was quite surprised as to how many gay people were in the Welsh Language Society and involved in the nationalist movement. I could not believe this. There was a time where I actually thought that nationalism drew homosexuals for some particular strange reason. And I remember telling that to Alwyn Roberts, who was a lecturer in the sociology department, and I remember him laughing and laughing about that, and he must have gone back to the Senior Common Room, because other lecturers said, 'Oh, Tecwyn, people are telling me that you think that Plaid Cymru is all full of poofs!' to embarrass me in a class situation.

I joined the Welsh Language Society in my first year as a student; I went to Bangor University in 1970, at the height of its activities, and was very much involved with the protests at that particular time. It was a very strong society at Bangor University. I think almost all the Welsh-speaking students joined Cymdeithas yr Iaith and we were coerced to go on protests: 'It'll be alright, it'll be alright.' When we were arrested my parents got pretty upset, but it was slowly crystallising my identity. Being arrested does have an influence and a long-lasting influence, and of course you were in a bubble. I wasn't part of many large-scale protests; the protests I attended were mainly at the university itself against university authority. Over the years, I came and went with the Welsh Language Society. I haven't always been a member. The Welsh language has been far more important to me than any idea of political independence or political separation.

Menna Elfyn: In 1970 I was part of a group who went to London to protest. Ffred would arrange these buses and say we're going to sit at these croesfan, and I never knew what he meant: what he meant was a zebra crossing. We were walking by and suddenly Ffred said, 'Right, sit down here,' in Oxford Street. I suppose we were very naïve – the police that arrested us realised we were a bit daft and they knew that we didn't pose any threat physically to them, so we were treated quite kindly. And you'd have a lot of Welsh-language policemen in London, who'd say, 'Oh, where are you from, do you know my aunty?'

Angharad Tomos: Because Dafydd Iwan was singing about jail and that he'd been in jail, you took that as a part of the package. I remember the frustration of being aged fourteen through to eighteen and not being able to break the law, thinking that's the only way we're going to change things. My father said, 'Well, until you're eighteen, I have to take responsibility for you, so you can't break the law.' And we couldn't do anything. I remember going to meetings and the only thing we could do was refuse our O-level certificate because it was in English, but it seemed a very trivial thing to do. And you felt useless. I've heard so many stories of breaking the law at that very low level. I can't think there was any bit of the administration in Wales that wasn't attempted to be broken: parking fines, exam results. It didn't matter how petty it was, it was all part of the movement's energy to make the point. I remember an interesting conversation when we were in the sixth form, and having the university entrance form and you had to label what nationality, and there was a great conversation in the sixth form, am I British or am I Welsh? I refused to fill them in because they were in English, and then I asked the headmaster could I send a form in Welsh and could I translate my own education certificates, so the teachers were trying to put up with that.

Dafydd Iwan: The campaign for language, for Cymdeithas yr Iaith, was very much tai a swyddi – houses and jobs – for the language. It was very much driven by the need to show that the language had economic value as well, and especially in the Welsh-speaking communities in the west and north, which were on the whole poor communities. We saw the language as a driving force for economic benefits in the Welsh-speaking areas.

Ffred Ffransis: The idea was that we weren't just tactically a non-violent movement, tactically not using things which could injure people, or being reckless of injury to people in demonstrations, we also wouldn't deliberately – although it did happen – insult or belittle people. In Cymdeithas the philosophical basis was that violence is an inherent part of the colonialism which we were campaigning against, and therefore we would be imitating and aping our very political enemy if we used violence as well. The idea was that we should not just refrain from violence, refrain from saying and doing a number of things, but that we should look at it positively, for everybody – the struggle for justice and peace aren't things of any particular faction in Wales, they should be something which you want everybody to embrace. If we want everybody to embrace it, then we must embrace everybody and look upon everybody as a potential supporter. Being part of the movement would come from the heart and the outward manifestation of that would be the words that we say and the actions that we take. I can't say that all of Cymdeithas yr Iaith lived up to it 100 per cent, nothing like 100 per cent, but probably far closer than practically any other political movement over a period of decades, with the possible exception of CND or the Greenpeace movement.

Rhys Mwyn: For myself and my brother there was always a question of at what point do we stand up and disagree with certain narratives within Welsh nationalism? Plaid was seen as mainstream; Free Wales Army and Mudiad Amddiffyn Cymru took direct action in the sixties. Cymdeithas yr Iaith Gymraeg were different. They were a language protest group, they did recognise the economic effects, but Cymdeithas started as a language campaign group. With them, we've had a very interesting relationship, as bands; we've all done a lot of benefit gigs for them, but politically, in terms of the debates and the discussion, I don't think they ever quite understood what we were doing. One of my first memories would be Gwynfor Evans becoming an MP and then, soon afterwards, you've got Dafydd Elis-Thomas and Dafydd Wigley, so that's Meirionnydd and Carmarthenshire, and we understood that they were visible. With Wigley, Dafydd El and Gwynfor, we had three of them, three Plaid MPs; they were known, identifiable. The other things we'd have been aware of would be from '71-ish onwards, people like Dafydd Iwan, Huw Jones, Meic Stevens, singing nationalist songs. That certainly contributed to the awareness.

Philippa Davies: A lot of my friends were Welsh first language, and I was in that culture by default in the Chapel – we all thought Cymdeithas yr Iaith were very romantic. Even though they were Welsh-language they were regarded as rather dashing and heroic, slightly romantic rebels.

Dafydd Iwan: From the mid-sixties to the mid-seventies I never ceased being a member of Plaid Cymru but my energy was in Cymdeithas yr Iaith, almost totally. Then I stood for parliament in '74, which was quite a big step for me, and perhaps damaged my image as far as the young revolutionaries of Cymdeithas yr Iaith were concerned.

Dewi Prysor: Up until 1974 Blaenau Ffestiniog was almost totally Labour. Dafydd El turned Plaid Cymru into a socialist party – he was almost a communist in those days and a lot of hard-working local people got him elected. Dafydd El became the first Plaid MP in Blaenau. Before then everyone was Welsh-speaking Labour and into poetry and everything Welsh-speaking people enjoy, but they were Labour, and they hated, hated PC because they could see the advance they were making in Wales. They absolutely hated everything about Cymdeithas and anything that promoted the Welsh language, even though some of these people couldn't speak English very well. The North Wales Quarrymen's Union only operated in Welsh – all their literature and minutes were in Welsh, which was remarkable given Welsh is an oral language and all commerce and legal matters were in English.

Ffred Ffransis: I had become the national secretary of Cymdeithas yr Iaith, and I proposed that we develop the non-violent philosophy further by adopting a motion that we should accept responsibility for our actions as Cymdeithas yr Iaith. The argument that was put forward was that we should bear the brunt and the burden of the battle, not cause problems to other people because of our beliefs. By taking it on our own shoulders, by taking responsibility for our actions and by being willing to accept all the consequences, we would show people how seriously we viewed the issue and that would then persuade people in their own way and in their own fields of life to accept responsibility for the future of the language themselves, not by doing what we were doing, necessarily, but in their own fields. And that was a logical extension of the non-violent principle.

Cymdeithas yr Iaith as a movement of still overwhelmingly young people at that time had developed and matured; the discussion which you had at an AGM was nuanced. Somebody had to take responsibility. It could be, for example, in the most basic campaigns, that the AGM took responsibility because it had voted for it. More often than not, it could be the Senedd of the society which would take responsibility, or the particular group who were organising the campaign. And the way in which this was put, and it was a difficult argument to argue against, was, 'Well, is it right, then, that maybe we, as officers of the society, think up these plans for direct action, we ask members to implement them, to take the direct action, and then they have to take the responsibility for it and face all the consequences, not us who organised it? Is that right? No.'

Ned Thomas: The ruling body of the Welsh Language Society took responsibility and that led to conspiracy trials. There were two, I think, and I attended those as press, and of course it's very difficult to prove things. Obviously, the Welsh Language Society had conspired in the sense they said, 'We take responsibility,' but the police had to establish a conspiracy, and the only way they could do that was on the basis of confessions, so they had to interview people who were fairly sophisticated officers of the Welsh Language Society, who just kept saying, 'No comment.'

The organisation's strategy included drawing attention to their objectives by taking direct action outside Wales, at locations of institutional authority such as the Old Bailey. As the decade progressed these protests took place against the backdrop of developing unrest in Northern Ireland and drew increasingly harsh prison sentences. The decade also saw the development of the campaign for a Cymraeg television channel that would reach fruition in the early 1980s, over the course of which a thousand members of Cymdeithas yr Iaith were incarcerated in prison and in police cells. Within the Welsh Labour Party these activities were frequently considered to be a source of irritation.

Neil Kinnock: The more aggressive tactics of Cymdeithas yr Iaith and one or two other groups were resented, and there was a mixture of embarrassment and amusement. Don't forget, this is against the background of real blood on the streets in Northern Ireland. That figured to an extent, especially in families with boys in the military.

Ffred Ffransis: It's not just the chair of Cymdeithas but everybody organising things. For example, in 1973, when I came out of prison after serving a two-year sentence, I announced on coming out we needed a further boost for the campaign for a Welsh-language television channel. They'd recently set up a commission and were undecided, so we were going to take three months of direct action, to take action twice every week for three months for a Welsh television channel, and that was an unprecedented series of activity. It was June 1973. I wasn't chair of the society, but I was on the board for campaign activity. I was organising lots of the action. We'd meet up every week and four people would be delegated and plans approved to make sure that the plans were implemented.

I remember meeting a group of four people who were going to take the action in Wrexham in 1974 one evening and I brought all the plans there. I'd done all the research into the Carmel TV transmitter mast near Cross Hands. It was a particular target because they were broadcasting English television to the north of Wales which had no Welsh-language content whatsoever. I'd done a map of the area, of how to reach the area, and where the entry point would be – not how to get in, they worked out that for themselves – but just a map of the area of how to reach it, being in a remote location. And I went over the plans with the four of them, and Ifan Roberts, one of the people who took action that night – [he] later became a minister of religion – they were just going out of the door towards the car, and he looked back at me and he said, 'This bit of paper, Ffred, with the map on, what do you want us to do with it afterwards?' because they were going to take action then from within the mast, to make sure that the authorities were telephoned to tell them that the action had been taken. And he said, 'So what do you want me to do: do you want me to throw it away or to give it to them?' and we hadn't planned [for that]. They were all happy to take the action; they were going to take the responsibility that time, and that went right to my heart. I thought, 'I can't send them out. I'll take responsibility.' So I said, 'No, just give it them.' He gave it to them and I got twelve months for that. It was so unfair, conspiracy to trespass, when they actually did the damage in the mast itself.

Menna Elfyn: Wynfford James, my husband, was Chairman of Cymdeithas yr Iaith at the time, and what they decided in the

Cymdeithas Senedd was to take a different path and accept responsibility on behalf of the Senedd and not take individual responsibility – there was a bit of a debate but they decided the Senedd should take responsibility, and a man called Rhodri Williams who was the media leader or whatever. And so what the police did was arrest Wynfford and Rhodri for conspiracy to cause damage to the Blaenplwyf transmitter mast. Wynfford and Rhodri obviously didn't cause the damage, that was other people, including still very famous names, who took part, but remain anonymous.

A trial was put on in Carmarthen and it lasted for about a week, or two weeks, and there were protests every single day there outside the court and people were arrested and so forth. I was eight months pregnant at the time. My daughter Fflur was due in August and this was in July, so there was a month to go, and they couldn't reach a verdict. So of course, they got let off, but the authorities then said there would be a new trial in the autumn. They were then put on trial in the autumn and Peter Hain later raised the trial in Parliament in connection with conspiracy trials, political conspiracy trials. He also raised the fact that what they did for the second trial was get a lot of people with English surnames, so that they would not get a jury that would be sympathetic to the cause.

I remember walking back when the first case finished, and one of the jurors turned to my husband and said, 'Good luck to you all now,' so that was that juror more or less saying, 'This isn't fair. We understand why it's happening, and we need a Welsh channel and so forth.'

So in the second trial, they were given six months' imprisonment each, and I visited him many a time, every month, and I took Fflur one time, and I remember one of the screws saying, 'Oh, you've brought in a baby, that will taint her for life!' That was Swansea Prison. And Wynfford, because he had been to prison about four times before, he took it well and he became the tea-boy for the screws, making toast and tea, and he had quite a good time.

Ffred Ffransis: We took the strategy of limited damage to property, so it was symbolic rather than actually putting something out of operation. We got into the control room of Granada TV because that's when the night porter made his brew every night and he'd left the door open. We got into there and we saw these big monitor screens, and we were saying, 'So, what's limited action?' We smashed four of them and we let four of them be, and we phoned the police. The important thing about that was that we phoned the police. They came in and the first thing the police did was let the security officers lay into us, because they were scared that they were going to lose their jobs, get laid off and so on, while the police watched. Then the next thing that happened is we showed the police exactly what we'd done. When we got to the police station, we said, as we'd always say, 'These are our names and our addresses, and we took this action which we've shown you, as part of the campaign for a Welsh television channel, and we're not going to answer any other questions,' because it wasn't our business to implicate other people who weren't there at the time. They started roughing and beating everybody up. They know where to hit you, where the marks don't show, and they went through the whole of that rigmarole.

Then they went out and came back again, and the chief police officer announced to the others, 'This case has to be done by the book.' They'd made one or two phone calls in the meantime, established that probably we had certain connections and that it wouldn't be a good idea to treat us as they treated most people who were in for criminal damage. In the court, the police officers that had been doing the beatings came. They smiled; they were very friendly. We didn't ever complain, because we thought possibly they had a legitimate concern: by that time, 1971, the IRA had just started activities and they didn't know who we were and whether we'd planted explosives, and maybe they were trying to minimise the risk to life. We gave them the benefit of the doubt and, with non-violent hearts, we didn't complain. You had to work out the implementation of things as you went on. Everybody who became chair of the society, and not only the chairs but the planners of the action, realised that this sort of treatment was on the cards, right through to the new millennium.

Dafydd Iwan: My main imprisonment was in '71 in Cardiff Prison. I spent a few days here and there in Swansea, during the big trial in Swansea, and I spent a couple of days in Walton Prison after non-paying my television licence as part of the S4C campaign, but the main imprisonment was three months in Cardiff. I was released after a month or so. The Archbishop of Wales came to see me, Glyn Simon, and that's the only time I remember the chief warden of Cardiff jail showing me some kind of respect, because I was summoned to his room in the prison to meet the archbishop, and the archbishop brought me the message that magistrates wanted to pay my fine, but was I willing? I was caught between two minds, because while I was in, there were many, many protests and, in fact, my imprisonment led to many other people being imprisoned, but also a very high profile for the whole cause, so I was torn between two things: accepting a payment of the fine by magistrates was in itself a very strong symbolic message of support, and eventually I did decide to accept the fine, but in doing so, in coming out, many of the actions planned during my imprisonment were put on hold. So there was an argument for staying in as well.

They were very exciting times, and we really thought that we were succeeding to bring the language into the forefront of the political agenda, and of course it signalled the end of the period when politicians could say, 'I'm all for the language, but . . .' – it then became necessary for political parties in Wales to put action where their words were, and to show they were in favour of full official status for the language or not. And it was a case of forcing the issue and making political parties show their support in a practical way.

Ned Thomas: These things spread out into the community. One of Gwynfor Evans' daughters, Meinir, was very photogenic with long, blonde hair and she invaded the House of Commons visitors' gallery and, if I remember rightly, swung from the balcony. In that period I was teaching in Aberystwyth but living near Tregaron, and so each evening I would be driving home and I remember giving a lift once to a girl who worked in the garage and lived in the next village to me, and to pass the time I said, 'Oh, I'm coming to your village to speak to Merched y Wawr ['Daughters of the Dawn', rough equivalent of the Women's Institute].' She said 'Oh, I don't go near Merched y Wawr, they're all raging nationalists.' She was a Welsh-speaking girl and a few months later, after these events, I gave the same girl a lift, and she wore a Cymdeithas sticker, saying 'Cymraeg!' and she said, 'Ah, you know, that Meinir, she must be so in love with Ffred Ffransis, she swung from the balcony in the House of Commons!'

Meinir Ffransis: That was the first time I went to prison. We had occupied courts of law throughout Wales. We were protesting against the imprisonment of Dafydd Iwan, and we stayed overnight. We went into Lampeter Court and the local chippy brought us loads of chips. They were so supportive. We really enjoyed the experience and it was a bit of an adventure.

Menna Elfyn: I'd been pushing them to send me to prison because I had received a fine for painting a slogan about British Telecom, and I wrote a poem about BT which R. S. Thomas translated so that I could send it to the courts in lieu of my fine. Of course, that didn't work. But I said, 'I'm happy to go. I want to go to prison,' and twice or three times I went to them and they said, 'We'll give you another month to think about it,' and I would say, 'There's no need to think about it: I'm not going to pay the fine.' They said, 'OK, we'll send you to prison for one week.' They took me to the cells, and the policemen are there – 'One week? Perhaps we can keep her here overnight for two days. Would that work out as being the same as in prison for a week?' and they were debating this, and the woman police officer was like, 'Oh, that means I'll have to do overtime; we'll have to take her all the way to the women's prison in Bristol.' So they didn't want to send me to prison. In the end, they said, 'Well, she hasn't had any lunch; go and get her some fish and chips,' so they went, got me fish and chips, and then I was on the way to Bristol with two women police officers, and I said, 'I'm sorry – you want to go home.' They said, 'Oh, it's OK, it's OK. Now, I don't know if you can have supper there: we'd better stop to have sandwiches on the way.' On the way, they stopped at a service station to get me sandwiches, I wasn't treated like a felon or a criminal. I think they were sympathetic because, well, they couldn't be arsed to take me to prison, basically.

Meinir Ffransis: Ffred decided nothing was happening, nobody was being arrested, and everybody was enjoying it too much. So Ffred decided we would go to the highest court in the land, in England and Wales, and interrupt the proceedings at the Old Bailey. Several of us went up into the public gallery, and there was a very important case being heard about something following the war: it was something about submarines called PQ17. It was being followed in the *Times* newspaper. And the judge was Justice Lawton, and Ffred and two others went up behind where he was sitting and started shouting for justice for the Welsh language, and then we all stood up in the public gallery and started singing hymns, and then were dragged out. Justice Lawton, I can still see his face, beetroot red and very angry. He left, then the police came. Lots of us girls had long flowing hair, and the police dragged us down these stone steps by our hair. There was no tradition of protesting in London at that time, everything was open, you could go up Downing Street and into the Houses of Parliament, not like it is now, after the IRA. But the police didn't know what they were dealing with, really, and in fairness to them, they didn't know that we were non-violent people and we had been told to go limp and let the police drag us.

Then we were taken to some cells underneath the court. There were about twenty or thirty of us there, and my father came to see us, because he was a Member of Parliament. Then we were taken individually before the judge – Justice Lawton again – and he gave us the offer, 'If you apologise, you can go home, that is you'll be fined for breach of the peace or contempt of court, but if you don't apologise, you will go to prison for three months.' And most of us apologised, but I think five of the boys and five of the girls refused, and the girls were taken to Holloway and the boys were taken to Pentonville. So that was that protest. It was then a big legal issue: the judge had been the wronged party, but he was also doling out the punishment and the fairness of that and the legality was an issue. I don't remember what conclusion they came to, but I remember it was being discussed. My father organised Dewi Watkin Powell to appeal for us against the three months' imprisonment, and we went to court every day, for the appeal proceedings, and the name of the judge in those proceedings was Lord Denning. There were three judges, Lord Denning and two others. One of them was a Welsh-speaker, but he was the most antagonistic of the three, ironically. But Ffred and Arvon and Rhodri decided that they weren't going to appeal and that they were staying in Pentonville for the three months, and I think Ffred got an extra month as well, for some road signs that he had taken down somewhere.

We were in the Court of Appeal for I think it was about seven days, and then Lord Denning decided to release us and I've got a copy of the letter. Tom Parry was our principal in Aberystwyth, and I've got a copy of the letter Tom Parry sent to Denning to thank him for releasing us, because we were still his students and Denning replied and said something like, 'When I saw those five innocent young girls, I couldn't think of sending them back to prison!' I don't think he disagreed in principle that we should have got three months, but he let us go, anyway. That's the first time I was imprisoned.

Menna Elfyn: We were to spend three months, but the judge let us out after the end of the court case. It showed how vulnerable the judicial system was and how very nervous it was about the growth in feeling, not from the likes of us youngsters, but from the class of doctors and lecturers and ministers of religion and so forth.

Meinir Ffransis: Being imprisoned is not an easy thing, but then five of us were together and we were full of the justice of our cause and actions, although I was in prison later once in Pucklechurch Prison at Bristol and when some people, my lecturers, came to see me and my father came to see me we weren't allowed to speak Welsh, so that was very, very difficult. I suppose the wardens couldn't listen in to what we were saying, but my lecturers were there because of college work. And at that time my father was still an MP. Menna Elfyn was in Pucklechurch Prison in Bristol at the same time as me, and another person, Nan Jones, and we were not allowed to speak Welsh to visitors. In Holloway, when I was there during the Welsh-language television campaign, the letters I received were censored, but the chaplain of the prison was a Cornishman, Mr Saunders, and he pretended he could speak Welsh because he could speak Cornish and he passed on all our letters.

Menna Elfyn: When Meinir and I were in prison, with Nan Jones, we decided to go on a visit strike. We were not allowed to speak in Welsh to people, and so we decided, 'Well, OK, we won't take visitors.' Well, you can imagine the anger from prisoners, some saying, 'How dare you; nobody's come to see me in three months and then you are able to choose not to see people, how dare you?' kind of attitude, and again, you had to agree with them, how precious we were to be able to be in that position, and yet, in prison was the first time ever I spoke to my mother and father in English. And that was quite a difficult conversation.

Angharad Tomos: When I was in prison all my letters were in Welsh, so they had to go through a censor. I wasn't allowed to have Welsh radio, because they said it was VHF and I could pick the police radio up. I think it would have been very different if I was imprisoned in Wales; there would be more of an understanding. I was mostly imprisoned in Risley Remand Centre. When I was eighteen, I thought it would be much more efficient to be undercover, because we had so few protestors or activists. I thought if you didn't take responsibility, you could be much more active, and then had long debates with Ffred about why the non-violent principle and taking responsibility for your action was so important.

Helen Prosser: I think I was first arrested at the end of my third year at university. I'd been active the night before our degree results. I was arrested painting signs in Powys, and had my degree results read out to me with a policeman holding the phone, because they kept us in overnight, and I was later imprisoned following on from that.

There are no women's prisons in Wales, so I was taken to Pucklechurch in Bristol. I went to the court in Aberaeron, so that would have been the closest prison to Aberaeron. It's closed now, I think. What happened to me was, I was taken to prison, and I wouldn't pay a fine. I can't remember how long for, it wasn't long imprisonment. But someone local – and to this day, I don't know who, well, I've got an inkling, I think it's a non-Welsh-speaker with plenty of money – actually paid my fine. The morning after, I was released, although I knew nothing about this. All I remember is, and Angharad says this, even though perhaps she hasn't done it every time herself, once you're in prison, in a sense, you need to conform, or you get a tough time. It was really interesting going into prison, even though I was there a fairly short time. Maybe about six of us were admitted that day: the other five knew each other well, there were hugs and kisses between them, and it made me see life in a different light, in a sense, that it was easier for those people to be in jail than to live, and we're talking about the eighties, not now. Now it must be far worse.

I was sticking out there terribly, because in prison women don't have to wear prison clothes, and I'd just been for an interview to do a teacher-training course, so I was there in a little dress, in this prison. And they even treated me differently, because they gave me sums to do rather than sewing, they got me to do the accounts.

Arriving there, you have a bath and there's a spout coming out of the wall, no taps, in case you try and kill yourself, obviously. It's so degrading. I remember the question, 'Which drugs do you take, how many abortions have you had?' Lots of these things have really stayed with me, even though it was such a short time. I had a pretty bad experience. Because the jail was full, they put me in the high-risk area. I was on the bottom bunk and there was this other lady on the top, and she said to me, 'Oh, when I was here in the summer, there was a fat woman above me, and every night she got closer,' and then there was a strip cell opposite and this woman screamed all night.

I think the lessons were life lessons, about injustice, that so many of these women just didn't have life skills, rather than being evil people doing bad things; I'm sure there were some there, but it was a really interesting process.

Menna Elfyn: There were a lot of women taking part in campaigns, but somehow, I can well remember, we had a lot of people who were parchus evangelists, who said, 'Oh, Cymdeithas wouldn't tolerate, wouldn't accept having a woman as a leader,' and of course that was later shown to be false. After going to prison, I've said before, that I went in as a language activist, as a language campaigner, and I came out realising that I was a feminist. My feminism was born in prison, where I realised there were women there who had no language at all: they were disempowered by language. [I saw] all the privileges we had as students, to start with, the educated class, and I started to read feminist writers and became a feminist.

I became a feminist at a time when Cymdeithas wasn't quite ready – well, we'll do that later, that was the attitude. It has always been, 'Let's get the language equal first of all before going on to gender politics'; it seemed something quite alien to so many people who hadn't read or witnessed or realised the inequalities. And so, that became also part of why I did other things with CND and the peace movement, where women didn't have to question why they were there: they weren't only there to take part in campaigns; they were there to be equal.

Angharad Tomos: I had police in England thinking that we were the IRA; they had no understanding at all of Cymdeithas, that was in the late seventies. There were four of us, one was named Sean, one was Theresa, I was Angharad and they asked, 'Why have you got Irish names? Are you the IRA, where are your explosives?' and we were trying to say we're a non-violent movement, we're the Welsh Language Society. We were in Manchester, but they didn't believe us at all. We'd broken into a transmitter, so they straight away thought, 'Oh, they're going to blow it up,' while in Wales, if you were in the middle of a protest and you say, 'We're Cymdeithas,' then the police would know the difference. I was in prison six times altogether, the first time was in London. We'd just climbed the mast in Crystal Palace, and they asked us to keep the peace and my friend said, 'Don't,' so I listened to her. I said, 'No, we're not keeping the peace,' so five days in Holloway straight away.

Menna Elfyn: I think if we want the language to prosper, we have to be sympathetic to different levels of Welsh. There's nothing so harming or disarming to people than people correcting their Welsh: this is another phenomenon of the Welsh. 'Oh, you can't mutate.' Or somebody will phone in to the radio and they've learnt Welsh, or they haven't learnt Welsh. Who cares? I think there's a lack of empathy from some Welsh-speakers towards people who speak Welsh at different levels and abilities; a lack of patience or understanding. It's back to our sense of insecurity, of being inferior somehow. We have two languages, after all.

FOUR

TOMEN RHIF 7 / TIP NUMBER 7

Voices

Mansel Aylward

Marilyn Brown

Rosemary Butler

Bob Croydon

Phil Cullen

Philippa Davies

Ron Davies

Jeff Edwards

Arfon Evans

Bob Griffiths

Len Haggett

Edwina Hart

Calvin Hodgkinson

Kim Howells

David Hurn

Tecwyn Vaughan

Jones

Neil Kinnock

Tom Marston

Kevin Morgan

Max Perkins

Christine Powell

Michael Sheen

Hettie Taylor

Alan Thomas

Bernard Thomas

Karen Thomas

Ned Thomas

Rowan Williams

Tony Winter

———

Though mining remained the principal form of employment in South Wales, by the mid-1960s the industrial base had diversified considerably.

The sector that had once provided the area's primary source of work was now in competition with the newer growth industries of steel, petrochemicals, tinplate manufacturing and their many and varied support services. Large-scale plants such as the British Petroleum oil refinery near the village of Llandarcy, Neath, and the steelworks of Port Talbot and Llanwern in Newport occupied a totemic position in their communities.

Under the auspices of the National Coal Board, mining still remained the region's principal form of employment. The industry was experiencing substantial changes as it entered a period of decline, accelerated by a fall in demand for coal. Between 1960 and 1965 thirty-five collieries closed in Wales, with the loss of 15,000 jobs in what was a nationalised industry. This process continued despite the election of a Labour government in 1964. The decade concluded with an estimated 50,000 redundancies in the South Wales coalfield and a reduction in the number of collieries from 121 to 52.

The new cooling towers that loomed across the landscape were visible reminders of the scale of the industry undertaken at the steel and oil sites and emblematic of a country experiencing, by the standards set earlier in the century, a high rate of employment, much of which was work that held the incentive of taking place above ground. Llanwern Steel Works, which opened in 1962, quickly grew to a workforce of over 6,000 employees. The oil refinery at Llandarcy was the third biggest in the United Kingdom and processed several million tons of crude oil annually. As well as employing thousands of workers, the refinery was noted for its onsite amenities including squash courts, gymnasiums, accommodation and outdoor sports pitches. Secure employment and the high standards of the facilities in these workplaces created an atmosphere of optimism supported by the institutional networks of clubs, libraries and halls established by unions and other associations, which remained a mainstay throughout the South Wales Valleys and within its mining communities in particular.

Neil Kinnock: From the Tredegar Medical Aid Society at the turn of the century growing in strength in the wake of the First World War, to the libraries, the workmen's institutes, the snooker halls, the thespian societies, the local operatic societies, everything in terms of erudition and cultural activity developed from the realisation that collective contribution, universal contribution, could produce wonderful results for individuals. And that understanding became applied in just about every sphere, from sport to entertainment to what could be called deep culture, and certainly to education and the opportunities for school-children and adult education. Right through, there's scarcely an area of life in the industrial areas of South Wales that couldn't be traced to that dawning of the realisation that if we all chip in a tiny amount, we can get the best that's available.

Arfon Evans: In Maerdy and Ferndale we referred to the institutes as palaces of culture. I remember walking into the library in Maerdy in awe, because you could pick up any book on any subject. You could read, you could get self-taught, because it was all available, bearing in mind that most of the population probably couldn't afford to buy books. We didn't have a Workers' Educational Association there, but then you had the strength of the Communist Party, which, not replaced it, but ran alongside it, and people could learn politically through that medium. But I was overwhelmed by the availability to such a small community of this massive palace of culture, with choirs coming out of there, snooker hall, small sports in the boxing gym; it was absolutely fantastic. They were six-, seven-storey buildings, paid for out of the subscriptions from miners.

Neil Kinnock: By the time I was about thirteen or fourteen, I'd seen in the Tredegar Workmen's Hall most of the great operatic stars of the era, and that was because from the period before the First World War, when the coal industry was relatively thriving, they had a universal system of payment for everybody working in the area. It spread through shop workers, steel workers, transport workers – everybody contributed a penny a week, and later tuppence a week, towards the Workmen's Hall, so that they got this wonderful, palatial edifice with a huge library where Nye Bevan and several other developed minds did their reading; to the snooker hall where we produced world snooker champions and on the last Sunday of the month, right through the winter months, the best concert artists that money could buy. They were paid Covent Garden fees to appear with the Tredegar Orpheus Choir, or the Tredegar Town Band or both. As a boy I'd seen Kathleen Jones, Jussi Björling, Joan Sutherland, all the stars of that period, along with a crowd of 2,000. It wasn't a few enthusiasts. I mention it to illustrate what people understood to be the power of collective contribution for individual emancipation, individual enjoyment, individual security and care.

Michael Sheen: My family had all been a part of that, and that was very much to do with not just being a performer, but also as a social cohesive thing as well; my family were very involved both in Port Talbot and in Newport, my father's brother, John Sheen, remained in Newport, whereas my dad came back to Port Talbot. I remember going to watch shows at the Dolman Theatre in Newport. It was Cwmbran Operatic Society. I think I was something like seventeen before I saw a play, but I'd seen loads of shows, because of the amateur operatic societies, watching all those shows – *Fiddler on the Roof* and *Carousel* and *Brigadoon* – my parents had been in the amateur operatic societies around the Port Talbot area as had my grandfather and my great-grandparents.

Edwina Hart: Years later when I was in the Assembly we were once having a discussion about support for opera in the Labour Group and for the arts and culture. A minister said, 'Oh, well, we don't want to bother with that, ordinary people aren't interested.' I said, 'Pardon? They're not interested in opera?' I said, 'Hang on a second, I know miners who know more about bloody opera than anybody in this room. Do you think because they worked down a pit that they weren't interested in opera, they weren't interested in classical music, they weren't interested in literature? What do you think they sought to achieve?'

Arfon Evans: My father worked for Powell Duffryn's in the No. 5 Pit in Ferndale and was disabled out of the pit at the age of twenty-nine, with what they called then early stages pneumoconiosis and silicosis. In front of my very eyes, I saw a young man deteriorate so rapidly into an old man – he was only in his forties and he looked like a man in his seventies – because of the nature of pneumoconiosis, silicosis is a progressive disease. And at eleven, twelve, thirteen, that had a significant effect on my psyche, on the way I thought. It started to provoke me into thinking what a terrible world this is, where a man was down the pit at the age of thirteen, comes up at twenty-nine, ends up with 100 per cent pneumoconiosis, and dies a young man.

As a very young man then, I joined the Young Communist League, I became very active in the Young Communist League: it was nothing for me to be seen in Maerdy going around, on my own, at the age of thirteen, fourteen, knocking doors, selling the *Daily Worker*, later to become the *Morning Star*, and selling *Challenge*, the paper of the Young Communist League. I was having debates with men who could throw back the Hungarian Revolution of 1956, but I could hold a debate at that age with those people.

Then, at the age of fifteen, I left school without any qualifications and went to the pit. I started in Maerdy. I worked on a conventional face with just wooden props and wooden flats, a compressed-air conveyor in the face, very antiquated. But one of the things you had to do, as a little butty bach, was to shovel fifteen or twenty tons of coal onto a conveyor. I was about 5ft 4in, weighed about 8 stone, and it really reflected back in my thoughts of how my father had to work in those days where you couldn't actually see an oil lamp or the flame of an oil lamp stretched with a straight arm.

Christine Powell: A lot of my family were involved in the mining industry over a long time, and my husband was a miner. My dad started his working life underground, but he had O levels, and in 1950, '51, if you had O levels, well, you must be bright. He ended up working in the offices for quite a long time, in different collieries.

My father's father worked in mines all his life; it was pneumoconiosis that dispatched him in the end, and my grandfather on the other side worked in a lot of private mines amongst other jobs he did through the course of his life. Anthracite we mined in this valley. My grandfather and my father and my two uncles began their working lives in Banwen Colliery, the correct name for that was Onllwyn No. 3. Banwen was on the hit list to close, so they advised [my father] to come to Seven Sisters Colliery, which is sort of halfway down the valley, because he was marrying a Seven girl and they told him that Seven Sisters Colliery would see him through the rest of his working life. Well, that didn't happen because, a few years later, that shut. Then he went to where Blaenant Colliery eventually was and that shut, then he went over to the Maesteg area, to Caerau Colliery. But he didn't own a car and it was very difficult for him to travel there, so along came the calling of the Ford Motor Company and he went in the mid-1960s to the Ford Motor Company and he worked there until he was sixty.

Arfon Evans: After a number of years, my father decided that, with the cooperation of the colliery manager, I would be sacked, and I went to the colliery manager's office, he presented me with two envelopes, and he said, 'You have decisions to make today.' He was quite aggressive, like they were, because this was in 1962, they hadn't long come out of the private enterprise system, because nationalisation was in 1947. I said, 'Yes, Sir,' and because of my politics, I'd learned to keep my mouth shut and respond when necessary.

He said, 'There's two envelopes, make a choice,' and I thought, 'Well, he probably knows more than me about these envelopes,' so I said, 'Can you suggest which envelope I should take?' and he threw an envelope at me, which was an application for a National Coal Board electrical engineering apprenticeship scheme, and I studied and finished at Treforest Mining School at the age of twenty-five.

In the meantime, within three months of me going into the pit, I was on the lodge committee as a youth representative, and then gradually I worked my way through as a craftsman representative, as the vice-chairman, until I probably was one of the youngest chairmen in the coalfield.

People like Arthur Horner, Charlie Coch-Jones, Hayden Matthews, Emlyn Williams, who was the chairman of Maerdy before me: all these people had invested their lives. The grandfathers and the fathers could testify that the union was always there to defend you. The union was a body which was progressive in many ways, in terms of your politics. It would help you decide how you voted in your local election. It would help you decide how you voted nationally.

Christine Powell: There was a campaign to stop the mine closures in the sixties. Harold Wilson came down through the valley, on some visit to something or other, and I remember sitting on the front wall of my parents' house, watching him go past, and the boys in Cwm Coed Colliery had spray-painted 'Coal not Dole' on the road to the colliery. That's the first time I recall the phrase being coined.

Bob Croydon: The early sixties was when things really got under way. You tend in your head to arrange it around Wilson, the white heat of technology. But in the mid-sixties, you had relatively full employment and with those large industries you had huge apprenticeship pro-grammes which rolled down into education, all the technical colleges. Kids were leaving school at fifteen because you could go into an apprenticeship with British Steel across a range of professions. The same with British Coal, and BP particularly, Ford in Swansea. It was Prestcold before that, making refrigerators, before Ford took it on. All these highly skilled apprenticeships were feeding back into that end of education; the universities were thriving and expanding. The impact of that level of industrial activity fed right back through society. The unions were on the up then as well, and people were earning relatively more. You could buy a semi-detached house for three grand.

Kim Howells: I was born in November 1946 in the hospital in Merthyr because there wasn't a maternity ward at the time in Aberdare. There was a terrible housing shortage and when I was very little my mother and father lived in rooms like everybody else. They found a council house, a brand-new council house on a brand-new estate, Penywaun, which is half-way between Hirwaun and Aberdare, and we moved in there in 1951. My mother lived there until she died almost seventy years later. It was a wonderful house in a terrific estate, though it was a very tough place. It consisted mainly of families who were coal miners or, like my father, men who'd packed in the pits very early on and become long-distance lorry drivers. My father worked for Dunlop in Hirwaun. There was a big industrial estate up in Hirwaun then which had been built more or less at the same time as the Treforest industrial estate, and so light engineering, manufacturing, electrical manufacturing were already the equal of coal mining in terms of employment, even in Aberdare. Mountain Ash itself had the highest percentage of coal-mining anywhere in South Wales but it wasn't dependent on the coal industry. Coal was still a very significant employer, but even by the 1950s the employment that was provided on the industrial estates was growing and at least as significant as the coal-mining industry in places like Aberdare.

Tony Winter: The economic development of Wales had been distorted, like in many countries. We ended up with the finest steam coal in the world, and my family is very typical. Going back to my grandparents, half of my family came off the land, literally peasants in North Wales, and the other half of my family came from the West of England, from the land. I'm going back now to the turn of the last century.

I think it had to be recognised that if the South Wales industrial belt, not to diminish the North Wales industrial belt, but without the industrial South being won over to progressive ideas about working conditions, the battle was lost. The explosions in mines were horrible things. I can remember nearly forty people in the Rhondda being killed when the explosion in Clydach took place in 1965; some were people I knew, as recently as that.

Kevin Morgan: I was born in 1953, and when I was living and growing up in Wales, it was boom time. I grew up in a small mining village called Rhigos; it's the end of the coalfield and it's the beginning of rural Wales. Our family council house had a vista to die for, because there were the Brecon Beacons. For a mining village, it had this hybrid quality of an industrial culture situated in a rural idyll, so growing up there was idyllic. It was full employment because Rhigos is the home and the host of the Hirwaun Industrial Estate, and dozens and dozens and dozens of buses would bring people to work from the whole of the Valleys there, and then come back at five o'clock, pick them up and ship them home.

Kim Howells: Mountain Ash had the highest percentage of coal miners anywhere in South Wales in the population, but it was not dependent on the coal industry. It was still a very significant employer, but even by the 1950s the employment that was already provided and was growing on the industrial estates was at least as significant as the coal-mining industry in Aberdare.

Bob Croydon: If you look at something like British Steel in Port Talbot – the Steel Company of Wales as it was then – or at British Petroleum at Llandarcy, they were running out sports teams across a range of disciplines. You had an A, B and C team in the rugby; a B team in the cricket; you'd have rifle clubs, archery clubs, judo teams. The sheer numbers of people who were employed in single sites and the way that that fed back into the communities was astonishing. In sport, the incubators were there, people were effectively being paid to play for the British Steel or BP teams at rugby.

BP Llandarcy employed a team of gardeners. I wouldn't say it ran into dozens, but there were probably a couple of dozen guys working there as groundsmen doing landscaping in and around the refinery; as well as rugby and cricket pitches they had bowling greens and tennis courts. Three or four people working full time maintaining bowling greens at an oil refinery and some of them were people who'd been affected by the war, what we now know as PTSD. BP didn't get rid of them. They found a job for them. The level of amenity that was provided by those sorts of industries was staggering compared to today.

Edwina Hart: I remember doing a course with the union reps from Llandarcy many years ago, while I was training for my union education, and I was fascinated, because I came from banking, and the banks to a certain extent did similar things with rugby and football, they supported sports like that, but not to the extent that somewhere like Llandarcy did. I was absolutely amazed at the facilities that they had in terms of support and what they did with them. You could say that BP was almost a model employer in some ways, but quite hard-nosed in the ways they negotiated with their employees. On the one hand, they were giving you these type of facilities, so you got that bond, that family feel, together, but you also got, I also felt, listening to the stewards, that there was often an alternative agenda that almost kept them beholden at the same time. Before the nationalisation of the steel industry, individual employers like Thomas Bolton who were in Gowerton, near Swansea, in the Albert Works, helped provide amenities for the rugby club and the cricket club. That was quite normal, their association with activities in their village.

Tom Marston: I worked in the steel industry and I belonged to a group of high-flying managers, so to speak, and we met up at various times with all the leading management theorists of the time, mainly American. I disagreed entirely with the views of these American managers who came across, giving us advice. They were heartless, unscrupulous people. BP Llandarcy was run by ex-military men, nearly all the management were Colonel This and Captain That and Major So-and-so, they all carried their military title still: you always addressed them as Major So-and-so even when they were in industry.

I was sent abroad to work in the steel industries overseas, to study their methods, and I worked in Germany for a short time. It was very efficient, but we were equally as good, if not better in some instances. My own department at Port Talbot was far more efficient than any I saw in Germany; from the very early sixties the steel company was training itself and adapting itself to become top-notch.

Kim Howells: One of my brothers played for Aberdare cricket club and that was a big game for them, to go down to BP Llandarcy, because the pitch and facilities were so serious, compared to what they were used to. Those companies took over some of the responsibility for silver bands and social functions; the only parties I can remember as a child were the works Christmas parties for Dunlop's and that was quite a big deal. Before he went to work for Dunlop's my father worked for a firm called Harfoot's and they were taking coal off the open casts, and open-cast coal mining was a very, very big industry in South Wales at the time, all the way from Cynheidre right across to the north-eastern rim of the coalfield, up above Brynamman. It was right the way along the northern rim, it was a big industry. My father suddenly had the opportunity to earn a bit more money driving hard core from abandoned tips, especially the tips of the ironworks in the Merthyr valley, down to lay the foundations for the Llanwern steelworks in Newport.

I can remember very well us all having tea, as we called it, the evening meal, when my father got home from work saying that one of the trucks, a Thames trader, had broken down on the Llanwern site as they were dropping off the hard core and they just bulldozed it straight into the ground. There was so much money to be made by these firms from shifting all these old iron tips and slagheaps down to Llanwern. It seemed like a fabulous image of a society that was changing at an incredible rate that someone could do this in what were still the post-war years.

Bob Croydon: The notion that you wouldn't get a job or couldn't get a job was alien. They were over-employing people at British Steel and then, as the unions got hold, it became increasingly hard to get rid of them. I can remember doing holiday jobs at BP where I was paid but I didn't do any work. You'd go into the labour exchange in Neath, you wouldn't sign on as a student and be stacking deckchairs; you'd sign on as a labourer and get a man's thirty quid a week or whatever it was. Nobody had a clue who I was, or what I was doing there; you'd wander round the steelworks, find a comfortable corner and read a couple of science fiction books for seven weeks.

Max Perkins: My journalistic career began in Pontypool, working for a local paper there. I started at a time when it was a very different scene industrially; you had three or four mines still working in the valley, and you had great diversity. You had the ICI Fibres factory just outside Pontypool, you had the Panteg steelworks, you had Girling's brake factory in Cwmbran, so it was a pretty thriving area and the miners were well above the average earnings level at that time, so they had plenty of money. Pontypool was quite a thriving little market town, which it is not now.

I shared a flat with some of the people from the research department of the ICI factory and they were very much at the forefront of research into nylon. They had a wonderful garden all year round, which they would open to the public; there was a fantastic social club which ran drawing classes, art classes, all sorts of things like that. Panteg steelworks had a really good cricket team and I spent a lot of time in Blaenavon, and the thing that I remember mostly was the miners' library and how well it was used, how well-informed they were. I used to go to local council meetings and there were some amazing people there, the level of debate and eloquence was exceptionally high.

Kim Howells: We weren't brought up assuming that the apotheosis of Welsh culture was choirs and silver bands and things. I was brought up in a house that was full of Dizzy Gillespie and Charlie Parker and Duke Ellington. My father, during the war, had met a family from Chicago, the Salazars, they were GIs, and for many years afterwards they would send over LPs and records and photographs of Chicago and music, jazz that was not available in this country. I can remember very well on summer afternoons and evenings, our front windows being open and my father playing Duke Ellington or Django Reinhardt with the windows open and all the kids and some of their parents sitting out around listening to this music, outside our window. It was an environment which was changing very rapidly. It was never, ever limited to those visual clichés and aural clichés of South Wales.

Max Perkins: From the cultural point of view there was a lot of anti-Welsh feeling, especially of course from Leo Abse, the MP for Pontypool. I remember going, in the days when they used to have public meetings during election time, to one such meeting. The Plaid Cymru people were sitting at the back, and they started stamping their feet and Abse said, 'Yeah, listen to them. They're all wearing jackboots!' and they all sort of stormed out, and there was this great tension. In south-east Wales, particularly within what was then Gwent, or as some like to call it Monmouthshire, there was this tremendous suspicion about the rest of Wales.

Rosemary Butler: The joke was that the First World War was declared by England, Wales and Monmouthshire, and the peace treaty was signed by England and Wales, so Monmouthshire is still at war with Germany. I think it was the fact that you couldn't speak Welsh at work in the Industrial Revolution and it came from there, and that was it. They used to talk about the Welsh heartlands. I always said, 'Where are the Welsh heartlands? I live in the Welsh heartlands.'

Ned Thomas: There was the very strong Valleys Welsh identity, but it wasn't entirely separate from a British identity.

Tecwyn Vaughan Jones: I was born in Bangor, in St David's Maternity Hospital, not that I had any relationship with Bangor until I was a student. I was brought up in Blaenau Ffestiniog in north-west Wales, and that's where my home is and I still consider my roots to be. Blaenau suffered a period of deindustrialisation in the 1960s, a bit earlier than happened in the Valleys, because all the slate mines were closed in the 1960s, leaving a remnant which still exists but there was mass unemployment there, and people were moving away from the community in droves at that time and young people no longer had the choice of going to work in the quarry. A lot of them still did, because there was some work remaining there, but I remember my mother telling me, 'Oh, so-and-so's mother was telling me that so-and-so is going into the Army; I hope you don't go into the Army. I hope you do well at school, so you don't have to go into the Army.' It was seen as something to keep them off the dole, at that particular time.

Philippa Davies: My father was liberal and he rose in the education department and ended up being the only man to be a director of education in Britain who hadn't gone to university, because he fought in the war, in the RAF. He was as rational and of the Enlightenment as my mother was bonkers. He joined book clubs and liked classical music. When I was in the Girls' Grammar and we were chosen to be on *Top of the Form* on the radio, the radio producer asked us what music we liked, and I said I liked classical music, and my friend was astonished, because she knew this was an absolute blatant lie. And the producer said, 'Well, what do you like particularly?' so I said, 'Oh, I like Stravinsky,' and she said, 'Well, what do you like best of Stravinsky then?' and I remembered my father had the *Rite of Spring* so I said, 'I really love the *Rite of Spring*,' and I'm sure that was the clincher with me getting the gig. It was still the post-war era, people were very interested in liberal ideas.

Tecwyn Vaughan Jones: Living in Blaenau in the 1960s, I saw poverty there which I've never seen since, in Wales, nor in Britain. In the same street as we lived there were exceptionally poor people. I don't know where they were getting money from – my mother told me afterwards, that every single child there never, ever wore new clothes. They all had second-hand clothes, cast-offs, from people that were helping them quite secretively. I don't think even the husbands knew: it was a woman's thing that they were helping each other then, and that was the kind of community. I used to play with some of these kids: there were no carpets, just a bosh [outdoor toilet] in the back; where they washed, there was damp on the floor. It was really, really awful. We weren't a rich family at all, but the clothes my friends were wearing, well, they looked like ragamuffins. They looked like photographs of the East End of London from the 1930s. I hope I never, ever have to see it again. Eventually, my father got a car, and we'd go to Llandudno for a drive on Saturday, and the car was filled with friends of mine who had no cars, and so we were three or four of us, sitting on the back seat of the car, going for a trip to Llandudno for the afternoon and we always passed other kids who were crying because they couldn't come with us.

I have lots of photographs of my father when he was growing up in the community. He was very much involved with the WEA, the Workers' Educational Association, and my father studied economics – never went to university or college or anything – but he studied economics, and that was repeated to me by his brothers: 'Oh, your father studied economics.' And I thought, 'Well, he only went to a WEA class,' but that was important in that community. And when I came to teach WEA classes and talk about and discuss issues with people like that, I realised how good it was for these people to get things off their chests. We had really incredible discussions, like we did in the sixties, when I used to attend them. They were very important.

Rosemary Butler: My father had to leave school at sixteen so his brother could go, and the only job he could get was in the pit, so he went down for six years, came out eventually and went in the army. He rose up through the ranks very quickly but he was deafened at Dunkirk, so he had to come out and he had no relevant qualifications. And when you look at that generation of people, he should have gone to Oxford or Cambridge. It's a bit like the miners who started the reading rooms. They were very bright men. My grandfather was a champion chess player, but they didn't have any opportunities and that's why the Workers' Educational Association was so important.

Edwina Hart: My father was a very active trade unionist. He was in the engineering union and he used to attend his trade union meetings in the institute in Gorseinon once a fortnight and the WEA ran courses there as well.

Neil Kinnock: I'd started to work for the WEA in 1966, and one of the first classes I established, these were evening adult classes, was in the Social Democratic Club in Aberfan, which was founded by the Social Democratic Foundation around 1900. It was a genuinely political but immensely popular club, so I thought that was a promising place, and so we filled out the papers. By the time of the disaster, I'd been running the class for five weeks, six weeks, and I had a class of about forty and I obviously socialised, got to know them – they were nearly all men in the class, there were only two women coming to the class. It was one of the highlights of my week.

Tom Marston: I attended a lot of the WEA classes. I can recall when I came to live in the village there wasn't a house that didn't have Workers' Educational Association books and Odhams Press books were also very important: *The Complete Self-Educator*, *The Complete Shakespeare*, the Bible, these were the books which you relied upon and you gave to your children, before they went to the county school or the grammar school or the secondary modern, you gave them *The Complete Self-Educator*, so that they had a pathway to the curriculum.

Christine Powell: I think the working class, particularly the miners, wanted their children to be educated because they didn't want them to follow them down a hole. I think my dad would have gone without to buy me a book.

Where else was the education going to come from? It was Sunday schools and unions. Nobody else gave a damn. I live across the road from what was Seven Sisters Miners' Institute, which was a reading room – they then extended it. In our valley, I think that's the oldest institute. Next to it is a bowling green, and I can remember seeing people in their whites playing bowls, and lower down our village we had the recreation ground, where there was a lido. There was a bowling green in Onllwyn; there was a bowling green in Seven Sisters. We had three swimming pools and a lido, as a kid I used to go there; they were still open then. We had wonderful amenities, wonderful amenities. In the 1960s I can remember eight collieries: Banwen, Onllwyn, Seven, Tonteg, Dilwyn, Treforgan, Cefn Coed, Blaenant, with men paying towards the welfare halls out of their wages every week.

There was so much there. They weren't the absolutely magnificent buildings you see in the Rhondda or over in Ammanford. They were smaller. In a way, I'm glad, because when you go to places like Merthyr and the Rhondda and Ammanford, and particularly if you go through Brynamman and go to Garnant, you see these beautiful buildings in disrepair.

Kim Howells: There was a very different kind of feeling then: one of great optimism, and what grew out of that, certainly as far as my family were concerned, was that none of us boys were going to go and work in the pit. That was a real theme throughout my childhood, and passing the eleven plus. Both my brothers and I passed the eleven plus; they went to Aberdare Grammar. God knows why I went to Mountain Ash Grammar, but I was forever grateful for it, because there were girls there. And as far back as I can remember, we were encouraged to go to libraries, first to the Miners' Welfare in Trecynon library and then the much grander Aberdare Public Library, which became a fixture in my life.

David Hurn: There is absolutely no doubt that if you do a job where you are likely to rely on your neighbour for your life, it builds an extraordinary sense of community. You get it in the steelworks, you get it in the slate mines, you get it in mining. You have that sense. But against that, it's a bloody awful job. You're balancing the argument of the people that are doing it, who I would suggest build round them a community spirit so that they can justify to themselves that they're doing something which they actually want to do: 'This is our community and we miners, or we steelworkers, get together.' You only have to move slightly outside of that to say, 'To be on your bloody knees down the bottom of a hole and moving seven ton of coal a day is a job? I mean, it's obscene that we're doing that.' And then, of course, it goes out from there, cleverly justifying that job by means of what we call community, so that you're not every day being destroyed by, in your own mind, what you're doing; you feel it's a job, but against that, is the realisation for a lot of people that this is a lousy job.

Kim Howells: Some of my mother's relatives had been badly injured in the pits, and my father's relatives. I remember my grandfather and his friends, they must have been in their sixties, sitting around what we call the Park Pond in Aberdare and all of them coughing and spluttering and spitting with pneumoconiosis. My grandfather died very young of it. There was also a sense of being cheated. The pathologist, the doctor, would always write 'Heart failure' on the death certificate, so the compensation was minimal, and that was very often the basis not only for the lack of enthusiasm to go and work in the pit, but of real resentment about the collieries and the coal industry and the owners.

Rowan Williams: If you put side-by-side the general secularising of British society with the levels of income, availability of entertainment, and all those other factors, all of that going on in the sixties, and map that onto the dissolution of traditional communities at a fantastically rapid rate, it's not entirely surprising that these communities, which had been focal of people's identity, didn't have a place to sit any longer in many people's eyes. And although the Anglican Church had had quite a good, active and flourishing period in the era from, say, '45 to '65, it, too, was beginning to feel the chill. It had good leadership in Glyn Simon as archbishop: he was a very significant figure. He was archbishop for a very short time and was of course archbishop at the time of the Aberfan disaster.

The village of Aberfan, which lies four miles south of Merthyr Tydfil and sits equidistant from the bottom of the western valley slope of the Taff Valley and the eastern slope of Mynydd Merthyr, was typical of the communities that had experienced the adjustments taking place in the mining industry. Aberfan and its neighbouring settlements of Merthyr Vale and Mount Pleasant, known collectively as Ynys Owen, had once provided a workforce almost 2,000 miners strong to its local collieries, roughly a quarter of the community population. By 1966 this figure had dwindled to 800. The use of spoil tips in the area was also in commensurate decline.

Only one of the seven tips in Ynys Owen, Tip 7, whose arbitrary construction had begun in 1958, was still in commission. Over 34m in height, the tip was assembled of 227,000 m³, or 270 million litres, of spoil, 23,000 m³ of which was tailings, the fine particle residue left from the refining, smelting and water treatment processing of coal, a residue which turns to the consistency of quicksand when saturated.

Tip 7 was built on highly porous sandstone permeated by underground springs. A shift at Tip 7 was detected in May 1963. Six months later, in November, a more substantial slide was noted, which had resulted in the previously even surface of the tip being replaced by a crater, whilst a forbidding bulge had formed at the foot of the tip. When pressed for a response to this ominous development, the National Coal Board asserted that, in their estimation, Tip 7 had not experienced a physical disturbance and provided assurances that the movement was a result of a tailings run off, of residue detaching itself. Residents of Aberfan made formal complaints to their statutory authority, Merthyr Tydfil County Borough Council, who subsequently wrote to the NCB regarding the 'Danger from Coal Slurry being tipped at the rear of the Pantglas Schools'. It was agreed that tailings alone would be deposited on Tip 7 with immediate effect. In 1965 the council and National Coal Board met to agree a further course of action to address the clogged draining ditches and pipework that were an ongoing, visible threat to the tip's stability.

No action had been taken over a year later when, on Friday 21 October 1966, Tip 7 collapsed, and its contents followed the course of the slope of the Taff Valley downwards to Aberfan. The black tidal wave of slurry first destroyed a farm cottage, instantly killing its occupants. At Pantglas Junior School, the morning assembly had concluded with the communal singing of 'All Things Bright and Beautiful' when the wave engulfed the school and several of the village houses nearby, before coming to rest and forming a thick, dark quagmire. Eyewitness accounts mention the total silence that immediately preceded and followed the disaster. Due to the consistency of the slurry, it took a week to retrieve all 144 victims from the quagmire, a figure that included 116 school children.

Alan Thomas: If you can imagine those tips, to a child they were huge. I walked on them, I played on them. I got a row many times for getting dirty and getting holes in trousers ... Our favourite things were the

leather conveyor belts that pulled the trams carrying everything that
went up that mountain.

Jeff Edwards: There were springs that came down the mountainside
and fed into the canal. As kids we used to dam up those springs and
paddle in them, looking for sticklebacks and tadpoles. We put them in
jars, took them home and waited for them to become frogs . . .

We played in the woods all around that area by Tip Number 7, built
dens and blocked up the stream. Coal Board said they didn't know
the stream was there, but we knew about it. Used to dam it up, make
a swimming pool, not far from the tip and swim in it. The water was
freezing cold.

Hettie Taylor: It was suddenly growing darker, and we couldn't
understand it. It was a rainy day and there was a mist going down,
so we thought, you know, it's just that. I think I'd finished marking
the register and there was this terrible noise, like a growling noise, a
dreadful noise. I started looking around – I couldn't see anything out
of my window – I thought something had gone in the roof. I couldn't
believe what I could see. Our end of the room was still standing but
there was black behind where the other classrooms were. You couldn't
see anything. It was as if the mountain was right up against the
school.

I took the children down onto the road. I said, 'I want you to run
home, tell your mams and dads that something dreadful has happened
in the school. But,' I said, 'don't look back, just run on home.' My
children were first year juniors, so it was alright for them to go home.
And they did, they went.

Karen Thomas: I was the last one at the table to pay dinner money and
while we were in the hall there was like a terrific noise and flying glass
started coming down the corridor from the headmistress' room. And
Nansi Williams, the dinner lady – her reaction was very quick – she

said to get on the floor on top of each other, but before we could even do that everything just caved in on top of us and she was on top of us. We didn't know what had happened. There was just this big noise and then the glass was flying from the headmistress' room and then the wall from the classroom just seemed to fall and all of a sudden it was just there, and we were buried.

Jeff Edwards: The next thing I remember was waking up with all this material on top of me. There were shouts and screams and 'Get me out of here!' I couldn't move at all because my desk was against my stomach and it really hurt. On my left-hand side there was a girl's head, and that head was straight here, just next to my face really, and I couldn't get away from it. She had died and as time went on, her face became puffier. My right foot was stuck in the hot radiator, because my desk was against the wall nearest the hall and this material was above me. All I could see was an aperture of light and you could see through the roof – the roof had collapsed.

The screams then got less and less as time went on and I just couldn't move. I was stuck. It was a panicking kind of concern and I really wanted to get away from this head. I knew she had died. I didn't know what was happening. One minute I was in a maths lesson, next there was all this. It was totally unreal.

Bernard Thomas: When I came round, the first thing I remember was the other children, screaming for their lives, with fear.

Mansel Aylward: He said, 'Are you a Doctor?' I said, 'No, I'm not a doctor – I'm in my final year.' He said, 'Well, I think you'd be useful in getting down to Aberfan.' He knew I had relatives there and we had a short chat. Then I realised it was the school . . .

I had great difficulty getting into Aberfan . . . there was slurry on the road about a mile or so before getting to Aberfan. But I drove through it – and broke the axle on my car! Then I had to walk. And when I got up into the site I didn't expect to see what I saw. The slurry, the coverage of the houses, many of which had been just taken away – and then the school. And they knew I wasn't a doctor, so they said, 'Well, give us a hand. We're going to examine the kids as they come out and get them off [to hospital] as soon as possible.'

Bob Griffiths: It started filtering through via our radios that a tip had slid into a school in Aberfan. Well, the first thing we said was, 'Where's Aberfan?' If they had said the village in Merthyr Vale colliery we would have known. On approaching I looked out of the window and the first impression I had was of a large-diameter pipe, actually bobbing on the slurry from the tip, actually bobbing along as if it was a lump of timber on waves. Couldn't believe it.

For the first ten minutes we were moving stuff out of the way, to see if we could find any casualties. It was a lot of people doing a lot of digging at the time, basically with their hands. We were digging with our hands because we didn't have any tools – on the van they were equipped with breathing apparatus not with tools for digging.

Neil Kinnock: It was the last Friday of Glenys' half-term – she was working for Monmouthshire then, in school. We heard on the news at ten o'clock that the disaster had occurred, although there were no confirming facts about it, and I said, 'I'm going to go up to Aberfan, because it sounds as if something awful is happening in the village.'

Len Haggett: If you're ever asked what resources would you want in an incident of that nature, we had the best in the world. We had the miners. They were the boys that could shift the slurry, who could support the roof and who could continue to search to see if there were rescues. I always admired [the miners' skills] – in the sense that the roof was hanging down, it was dangerous, Yet they came and a repairer as they called them would look at it, grab a length of timber, wet it with his thumb and say to his mate, 'Saw that.' And he did and it went up

105

perfectly. And that occurred a number of times. No measuring tapes, no nothing. Just looked at it and assessed what length he wanted, where it was to go and it went. And this is what was going on to protect the people who were still working in that area to try and find children and to make it reasonably safe – and this is what they did. And though everyone were heroes that were there that day, members of the public, everybody else, the miners were probably the best men you could have at that scene.

Marilyn Brown: There were quite a lot of people there by this time. Quite a few of the women were onto a heap, the old part of the school, passing bricks and stones, and it didn't seem real somehow. I thought the children must be out of the building, they must be somewhere. They can't be in the school. I didn't realise how bad it was, I really didn't. I must have been dreaming or in denial, because I didn't want to think that they were in that school, and a lot of people felt the same way.

Len Haggett: When we arrived in Moy Road – I had lived in Aberfan – I realised that a complete row of houses had collapsed and right across the road there was a twenty- to twenty-five-foot wall of coal slurry. Initially I was not aware that the school was involved. We were dealing with rescues in Moy Road and we couldn't see over the slurry. Leading Fireman Bill Evans on the first appliance was there with me. We could hear people calling out from beneath the rubble.

Calvin Hodgkinson: I was digging away with my hands ... All of a sudden I can see a hand. I shouted to the workmen, 'Quick, there's somebody over here!' They said to me, 'You've done well. Move away now.' It was a little girl they had out of there and she was alive.

David Hurn: If you were doing a lot of current affairs work, journalistic work, whatever you like to call it, you listened constantly to the radio; suddenly it came over about Aberfan. I was with Ian Berry, who is a very great photographer, and immediately, we didn't question it, it was our job: we turned around and went there. For me, it was slightly more emotional than I suspect it was for Ian, it was something that had happened which you ought to cover; for me, it was something that had happened which I ought to cover which also had an emotional impact.

Neil Kinnock: We took my father's shovel from the coal cwtch and threw it in the back of the Mini, and both of us went over to Aberfan, we got there by about, I don't know, ten to eleven or something and it was total devastation. I was the constituency MP and we arrived at the site within the hour.

You can see the photographs, but even that doesn't really convey how transformed the whole place was. We realised after an hour or so that there was nothing we could do, and the boys were starting to arrive from the pit, so I said, 'We'll leave it to the people who know what they're doing,' and got in the car and drove home. The tip had washed up to the doors of the Social Democratic Club in the main street in Aberfan. Everything from there right to the top of the tip was completely flattened and covered in slurry.

David Hurn: We got there quite late in the day, and immediately you realised that this was emotionally a different event. This was a lot of kids – 116 or whatever it was, who had been suffocated to death by crap; by crap which shouldn't be there. Slip, they call it. It should never have been there. It should never have been built on the place; it was totally incompetent. On top of that, you had their parents and their grandparents trying to dig them out, of a situation that you couldn't dig people out of. Slurry, you dig it and as quick as you dig it, it fills back in again. You had this unbelievably emotional situation where people were pushing themselves physically to the absolute extreme to do something which was impossible to do.

Tom Marston: I was in the steel company at Port Talbot and I ran a chemical engineering department and I received a telephone message at work: 'Could I supply shovels?' I said, 'What do you want shovels for?' 'Oh, we want 300 shovels.' I said, 'Yes, OK,' I went round the stores, and gave them the shovels. They didn't tell me what it was for; I was just asked if I could supply 300 shovels. I put the phone down, and within two minutes I was asked 'How many sacks have you got? Can you give us sacks?' 'Yes, OK.' The next thing: 'How many lorries have you got and how many men can you spare?' and I went down and then I realised what it was, then, when the full information came out. It was terrible. Terrible.

David Hurn: By and large, if you had any sensibilities – I don't know about other people, but certainly I felt – the residents of Aberfan didn't want you there. You were being a voyeur at something which to them was deeply, deeply emotional. Against that, I had enough experience by that time to realise that this needed to be recorded for historical reasons. All you can do in that situation is to try to be a decent human being. You try to keep the balance between trying to not offend the people you're pointing the camera at and your own judgement – whether that be good or bad judgement – that this has an importance that needs to be recorded.

I'm a great believer that the second that somebody says you can't photograph something, you ought to be photographing it, in the same way as I'm a great believer that if you see masses and masses of national flags, there's something dodgy going on, or lots and lots of big photographs of one particular person stuck up on every wall and poster, there's something dodgy going on. The advantage that I had was that quite a lot of the people there were newspaper photographers and they're used to taking and getting their one picture. I had worked for magazines and my first thought was, 'How big a layout is this going to need?' 'If you need twenty pictures in your story, then you need this sort of picture, that sort of picture; don't forget it's very important

108

who's supplying the sandwiches,' that approach to things. You don't miss those things because your experience tells you that they are part of the story. If you're not experienced, you don't think about that, and if you're not experienced in magazines, you think in terms of the single newspaper picture. Then, when that series came out, it went in *Stern* and *Paris Match* and didn't go into the local English papers.

The difficulty was the emotional aspect of how you deal with the knowledge, or how you deal with the feelings of the people doing the digging in the slurry.

Philippa Davies: I remember the day. Everybody, all the mothers, out on the streets, outside our house, because everybody knew somebody who was connected to Aberfan. I can remember it totally, coming home from school and women and men crying everywhere outside our houses. Everybody did know somebody. It's much more vivid than Kennedy dying in my memory, because it was very live. And we couldn't believe it, watching it on the news.

Phil Cullen: My father, grandfather and great-grandfather all lived in Cinclid and I have a photograph of a tip slip that came right across the Cinclid common, which blocked the main Merthyr to Cardiff road. It diverted the River Taff and blocked the canal. That was during the war years. Mistakes that had been learned from then had never been acted upon. The practice of dumping on the side of the mountains was implemented by the private sector, and when the Coal Board inherited the legacy of those tips after nationalisation in 1947 they continued very much as the private sector had and hoped for the best.

Philippa Davies: I wrote a poem on Aberfan which has gone into the *Poetry of Places* anthology. I revisited the report in my research and my God, it makes you angry, the way Lord Robens behaved, the warnings that had occurred before. There's a whole series of little acts that build up to quite a big picture of guilt and then the subsequent stuff that happened with the fund are incredible, really incredible. It was really dreadful. Interestingly, one of the people who challenged Aberfan and what happened subsequently, very effectively, on the floor of the House of Commons, was Thatcher. She did a really thorough analysis of it.

Phil Cullen: Back in 1966 whoever was the NUM lodge chairman or secretary at Merthyr Vale probably knew nothing about that tip. At the end of the day the responsibility for that tip sat with the National Coal Board. It wasn't the union's tip; it wasn't the men's tip, it wasn't the village's tip. The tip belonged to the National Coal Board and that's where responsibility lay.

The chairman of the National Coal Board, Lord Robens, was alerted to the disaster at a meeting that same morning. Robens decided that the response should be deputised to the company's Director-General of Production and Chief Safety Engineer, who immediately made their way to the village, while Robens kept his afternoon engagement to be invested as the first chancellor of the University of Surrey, Guildford. When the Secretary of State for Wales, Cledwyn Hughes, contacted the NCB later that day, for confirmation that Robens was personally overseeing the relief work, his colleagues fabricated their answer.

The Magnum photographer David Hurn captured the immediate grief, madness and rage of the disaster, having arrived at Aberfan around midday. His photographs would later be reproduced in editorials around the world and used in evidence during parliamentary debate. In statements to the press that were met with disbelief and anger by the village residents, Lord Robens asserted it was 'impossible to know that there was a spring in the heart of this tip' and dismissed the media coverage of the disaster as 'ghoulish'.

Robens' attitude and easy reliance on half-truths confirmed the sense that the National Coal Board had failed to engage with the condition of Tip 7 with any seriousness, despite the fact it had been made aware of the site's numerous problems three years earlier. The Queen visited the village eight days after the disaster, having previously sent Prince Philip to represent her in the immediate aftermath; she later spoke of her decision not to visit the village immediately as 'her biggest regret'.

Five days after the disaster Cledwyn Hughes appointed a tribunal to inquire into 'the causes of, and circumstances relating to, the Aberfan disaster' to be chaired by Sir Herbert Edmund Davies, a South Wales barrister with detailed knowledge of mining laws.

David Hurn: There's no doubt that what Aberfan did was to point out that there were people in power who in the minds of a lot of people really didn't know what they were talking about and however well-meaning they were, or however they wanted to justify this as the greater good and all that sort of stuff, they were the enemy in a way. From my point of view, the fact that the pictures were mentioned in Parliament was, I suppose, significant.

Undoubtedly, if anybody helped with that, it was Cliff Michelmore of the BBC, because that was a man of extreme dignity, that could stand on the edge of the disaster and talk about everything without being in the least bit patronising. Obviously a highly, highly intelligent, sensitive, decent journalist who understood the context of what he was reporting.

Ron Davies: Tryweryn was obviously important in part of the Welsh community, notably in the Welsh-speaking heartland. I can remember the flooding of Tryweryn being on television, seeing it, but thinking, 'Oh, somewhere in Wales, what's that got to do to me?' that sort of attitude.

Aberfan was significant because it shook people in Wales. Aberfan, hitting the guts of the mining valleys, caused a stir, whether it was a resentment of the disaster itself, or whether it was the events surrounding that. I think all of that did shake the Labour Party. It must have been in '67, the Rhondda West by-election, where you would expect the Rhondda to have a majority of 20,000, and the Labour Party only just squeaked in by a thousand, and similarly then in Caerphilly, the majority was slashed to a couple of thousand from 20,000.

The tribunal attracted immediate controversy and there was an order by the Attorney General prohibiting media speculation on the cause of the disaster. The precedents of earlier inquiries into pit disasters suggested a tendency towards leniency and reluctance to lay blame at the foot of the executive. These factors exacerbated the tense atmosphere around the proceedings, which had been stoked by Robens' earlier, irresponsible remarks, and led to members of the public shouting phrases such as 'Mark the death certificate "Buried alive by the Coal Board"' and 'Our children have been murdered.'

The tribunal sat for seventy-six days, at that point the longest-running industrial inquiry in British history. The National Coal Board initially maintained the same specious defence exhibited by Robens and claimed that the collapse of Tip 7 was an act of God, citing heavy rains and the 'hidden' geology of the tip in its defence. During the course of the tribunal over 300 exhibits were examined and 136 witnesses called, including schoolchildren, miners, geologists and academics.

The local community's previous anxieties about the safety of the tip were made clear and Robens' claims of waters below the tip being undetectable were proven to be false. A contrite Robens finally gave evidence near the end of the tribunal after his absence had been noted by the QC representing the Aberfan community. His admission that the Coal Board was culpable was finally delivered six months after the disaster, though an earlier acceptance of responsibility would have precluded the need for the inquiry and spared the population of Aberfan untold sorrow.

The tribunal report was published on 3 August 1967. It stated, 'The Aberfan Disaster is a terrifying tale of bungling ineptitude by many

men charged with tasks for which they were totally unfitted, of failure
to heed clear warnings, and of total lack of direction from above.
Not villains but decent men, led astray by foolishness or by ignorance
or by both in combination, are responsible for what happened at
Aberfan.'

In conclusion the report decided, 'Blame for the disaster rests upon
the National Coal Board. This is shared, though in varying degrees,
among the NCB headquarters, the South Western Divisional Board,
and certain individuals . . . The legal liability of the NCB to pay
compensation of the personal injuries, fatal or otherwise, and damage
to property, is incontestable and uncontested.'

The local authority and the National Union of Mineworkers were
absolved of any responsibility due to the assurances they had received
from the NCB, nine of whose officials were referred to as being
especially worthy of criticism. However, no member of staff was made
redundant, demoted, or was subject to any formal disciplinary action,
let alone retribution.

The Aberfan community would experience further injustices at the
hand of the authorities. On the night of the disaster, the mayor of
Merthyr had immediately launched an emergency appeal to assist the
village and the bereaved. The appeal was formalised as the Aberfan
Disaster Fund, although its constitutional status remained unclear.
When the appeal ended in January 1967, less than four months after
the disaster, it had raised a figure approaching £1,750,000 from almost
90,000 contributions. As neither the National Coal Board nor the
Treasury would accept full financial responsibility for the disaster,
it fell to the fund to contribute £150,000 from its own monies to
help pay for the removal of the remaining six tips that continued to
overlook the village. Three decades later the amount was repaid,
without interest, by the newly elected Labour government.

The dense rows of terraced housing that follow the north–south coal seam throughout the Valleys were originally sited in close proximity to mine pitheads. Villages such as Aberfan were created by mining and still, in 1966, greatly associated with and reliant on the industry. The disaster of Tip Number 7 placed the role of coal mining in Welsh society in stark relief. It was an industry with a history of deadly accidents, one that was responsible both for poor health outcomes in its workforce and destructive and detrimental to the environment. The communities of the South Wales coalfield nevertheless took great pride in the mutual reliance, determination and resilience that bound its workforce together as they laboured underground in challenging conditions near to their homes. The contract between the mining communities of Wales and the industry they served was broken at Aberfan. Although subsequently repaired, it was perhaps never honoured again with the same degree of commitment.

FIVE

ADFERIAD / RECLAMATION

Voices

Rosemary Butler   Kim Howells   Kevin Morgan
Bob Croydon   David Hurn   Richard Parfitt
Phil Cullen   Patrick Jones   Davinder Singh
Andrew Davies   Neil Kinnock   Phil White
Ron Davies   Tom Marston   Nicky Wire
Richard Frame

———

*In the wake of the Aberfan disaster the Mines and Quarries (Tips) Act
was passed in 1969. The act led to the renovation of many collieries
via the introduction of new mining technologies and strict inspection
regulations. Another effect of the tragedy was the series of tip clearance
and land reclamation schemes undertaken across South Wales. Several
of these drew on the successes of the earlier, pioneering Lower Swansea
Valley Project, which had been established in 1961 in response to the
dereliction left in the wake of the smelting and tinplate industries that
had previously thrived in the region.*

*Copper smelting had been a feature of the local economy since the
eighteenth century; its decline had left significant residual deposits of
the metal, as well as by-products of nickel, zinc, iron and steel smelting
throughout the Valley landscape. After the Second World War, during
which the copper industry had been temporarily revived in the area,
the visible signs of dilapidation included abandoned mills, metal*

works, forbidding spoil heaps and resinous ponds that were frequently contaminated with toxic waste.

The Welsh National Development Agency was launched in the early 1970s in recognition that the economy of Wales, so heavily dependent on industry, was vulnerable to the destructive forces of long-term contraction. Rather than deliver an overarching economic strategy, the agency, renamed the Welsh Development Agency in 1976, was established under an Act of Parliament by John Morris, Secretary of State for Wales, Labour MP for Aberavon, to create and deliver secure long-term employment, growth and competitiveness by providing direct financial assistance or attracting investment from diverse sectors, such as the automobile and microprocessor manufacturing industries, as well as finding a purpose for the significant property holdings owned by nationalised industries that now fell under the agency's jurisdiction. For many in Wales, the most visible purpose of the Welsh Development Agency was its land reclamation programme, which oversaw the clearing of derelict industrial sites and a restoration of the landscape, an entirely successful and transformative project for which the agency deservedly gained an international reputation.

The landscape of South Wales recovered; the safeguarding of future employment for places of high population density such as the Valleys remained a more onerous task. Light industry and manufacturing services businesses appeared across South Wales. This represented a shift in the region's economy away from heavy industry and was accompanied by other developments in the character of the area.

Tom Marston: Aberfan had some consequences because they did clean up the environment afterwards. You could stand in my village, Banwen, and look in any direction and you were completely surrounded by tips: if you looked north, south, east, west, there were tips all over the place. There's nothing there now, you can't see a thing. The aftermath was that we became more environmentally conscious; we put tips in the right places. If you were going to put a tip, you made sure it wasn't over a spring and things like this, a situation where the whole tip was self-lubricated and will flow away after a heavy shower. It woke a lot of people up.

Phil Cullen: I was at school when Aberfan occurred but I was in the mining industry from 1973 onwards. There was a mass of regulations that we had to be aware of in the wake of Aberfan. The law regarding tips changed completely; it was shocking before Aberfan.

Neil Kinnock: The greening of the Valleys really started in the late sixties, early seventies, in the wake of Aberfan, because the Labour government introduced the Industrial Investment Pact, direct subsidies to local authorities for a variety of things, including tip clearance, renovation of housing stock and several other developments, and, certainly, the reclamation of land was a direct product of the Aberfan disaster.

Bob Croydon: In Barry and Swansea there were still coal hoists operating when I started work: they tipped the whole wagon into the hulls of ships. Port Talbot had more or less closed by then because they were building the new tidal harbour. The WDA started as the WNDA, the Welsh National Development Agency, in the early seventies. I can remember going for an interview with them. They were pushing us all from college towards organisations like that. They were in Treforest. At the interview it turned out I didn't play rugby in the right position to get the job, because, joking aside, that still informed employment policy in South Wales. There was the Welsh Development Agency and the Development Board for Rural Wales and also an outfit called the Land Authority for Wales fitted in there somewhere a little later.

The WDA was organised in geographical divisions, which was stupid, because the problems that faced Pontypool were the same problems that faced Llanelli, so having territorial divisions made little sense.

They should have had disciplinary divisions. But you had excellent things within the WDA, like the re-landscaping and the re-greening of the Valleys. D. Gwyn Griffiths, who pioneered the initiative, is one of the unsung heroes of Wales. If you think of what it was like to drive from Cardiff to Merthyr even in the 1970s, there was no A470, you were weaving up the Valleys, driving through collieries and through coal tips. Aberfan was a trigger in that. Part of the response to Aberfan was the re-landscaping and the reclamation of the landscape, which was funded by the government.

Gwyn once gave me a slide that I used to use. It showed two little kids proudly planting a tree next to which a sign read 'Old Arsenic Works, Keep Out'. The Swansea Valley was full of heavy metals, it really was contaminated.

Kevin Morgan: D. Gwyn Griffiths had delegations from all over the world coming to Wales to study its land clearance, rehabilitation and remediation schemes; it was the benchmark.

Bob Croydon: A lot of local authorities like Swansea had set up their own initiatives, or even community initiatives in some cases. I can remember as a kid in the Lower Neath Valley we used to play in the ruins of an old copper works. I've got maps which show them as being derelict in 1840, and they were still there in 1960 – the copper industry went from there over to the Swansea Valley.

They all went in one sweep when they built the extension of the Heads of the Valleys road. The levels of dereliction in the Swansea Valley were right across the piece and places like south Llanelli were still like that even in the 1980s.

Andrew Davies: The Lower Swansea Valley project was a joint initiative between Swansea University and the local council, and it was a pioneer in the restoration and regeneration of polluted areas. Swansea was known as Copperopolis in the nineteenth century, when the district produced a third of the world's smelted copper, sometimes more. The result of that was that non-ferrous metal smelting left a huge area of the Lower Swansea Valley deeply polluted by heavy metal pollution and as a result there was no grass, no trees, and it was a huge area. If you came in on the railway from Cardiff into Swansea, down the Swansea Valley, over Brunel's viaduct, you would just see spoil tip after spoil tip, of white, or grey soil where nothing would grow. I remember being a very callow, scared student, coming in on the train into Swansea and seeing what was essentially a moonscape, the largest area of industrial dereliction in the whole of Western Europe.

Bob Croydon: My first job after graduation was at British Transport Docks Board, one of the largest landowners in South Wales, whose portfolio included endless former railway sidings, which were completely and utterly redundant. These were vast areas of land, not big warehouses like in Bristol or Liverpool. Nobody wanted to rent any of it commercially. I thought, 'This is marvellous, I'm getting paid 30 quid a week and I don't have to answer the phone. It never rings!' And that was in a nationalised industry in 1973.

There were still hierarchies in those organisations: you had a management canteen, a staff canteen and a works canteen. There were white-collar divisions and the guys who went to the staff canteen sat in the stand on a Saturday afternoon. If you went to see Neath playing Aberavon, you could tell who was supporting who by the colour of the free protective clothing that they'd had from British Steel.

The strong links that bound the corporatism of South Wales Labour to Westminster had provided the area with high employment. In national politics, Wales had benefited from the epochal change in macroeconomic policy that followed the Second World War. The government had either invested in existing steelworks such as those at Trostre, Felindre and Ebbw Vale, or created new sites, such as at Llanwern, Newport. Other national and commercial industries, often those producing new consumer goods, had been encouraged or directed to invest in premises in South Wales, including British Nylon Spinners in Pontypool; Hoover in Merthyr Tydfil; Mettoys in Swansea; and BP's petrochemical works at the nearby Baglan Bay, established in 1963. In local politics, Labour council leaders held positions of great authority and were occasionally associated both with accusations of corruption and an antediluvian attitude towards the societal changes that had occurred since the 'white heat of technology' industrial strategy of the 1960s.

Ron Davies: There were straws in the wind of a disaffection with Labour by the early 1970s. Certainly, I fell foul of people in the Labour Party early on – I think it was probably because I was young – but in the local Labour Party I fell out with the guy who'd been chairman for years, who accused me of something or other and told me that he'd never been spoken to like that before. There was a group of people around Neil Kinnock, some of whom were very good friends of mine, and they were refreshing. The big issues at the time were the anti-apartheid movement and protesting against the South Africa rugby tours, and we were all active and committed to those causes, whereas the old guard, for want of a better word, were more concerned about who was going to be chairman of the allotments committee. It was an era when people who you wouldn't have automatically assumed to be of the highest ability emerged as head teachers at local schools and then, lo and behold, they were members of the Labour Party.

Rosemary Butler: I got on the council of Newport in 1973, just as there was an amalgamation of districts. I had two small children, I was a young woman, and it was quite interesting, because you go off to a meeting as a councillor, and they always assumed you were the secretary, and you'd go to a conference and you never had to queue for the toilet. It was interesting like that. There were very, very few women. In the early seventies, we had a selection for a Member of Parliament, and this fantastic woman came up, but she didn't get it, and then she rang to ask 'Why not?' and we had to say, 'Well, it's because you're a woman,' which is an awful thing to say. But things began to change from there. It was difficult, because I didn't have a job. I had two children, and I remember thinking, 'I really ought to claim for babysitting,' because if you were a man and you were on the council and you had a job, you had your pay reimbursed, it covered your work. As a woman, you had nothing, absolutely nothing. I remember making a claim for 50p for a babysitter. Oh, there were huge debates as to whether I should have it, and I managed to get it in the end. Things like the telephone bill, which the council would pay, was in my husband's name, and therefore they weren't going to pay it because I was using it. It was very difficult; as I say, there weren't very many women.

It was a small issue that finally made me stand for the council, which was that you'd go to the park and there was nowhere for the mothers to sit, because the fathers didn't go to the park then, mothers went, and I tried to get a bench from these male councillors and they didn't see the justification for one. There was an election coming up, so I got selected for the Labour Party and I thought, 'Right, I'm going to try to get this bench now.' We got a bench in four weeks. As I say, it was a small issue, but it was that kind of mentality: a bench wasn't important. And all the significant committees, like Economic Development and Education, you just didn't get a look-in on those sorts of things.

Davinder Singh: My father was an open-cast mine engineer. He was shipped into the UK in the wake of independence in India by the company he worked for to upskill, and he stayed. He shifted around before they eventually sent him to a mine near Ammanford. We lived in a lovely house in Swansea, by the sea, because we could: he was a civil engineer. You got inured to the racism, or you dealt with it through humour, and the fifth time you're called a 'Fucking nigger' or a 'Paki bastard' you just think, 'Well, that wasn't delivered very well, the timing was all off. You could have added in a few more adjectives to make it more impactful.' I think that the hostility, the anger, the fear of communities was because of ignorance, bred of a lack of instruction and education. No child is born a racist, that line is absolutely right. In other families we knew in Swansea, racist attacks and deaths occurred. There were deaths based on colour, which is always mixed in with jealousy, which is always mixed in with resentment.

Andrew Davies: When I was at Swansea University, there was an organisation, or a club, called Soc Soc, the Socialist Society, and I don't even think then, in the 1970s, the Labour Party even figured. The 1974–79 Labour government, which was headed by Wilson and then by Callaghan, was uninspiring, and obviously they were dealing with huge challenges, such as the aftermath of the 1973 OPEC-induced global inflationary crisis; there was a huge amount of turmoil – industrial, economic and social. For a lot of young people on the left the Labour government was a deeply unattractive proposition. More locally in Swansea, which is where I was living, as elsewhere in the UK, such as Newcastle with the T. Dan Smith and John Poulson scandal, local government corruption was quite endemic. Swansea was archetypal, in that the Labour leader, Gerald Murphy, was sent down for corruption and then Labour lost control of the council to the Independent Rate-Payers Party, and then not long afterwards, the leader of the Rate-Payers Party was sent down for corruption as well.

Davinder Singh: In the Lower Sixth and you had to fill in a form about what job you wanted to do. I wrote out the form, sent it in and went to see this careers advisor, who saw the form and said 'Oh, right, OK, this is very promising.' I had very blocky sort of writing; he really had to decipher what I'd written. He said, 'I think we can organise something very quickly on this front for some work experience for you.' On the form I'd written: 'writer', I wanted to be a writer. He said, 'Right, OK, I know of some people that will be able to help you if you want to get some experience in this field, Mr Singh,' and then quickly asked me, 'By any chance, do you know of any contacts?' I asked: 'How would I have any contacts about this?' He thought I'd written 'waiter' and didn't even question it. I'd written writer but he saw waiter, and thought, 'OK, yes, I can understand this.' There was a community of educated, literate, well-connected brown people – I can only talk about Asians, it's what I know – who made their presence obvious and these groups tended to be run by professional Asians who wanted to be part of the golf club in Swansea, because it suited their own particular craving for acceptance and recognition. None of the market traders went to these events but the white liberal intelligentsia and associated media individuals would target these very erudite black or brown faces for commentary, for input, for a view.

Rosemary Butler: You had to serve your time on the council; you had to put up with some terrible stuff. Ridiculous now. It was vicious stuff at the time, but you eventually begin to realise, well, something's not quite right here. You stick it out and you keep going. There were never that many women on the council, never. I can't remember how many there were: six, seven, something like that. We used to try and get more women onto the council, but it was very difficult, and you'd go knocking on doors and ask people how they're going to vote, and they'd reply, 'I'll have to ask my husband.' Politics was the man's place. In order to become a councillor, you had to wait for somebody to step down or die. And the same for Members of Parliament, it was very difficult.

Andrew Davies: Both local and national politics were deeply unattractive. When Mrs Thatcher became leader of the opposition in the mid-1970s, I was really scared about what she would do. The fact she'd grown up in Grantham, a small market town in Lincolnshire, was telling. I was born and grew up in Hereford, of Welsh parents, and I knew loads of people like Margaret Thatcher, who knew the price of everything and the value of nothing. The havoc she wreaked on Wales is something which we're still dealing with in many cases. We have continually had some of the worst health indicators in the whole of Western Europe.

Ron Davies: Wales, particularly South Wales, had done quite well on the strength of Labour Party influence. We got the steelworks at Llanwern, rather than it going to Ravenscraig in Scotland, because of the need to do something about the unbalanced Welsh economy. By then the mining industry was already starting to feel the pressure, and that led to the events of 1972, '73, '74.

In January 1972 British miners took united industrial action for the first time since 1926. The catalyst was a pay dispute between the miners and the Conservative government that resulted from the wider issue of inflation that Westminster, in an ill-fated policy known as the 'Dash for Growth', was struggling to control. In South Wales the strike spread to other industries as dockers in Newport and Cardiff refused to unload ships whose cargo included coal. In February the miners reached a pay settlement with the government. The strike had demonstrated the United Kingdom's reliance on the coal industry, which was brought into focus the following year during the OPEC oil crisis precipitated by the Arab–Israeli War. The global price of petrol increased dramatically as crude oil rose from $3 to $12 a barrel, leading to higher interest rates and further inflation.

In response, in early 1974, the miners once again demonstrated the unanimity of organised labour and entered a strike over their pay levels, which, they argued, had decreased substantially, prompting the Conservative Prime Minister, Edward Heath, to institute a three-day working week and then call a general election at which he was defeated. The Secretary of State for Employment in the new Labour government, Michael Foot, implemented a Pay Board report and other benefits to the industry.

*Around this time the National Coal Board regularly ran recruit-
ment campaigns for the industry, often produced by its own NCB
film unit. One striking recruitment advert used in 1975 was titled
'People Will Always Need Coal'. Produced out of house for the South
Wales coalfield, it juxtaposed images of work in the pit with the life of
a miner, who filled his leisure hours with activities such as canoeing,
playing squash, live music, and the wining and dining of female
company. The accompanying jingle promised a job with 'lots of money
and security'.*

*At the mid-point of the 1970s, the UK experienced both a historic
peak of income equality and a balance of payments crisis during an
era of strength for a unionised workforce that future Conservative
governments would reverse, along with the secure, long-term future of
industrial employment promoted in National Coal Board advertising.*

Bob Croydon: Industrial South Wales hit its peak when Britain hit its
peak, which was just before 1914. We've been in decline since 1914 and
a lot of people would disagree with me on this, but I think the endgame
kicked in in 1973, with the setting in of the oil crisis and the secondary
banking crisis. In 1914 shipping went over to oil rather than coal, so
Welsh steam coal was in less demand globally, but other industries
came, as the coal industry declined in Swansea Bay. Swansea, Bargoed,
Llanelli, these places in the early sixties were still pretty prosperous,
pretty bustling. Heavy industry was still going, but of course 1973 saw
the end of that lot, and they started to decline.

Phil White: I started with the NCB in 1969 at St John's Colliery, in
Maesteg. The National Coal Board at the time had an awful lot of
advertising, marketing, trailers in the cinema. When we went as fifteen-
year-olds the big trailer came up, 'The NCB is the industry for you,
the job for you,' so three of us at that time decided we'd apply for
apprenticeships at the National Coal Board. All of us were successful,
and that's when I started in an electrical engineering apprenticeship,

the very first day I got there was the last fatality at St John's Colliery. I started on the Monday in October, and they brought up a body from underground; he died as a result of being crushed on the Sunday night shift. And then, within a couple of months, I was on strike with the surfacemen's strike.

Phil Cullen: In the National Union of Mineworkers we had a strike for wages in 1972 and another one in '74. Now, the miners united will never be defeated, and of course we weren't, because we were very united. Everybody's pay was the same, the National Powerloading Agreement had come in, which meant from the north of Scotland down to the south of Kent, everybody had the same wages, and whether you were working in difficult conditions or good conditions, you had the same wages. And, of course, we won the '72 strike and we won the '74 strike. And the seeds, historically, they say, were then set for what happened in 1984. It wasn't the NUM that kicked the Tory government out; it was the British public that actually kicked the Tory government out, but you could say that we set the stage in order for them to do it.

Kim Howells: The National Powerloading Agreement made all the difference because it united everyone. Until the National Powerloading Agreement the Nottingham miners were way ahead – not just Nottingham, but some other coalfields as well, where it was possible to mine a lot of coal quickly. The output was so much bigger than most pits in South Wales or some of the Scottish coalfields, but that National Powerloading Agreement had really brought everyone together, and you got more or less the same rate for doing the same job, regardless of which coalfield you were in, and regardless what the output was.

Phil Cullen: For the first time in the modern era, you had a generation like myself who had gone into the mining industry and were told, 'You'll have a job for life,' and mining had now become a modern industry – I went in as an engineering apprentice. If you look at the later union officials of South Wales, they were practically all craftsmen.

The dynamic had changed within the mines themselves. The collier was really no longer king. Underground had not been very heavily mechanised, and that all changed, so the philosophy changed as well: the industry and the men working in it changed.

You had a chairman of a British nationalised industry, the chairman of the Coal Board, and you had the president of the NUM, who were both getting paid the same. The president of the NUM – it wasn't Scargill, this was years before – didn't feel he was on equal terms going in to negotiate with the Coal Board unless he was up there with them in terms of pay. Therefore, whoever was the president of the NUM was, de facto, a millionaire; that may sound incredible, but it's true.

Kim Howells: By the late seventies, because it was their job to try to increase efficiency, the Coal Board didn't like it; they'd seen what that Powerloading Agreement could do for solidarity during the seventies and they knew that if they were going to institute this big pit closure programme, they had to destroy that solidarity, and they did.

As employment levels in heavy industry decreased in South Wales its jobs were replaced by those in services and light industry and manufacturing, including a high cluster of factories surrounding the new town of Cwmbran. The growth in the service and light industrial sectors ensured Wales remained a country of relative prosperity even as its traditional forms of employment started an inexorable decline.

The changing social texture of the area was recorded, usually in austerely printed black and white film, by students attending the documentary photography course at Newport Art College. The course was founded by the Magnum photographer David Hurn in 1974, and was the first of its kind in Britain. Its creation marked one of the final moments of the spirit of egalitarian education promoted after the Second World War; the course in its unlikely setting of a fading docks town in South Wales developed an unparalleled international reputation.

Bob Croydon: The initiative to build Cwmbran was led by a quango, the New Towns Commission, which relied on private people coming in and doing some of the commercial development in Cwmbran. Relatives of mine worked for British Nylon Spinning and had houses in Cwmbran; they were almost council houses for key workers. Half the cul-de-sac would be travelling to the same place for work in the morning. It was all very, very shiny, all very bright, all very optimistic, and people who'd been living in terraced houses with the toilet at the bottom of the garden suddenly had these nice houses with a porch.

Richard Parfitt: I was born in Wales's first New Town, Cwmbran. My mother was from Glasgow, so it was like Hollywood to her: she had her own house. My dad was from Newport, and he loved it. Everybody worked at Girling's the brake manufacturers, or at the nylon factory, or at the biscuit factory; they were the big employers.

Bob Croydon: My generation, the post-war fifties' kids, all suddenly wanted a house, and we hadn't built that many. People used to scorn Wimpey houses then, that they were little boxes, but they're exemplary compared to what's been built since. The council estates were Parker Morris standard, and you look at some of those post-war council estates right across South Wales and the quality of the building and the layout, and the amenities and space that they were given were quite staggering.

Richard Parfitt: My dad worked in Newport and we moved there when I was ten, because travelling three miles to work in those days was too much effort. It was all happening in Newport; it was a really hard town. My mother worked in Newport as well by then, a really hard-working town: everybody I knew, their parents were working.

Nicky Wire: People were really well paid. The pay levels in the sixties and the seventies were brilliant for working-class people. Everyone in our valley was wearing suits and going to Tunisia on package holidays, mad things like that. My dad just worked his bollocks off; he was one of the great workers. When he passed away, we had 'Father, son, brother, worker' on his memorial stone, because that's what he did. But the opportunity was there to work. It never actually felt like there was that much unemployment.

Patrick Jones: Our parents came out of the post-war period and their families having no money. Then, having a little bit more money, my parents had bought their house in the Valleys in the 1960s, outright with a mortgage for only a couple of years or so. My dad worked with his hands every day; probably right up until the week before he died, he was doing something. That generation. He would finish on a Friday, he would talk about that, finish on a Friday, start on a Monday – it was always labour work, building.

Richard Parfitt: The shops in Newport were proper shops; there were no empty shops, no charity shops. It didn't seem like there was any homelessness – there must have been. It was a hard-working town, and the Llanwern steelworks absolutely dominated. Everybody's dad – except for my dad – worked at Llanwern steelworks.

David Hurn: I was invited to lunch with John Wright, who was the head of the art college in Newport at that time, a very progressive sort of person. The whole of the top floor was a painting and decorating course, and an exceptionally good one. And what they did was to get a lot of bricks and cement and show somebody how to make a wall and these people teaching them were skilled builders and decorators. And I got a lot from that, talking to the guys there about how they taught painting and decorating. My feeling was, 'Well, they turn out painters and decorators, so if you think a little bit about what they do, maybe you can turn out photographers.' It was what your fantasy of an art college is. It had a pantomime; it had an arts ball; it had people that started pop groups.

I was very friendly with Sir Tom Hopkinson who had been the great *Picture Post* editor and then *Drum* editor. And I sat down with him and talked to him, and then there were other people I knew, like Stuart Hall and Raymond Williams, and these were all people that in some way had an influence. I loved the precise thinking of Raymond Williams and Stuart Hall. I've always in my own mind argued that perhaps some of the best training for photographers is not to do a photographic course but to do anthropology and sociology, that the photography side is easy. What is difficult is the sociology part, the understanding a little bit of your view of the world.

I talked to all these people, and I said, 'Wales is in difficulty, the steelworks are closing down, the mines are closing down, everything's closing down, and photography is something that people could do.' I said, 'If I was going to run a course, the prime thing you would be saying to people is "Come here, you can retrain as a photographer."' That would be the prime thing. Newport was very rough, very tough, which turned out to be an incredible advantage. Clarence Place, where we were, was right in the middle of what was then a town, now a city, and there was so much going on there.

You could get people to go out and, within ten minutes, they could be shooting stuff and you could get them back in an hour, you could crit them and then send them back to the same place to redo it, having some sort of understanding of how they could do it better. So that had an incredible sort of advantage. But it was undoubtedly a rough, tough place. We started the course in 1972.

The first thing we said was, 'Look, I don't want to look at portfolios. We'll interview for the course.'

And in the case of Tish Murtha, who was a wonderful photographer, she was the shortest interview we ever had. I've mentioned it many times before, but she came for interview, and I said, 'Tish, what is it you think you want to learn to photograph?' She said, 'I want to photograph policemen kicking kids.' 'You're in!' Anyone who has that kind of clarity and passion is going to deal with all those social issues very well. I can teach her how to get the damn picture in focus, and how to put together a group of pictures to make a story, what I can't teach is that passion. I paid the deposit on Tish's first camera at Dixon's in Newport as she didn't have the means herself.

Richard Parfitt: The docks started to close in Newport in the seventies, but we used to go down the docks; my dad used to take us down. There used to be a big outdoor market in Pill on a Sunday, a cattle market, it was terrifying! It stank, it was noisy. And there was visible poverty, absolutely. My parents used to warn us not to go there. You were warned not to go to Pill.

Richard Frame: At that time Newport Art School was great. There was a students' union on Stow Hill, students all living in Newport and the sort of students that had the luxury of student grants, not worrying about anything. There was a fashion school in Newport, and so the girls would make their own clothes, a lot of them. There was a very small group of mostly blokes, youngish blokes, who were interested in music, and they'd come up there to the union, every week – we'd have a band in the hall at the back. I think Shaky [Shakin' Stevens] must have come over at some point, because we were friendly with him in Cardiff. He used to hang around with us at the art college; he was another person who hung around with the art students. He had a Transit van, and he used to take us to the Severn Bridge services in the evenings, you know, just to hang around at the Severn Bridge.

SIX

MUDIAD ADFER /
THE RESTORATION MOVEMENT

Voices

Cian Ciarán

Carl Iwan Clowes

Cynog Dafis

Menna Elfyn

Ffred Ffransis

Meri Huws

Dafydd Iwan

Tecwyn Vaughan
Jones

Ben Lake

Rhys Mwyn

Gruff Rhys

Ned Thomas

Rowan Williams

———

*The struggle for the survival of Cymraeg during the 1970s was
considered to be a struggle for the survival of the communities in which
it was the dominant language. The north-western and south-western
counties of the country, especially for those of their inhabitants who
could claim ancestry in the regions, were held to be the quasi-mythical
Y Fro Gymraeg, the Welsh Heartland. Other than agriculture and
its attendant service industries these rural areas offered little in terms
of employment to the indigenous population, but were attractive to
people from outside the communities in search of holiday homes, whose
purchase of the local housing stock drove up property prices. By the end
of the decade the phenomenon of property remaining unoccupied for
the majority of any given year at the expense of local ownership was
considered to be reaching a point of crisis.*

*Solutions proposed to address the issue were varied. Several
independent housing associations were created to ensure indigenous
families could remain in their place of birth; a more radical idea,*

one explored by a group known as Mudiad Adfer [Restoration Movement], was the establishment of a putative Cymraeg colony in the nation's interior, a settlement for true Welsh people.

Emyr Llywelyn, a leading member of Cymdeithas yr Iaith Gymraeg and the charismatic founder of Adfer, had previously been imprisoned for attempting to destroy building equipment used in the construction of the dam at Tryweryn. Within this new organisation, he now explored the opportunity of transforming Y Fro Gymraeg from an abstract ideal of place to a defined hinterland for a separate, monoglot region of Welsh-speakers, a singular interpretation of utopia.

Cynog Dafis: Adfer was established first of all as a kind of housing movement, that was what it was about, buying property and renovating it, then letting it to Welsh-speaking local people. And I was involved with that, I was involved with the first two purchases. We bought houses in Tregaron.

Ned Thomas: Adfer's impulse was, in the sophisticated version, which I had a lot of sympathy for, that if you lost the reservoir of native and normal Welsh-speakers, then you would also lose the reservoir from which teachers of Welsh in South Wales and in the more anglicised areas came. The leading Adfer figure, Emyr Llywelyn, was also one of the Tryweryn figures, one of the people who spent time in prison – it was a very minor kind of sabotage, late in the day – but he was a kind of hero figure because he'd spent time.

Ben Lake: The way that I've understood Adfer was that they were not exclusively, but often university-educated, very knowledgeable, well-read, had a keen sense of understanding of Wales's place in the world; also it's quite striking how often they would know about the suffering and the struggles of other nations and peoples across the world. It was a very internationalist sense of 'This is an injustice on any level, and it's justified for us to take this action to bring together, to come together.'

Ned Thomas: Adfer was a breakaway from Cymdeithas in the 1970s and in my view, it had a very positive impulse which wouldn't have needed it to break away. And that impulse was that a lot of the campaigns of Cymdeithas were directed at the British government and to an extent the Welsh Office, in order to have forms in Welsh, to have road signs in Welsh, and then the television campaign, which took ten years, began in a small way and then worked up. All these things were directed at what you might call rights, which to some people seemed very abstract, meanwhile you had the question of 'What is happening to the Welsh-speaking areas?'

Rhys Mwyn: 'Adfer' means to restore. If you look at the context of the late sixties, early seventies and the hippie commune ideal train of thought, you do see where these people are coming from. It's really idealism: it's the remnants of sixties idealism before the reality and the absolute shit and horror of the seventies. There's one side where I can understand intellectual Welsh-speaking, university-educated people, involved with culture, involved with bands. You're talking about people like Tecwyn Ifan, the folk singer, and Clive Harpwood. A lot of these characters started thinking that the best way to preserve the Welsh language was to head out west, to what are allegedly the heartlands of the language, although we've got to be careful with that. It is in terms of percentages of Welsh-speakers, not in terms of numbers. But Gwynedd and Dyfed, north-west and south-west, were arguably rural areas where, in an ideal vision, it would be a little bit like the Gaeltacht in the west of Ireland, where you have these areas where the language and culture are preserved.

Dafydd Iwan: Adfer became a kind of splinter led by Emyr Llywelyn based on this idea of dedicated clean living, monoglot Welsh-speaking people forsaking all to do with the English way of life, and back to the land – Emyr was a very persuasive and emotional speaker – but it fizzled out in the end, and for a time there was quite a nasty animosity growing between Cymdeithas yr Iaith and Adfer. Adfer didn't like the fact that Cymdeithas yr Iaith did things bilingually: they wanted everything to be kept monolingual Welsh, and for a time the feeling in the Welsh-speaking community in Bangor University especially, but to some extent in Aberystwyth as well, put forward by the Adfer movement, became quite aggressive towards Welsh learners. This was not the fault of Emyr, but some of his followers.

I stood against the ideas of Adfer from the beginning and yet of course I agreed with a lot of things they were saying, and some of them are still telling me, 'At heart, you're an Adferwr.' The term is still used, but it doesn't exist in any meaningful way. The biggest thing that came out of it as a lasting influence was papurau bro, the local Welsh newspapers, which are still going strong, and *Y Faner Newydd*, the independent magazine run by Emyr Llywelyn and his mainly Adfer colleagues, and it's developed into a very good magazine. It's about the only thing produced in Welsh that is not supported by the Welsh Books Council.

Ned Thomas: It was a man called Owen Williams, who was one of the Tryweryn saboteurs, who invented the idea of Y Fro Gymraeg. This philosophy, which is there in print in a pamphlet called 'Adfer, Y Fro Gymraeg', more or less said you couldn't be a proper Welsh person, even if you spoke Welsh, if you didn't belong to Y Fro Gymraeg. He proposed really rather fascistic things, I thought: 'Who represents Y Fro Gymraeg and who will set the rules of what you should do?' 'Well, we, Adfer, who are not elected or anything, say aye.' This was a very negative aspect. My daughter did her philosophy degree through Welsh in Bangor. On the one hand they were fighting the authorities to be able to study things in Welsh, but on the other hand they had to contend with this Adfer section who didn't want Welsh learners, because how could they be proper Welsh people? It was very negative in that aspect.

Cynog Dafis: Adfer then morphed into a political movement, which was all about concentrating entirely on Y Fro Gymraeg and seeing Y Fro Gymraeg as the overwhelming priority, and notions then of a self-governing Wales and indeed, Wales as a significant entity, really, would have to be sidelined, to some extent, with this intense concentration on Y Fro Gymraeg.

Ned Thomas: Emyr Llywelyn, he turned the idea of Y Fro Gymraeg into a philosophy. I think he was influenced by J. R. Jones, who was a professional philosopher, and I don't think Emyr Llywelyn fully understood the ideas of J. R. Jones, but J. R. Jones bears some responsibility.

Ffred Ffransis: There was a booklet we published at the end of the 1970s, it was called *Cymdeithas yr Iaith: The Second Front*. Cymdeithas yr Iaith can't readily be translated. It isn't a literal translation of socialism as such; it is literally communityism or societyism, communitarianism, some people have said. The basis of the philosophy was that a key criterion informing socio-economic policy should be the test of whether it is helping to develop or undermine community life. In other words, if one was undermining communities, one was undermining the language as well. The movement Adfer, which talked about Y Fro Gymraeg and Wales, now we actually rejected that whole philosophy, especially the Christian element, we thought it was a very dangerous philosophy, the way it was developing. But what we did take on board was the importance of community, that saving the Welsh language and saving community life went together, that if the language was declining, it's a litmus paper that the community was declining; you'd almost certainly find it was declining in all sorts of other ways. The revival of the language would have wider support if it were part of the wider community revival, if it were becoming a more interesting place socially, culturally and so on. There were economic initiatives, political changes coming, and the language was all a part of this.

Dafydd Iwan: Dic Jones, who was a leading member of Plaid Cymru and a theologian and historian and a very able man, came out publicly against Adfer, accusing them of being fascist-orientated, and it caused quite a bit of a stir, but he was right, basically: there were elements in their way of thinking which could have led to dangerous things and it showed for a while in the attitude of some of the members towards people learning Welsh or because they didn't speak proper Welsh.

Ned Thomas: Dic Jones, who was older and one of the great intellectuals of the previous generation, with one article in *Y Cymro* went slightly over the top, but he knocked this idea on its head and said, 'This is neither democratic and it has terrible echoes of saying the *Volk*, the people, we know who they are, and we represent them, but in no way have they been elected or anything.'

Rhys Mwyn: The other side of it, and this is the one that was certainly contentious at a time, is some of those characters involved with Adfer were probably further to the right than would be acceptable to somebody like myself. Within Welsh nationalism, it's a spectrum that goes from hard-core Communist/nationalist, working classes in the South Wales Valleys right through to the Saunders Lewis kind of vibe, 'Let's breed more Welsh-speakers.'

Rowan Williams: I can remember arguing a bit with my parents as a teenager about this. I was very keen on Plaid as a teenager, and what they were saying was, 'We don't want exclusivist nationalism,' and my father said, 'I fought in the war against nationalism,' which for him, not a very political person, was quite a strong thing to say. And I suppose there is a tension there, because that strand of Welsh national identity which sees itself very much as part of a global commonwealth of small nations, that's one end of the spectrum; the other end is that rather more fascistic one. Certainly, in the sixties, in my teens, what appealed to me about Welsh nationalism was I think that strand of the commonwealth of small nations idea, that was what I thought I was signing up for at the time.

Cynog Dafis: There was friction between Adfer and Cymdeithas yr Iaith, because Emyr was in effect saying, 'This is the thing we've got to do, and other things are not important,' and I felt at the time that Cymdeithas yr Iaith was important and I felt that we had to have an all-Wales, we had to have a national framework to what we were doing, and I accepted, of course, the significance of Y Fro Gymraeg as a territorial base for the language – language needs a territorial base, all of that kind of stuff. Later on, I studied a fair amount of sociolinguistics and sociology of language so I understood that perfectly well, but I wasn't prepared to have the national issue sidelined.

Menna Elfyn: For a few months, I thought, 'Oh, this is a good idea,' and I think I went on one of the Adfer campaigns to try to build or rebuild some home or other. I was totally useless, by the way. And then I realised that their philosophy was so different from Cymdeithas yr Iaith, because their philosophy was inward-looking; it was very conservative in view. I remember someone saying that someone in Adfer was dismissive of his sister wearing 'city clothes', this kind of mentality. I think we saw it more as a cult – perhaps 'cult' is the wrong word, but a group of people who felt enamoured by someone like Emyr Llywelyn, who had the gift of oratory and was able to inspire people.

Rhys Mwyn: I grew up in east mid-Wales, near the border, in Montgomeryshire, Llanfair Caereinion, and for me, becoming a teenager in the late seventies and hearing this stuff about 'Let's move west', that immediately got me going, 'Piss off! I don't want to leave Montgomeryshire!' I was actually active in Montgomeryshire, promoting

Welsh music and putting on gigs, even trying to do things for Cymdeithas yr Iaith in the east of Wales in Montgomeryshire. What I found was once you get into hard-core nationalism, it's hard to pinpoint, but there were people in Adfer that were borderline what we would probably call fascists, not that they were organised fascists, but it was getting dangerously close to something that we opposed. Our viewpoints, coming at it hand in hand with gay liberation and Rock Against Racism and all these things that we picked up from punk, meant it was a difficult ideology for us.

Ben Lake: Emyr Llywelyn told me of a visit he had to Tregaron. There was a weekend with his first wife in the Tregaron area, on one of these weekends away restoring a building. They had been working now on a particular house and had gone either to a pub or a café in the town, to rest after the day, and they had a lot of hostility from the locals, young locals as well as the old. In Tregaron the elder generation might look down on that sort of thing, anyway, because it wasn't the done thing; it was a bit odd and different and you don't do things like that. He mentioned how even some of the young local people were quite hostile to what Adfer were trying to do, even though they would have been amongst those who would have benefited the most from their objectives.

Meri Huws: I knew some of the Adfer people. I did agree with them in terms of the importance of housing and homes, but I didn't agree with them in any shape or form with this idea of creating ghettoes in West Wales, not at all.

Tecwyn Vaughan Jones: I was never part of Adfer, I was terrified of that, because they were all very respectable, married couples with two and a half children, and I couldn't fit into that at all and I realised that. I didn't believe in the sense of Y Fro Gymraeg as this division of Wales into a Welsh-speaking and a non-Welsh-speaking area. Any vision of Wales to me had to include the South Wales Valleys, it had to. Cardiff I found problematic: Cardiff people would talk – we'd take a trip out, maybe go down to Pembrokeshire, to somewhere for the day, 'Oh, you're going to Wales, are you?' this sort of attitude. And then, 'Oh, the Welsh will be down,' because we used to go clubbing in Cardiff on a Friday and Saturday: 'The Welsh come down on Fridays and Saturdays.' And I said to one of them, 'Well, what do you mean by Welsh? I mean, you're Welsh, you live in Cardiff.' 'Yeah, but they're a different sort of Welsh. You'll see what I mean; you haven't lived here for very long. They're short, stocky, hairy and dark-haired.' I remember being told that. And a guy in Cardiff who I'd see him all the time would say, 'I hate the Welsh, I hate the Welsh.' And I said, 'Well, you're Cardiff, you're Welsh yourself,' 'But I hate the Welsh,' and in the end, I got angry with him and said, 'Well, if you hate the Welsh, you hate yourself and don't expect me to like you, either.' Identity has a remarkable discourse in Wales. It's really, really complicated.

Rhys Mwyn: Where Adfer became extremely unhealthy is when the younger students, the second generation, picked up on it. They were mainly students in Aberystwyth and Bangor University, and they were pure thugs. I was physically threatened several times. I was in a toilet in Bangor once, and one of these Adfer guys comes up to me and goes, 'Fuck off back to Cardiff, you cunt!' and I went, 'I don't even live in Cardiff. Know your geography! Get a map out with Montgomeryshire!' But it was that raw. My brother was actually thumped: he's still got a cut lip, one of them hit him. These people were absolute thugs. Today, you see them around as teachers and lawyers, and when I see them, I always smile, never say anything. I smile because I know what you are. And they're so embarrassed about it today, some of them, but it was unhealthy. So that's the early eighties, around '83, '84, it had become mainly a student thing, and it was dangerously close to English-bashing. Absolutely unhealthy.

Tecwyn Vaughan Jones: A long time ago, there was a programme on Welsh identity on the television, and they were interviewing Neil Kinnock and he had to name three things that were important to the Welsh people, and Kinnock said, 'Singing in a choir, beer-drinking and playing rugby' – those were the three things. And then they went to this very respectable old lady, in Nefyn on the Llŷn Peninsula, and she said, 'Speaking Welsh, going to Chapel and attending eisteddfodau.' In between that, on that continuum, you've got 3.1 million different views of identity.

Menna Elfyn: I think poetry at that time wasn't what it is now, where we all have to be public poets. I knew Gwyn Alf Williams. I had written a play on Simone Weil, the French philosopher, she wanted to teach the *Iliad* to people in factories – that would have gone down well, wouldn't it? But I thought, with Gwyn Alf Williams' power of persuasion, we could go round factories and combine poetry with our political beliefs, but it never happened. And then Gwyn Alf got ill and the rest of it. There's always been a need for poetry to be seen as being not something elitist, something that is far apart from the world that we live in, and of course the Eisteddfod is another stumbling block for people who don't speak Welsh. It's modernised in the last couple of decades in allowing people to be able to take translation equipment around and listen to things, but it's still seen as being something that's alienating to people who don't speak Welsh and therefore wouldn't be able to appreciate Welsh or Welsh poetry.

Tecwyn Vaughan Jones: People who promote the Welsh language have made people who are not Welsh-speaking, not second-class citizens, but not included. And this is how I felt in Cardiff, that they were neither English nor Welsh. They didn't like the Welsh community living up in Whitchurch and Rhiwbina; they were middle class, but they were not inclusive. I did Welsh as a subject in my first and second year at university, and I think this was drummed into us. There was a

141

preciousness about us who spoke Welsh: we were very special in that sense, and I hated that. I have hated that ever since I was told about it. And especially with my views of the South Wales Valleys, I think those people who live there are more Welsh than any of the people that live in the rural areas of Wales.

Mudiad Adfer had correctly identified that Wales was enduring a housing crisis, although the organisation's more militant stance resulted on occasion in a less than unified sense of purpose in addressing the need for more houses in rural Wales.

Carl Iwan Clowes: My experience is it's not the Health Service that dictates health, it's about good housing, it's about a decent income, decent occupation and decent work and confidence.

My wife Dorothi was from Ireland. The pair of us had been on Oileán Chléire, Cape Clear Island, in West Cork in the 1960s and had become aware that the island was trying to do something to help itself. It was a Gaeltacht area, very much an isolated Gaeltacht, and appreciated that they had this community cooperative, as it was called. We thought this could be a model for us and came back to Llanaelhaearn and introduced it to the village hall gathering: it was well supported, well appreciated and became a community cooperative, the first in the UK, called Antur Aelhaearn. It was January '74, Antur was established, everybody was involved. Everybody on the electoral list could buy a £1 share in the organisation; there was an annual meeting where they elected a senedd, and that senedd then determined developments which we would try and secure for the village in the next twelve months or so. That still goes on today, whatever it is, forty-five years on, never an easy journey, but still going. We built our own factory, at a time before the Welsh Development Agency or economic development officers existed, before there were any grants worth having. We got funding together from contributions locally and wider, loaned stock. We got a loan, it would have been from the local authority, and we finished up with

£11,000, which was a fair sum of money in the mid-seventies. We put up our own factory with that money.

It was a building and we felt there was an opportunity to attract somebody to it to create something. In tandem with that, we'd established a potter in our garage, a young lad who was working in Aberystwyth at the time, so that was ongoing. We'd established knitwear in people's homes and the factory initially was used for that. The publicity that Antur Aelhaearn had as a self-help organisation in the 1970s was incredible. I was spending as much time involved in PR as I was in my GP practice. The *South China Morning Post*, television from Norway and Holland, the *Telegraph*, *Times*, you name it, I was bombarded, and of course the Welsh press, which was far more active in those days. It was a good news story: people helping themselves.

Rhys Mwyn: Adfer would certainly have looked at Welsh-speaking communities and saw them being destroyed by second homes. We were all aware of this idea of villages that were basically unoccupied for seven or eight months of the year. That issue went across the board from Adfer to Cymdeithas to Plaid Cymru; you could see it, there was an obvious direct effect of second homes.

Carl Iwan Clowes: One of the things that really hit home for me during those first few years in Antur was the lack of confidence. It's not surprising, is it, when many of your contemporaries have left, you've got pretty crappy housing – and it was, for the most part, pretty terrible: no hot water, no toilets, no baths in many of those houses in that village at that time. You had all the criteria for poor confidence, and their language didn't have any status in that period, the early seventies, nothing of any significance and it was still being subject to mockery at times by those who wouldn't know better. And Antur really did change the whole atmosphere. People saw media coming in from outside, taking an interest in this self-help organisation, and the confidence became far more than it was.

Gruff Rhys: I was born in 1970, and lived in Maenclochog till I was three. My parents had been part of Gwynfor's campaigning in 1966, because they were fairly local and I think they were quite heady times. Then we moved to Bethesda, which was a Labour-voting quarry town in the 1970s, whereas the next constituency along had gone to Dafydd Wigley, but I think after Wigley's campaign to get compensation for silicosis victims among quarry workers, the Labour vote switched to Plaid Cymru. My father was politically active when he was younger, and then he worked for a series of county councils, so he always tried to stay neutral publicly, whereas my mum didn't – she could wear the stickers.

Adfer were really active in Bethesda. I was a music fan – both Cymdeithas yr Iaith and Adfer had an influence on the music scene. In my early teens, the biggest Welsh-language pop paper was *Sgrech*, which had an Adfer slant. My favourite band when I was about four was Ac Eraill, a folk boy band with political lyrics about going back to Y Fro Gymraeg and rebuilding the houses. There's a lot to be said for the idea of buying up housing stock and fixing them up and making cheap housing available for local people. Adfer had a presence and, to generalise wildly, the emphasis concentrating on Y Fro Gymraeg and giving up on everywhere else, was maybe a faultline in their outlook.

Ned Thomas: I went to a small meeting in the bar of the Belle Vue in Aberystwyth, fewer than twenty people, where they were wanting to collect money for Adfer. There was a lot of rhetoric about young people trying to find somewhere to live and so on. Then we had questions: I remember asking, 'Well, presumably if we manage to buy one house and then a second house, these will be rented to people.' 'Oh, no, Sir, they can buy them.' I remember saying, 'Well, people have to move, they have to go into new jobs. When they sell them, does it go back on the open market? What's the answer to this?' It all went ahead, I think they had one house in Tregaron.

I remember leaving that meeting; and I lived at the time near Tregaron and it got rather late, so I went into a telephone kiosk, as one did in those days, and phoned home to say, 'I'm managing to start back at last. I'm on my way,' and as I phoned, I saw Emyr Llywelyn, who'd also left the meeting, walking to his car, and I think he must have thought that I was reporting on the meeting or something, because a little while later, he wrote two articles in *Y Cymro* mentioning no names, but describing a sinister person who had been in Russia, had edited the British government's quarterly magazine in Russian, so was probably in the pay of them, and had managed, as if by magic, to start a magazine in English, which purported to argue the case that we had to be very careful of people like this. I was completely identifiable. There were rather farcical aspects to this – I didn't have a television, but I had to get one in order to not pay the television licence, so we had to get the television electrician man from Tregaron to come.

He was the kind of Welshman who played it every way, and he told my wife, 'Emyr Llywelyn came to see me and said, "How do I listen in to Ned Thomas' telephone conversations?"' So this electrician said, 'I did three things. I told him every fifth telephone post has a coil on it and you can get up there with proper equipment and earphones. So if you want to do that, I've told you how.' He said to my wife, 'Just so you know that I'm perfectly straight with you, I also mentioned it to my friend from school days who's an inspector of police in Aberystwyth.' Whether he did or not, I don't know, but I had this nightmare image of Emyr Llywelyn on top of a telephone post, the police come and arrest him, and this confirms all his insinuations about me being a spy.

Carl Iwan Clowes: The wider determinants of health as they call them now, are the economic background you have, your housing, lifestyle and so on, and I began to realise, as the years went by, that despite my best efforts, our best efforts as a community, many of the leading determinants of health, if not most of the leaders, were not in our hands, but in the hands of politicians. The Welsh government today, or

London, has a huge responsibility for the state of health of the people of Wales. The fact that we are at the bottom of the heap in many, many statistics throughout Western Europe is a great worry to me. There's nothing innately inadequate about Wales, or our environment, or our people, or our genes. It's the way an environment has been created which has not been conducive to developing good health.

Dafydd Iwan: Carl Iwan Clowes set up a village cooperative in Llanaelhaearn and it has been replicated in various forms in other places, and we grew out of the same period; we set up Cymdeithas Tai Gwynedd, a housing association which was completely independent of government and is still an independent housing association. We only have about thirty houses, but we are in complete control of who gets them and we're all working voluntarily. It was part of that cooperative mindset, that community ventures like that were very important to the same movement as the language.

Carl Iwan Clowes: We formed the cooperative as an attempt to try and give confidence. We tried to have an impact on planning applications and influence planning opportunities in the village – there hadn't been one new building, let alone a house, in the previous forty-five years, so that was the state we inherited. We were also looking at things like television reception in the area, pavements through the village, an eisteddfod was established, the first one for fifty years, all in that period. The local authority wasn't really helping us, and you ask why would they help a small village of a couple of hundred people, as I suppose we were, more than any other village which was in a similar position?

Ned Thomas: One of the things Adfer did, that Dafydd Iwan also did, was to help local people to have housing when people with a lot more money from outside were making it impossible. This is before we had state-aided housing associations – I'm not sure who did it first; they had them I think at about the same time, but perhaps Dafydd Iwan may have been the first with Cymdeithas Tai Gwynedd – like many other people, I put some money into it. Adfer had this idea, too, but the leadership was not as intelligent, in my view.

Cynog Dafis: Cymdeithas Tai Gwynedd was established by Dafydd Iwan, and others. Dafydd Iwan and Emyr Llywelyn are related: they're second cousins or something. But that caused a little bit of bad feeling, actually, because Emyr saw Cymdeithas Tai Gwynedd as being set up in competition, as it were, with Adfer, and I don't think that was the intention at all. There was a little bit of bad feeling about that.

Ned Thomas: Cymdeithas yr Iaith. Except in one short period it was in the hands of quite young people, many of them students, though not all, so you got a turnover. There remained people like Dafydd Iwan in what one might call the national movement, but they went into Plaid Cymru, or they went into jobs where they could do something. Dafydd Iwan was trained as an architect, so it was natural for him to start Cymdeithas Tai Gwynedd, because he knew about planning.

Carl Iwan Clowes: Dafydd Iwan became a friend through Cymdeithas Tai Gwynedd, the housing association I joined in that period, and Dafydd was one of the main motivators and the administrator and architect certainly for the association.

The village we lived in was very much a quarrying village, granite quarrying, in terminal decline, and that had meant a lot of people had moved away over a period of years. There was an image, I think, I'm going to say perhaps a feeling, in more urban areas, Cardiff perhaps, that holiday homes were an issue for isolated or abandoned cottages on the side of a mountain, but there in Llanaelhaearn you had a whole terrace of cottages, right in the middle of the village, I think there were five or six in the row. In a sense, they typified what was happening: there was only one that was lived in, and you could walk by one evening outside in the summer and there wasn't a light: it was that unwelcome, alien feeling that this village was disappearing rapidly. And that was partly a lack of employment, obviously, but it was also partly a lack of opportunity for young people to buy these houses. Their salaries were the least competitive in the market. Those young people who chose to remain tended to be those that earned the least as well.

And that was quite typical of much of Gwynedd in the seventies, and that led to Tai Gwynedd being a very successful housing association in setting an agenda, because what it meant was people the likes of myself and others contributed their 200 quid, 500 quid, or whatever it was until you got sufficient funds together to buy a house, and it gave some momentum then to the notion that we could do something to help ourselves.

Dafydd Iwan: I remember a German coming to stay in this area when I was running Cymdeithas Tai Gwynedd at the beginning, in the mid-seventies, and he'd been one of the people who later became the Baader–Meinhof Group, and he obviously disagreed with them at that point; he said, 'Oh, they lost their way and they went into violence, but we started at the beginning with a housing group and a publishing house and a printing press and a local community venture,' and he liked what we were doing with Cymdeithas Tai Gwynedd and he said, 'Why don't you let some of the houses as holiday homes for people like me, who could come here and pay you the rent we are now paying to these agents, and you could use the money from those houses to build more homes for local people?' And I could see his argument, it made fine sense, but because of the hostility to the idea of holiday homes, if we had started letting our houses as holiday homes, people would have attacked us. We didn't go on with that idea. But he said, 'Oh, people like us would like our money to help you build more homes.' It's a fascinating argument and it's a fascinating sector, housing. But as long as houses are used as investments and not as homes, we'll always have a problem.

Carl Iwan Clowes: The next thing that became a significant part of my life was Nant Gwrtheyrn, a totally deserted village on the north coast, which had been part of my practice when people had lived there. I became aware that Nant Gwrtheyrn was very much, how can I say, a really potentially significant asset in the area, an amazing bit of coastline, a totally deserted village, and I, at twenty-six years of age, perhaps twenty-seven by then, initially had a word with somebody in the village who'd worked with the company who owned it and said, 'Do you think there's any chance of us buying this?' He looked at me a bit sideways: 'What are you talking about?' Because there was no road into the village, there was no water, no electricity, nothing. And half the houses were without roofs and the windows had all gone. The hippies had moved in in the mid-seventies and burned whatever wood was to be had.

Cian Ciarán: There was a lot of work. It used to be a quarry village that died in the fifties when the quarry closed. I think the last residents moved out in '58 or something like that, but it quickly fell apart. Hippies moved in in the sixties and it got left to rot, then my father got a cooperative together. They bought the village, a bit of the surrounding land and then started to renovate each house in the village. That was through the late seventies, all the way through the eighties. I'd go there when I was a kid.

Carl Iwan Clowes: I badgered the company, got a few friends close to me. Nobody, but nobody believed that anybody could do anything with it. 'Why Nant Gwrtheyrn? It's deserted, it's inaccessible. What's the matter with you, you must be mad?' I suppose there was an element of that. I plodded on, I got a few – one, two, three – people to semi-believe perhaps that this could be a possibility, and in '78 the company decided to sell it to an embryonic trust that I created. There was a lot of competition by then, because the *Guardian*, particularly, the *Telegraph* and other press, the *Western Mail* was a big one, all gave a lot of publicity to the fact that it was for sale. The company was called Amalgamated Roadstone Corporation, and in '78 they decided to sell it to us.

Once it had gone public that it was for sale, we had all sorts of people interested in it, there were 106 different organisations, individuals, trusts, whatever, interested in buying it. For what purpose? Well, holiday homes, you might imagine, which were very much rife in that period, but there were things like BP, at a time when what was called Celtic Sea oil was literally in the pipeline, they wanted to hide their oil tanks in the village, in the valley. There was a trust in Liverpool who were interested in rehabilitation of offenders, a trust in Manchester, rehabilitation of drug offenders. We were the only organisation from Wales, out of the 106. There were two main aims. One was to give a big boost to the language, and the second was to create employment. We employ thirty-three people full-time now, and tens of thousands of people have been through the place. Nant Gwrtheyrn is now the National Welsh Language and Heritage Centre. We have something like 40,000 visitors a year by now. It was a national cooperative effort: people from all over Wales came in to support it and help finance it.

Ffred Ffransis: Towards the end of the 1970s, that's when our first venture outside purely linguistic campaigning in Cymdeithas yr Iaith would have been the housing campaign, especially the campaign regarding second homes.

From the late 1970s onwards, it was immediately obvious why holiday homes were a threat to Welsh-speaking communities and the language. Not so much because second homes in themselves meant any hatred of second homeowners, but the fact that their higher purchasing power meant that they were injurious to local communities, that local young people couldn't buy the houses, and injurious to the local economy, in that they didn't purchase much in local shops or contribute to the local communities, that was the main reason.

We started campaigning seriously in that field, and when I was chair of the society, in 1976 I think this would be, I remember there was one village in the north of Wales called Rhyd. It was a small village, but every single house but one was a holiday home, and we occupied the entire village and we set up roadblocks in the village. The sole remaining house was the home of somebody who wasn't a holiday-home owner. He was in his eighties and, it's so sad, he was a part of that generation: he opposed what we were doing.

SEVEN

MEWNFUDWYR / INCOMERS

Voices

Kirsti Bohata	Steve Eaves	Ben Lake
Dewi 'Mav' Bowen	Menna Elfyn	Julian Orbach
Jane Bryant	Nick Hand	Ann Pettitt
Cynog Dafis	Meri Huws	Terry Stevens
Philippa Davies	Dafydd Iwan	Karmen Thomas
Nigel Dudley		Ned Thomas

———

For the first time in the twentieth century, late 1960s Britain witnessed an increase in inward migration; even if the difference in the number of inhabitants was at first negligible, the population of rural areas grew and due to their inaccessibility parts of rural Wales became desirable for those who sought a new life by taking to the hills. Even if they were in a state of disrepair, by the standards of the day Welsh smallholdings and hill farms were inexpensive to purchase. For those with the means the Good Life was achievable in rural mid, West and North Wales, the regions regularly considered Y Fro Gymraeg and traditionally accepted to be the heartlands of the country's Welsh-speaking communities.

To outsiders such communities could appear insular and socially conservative, while some members of the indigenous population regarded these new incomers and their ideas and ideals as curious.

Steve Eaves: Hippie incomers, Lampeter was rife with them. And there was a tension between the locals and those incomers, mostly it must be said, people with middle-class accents, and I don't know if I can explain this, middle-class confidence. What I noticed was that people who weren't from my kind of background were all more self-confident; they had a self-belief that the people that I knew didn't have. They were really quite alien in Lampeter. They were around in Tregaron and outlying areas between Lampeter and Carmarthen, Aberystwyth, these places.

Dewi 'Mav' Bowen: When you look at the population as a whole, they were quite a small number but when I think about it, every town had pubs where the hippies hung out. Recreational drugs and particularly psychedelic drugs were quite important, because it changed consciousness, and that's a revolution in itself. It's a different nationalism; it's a different type of pride, because Wales has a lot more mythological roots than England. I think it's always been there, since Iolo Morganwg and the bardic tradition – it comes down through the ages, but it's almost too prevalent in a way and everything melts into a Celtic hwyl, and before you know it, you believe in ley lines and all this sort of nonsense and it does get a bit OTT. It all becomes a bit of a laughing stock, this Celtic nonsense, but there is a proper hwyl, a real sense of belonging.

Philippa Davies: The association of psychedelia and of romantic ideas and the Welsh language is a really interesting one. The *Mabinogion* can easily be read in that context, there's a yen for it I think.

Dewi 'Mav' Bowen: I was up in Aberystwyth, this was 1970. I took a thousand tabs of acid up there and I'd sold about 200, and I had an instinct. I put them in a box, I bought something like a toothpowder box, chucked the toothpowder, put all the acid in it, and sealed it up and put it in a Jiffy envelope and posted it to a very innocent friend of mine in Swansea who was actually a lecturer at the university. And on the way back, I was in Lampeter, and I got taken to one side by the police and searched. They were definitely on to me and after that I was a bit more circumspect. I didn't know Richard Kemp, the Acid King, but I knew Buzz and Smiles [two local and popular men associated with the distribution of LSD across mid and West Wales, and beyond] and that crowd that got busted in Operation Julie, who were around him. I was in the second division and they were in the first division. There was loads of LSD in Wales and if you knew the right people the economics of it were favourable. You'd buy them for half a crown each, you'd lay them on people for five bob each, and they'd sell them for ten bob each. And we flooded the market with LSD, almost in a messianic way, thinking, 'If everybody took LSD, and listened to the Incredible String Band and Love, we'd change the world.' It wasn't as simplistic as that: a lot of people went nuts and then the gangsters moved in.

Philippa Davies: In school, we had an election, I must have been about sixteen, and I stood as the leader of the Liberal Party, with the amazing slogan, 'Vote Phil for future freedom'. We were very influenced by the hippies. And one of the hippy boys, my mother used to take visitors to go and look at him. He was Elizabeth Taylor's son, I think it was her son from Michael Wilding, who was very beautiful. My mother befriended him and would take people to meet him. He was up in the hills and he had a stall at the market, selling joss sticks and patchouli.

The hippies were very friendly and the opposite of the ladies who were still wearing their hats and gloves to Chapel. When I was about fifteen, I had this great idea that I would stage *Jesus Christ Superstar*, or extracts of it, in Tabernacle Chapel and I asked the minister and the teachers in the Sunday school could I do it, and they said yes. It was myself and three or four other fifteen- or sixteen-year-olds, and we donned black leotards and tights and came shrieking like banshees, running through the main bit of the chapel, going, 'Jesus Christ, superstar'! And the next day, in the evening, by six o'clock, there was a knock on the door and my mother went to answer and it was a deputation of the deacons to talk to my mother about the possibility that I'd been possessed by the devil. There could be no other explanation for me leading these other nubiles astray and exposing the deacons to us wearing leotards and tights.

Kirsti Bohata: My parents were probably unknowingly part of that first wave of incomers. They came in 1972. My mother was a telephonist at the time and so, on her breaks, she could phone around estate agents and I think she phoned Guernsey, Cornwall or somewhere down in the West Country, and the only place they could afford land was in Wales, so they came to Wales. I don't know how they found the house that they bought, but it didn't have a road and it didn't have a roof, I don't think it even had four walls. It was a ruined cottage in the middle of farmland, which they bought and did up and it took them a couple of years to make it habitable. They saved up and they came down, and I think they paid more than the place was worth because they were a bit green. As they tell the story, they told the farmer how much money they had and he went, 'Yep, that'll do.' But there were some grants for doing things up at the time, and I know that, occasionally, when they ran out of money, they'd go back to London and pick up work as it was available – my father as a carpenter, my mother as a switchboard operator.

The areas around the west coast of Wales in particular became a popular destination for a generation seeking a life on the land, one often inspired by the writings of the author and broadcaster John Seymour, who from the mid-1960s onwards lived in the Preseli Hills overlooking Newport, Pembrokeshire. Seymour's works popularised the idea of self-sufficiency, an approach to life that was provided with spiritual and philosophical scrutiny and leadership in the pages of Resurgence *magazine, which was published and edited by Satish Kumar, a former Jain monk, environmentalist and Preseli neighbour*

of Seymour's during the 1970s and something of a folk hero among
many of the new incomers. The deepest countryside of Wales was
also considered a suitable location for the numerous communes and
intentional communities that were established, then dissolved with
equal regularity during the decade and for much of the one that
followed.

Ann Pettitt: One of the things that I've always found very interesting
is that I'm part of a wave of people who moved to West Wales from
London and other cities in the seventies, sometimes as far back as the late
sixties, and we were part of that wave of sixties counterculture. It's only
when I came to live here, I realised that wave hadn't really happened in
Wales; it was very much a London and urban phenomenon of England.
We read *The Fat of the Land* by John Seymour, as did loads of people.
And unbeknownst to us, we were part of a kind of movement. I think
it wasn't until we began organising anti-nuclear activities that all these
people came out of the woodwork, and you realised that people with
very similar motivations to us – were English, had moved, some with
Welsh roots, many not – had moved to live in West Wales.

Julian Orbach: John Seymour's book was well-thumbed in our
collection before we came to Wales, and nearly everybody had a copy
– it was a mark of a hippie household, that you had one of his books on
self-sufficiency somewhere prominent. Mostly we had the little ones
with the nice illustrations by his wife Sally in them. I think there was
one called *Self-Sufficiency*. *The Fat of the Land* was the story of the
Suffolk one. A very romantic book.

Ann Pettitt: The romance is important because the life in these places
was hard going. We didn't have a Rayburn, we didn't have any radiators,
there was no central heating. There was an open fire in the back, which
was the original open fire. It had a massive great chimney and all the
heat went up the chimney. You needed the romance in order to carry

you through the thing of replastering walls and living with rooms full of rubble and heating the kids' bedroom with old paraffin heaters. You had to have a romantic vision of natural beauty that you wanted. You wanted to grow your own food, know where it came from, bring up kids on wholesome food, a lot of which you'd had a hand in growing yourself, vegetables, keeping animals and so on, and I wanted to be in contact with the natural world. I wanted to see the stars. I wanted real fires. I wanted to experience the wind and the rain and the sun and the cold. You wanted to experience it and not just as a holiday. As a life and certainly not as a lifestyle.

Julian Orbach: John Seymour had very good stories about being in a West African regiment during the war. Most extraordinary stories. My partner and I finally arrived there in West Wales, very near to where Seymour lived. Our baggage was home education, not Steiner education; it felt that, in a way, home education could sit quite happily next to Steiner, and we tended to know most of the Steiner parents.

Brithdir, our place, was up for auction. It had been an amazingly run-down farm and had it not been sold to us God knows what would have happened to it. It didn't even go for its asking price; it was that run-down, it would have fallen to the ground. Before we bought it, John Seymour used to go over to Brithdir and sit around with the three brothers, who were romanticised by Seymour as being the salt of the earth, while their immediate relations and other people around said that when their mother died, they became lazy bastards and they basically ran the whole place into the ground, and they liked drinking with people like John Seymour rather than working. It led to the failure of that farm, and the building was falling in on their heads.

Ann Pettitt: There were quite a fair number of pretty derelict small-holdings to be had, and this was not true of other parts of Britain. Wales was unique in that respect. And the reason they were affordable to people like us, who could manage to scrape a couple of thousand quid together, and that's what you were talking about, was because they were in such a terrible state: no running water, sometimes no electricity, long tracks, long rubbly tracks to be negotiated, far from any kind of form of services at all, on the outskirts of villages, and a struggle to live in, and understandably abandoned by the sons and daughters of the farmers who had struggled to farm these places. The land wasn't necessarily poor, but you would struggle to grow a crop there. It was grassland; you could only run animals on it. So our farm, for instance, it had stalls: where our workshop is was the cowshed, and there were stalls for eight cattle: a few sheep, a couple of goats for milk, a horse to pull stuff.

Quite a lot of people fell by the wayside, when they realised this way of life wasn't sitting back, smoking dope and strumming guitars: it was bloody hard work. We ran a house cow for a while on our neighbour's fields, because our Welsh neighbour was very good and very kind and very helpful to us. We were able to have a cow. We did the whole small-holding bit, the cow, the pig, the goats, the chickens, the sheep.

Ned Thomas: It's an old tradition, isn't it, from the time of the romantic poets onwards. There are waves. The first wave was when the Napoleonic Wars stopped people going to the Alps to find sublimity, so they came to Wales and they didn't only come from England; they came from Germany. I remember publishing a very interesting article in *Planet* some time in the seventies by the late Tecwyn Lloyd. He had discovered a German student in the Romantic period visiting Wales who eventually talks to one of the locals and he's taken aback and wishes that he hadn't had this conversation, because he wanted the people still to be what they were in his imagination. There is always that friction.

You can argue that the best thing that can happen is to have the friction and to come to some kind of accommodation and to learn from that intermingling. But of course, it's a tricky business. I think people brought some form of idealism with them, but many, many returned to

England, particularly perhaps the kind of people who wrote books, or were prominent in the back to the land movement.

Kirsti Bohata: For my parents' generation, the people with small children, there was a divide and a suspicion, and the two communities didn't want much to do with each other. The hippies didn't want much to do with the local Welsh people. They had their own community; you had these two parallel existences in the same territory. That's not to say there weren't cordial relations when you went into a shop, for example, but there was no effort to mix socially because there was such a gulf culturally and socially.

Later, we had home helps coming in a lot, because my mum became disabled, and we had a carer called Hedydd, which means 'lark' and I remember my dad saying, 'Oh, actually, all these Welsh names, they're not that different, are they?' Over time there was an acceptance, but particularly in the early days it was very much thought that the Welsh were a bit backward, they didn't really have anything to offer and it was all a bit laughable.

That said, my father would go to farm sales – men integrated more around the practical side of things. There is a male world in which people do business or do practical things and talk, which was perhaps a bit more integrated than the wider social world. But what I'm really saying is that there were two very distinct groups that rarely tried to mix.

Julian Orbach: I remember having a mournful conversation with one of the farmers in the Gwaun Valley, saying that when he was a child, he knew who lived in every single farm and cottage on the way round the valley and back into Newport, past the Brithdir entrance. And what was interesting was that as far as he was concerned, history had stopped. As each one of these cottages was bought, he had no interest whatsoever in who had come there; he saw it as basically it had passed out of a local history into some other story.

Meri Huws: My father was John Seymour's bank manager, and looking at dad's books, there's a book there, John's first book, inscribed to his bank manager. I think that epitomises some of this divide which we did not bridge at that time in the seventies and eighties. Satish Kumar as well, living down in Pembrokeshire, who was never really absorbed into the community, was never seen as fighting the same fight as the community – and he was, essentially. If you were to characterise the 1970s and 1980s in Wales, it's a period of change, but it's a period of lost opportunities, when we didn't create those alliances that we could have created, and I actually think that there are two issues and language is the second issue. I really think that it was also about lack of confidence amongst Welsh people, that we felt safer and used the language as a defence: 'You're not one of us. We think you're doing something which is vaguely interesting, but you are not of us.' And I don't think that was alienation; I think a lot of it was lack of confidence in ourselves at that time. Another aspect of that, that went along with a lack of confidence, and it's probably the same thing as parchus [respectable] – we are respectable people. And I think that is also part of that lack of confidence or inferiority. It emerges as 'We are respectable; we are Chapel-going; we are this; we are that; we speak Welsh; if we're not well educated, we want our children to be well educated,' and to some extent, we've hidden behind that for years and years.

Ned Thomas: At the time I remember running a series in *Planet* called 'Living in Wales', which was open to people from whatever group or position who had moved into Wales and open to green ideas. Of course, every magazine tends to attract the people who agree with it, so it probably didn't really represent a full range; it was probably perceived in South Wales Labour as nationalist, but also perceived among many English people who moved into Wales as more radical than Welsh Labour, which was very Old Labour industrial at that time. I think then, I probably became aware of the tensions. Satish Kumar was in Pembrokeshire, and I got on quite well with him, and I think

I may have contributed to his publication *Resurgence* and he may have contributed to *Planet*, but having said that, there was a big gap of understanding between him and the local community, one in which a neighbour might help a neighbour and nobody keeps a logbook of Favours Given and Received, but it's a lifetime kind of relationship in which there's giving and taking and you don't become overnight a member of that community and even less so if the language difference is there.

Menna Elfyn: We were aware of someone like Satish Kumar in Carmarthen, who was a bit of a hero of ours; we'd go to different meetings. And I think what we must remember is people like that, they did enrich the life of Wales. Forget the language: they brought in a new language of how to live and prosper in a different way. I think it's very dangerous to lambast incomers coming into Wales, because they do bring something. Do we want a village to die, so that it retains its Welsh past? Or do we want a thriving, living land where there's the possibility that they might learn Welsh and they might send their children to school in Wales, which has happened at a great level? We'd go to Newport Pembs and there'd be a day school about environmentalism and Satish Kumar would be there, and of course he then moved away and I hate the idea that perhaps he moved because he didn't feel welcome in Wales, he didn't quite feel he fitted in – but who does fit in? We're all fractured souls.

Ned Thomas: Rural agricultural communities have many, many of the virtues of the face-to-face community, but they don't live in a kind of philosophic cloud. Estate agents say, 'Village house in close-knit rural community', and the idea is, 'If you move here, everybody helps each other and so on.' Yes, they do, but they do it, in my experience, on the basis of life-long mutual favours; in other words, it runs in families, you remember the help your father got, or your retired mother got from the neighbouring farm.

Kirsti Bohata: There were lots of people coming in in the seventies and a lot of them had had private educations or private means, but they weren't all massively wealthy. Some people might have been, but my dad was a Czech refugee and had gone to grammar school in London and was a carpenter – he had nothing behind him. And my mum had been to secondary modern and was from a very poor, working-class family from Birmingham. They might not have been typical, but they weren't that unusual, either. Not everyone was rolling in it and a lot of people were living very frugally as well. A friend of mine has a theory that this was what endeared incomers to Welsh people, or at least made them tolerate them: the fact that they were buying up ruins and nobody else was touching these places. They were living without electricity or running water – we had a spring to start with. Perhaps there was an element of respect for the fact that they were not coming in and building a bungalow. I think the 1980s in-migration of another wave of people, often from the Midlands, was slightly different. That early group, I think they were privileged in lots of ways, but I don't know if I would say that they were all rich. And they're weren't all English. In my little area, my dad was Czech; over the woods at the time was someone called Martina, who was German; up in the gardener's cottage there was Brigitte from Brittany, who was the mother of my best friend; and then, when I was eleven or twelve, my best friend's mother was from Holland, although she was not necessarily part of the hippie diaspora. Up the road there was my first boyfriend; his mum was from Sweden, and he spoke Swedish with her. My father was restoring antiques then. He did 'Stripped Pine and Welsh Country Furniture': his labourer was from Germany. Over the valley our kind of local guru, Ali, was always described as a French Algerian. I think he might have originally been from Algeria and spent time in France – he was an amazing man. In this three- or five-mile radius there was that community around us; everyone else probably was English, but it wasn't only an English-incomer phenomenon.

Ned Thomas: At Aberystwyth there were students coming from South Wales to the university, which was part of identity reclamation. You got people from England who had one Welsh grandfather or something; but you also got people who had no connection and who are still here, and they had time to learn Welsh and did so. But I think there was a tension there. There were communes, and they were the usual mixture of idealism and exploitation sometimes. You very often got the kind of charismatic man with female hangers-on who were exploited to some degree. I remember sending somebody to write a piece about a commune near Lampeter and she came back appalled by the domination of this group, and of course they published a cyclostat magazine called *The Waning Moon* and, as you can imagine, it had a guide to rituals for the full moon and so on. It sounds pretty harmless but, combined with this charismatic figure, a little unnerving, and after a while, like so many of them, it collapsed.

Julian Orbach: There were several small communes that had come and gone by the late 1970s. One at Glaneirw in an old country house. There were bigger ones, including what is now the National Trust house at Llandeilo, Dinefwr Castle. We visited one which kept changing its orientation, Plas Taliaris which was near Llandeilo as well, it was vaguely Buddhist, spiritual. They all fall apart because people don't get on, that's the fundamental thing, and then the question comes up, who has, as it were, the voting rights? The main commune of that era was Glaneirw, which was a house and forty acres about eight miles north of Cardigan, which was income-sharing, a proper single business, which was mending Rayburns, which made the money for the community and home educating. They also had a self-sufficiency thing: that was their big number. At Glaneirw, somebody realised quite cleverly that the way that it had been passed on by the founders was as a housing co-op and if there were no more people being housed, the housing co-op owned the place. If they could make the community fall apart then there was nothing, so eventually they sold it and it's a private house now. There was no income being generated at other communes like Dinefwr and Taliaris – if you bought a nice great big cheap pile, you couldn't afford to do the roof.

Glaneirw was falling apart spectacularly all the time I knew it, even though there were plenty of people with reasonable skills, but it didn't happen, and later when our commune started to fall apart, I did quite a lot of investigation of why communes succeed – because why they fail is only too easy to spot. Once you were income-sharing and sharing all meals and sharing all cooking, then the arguments came up. This is my take on it anyway: the ones that allowed a degree of independence, and particularly independent family units within the structure, tended to last longer.

Wales was cheap. I don't think there was any other reason for people to try and settle there. Not the weather, not the land. Glaneirw farmed in a fairly serious way, in the sense that they grew wheat and they had tractors, so they were doing field-grade farming and they had cows. We didn't do anything of the sort. And I don't think the Glaneirw farming was at all successful and all those things they attempted worked, but they were absolutely fraught with ideology. Everything fell apart, arguments about how much time and energy had been spent by each person. That old thing, that resentment, is such a strong focus in communal life. Those micro-resentments and also to some extent micro-guilt, that somebody else is doing something and you're not. The two things are quite toxic. It's a very intense way to live your life.

Dewi 'Mav' Bowen: In the mid-seventies I was in Gower, living in a hippie commune. It was called Alansmoor, near Gannisland, and we were all members of the Divine Light Mission, doing yoga, but bringing up kids and having a normal family life as well, growing organic vegetables, that kind of thing. There was a guru, Guru Maharanji; he was a nineteen-year-old boy. This was near Fairwood Common airport, Swansea. It was mostly Welsh people, but not Welsh-speaking Welsh, just Swansea girls and boys. Of course, we had our kind of share of blow-ins. There were places like Dolwilym where this chap Giles Chaplin settled. He bought a place called Gwilym's Meadow, an old mansion, and that was full of characters.

Kirsti Bohata: Over the woods from us was Dolwilym Mansion and that was the location for quite a lot of the parties, and my father worked there for a while with Giles, restoring furniture, before he created his own business. I went to a Montessori school that was set up by a group of parents, people from Dolwilym, my parents, other people further towards Cardigan and maybe Pembrokeshire. We used to go and visit the Celtic cross in Nevern graveyard, because the school was in Nevern for a little while, in the village hall. Not for any spiritual reason, to play in the stream. My parents weren't at all spiritual, so the whole Celtic thing wouldn't feature in their world. And I don't think they knew anything about Wales: the fact that there was a language was a bit of a surprise – although that's hardly unique to them – and subsequent waves of people were shocked that there was a language here.

There was a loose collection of people at Dolwilym, because there were so many buildings and outbuildings and there were caravans in verges, and there was a scene going on there, although it wasn't a commune in the sense of being particularly collective, but there was a whole community there. I wasn't aware of any experimental communes, though in retrospect Albro, the Montessori school, operated a bit like one, and more than one local mansion was a place to score dope. What I was aware of as a child was eventually realising that all the couples that were together with kids weren't actually necessarily the parents of the children that they happened to be with at the time, so you were aware that there was a lot more movement of partnerships. There was this group of teachers and parents, and they were learning on the job. But it was an amazing school. It started off in Nevern, in the village hall which we had to put back every day, and apparently some of the villagers didn't like us there. Then it moved to Albro Castle, the Workhouse in St Dogmaels, we had a wing of it. Parents would take it in turns in the kitchens. But by the time we were getting to seven, I was pretty bored, it was a really long journey in a minibus, but it went all over the place, and whoever was driving would stop and chat with the parents, so you were desperate to get home. I was always getting car-sick. I do remember a Welsh child – a proper Welsh child – coming briefly. I can't remember her name. She spoke Welsh or came from a Welsh-speaking background, and that was the only time there was ever the question about 'What is the status of Welsh in the school?' and it didn't quite fit when somebody from outside that community, who obviously was committed enough to want to investigate Montessori, came enquiring. That's my memory of it, though I was only five or six.

It was a really vibrant community, lots of festivals and music and swapping labour to do up houses. There were quite a lot of hippies. They wouldn't necessarily call themselves hippies; my parents would call themselves beatniks. And they were; they were part of that earlier wave.

Dewi 'Mav' Bowen: We had about three acres of land, which we were growing. We put a lot of effort into it, and then the landlord wanted the place back for his family. We all moved to a place called Sandy Lane then, which was all wooden chalets and that was all developing, so it was a kind of natural extension for us, and then other places became completely gentrified because the properties were really cheap.

Julian Orbach: In the late 1970s and 1980s *Diggers and Dreamers* was the bible of knowing what was going on. It didn't have very much to it, but it had the address of communities and the number of members and an ideology and a certain amount of editorial, vastly optimistic normally, written up by each commune in the country. One of the things one could see very obviously were the ones that had a complete religious focus and the ones that had a single-guru focus.

Our house, Brithdir, near Newport, Pembrokeshire, was technically a commune, except that my then partner Emma and I owned the land,

and the initial idea was that we would give it to the community, and then it fell apart, or at least it did to the extent that it split in two.

Kirsti Bohata: I once went to Boncath with a friend, who was looking for a place down one of those long drives near where the Meigan Fayre free festivals had happened, where she used to live as a very young child, and we ended up knocking on the door of the retired postmistress. We were trying to find this place and we were not sure what we were doing and this retired lady came out. She was really friendly, and she said, 'Oh, yes, I remember. It was a commune, I think. I remember the people down there.' Then she said, 'Everyone was very suspicious of them, but I knew they were educated people,' and that's what she kept, as an educated woman herself, because postmistress is a high-status job. She was really keen to say that she could see from the kind of letters that they had received, that they were educated people; they weren't just crazies. It was a fascinating insight into the tension that she must have been aware of. They were probably naturists – there were a lot of naked hippies wandering around in my childhood – and that probably didn't endear them to the postmen and the other people that had to go and seek them out.

The Centre for Alternative Technology, initially titled the National Centre for Alternative Technology, was founded in 1973 at a disused slate quarry on the outskirts of the market town of Machynlleth, Powys, in mid-Wales by Gerard Morgan-Grenville, the great-grandson of the last Duke of Buckingham and Chandos. Originally an off-grid community, CAT, as the centre came to be known, pioneered a series of innovative solutions and responses to the widening environmental crisis. In an era when any form of green activity was still considered a fringe interest, CAT ran informative programmes to educate the public on the practicalities of building, planting and living without causing damage to the natural world. The centre's choice of location in mid-Wales strengthened the impression that the Welsh countryside was a suitable base for alternative, even radical, methods of existence.

Nigel Dudley: I went to university in Wales in 1973. I went to Aberystwyth. I chose Wales: my two first choices were Aberystwyth and Bangor, joint equal first choice. Given that most people in those days went to both of those on clearance, I was quite unusual. I went to the Centre for Alternative Technology as a student. We had a university environmental group and we did work at Ynyshir bird reserve and then someone got wind of CAT. I really liked it. I started going more and more, and got offered a job after I left university in 1974. It was completely chaotic. The blue-blood founder, Gerard Morgan-Grenville, had persuaded another blue-blood, the local landowner, to give this place on a peppercorn rent, but it had been abandoned as a quarry sometime in the 1950s, so it was empty. All the houses had fallen down; people were living in a few caravans and some of the slate miners' cottages were being done up when I first went there. They didn't have any power and it was a little bit anarchic. Odd people would come along and do stuff; it was all very 1970s.

I think it saw itself as a commune. Very much so. Everyone lived on-site, together. I don't know if people were being paid right at the beginning. There were lots of volunteers and, throughout the time I was there, people would come for both week-long volunteering and six-month volunteering. But we were paid – I was certainly always paid, thirty-two quid a week, not a lot, but a contribution of food, free accommodation – actually, at twenty-one, it was fine. I had money to burn.

Jane Bryant: CAT was a commune. I was there in 1976, really early days. Very few people had one role: everybody did everything. And it was an incredible learning curve, made possible by two English rich people: Gerard Morgan-Grenville, the founder, and John Bowen, who owned the land. That's the irony. I don't think anyone that I can think of when I was there at the Quarry was there because Wales was cheap, because no one was interested in buying property, or to find a family home, or the idea that one would stay there forever. It was really a shared passion for the environment: for me it was completely about trying to save the planet. It sounds very clichéd, but the Quarry was driven by the realisation that we have to try and live lightly on the planet, and this was a golden opportunity in community with others.

It was a way of living in a community and a lot of people there were only-children, without brothers and sisters. Unlike many communes we were trying to engage with the general public to say, 'You can do this.' We were trying to share things as well as researching, exploring and living it. You can't suggest to somebody else, 'This is how you should live your life' if you're not living it yourself. We were all incredibly idealistic and probably very naïve. It's very easy to criticise but we were passionate, without question.

Cynog Dafis: I remember visiting CAT as part of a day trip from our village where I lived, in Talgarreg near Llandysul, and enjoyed the visit. Many years later, after I retired, I became a board member of CAT. I was back and forth to CAT for ten or twelve years, until fairly recently. CAT is one of those contradictions; I could see how important an experiment they were conducting and how pioneering a thing it was and how innovative. Plaid Cymru, with its emphasis on community and decentralism and all that kind of thing, was actually going to find itself within a compatible wider framework and a wider movement: if environmentalism is the direction of travel, then that's good news for Plaid Cymru, and for our valley.

Nigel Dudley: There was a thing called BRAD, Biotech Research and Development, which didn't last very long and fell apart in awful mutual recriminations, everything you'd expect from a commune, and there were lots of other communes that collapsed. CAT was never really a typical commune, and I think that although we were always listed by the commune movement and people probably said community rather than commune, most people didn't come there to live in a commune. They came there to work on renewable energy or work on organic farming, and there was no particular distinction made between those who chose to live outside and those who chose to live on-site. We needed people living on-site at that stage – no one does now: it's all changed. So it wasn't as introspective as some of the others, and I think they're the ones that fell apart.

By the time I'd got to CAT the original founder, Gerard Morgan-Grenville, wasn't living there. He was living near Crickhowell by then. The Society for Environmental Improvement, which was his society, in theory had complete control over CAT, but it was really quite anarchic and there was a new project director every week and so on. Then a man called Rod James was employed as an architect, then he was employed as initially project director and then it became much more structured. Throughout the whole environmental movement in the seventies, there were a lot of rich people, that was a strain running through Friends of the Earth, Greenpeace, all of those, and it's easy to mock, but actually, they could have been hanging around on the Côte d'Azur, having a good time, but they were working, so good on them: there was no other money for environmentalism.

Cynog Dafis: The contradiction was that all of this activity in Wales was happening in English and among English people, and among people from quite well-heeled backgrounds. We've been living with that contradiction ever since.

Julian Orbach: In a sense, private income, family money, that was in the background of most of hippiedom across the whole of Britain.

Nigel Dudley: I think that's broadly right, but right from the very early beginning there were people at CAT who were not part of that. There was a guy called Bob Todd, working-class lad from Sheffield, very, very brilliant guy, who had been a lecturer at Southampton University. He and his wife were working on some advanced electronic stuff he felt was a waste of time so he moved up to CAT and lived on-site for a while. The three main directors there were Rod James, who was an architect who built his own house from nothing – it was a beautiful house; as I say, this guy Bob Todd, who was a former academic and from Sheffield, working-class; and a guy called Jeremy Light, who was certainly from an upper-middle-class background and had been with the British Antarctic Survey and was a biologist. All of them lived on a farm and were building themselves, and all of them had a real ethos of hard work. Machynlleth has always been about 50:50 Welsh-speaking, I think. They say 54 per cent Welsh-speaking. Machynlleth's a funny place, because it's not particularly welcoming. Other Welsh people say that, you know, they say, 'I came from twenty miles away. I'm still a stranger here,' but it's very tolerant, so they let us get on with it.

Nick Hand: When I was nineteen, I went to Machynlleth on a camping holiday near CAT and I thought it was like nowhere I'd ever been before. The area around Machynlleth was incredibly beautiful. We visited CAT, which had a tourist route you followed around the place, but you could see there was a lot going on in the background – people were living there. There were little houses hidden down the old railway line and I was intrigued by this self-contained world. When I finished art college, I wrote CAT a letter. It coincided with a project they were working on about alternative energy for primary schools, which didn't seem surprising but must have been radical for 1977, because no one was talking about renewable energy and how to make a wind turbine out of a bicycle wheel then. Nigel wrote a pack for schools and I went to CAT to work with him to produce it. CAT was a place where everyone had to do everything, so you had to cook and work on the bookshop and be part of the overall project. There were meetings with everyone on site and it was the first time I'd worked in that holistic way.

At a guess half the people who worked there lived on site and half lived in houses and cottages outside: we'd go and eat with them at weekends and get to know their children. There were some grown-up people at CAT, but the site itself, particularly the Quarry, felt like a commune, definitely quite a hippie feel, very relaxed, a lot of soft drugs. Mushrooms would be in everything. If there was a quiche prepared for supper it would have mushrooms in it. I had some quite odd experiences.

Dafydd Iwan: There was initially a lot of antipathy locally in Machynlleth, especially from amongst the farmers. They didn't take kindly to CAT.

Nick Hand: There were a few locals there who worked at CAT. I think quite a few locals in Machynlleth thought it was a free love commune, a weird sort of place. Some people were very suspicious of it, but Machynlleth was a very friendly place, and at CAT it felt as though anything was possible. I wasn't quite ready for it personally, but CAT was also quite ambitious. I think it really wanted to affect the way the world was going. There were some people there among the directors who could be intimidating, who played a headmaster role.

Machynlleth then in the late 1970s felt a little like it was on its way to what places like Frome or Totnes later became. There were cafés opening with children running around; I hadn't come across anywhere else like that. The town itself had a brilliant community. I played football for Machynlleth Town football club and they really welcomed me. It was the only football team I've ever played for that, when you got into the changing room, you didn't have to keep your mouth shut because you didn't want to get involved in whatever rubbish they were talking about. When we went into the pub after a game, people would get bought drinks; it was the only time I've felt that sense of community in a football team. Later the Quarry opened a shop in the town and integrated a little more after I left.

CAT gave me a deep love of Wales and Welsh people, I can't think of a word for it, but there's a particular Welsh embrace. I feel embraced in Wales and I don't feel it anywhere else. I'm from Bristol and I don't feel it there, but I felt it in Machynlleth.

Jane Bryant: Part of the backdrop were things like E. F. Schumacher – everybody had read his books – and Satish Kumar; everybody had a different inspiration in their own field. There were people who were concerned about the food chain and biodiversity, people who were passionate about energy and how we should be using sustainable energy, and there were people who were interested in buildings. There were those three hooks: biodiversity, energy and building, and everybody was mainly under one of those umbrellas. CAT never felt integrated with the town. We lived on an island. The whole idea was that we were going to be self-sufficient.

One of the reasons for opening the Quarry shop was to have a foothold in the town and some people from the town used to work in the Quarry. Some people at the Quarry tried to learn Welsh. We had very little transport. We were hippies, basically. We knew about John Seymour and people had visited him in Pembrokeshire. We saw ourselves as a bit of a cut above that ethos as we were interested in technology as well and we were interested in trying to engage with the wider public. We had several connections to organisations such as the Soil Association and were there to try and promote and engage. We didn't just want to live in the commune. It felt international. I worked on a fish culture project based on an integrated fish system developed in California, in which fish were grown and the fish waste was used to grow vegetables hydroponically and that was based on research by the New Alchemists in California.

Nigel Dudley: In environmentalism it's really difficult to separate out what was happening in Wales at the time from what was happening in Britain in general, because there was always a twin-track approach.

At CAT we did something called the Alternative Energy Strategy for the UK at the time of the Windscale Inquiry in 1976 or '77, and worked with a guy called Christopher Alty, who died very young but was a very brilliant academic at Warwick. He sat down and worked out one of the early proposals about how Britain could run without nuclear power. It relied a lot on coal, so in what we know now it wouldn't have been a sustainable thing, but it was quite new. I think as soon as that had come out, that showed a change in our attitude from demonstrating to starting talking about policy, and that's gone on with a strain of Zero-Carbon Britain and the books that have been done since. Gerard Morgan-Grenville's original plan was always that CAT would be the first, and then things would mushroom out to similar centres, which never really happened, but also that there was a kind of global policy aim. How much that happened in Wales . . . well, I think it did, not only because of CAT but all the things that happened in the seventies and eighties which did influence the Welsh government, no question, and certainly influenced Plaid very closely. When Dafydd Elis-Thomas was the leader of Plaid Cymru, he was very supportive of CAT and very supportive of what we were doing.

Cynog Dafis: When I went to Parliament, I worked very closely with environmentalists in Parliament, the Parliamentary Environment Group and Parliamentary Renewable and Sustainable Energy Group, I was chair of that. What depressed me at the time was the absence of awareness of these issues, really hugely significant issues for the age in which we live, among Welsh nationalists, among people who had a very, very heightened sense of Welsh identity: they were insufficiently aware of all of this. I think that's changed, and now you have a whole lot of Welsh-speaking people who are highly environmentally aware. It wouldn't have changed had it not been for the presence of initiatives like CAT in Wales, that's how it's worked out and, in the process, Plaid Cymru absorbed greenness into its ideology, but there were tensions,

174

all the time tensions. For example, I was an MP representing a rural constituency and one of the industries that Welsh-speakers were very successful at was road transport: operating big lorry road transport companies. And there was I, talking about the need to reduce road transport.

Nigel Dudley: Early on we had visits from people like the Duke of Edinburgh and Prince Charles. Does that mean it was taken less seriously? I don't know. In some ways, that made it worse, I'm sure, for the people who didn't like it. It made it much worse. I thought it was a crazy idea. The Duke of Edinburgh came, I think there was another one as well, possibly Prince Michael of Kent. I deliberately went away when Prince Charles came.

Jane Bryant: I have a picture of myself and Prince Charles feeding the pigs. We should have paid more than lip service to the fact we were in Wales. It was never a topic of discussion. We had all our printing done locally and were trying to engage with the community by using local suppliers, but I never remember a discussion about our Welshness – it was where we happened to be. It could have been anywhere really. We worked very hard. Most of my time was spent being freezing cold and soaking wet, building and making, printing. We did so much, as amateurs with a passion: I had no clue about the outside world. Everybody wore the same smock. I was the first ever information officer – there were constant questions. There was a hunger for knowledge. We were printing information sheets and trying to find the answers; it felt as though there was a community on-site and a wider community that was trying to support us.

Nick Hand: There was definitely a bit of a class thing going at CAT. There was an Oxford–Cambridge element in charge; the founder, Gerard Morgan-Grenville, was obviously an aristocrat. I never met him. He was in the background, and he appointed the directors, who were clearly ambitious. Everyone got the same wage, £32 a month, possibly not the directors who had families, and I'd say the workforce was fairly evenly divided between men and women. But the management all seemed to be men. I wondered if CAT was scared of becoming political, although I think quite a few of them there were Tories, which felt a little bit of a shock. I think that's why they ended up going into education, as it's an easier option than engaging directly with environmental politics. I suspect they thought the best route for them was through the royals rather than politics, which may have held them back.

Nigel Dudley: These days Montgomeryshire has, I think, got more wind power than anywhere else, and that very much came from CAT and from people who had been at CAT who got involved in putting energy together. It's like any kind of social movement: on one level, it was taken seriously quite early on by early-adopters, and then there's a much slower take-up by other people. I'm always really wary when people make that a split between the English culture and Welsh culture. I think it's a culture of people who move around and have been other places and done things and been exposed to more ideas that bring new ideas.

There were groups like *Undercurrents* magazine and Radical Technology, who also published a book, *Radical Technology*, in 1976, edited by a man named Peter Harper, who ended up working at CAT for a long time later on. He was part of a crowd, the people around the Open University at Milton Keynes, people working on renewable energy; they all thought we were crazy. Well, they were, at the very least, very suspicious. It was called the National Centre for Alternative Technology to begin with, because Gerard had ideas that it was really important. We dropped the National later, but that was a big debate. I used to work for *Undercurrents* magazine and they were suspicious, I think rightly so. It was a bunch of upper-class people playing games, but somehow, I think through the fact that CAT attracted different people from different backgrounds early on in the process, it solidified in a way when lots of other things fell apart.

Jane Bryant: *Undercurrents* used to do articles about us from time to time, they were sometimes a bit cheeky. I suppose if anybody could have been considered a guru at CAT it would have been Satish Kumar. As I recall, the reason he didn't come and live at the Quarry is because we couldn't accommodate his cow. We didn't have anywhere where it could have thrived. The three directors were all men, but the gender divide otherwise felt fine. Three of us who rebuilt a cottage were all women. It never felt in any way sexist.

Nigel Dudley: There might have been odd donations, but the idea there was loads of money . . . I wish. We were on our uppers, which is why we lived off tourism. We got donations of equipment and sometimes we got donations of food. People would give things: McVitie's gave biscuits for years. But there were no big injections of cash, because there wasn't an awful lot needed. We weren't paid very much; we weren't paying for the site though we had to buy building materials. There was a lot of fear about drugs – of course people took dope, but it was officially banned, because we were always worried about the police raiding and about our reputation.

Jane Bryant: Some people did grow weed, which we had to rapidly destroy once, when Prince Charles was coming, because an advance party comes and goes through everything before the heir to the throne visits, so we had to do the rapid disposal.

Nigel Dudley: And also, within that environmental movement, occasionally people would come as volunteers and really just want to sit around and be cool, and they were kicked out pretty quickly. It was pretty hard work, building stuff. The anti-nuclear movement felt highly developed in Wales, perhaps more the anti-nuclear dumping movement rather than the anti-nuclear movement, because the dumping movement came earlier. There were two organisations: there was Pandora, which was basically English-run, Powys Against Nuclear Dumping in Rural Areas, which had a nice little newsletter, and then there was the Welsh group, Madryn [Mudiad Amddiffyn Dynoliaeth Rhag Ysbwriel Niwclear/Movement for the Protection of Humanity against Nuclear Waste], which was much more in-your-face. They boxed people in and said, 'Get out!' Then they started thinking about renewable energy: 'OK, if we don't want nuclear energy, we need to think about renewable energy.' Then, when Chernobyl happened, depending on who you believe, either it was a lot of rainfall from Chernobyl on the Rhinogydd Mountains or it had been there all the time and no one had looked at it, but there was a lot of radiation. The sheep couldn't be sold off the Rhinogydd Mountains for many years because of radiation levels, and that was right in the heart of Plaid's interest, so the nuclear issue has always been there.

Ned Thomas: A long-running problem of Plaid Cymru is nuclear power. The policy, for as long as I can remember, has been no nuclear power, but, of course, in Anglesey, Plaid Cymru won an area where nuclear power is a source of employment for the local population. If you take away the retirees, there's historically been high unemployment among younger people, so that's the kind of problem that arises.

Terry Stevens: In 1975 I won a Churchill Fellowship to look at eco-tourism in the States, and I was supported by my employer at the time, which was Dyfed County Council, to go and do it. And I brought back ideas that were implemented. I was seconded to the US Parks Service, I worked at Santa Fé, Harpers Ferry in West Virginia, the US Parks Service office in San Francisco, and Parks Canada, and I would say that 90 per cent of the recommendations I brought back were implemented in Wales in some way or another. This was the beginnings of the Pembrokeshire Coast Path, the beginnings of community tourism. I wrote the manual for the Development Board for Rural Wales, and community tourism was alive and well in the late seventies. We were doing it, but it wasn't badged.

Nigel Dudley: CAT looked to America. Rod James took a sabbatical and went around to a lot of sites, places on Cape Cod, the New Alchemy Institute, places in San Francisco, the Farrell Institute, Portland, Sustainable Portland, the National Center for Appropriate Technology in Butte, Montana; there was a whole bunch, and we had quite close links with them for a long time.

Jane Bryant: Another loose connection was with Findhorn Foundation in Scotland. But they were more interested in their community and philosophy and way of life. We were much more pragmatic – 'You can build your house like this. There are solar panels you can use.' We weren't a spiritual organisation; there was no guru or philosophy of life.

Terry Stevens: In most things in life, there's no new ideas. It's that we badge them. Food and drink was always there, eco-tourism was always there, but we never called it that; CAT was ahead of the game. There were lots and lots of great initiatives, but we never calibrated them; we never saw a need to give them a title, because they happened, they were organic. There's a poster for the village of Rosebush in Pembrokeshire from the 1930s: 'For all who seek nature and repose' – it never needed to call itself a well-being resort, or spa resort, it just was.

Nigel Dudley: There was certainly a shift in perspective and CAT had to shift its perspective. We had a film at one stage which said something like, 'You may think the most important thing in life is going out and getting a good job,' and then kids came along in the eighties and said, 'Of course it is. Mum and dad haven't got a job!' There was a real shift in the way people perceived what we were doing. Did environment go on the back burner? I don't think so. A lot of the worst things happened in the seventies. The Forestry Commission had huge power: it could buy up farms; we had a nuclear power station bang in the middle of Snowdonia National Park, all sorts of things I don't think would happen even a few years afterwards.

Jane Bryant: I think the Quarry did influence environmentalism in Wales and offered an alternative industry for the country. There are people who stayed on who started off at the Quarry, who run book-shops and decided to make Wales their home. They learned Welsh and their children spoke it at home, I think they became naturalised. A lot of those at CAT felt an affinity to a Celtic idea of life as well.

Nigel Dudley: Is CAT recognised? I wouldn't have thought so. I think these things are very seldom recognised. There was a brief period when CAT was really quite big, and it employed a lot of people from town, which was interesting, because apparently it was a really popular place to work. People liked working there, which was good. But people still talk about the hippie place, you know, but then they talk about the art shop in Machynlleth as a hippie place.

The definition of a simple, timeless life sought by the generation that had moved to rural areas of Wales was not one necessarily shared by the indigenous population for whom change, however incremental, could appear dramatic. The differences in social attitudes between incomers and natives occasionally provided a source of tension, one that could boil over into open disputes that revealed the scale of the differences between the two communities.

Karmen Thomas: I was living in the north of England; I was living in Colne, which is near Barnsley, north of Manchester, east of Barnsley, a tiny little mill town, on the edge of the Pennines. I lived there with my husband and very small son – he was under two and he developed pneumonia, but he was allergic to the antibiotics, penicillin, at the time – this is 1977 – and the doctor suggested I move somewhere drier and warmer. I know that sounds mad, moving to Wales, but you have no idea how wet and bitterly cold the Pennines are.

When I came down to Wales for a visit to look for a house, we were all wrapped up in huge cloaks, coats, scarves, hats, because it was October time, and I walked down to Ammanford and everybody was in macs and quite a few people were in short trousers and short sleeves. I couldn't get over that. We found a place in Betws, an old ramshackle semi-detached cottage with a barn on the side of it. Up in Colne, in those tiny northern mill towns, there was almost complete unemployment at that time and my husband got a government grant to move to Wales because there was far more work down here. It was quite a prosperous area at that point, or seen as that by the government, so they helped pay for our moving and the hire of a truck to move.

That's what brought me to Wales, and it was quite weird, I knew absolutely nothing about Wales, I was brought up in English and with typical English stereotyping of Great Britain had no understanding that there was a Welsh language or Welsh difference, so it was a real, real shock. I was in Betws, which was just outside Ammanford, away enough to be a little bit different, but you could walk into Ammanford, which was full of little industrial places, the railway, the Miners' Association clubs and places like that. But Betws was mostly elderly people and they took me under their wing, because they couldn't believe I moved down with no family, 'family' meaning extended family, and I was a young mum. They thought it was quite brave, but they also thought it was daft.

Ann Pettitt: When we very first moved here, before it became a wood-working workshop, we had the idea of turning the outbuildings into some type of residential place where kids from schools in London could come – we'd both been teaching in schools in the East End of London: my partner Barry was remedial teaching in a school in Poplar and I was in Bethnal Green. We had the idea of bringing these kids whose entire experience was urban to be able to experience the countryside here, and to see animals and where food comes from. The house was still in a pretty bad state and as a try-out for the idea, a couple of times, we had kids come down and stay for a week, some of whom were Asian, and a couple of whom were West Indian, a couple were Chinese, as well as white children.

They were teenagers, and I think on one occasion, there was a little expedition to the pub. The next morning, a couple of local guys, who were very involved with Welsh nationalism then, came up and asked to speak to Barry. Two of these local kids went out the back, and were threatening Barry physically, pushing him, poking him: 'What are you doing, bringing in these blacks here?' It was racist – overt racism. I remember this little kid, who was a Sikh with his hair in a turban, and they started pushing him around – he was only about eleven, a skinny little thing – and they started pushing him around, these absolute racist bullies. I forget how it was resolved – I think Barry stood up to them, and I went out and we basically shouted at the bastards and told them to fuck off. I actually said that, 'Fuck off down the village!' They were saying to this kid, 'Fuck off back to where you came from,' and we were saying, 'No, you fuck off back to where you came from, and don't ever come up here again.' Afterwards, we found that they had a reputation for generally being unpleasant in the village, anyway. They'd latched on to Welsh nationalism as a kind of prop for their bullying behaviour and it made me think and it affected me, quite profoundly, and the effect was reinforced when, about fifteen years later, I began teaching and I taught in the Welsh school up in Llandysul, which was exclusively Welsh-medium. I could teach in a Welsh-speaking school, so I could hear what was being said, and it made me feel, 'Scratch a nationalist and find a fascist – and a racist' because I think nationalism is such a fine, fine line between being proud of your country and thinking you're better than anybody else.

Ben Lake: In parts of rural Wales, I think there has been, and still actually remains, a social conservatism, if I can put it like that, and what I mean by that is it's not very liberal when it comes to social matters. When looking back through the decades, you could perhaps include the one-eyed Welsh nationalists, who upon seeing black individuals come to the village, might act with quite some hostility and racism.

Kirsti Bohata: The hostility that we had in school, I don't know whether adults experienced it. Although it was a Welsh-speaking school, these battles happened in English, and there were definite groups: the English Ones and the Welsh Ones as we imaginatively called each other. My younger brother became friends with Welsh-speaking kids – and he integrated quite quickly through sport – but in my class we didn't mix, and we were culturally different: it was a genuine inability to get on and they probably thought we were horrible. But it was stoked by a nationalist headmaster who delivered Saunders Lewis 'Tynged yr Iaith'-type rants in assembly: 'The language is dying and it's your fault.' I remember him ranting about these messy properties that the incomers lived on and I think he was talking about our place, because my dad had furniture all over, it was pretty messy. We had that attitude from the very top, and one teacher in particular hated us incomers. We weren't incomers – the kids – I was born in Carmarthen, but the kids would say, 'Go back to where you came from,' and I'd think, 'OK, that's not going to work, is it?' but I did identify myself as English and Czech at the time, because you took your parents' nationalities and I think I might have subdivided it according to some German and other things going on in my father's background. English and Welsh, there was a real divide and the phrase 'Go back to where you come from' was often used.

The teachers were capable of being pretty nasty at times. There was one in the middle class, who was beloved by everyone, including me, but who I found out afterwards told the class that my mother, who had MS, was disabled because she had not prayed to God. This teacher then became headmistress of another local school and when some of the children went off to Glastonbury she would lecture the whole school on these bloody kids: 'Those children are outsiders and we don't like their lifestyle.' Chapel was part of it, but I don't know if it was a deeply held religious belief, or whether it was prejudice and intolerance. But certainly, we knew we were outsiders, we knew we were different; the teachers made sure we knew that. It's only a bit of an exaggeration to say that my whole career is based on that primary school experience. I'm a professor who studies post-colonial approaches to Welsh literature in English; really I'm still just trying to work out what to do about being told to 'Go back to where you came from' in Ysgol Beca although I was born in Carmarthen.

Julian Orbach: Occasionally, people would get drunk and call you a white settler, that was a favourite one. That was always there. 'Ifan!' [Gay], too, although it was quite rare. I remember mostly people who were drunk would get into an argument about something. A lot of the arguments I got into were about Brithdir and what we were up to, so they didn't tend to be racist particularly; they would tend to be more class-based, 'People like you coming down with your education.' Posh weirdos! And because I spoke Welsh and made the effort, that funny thing always happened: 'I'm not talking about you, but these other people.'

Ann Pettitt: The revival of the economy of West Wales and the role that we immigrants played in it, a lot of it comes from our exclusion from the traditional job market and the conventional job market. We couldn't get jobs with the local authority, and I couldn't get a permanent job in teaching very easily, because it tended to be sewn up by Welsh-speaking crachach [snobs, social elite]. Many people we knew were like us – they had to start a business of their own, they had to find a way to generate income. And all those little businesses, of course, ended up employing a few people. My partner Barry retrained on a very good scheme, set up by Margaret Thatcher in fact, which was a TOPS course. They were practical training in practical skills: carpentry, plumbing, cabinet-making, motor mechanics, and he went to one; it was a six-month course, shortly after we moved here.

Julian Orbach: Wales makes everything seem very stark and harsh and the Newport community was layered absolutely in three: Welsh-speaking, hippie incomers and retirement plus shopkeeper-type incomers. And they didn't really change over time. Our problem was that we were bad farmers in a hippie way and the things that we were trying to grow were unsaleable. We didn't grow enough to do more than feed the intentional community, and we didn't even grow enough to feed ourselves. We had polytunnels and a bit of a slug garden. I learnt the language and my ex-partner Emma learnt. There was basically quite a lot of Welsh in our community, but the whole issue about foreigners speaking Welsh is actually much more fraught than people give it credit for. To some extent, it feels like lots of people would rather that foreigners stayed foreign and didn't muck around with speaking Welsh, unless they get to the point where they're absolutely fluent and there is no clear difference. People making shop conversation in Welsh when both parties speak English [better] annoys Welsh people just as much I think.

Kirsti Bohata: We – the English-speakers – went to a Welsh-language camp for a week in Pendine and when we got back to school we barged in through the school doors chanting, 'Siarad Cymraeg bob amser' ['Always speak Welsh']. The headmaster turned round and said, 'That's baby Welsh'. And that was that, we were crushed. There was a hostility towards learners, or at best a reluctance to engage with them. 'Dysgwyr' ['learners'] was a derogatory term.

My parents had been outraged that we were excluded as children because we didn't have enough Welsh when we first went to school. They didn't think, 'Hang on, maybe we need to adopt the language.' But we went to Welsh-speaking schools, and they were educated otherwise by us, so when my mother was annoyed that my brother was having a conversation in Welsh on the phone in front of her, and said, 'That's very rude,' he said, 'Well, a) no it isn't, it's not your conversation, and b) I'm speaking in Welsh because that's the language I use with this person.'

Ann Pettitt: We got styled either as hippies or Communists, neither of which we were. It was very funny because we got on very well with our neighbours, who used to be around here all the time. There was an old settee in the corner and the nearest farmer, Handel, who was a single man – his wife had left him – was always coming round here because there were lots of women coming to stay – we had lots of visitors. He was our neighbour, in a caravan out the back, and he'd lived here all his life, a very funny man, he was always laughing and joking, and he'd say 'I don't care what they say' – we'd think, 'What do they say?' – 'I don't care what they say, Ann and Barry, they're good!' You'd think, 'Go on Handel, this won't wait. What do they say?' In fact, I learnt a lot of Welsh from him and from my neighbours, in order to speak Welsh with them. Handel used to walk down to the village every night, have a drink in the pub, or several, and after a skinful, walk back up the hill. I think that's why he managed to pass seventy, all this walking back up the hill. He was what they call a character, which is a code for drinks a lot, but he was a very good storyteller.

In the 1970s, more people were described as hippies than identified with the term, although the number of self-confessed hippies should not be underestimated. Many of the behaviours associated with those who arrived in the Welsh countryside seeking new ways of living became commonplace. It is relatively straightforward to locate a Buddhist retreat, complementary medical practitioner or reflexologist in rural Wales. The influence of the nascent environmental movement of the 1970s on Welsh government policy is certainly tangible, although

*the extent to which the new energies brought by the incomers of the
1970s and 1980s integrated with the existing culture of rural Wales is
hard to determine.*

Julian Orbach: A lot of those alternative therapies were what people
made their money from, shiatsu, reiki and acupuncture, all that was
already there, then reflexology turned up and then the back one, chiro-
practors, and homeopaths – you couldn't throw a stone in Newport or
Cardigan without hitting a homeopath.

The likelihood that people's religious affiliation would be Buddhist
was probably higher than anything else in those days. The Rajneesh-
puram had all been through West Wales by that time; they weren't big
in Wales, they were much bigger later on in the West Country.

Dance Camp Wales was an interesting phenomenon. DCW, as it was
known, was always held near Cresswell Quay on somebody's land. It
was fully fledged when I was going. It was hedonistic and then there
were moments of retrenchment, but when I first went there, nudity
was the big thing, and that's what excited the locals, very much – I had
friends who lived in Cresswell Quay and quite a lot of the dance camp
kids would go down to the pub, because there wasn't any drink sold on
the site. So they'd hang about, cause a nuisance, what have you – but
the locals all wanted to know whether there were pretty women naked
up at the top, and the answer was of course that actually it was the
middle-aged who were naked, and the children tended to find all that
nakedness quite embarrassing.

Everything was very, very familyish, workshops were run continually,
dance workshops were the main part of it, but then there'd be workshops that were more spiritual or for other arts. I always thought it
significant that it was called Dance Camp Wales, but apart from a few
curious onlooking locals, I seriously doubt there were that many Welsh
people there, if any.

EIGHT

MIL NAW SAITH NAW /
NINETEEN SEVENTY-NINE

Voices

Cynog Dafis	Kim Howells	Max Perkins
Andrew Davies	Meri Huws	Gruff Rhys
Ron Davies	Dafydd Iwan	Ruth Stephens
Menna Elfyn	Neil Kinnock	Ned Thomas
Ffred Ffransis	Sue Lent	Angharad Tomos
Meinir Ffransis	Eluned Morgan	Mary Winter

———

On Saint David's Day, 1 March 1979, a national referendum was held to determine whether there was sufficient support in Wales for an elected Welsh Assembly. The proposed institution would have neither legislative nor tax-raising powers, a weakness that made the idea of an assembly easy for its opponents to dismiss.

The No campaign, led by Neil Kinnock, achieved a substantial victory as only 20.26 per cent of the votes were in favour of the proposal. Within three months a new Conservative government came to power under the leadership of Margaret Thatcher. It was a government that less than a third of the people of Wales who were eligible to vote had chosen. Nevertheless, the consequences of its policies would be considerable in a country that had never returned a Tory majority, although several of the era's most influential Conservative MPs were themselves Welsh, including Geoffrey Howe (born in Port Talbot), Michael Heseltine (Swansea) and Michael

Howard (Gorseinon). The values of industrial Wales, in particular the strength of its unions, whether located in the North, South, or in areas such as those harbouring the residue of the slate industry in Gwynedd, were values a government led by Margaret Thatcher was determined to dismantle. As much as Thatcher disliked the values of Labourism, Labour itself regularly held the values of Plaid Cymru, who had achieved recent successes at by-elections, in contempt. As a party led by and under the influence of committed supporters of the union, Labour was equally sceptical towards any form of devolution for Wales.

Ron Davies: People asked: 'What is this thing about devolution? We're over-governed. We've got councils coming out of our ears right, left and centre.' The councils themselves were all saying, 'We don't want this new tier of assembly: what are they going to do, they're going to take our functions off us,' and there was a lot of discontent about that issue, as well as the fact that the Welsh language was simmering.

Neil Kinnock: Devolution was just wrong. Wrong at two levels: first of all, I've always been very, very distrustful of nationalisms of various kinds. I described nationalists once as people who think with their blood, which is a massive error of human nature. I also took the Orwellian view, a phrase which I used to use: patriots love their country; nationalists hate everybody else's country, and that was very basic to my feelings, ever since I was a kid. But the second reason was that I thought they were wrong in that there was no sustainable future for a separate Wales. In those days, of course, Plaid Cymru and nationalists generally were much more forthright in being willing to say that their ambition was quote-unquote independence. And I never thought it would come about, because of its unsustainability, but I thought that we would get the worst effects of semi-separation without any economic benefits, or indeed any cultural benefits.

189

Andrew Davies: Wales was very much still part of Britain. I think it was partly to do with the war, but it was also, I think, that people did still at that time feel genuinely that they were part of Britain. And I think the experience of the 1979 referendum and the rejection of devolution was symptomatic of that, and the 80 per cent voting against it was also a reflection that Wales had reached its apogee in the late nineteenth, early twentieth century with the power of coal and the traditional industries. With the long-term economic decline of those traditional industries, that sapped the confidence of people, individuals and communities, which then fed into the No vote in '79; people felt they didn't have that confidence to run their own affairs.

Ron Davies: It was traumatic as far as the Labour Party was concerned, but certainly in South Wales there was no appetite for devolution at all within the Labour Party, but also the feeling in local government was very, very strongly against it, because it threatened their patronage.

Neil Kinnock: The 1979 referendum was the last time I enjoyed politics. It wasn't just winning it – though winning was delicious – but the campaign itself was . . . I mean, it was house-to-house fighting, this!

Andrew Davies: 1979 was a turning point. Now you can see that it was the beginning of the end of the post-war settlement. It's interesting to contrast Wales and Scotland. In 1979 in Scotland there was actually a majority for devolution, but there was a minimum proportion of 40 per cent in favour required for the vote to pass, which the Scots didn't reach. In Wales, it was very different: the Labour government legislated for a referendum but the campaign against it was to a large extent led by Neil Kinnock.

Dafydd Iwan: The 1979 devolution campaign was grim because we had to swallow a lot of pride in Plaid, and said, 'OK, we'll back this weak assembly,' and despite the 40 per cent rule – our heart wasn't in it, but we went round, knocking doors, and I remember supporters of the Labour Party telling me on the doorstep, 'If this was a real assembly with powers, I'd vote for it, or even if it was for independence, I'd vote for it, but not this cobbled-together thing.' So, our heart was not in it.

Angharad Tomos: Cymdeithas's attitude to it was it wasn't worth having the powers of the assembly.

Mary Winter: The Communist Party was very active in promoting devolution and promoting the Welsh language. I was assistant editor with Dr Alistair Wilson from Cynon Valley of the magazine *Cyffro*, which was a bilingual Marxist journal, and we had anyone and everyone writing in it. At the time Kim Howells was a member of the Communist Party, briefly. And I think its role is often overlooked. We gave quite substantial evidence to the Kilbrandon Commission, and we were consistent in our arguments for devolution. *Cyffro* at the time was quite a groundbreaking journal because it was bilingual, it was Marxist; it was involved in the Christian–Marxist dialogue; it was very much involved with poetry and culture, but also with marrying the industrial background and history of Wales with that cultural aspect of Welsh life. People like Dai Francis [Communist Miners' Union official during the 1970s] were crucial in that devolution debate and in the promotion of Welsh culture, while at the same time, very much a leading light in organisations like the NUM.

Eluned Morgan: The Labour Party was quite divided in terms of being pro-devolution or anti-devolution. During the referendum in 1979 I was eleven years old, brand-new into a Welsh-speaking school, and I remember there was a little bit of a buzz about it. Everybody in school was pro-devolution, and in my particular circumstances I was from a Labour family who were pro-devolution and that in itself was quite strange, but acceptable within school.

At the time, Welsh-speaking schools were breeding grounds for nationalism, without question.

Max Perkins: I do remember the '79 referendum pretty well. In fact, I've got a document which Neil Kinnock sent to me: a very detailed press release, it's very interesting. It was published in February '79 and it's the detailed reasons for voting No in the 1 March referendum, and answers to the claims of the Yes men, devo fanatics, etc., etc. Very emotive. Basically, he was saying that all the claims that this would revolutionise the Welsh economy, we would get more than we were getting at the moment from central government, were inaccurate. He said, 'Wales will not survive as a community or as a culture if we cripple ourselves with the unwanted and unnecessary burdens of expense and disunity which will result from an assembly,' and 'We've been characterised as being anti-Welsh, but the truth is the opposite: it's fundamentally because we are Welsh, directly because we represent Welsh interests and strictly because we wish to maximise the opportunities of economic, social and political support for our country.' It goes on in that vein.

Neil Kinnock: The problem was, neither I nor those associated with me were against a decentralisation of government; we actually thought that the concept of devolution was a good idea. We thought it was such a good idea that it should apply to everybody and should apply to the English regions as well as Scotland and Wales. What really mortified me was the idea that in what I saw to be, accurately I think, a feeble gesture to nationalism, we would get what I called at the time 'sore thumb devolution', which would expose and highlight both Scotland and Wales's massive fiscal deficit with the English taxpayer and leave us much more exposed to attacks, reductions, questions, about the money which we needed and was justified in coming to Wales.

Kim Howells: I remember Neil telling me, 'No, we can't have one devolution, we can only have three.' In all seriousness, he said this to me, years before he came into power, but he thought we needed an assembly for South Wales and one for mid-Wales and one for North Wales, and people were talking about this stuff at the time.

Neil Kinnock: It became a fixation for me, especially when I devoted myself for a considerable period of time to getting into the detail, and the more detail I got, the more critical of this selective devolution I became, and my colleagues were similarly convinced. The first among them was Leo Abse, and about four or five others shared that concern.

Andrew Davies: Within the Labour Party, the Welsh language itself could be hugely divisive, so you had people like George Thomas – I'm not sure where that visceral hatred of the language came from. With George, you never knew, it may be to do with his sexuality. There was a very strong element, in south-east Wales in particular, which held a visceral hatred. It became deeply emotional and almost impermeable to rational debate.

Max Perkins: The first time I interviewed George Thomas, in the HTV studios in Pontcanna, we sat down and he said, 'Tell me, my boy, do you speak Welsh?' and I said, 'I'm afraid not, Mr Thomas.' 'I'm delighted to hear it,' he said. 'There are far too many people in this building who are only here because they learnt Welsh at their Mammy's knee!' He was a strange – well, he was a very strange man. And he obviously knew Welsh, but refused to admit it, because he spoke in Welsh at the investiture. But he would sneer – he was very good at sneering – I remember at one conference, he said, 'I've just been to Peterborough. I've got relatives living there, they're my quality relatives,' he said, 'Ddim yn siarad Cymraeg' ['Can't speak Welsh'].

Eluned Morgan: Growing up in Cardiff in those times, it was very different from growing up in Cardiff now. I was brought up in Ely, which was extremely anglicised, a council housing estate of 30,000 people and there were literally three families who could speak Welsh and sent their children to Welsh schools. If you spoke Welsh, you were quite isolated and almost a flag-carrier for the Welsh language, and it meant you left your area to go and get an education. The sense within school was that everybody was a nationalist and came from that kind of background. There was almost an assumption, if you were a Welsh-speaker, that you would fall into that camp.

Ron Davies: The Gang of Six. It was a big issue, the Labour Party had laboured the legislation through parliament requiring devolution, but then internal opposition not only forced the referendum, but forced a required majority on the people of Wales and Scotland, and that brought about the defeat of the proposals. But there was a lot of antipathy within the Labour movement, certainly in South Wales. You had Neil Kinnock as a prime leader of the No campaign along with Leo Abse, Fred Evans in Caerphilly, Roy Hughes in Newport, Donald Anderson in Swansea, Ioan Evans in Aberdare. At that time there wasn't a single Labour woman MP in Wales. They were all men.

Max Perkins: It was Neil Kinnock and Leo Abse, Fred Evans, Ioan Evans, all part of this backlash against devolution, which was part of the reason for the divide of the Labour government, there's no doubt about it. Leo Abse subsequently – many, many years later – agreed that it was a good thing to have had an assembly. I'm still not sure about Neil Kinnock.

Sue Lent: I was working in the old Unison building and Unison was continually sending stuff out saying, 'Vote No'. Neil Kinnock was very anti-devolution, a lot of the top people in Labour were all anti, whereas some of the people that later became quite prominent Labour politicians in Wales did vote for devolution. It was no wonder the vote was lost, because all the propaganda was against it. I think a lot of people latched onto the idea about not wanting any more politicians.

Ron Davies: During the referendum there was a lot of evidence English-speakers in the south of Wales voted No because they didn't want to be dominated by Welsh-speaking Northerners, and the Welsh-speaking Northerners voted No because they didn't want a devolved government to be dominated by English-speaking Southerners. So it was caught in the cross-fire.

Neil Kinnock: The Welsh language was vital to activists, a matter of pride and confidence to native Welsh-speakers. Amongst a very small minority of monolingual English, there was some resentment, mainly related to Welsh broadcasting, but you couldn't fill a couple of buses with the people who felt like that. And for the great majority of others, they were glad to sing 'Hen Wlad Fy Nhadau' but they didn't have any real intention of learning the language – but they thought it wasn't a bad idea if their kids did. It would be wrong to describe it as an upbringing, but it was an unassertive satisfaction with a distinctiveness of Wales and Welsh which didn't arouse much passion. In public generally, it couldn't be brought up as a source of division.

Meinir Ffransis: My father was very upset but Neil Kinnock says himself he never, ever spoke to my father or had any meetings with him, and some of the things Neil Kinnock said are plain wrong, saying my father was for violence and this kind of thing! My father was very friendly with Emrys Hughes when he went to Parliament. I think Emrys Hughes was on a trip to America or something with Kinnock, and had come to the conclusion that Neil Kinnock had a complex because he couldn't speak Welsh! And it was a chip on his shoulder, and when he said that the princes of Wales were no more than bandits and this type of thing, there's no pride at all in his Welshness, and he seemed to be ashamed of it. I think that's the inferiority complex or something that Neil Kinnock suffers from.

Mary Winter: My husband Tony and I and our two girls were thrown out of the Boot Hotel in Aberdare when we tried to attend a meeting that Neil Kinnock was addressing. It was the Labour Party that threw us out, because they knew, as members of the Communist Party, we were for devolution.

Cynog Dafis: I wasn't all that active in the referendum campaign, not as active as I should have been. I did some things, I attended meetings and I did leaflet distribution and knocked on a few doors and that kind of thing, but it was a very dismal campaign. There was no momentum, no enthusiasm, really, on the side of the Yes vote, and it was badly led, I think. Elystan Morgan was the chair – I don't think he was a particularly good chair. It was a pathetic campaign and you could feel the vibes, the hostile vibes, anywhere and everywhere.

Ron Davies: There was almost everything going against the 1979 referendum.

Ffred Ffransis: On the night of the lost referendum in 1979, Cymdeithas yr Iaith organised a gig. And I remember one of the local bouncers, him asking me, it was that night, 'How did the referendum go? What was the result of that vote, then, just as a matter of interest?' and I told him, and he said, 'Well, I didn't vote, myself. If I had have voted, I'd probably have voted No, because I don't think probably Wales should be completely separate from England, and having border crossings and so on,' and from his perspective, that was exactly what the referendum was about. The point is, he didn't feel strongly enough about it to bother going out to vote against it: if it happened, it happened, and so on. It is important to nail that one, whether non-Welsh-speakers had any feelings against the language essentially. It wouldn't be my experience.

I think it was mainly the Labour Party politicians in response to the threat of Plaid Cymru. From our point of view, in that period, that is when the political development began.

Ron Davies: A lot of the Plaid activists were literally incandescent, desperately disheartened afterward, and there was a sense of betrayal. They felt that they had gone into the referendum campaign believing that there would be a proper, united campaign in favour of devolution, only to find out that they were being stabbed in the back.

Cynog Dafis: I thought it was nearly the end, to be perfectly honest. That's how we felt: 'Well, it's finished. Welsh people have been offered a degree of self-government and they've said they don't want it.' But hope springs eternal, and there's that, but there's more to it than that: it's that we were so imbued with a sense of mission about Wales that we couldn't leave it alone; we couldn't let it alone.

Dafydd Iwan: The amount of the victory for the No side was gut-wrenching, and there was a period then when we really felt down, and was there any hope of getting Wales together again politically?

Angharad Tomos: People were devastated and thinking this is the end of the world, and we said, 'You've got to carry on.' And then within three months you had Maggie Thatcher coming in, which was much more serious.

Andrew Davies: 80 per cent of the population that voted, voted against devolution, and then of course Neil became leader of the Labour party, from 1985 to 1992, so given the result in 1979, 80 per cent against, that meant there was going to be little or no debate about devolution, certainly in the Labour Party.

Dafydd Iwan: The songs we wrote and sang in that time reflected this low period and despondency, but out of that grew things like my song 'Yma O Hyd' ['Still Here'] and more songs saying, 'Bugger it, we must do something about this.' My singing career grew out of that; my songs became far more optimistic and determined. We learnt a lesson in the '79 referendum, but we didn't give up.

Ron Davies: I can remember reading a report which was done by the then University of Glamorgan into attitudes amongst the people of the Valleys towards the Welsh language in the years following the 1979 devolution, and it claimed to demonstrate quite a remarkable shift in attitudes towards the Welsh language. People were becoming less fearful, less intolerant and more sympathetic to the language.

The first challenge to the Thatcher government from within Wales came in response to their decision to rescind an electoral pledge to create a television channel devoted to Cymraeg. In protest at the Tories' mendacity, Gwynfor Evans, now no longer an MP, announced he would undertake a hunger strike until Wales was granted what it had been promised. This proved a dramatic escalation in the tactics of the existing campaign for the channel that had endured throughout the previous decade. Evans' campaign found sympathy in communities outside Y Fro Gymraeg, including those in industrial South Wales experiencing the mass unemployment precipitated by the Conservatives' first term in office.

Cynog Dafis: After the defeat of the '79 referendum the nationalist movement shook itself up by the bootstraps and then, of course, the language came into the centre with Gwynfor Evans' decision on the hunger strike. And he told me that the reason he did that was not so much to get a Welsh-language television channel, but to save the nationalist movement from collapse and to save Wales, in a way. That's a very interesting example of using the language as a political instrument, so the very thing that Gwynfor didn't understand in the 1960s he certainly understood at the end of the seventies, beginning of the eighties.

Ned Thomas: When you came to the general election of '79, the one that brought Mrs Thatcher into power, every major political party had committed itself to establishing a Welsh channel, so that was in May, I think. In August the Home Secretary, William Whitelaw, announced that he'd thought again about this and it would be better to give some extra money to ITV and BBC to make a few more programmes in Welsh, whenever they could fit it into their schedules.

This produced some outrage. Every time there had been a recommendation for a Welsh channel, nothing happened. Then Cymdeithas upped their protests and these things had a publicity value in Wales, they got attention in the British press, which in those days had a full-time Welsh correspondent, which has gone now.

In the period after that U-turn, Cymdeithas asked various people of an older, more established generation if they would be willing to take some direct action. I had said yes, and so in the autumn of that year the late Meredydd Evans, who was much senior to me and had been head of light entertainment in BBC Wales and had been to Princeton and was a person with a lot of prestige and contacts, too, inside and outside broadcasting, joined myself and Pennar Davies, who was head of a theological college in Swansea. It always has to be three, because of Saunders – it was a possibly accidental re-enacting of The Three.

They were both somewhat older. I was the younger, I was a senior lecturer or something by then – we seem to be entranced in Wales by the need to have these titles – but we went and we turned off the Pencarreg broadcasting transmitter in North Carmarthenshire. It was a very Welsh occasion.

We were three academics, or whatever you want to call us, people who were not terribly practical, so we had afternoon tea at Llanybydder in the house of a bank manager, in his front room with the best teacups and scones, and then some students put their head round the door – one was the son of the house – he and his friends were members of Cymdeithas. It was getting dark now and they said, 'Well, we'll go ahead and we'll cut the wires to get into the transmitter compound, and we'll force the door for you and then we'll depart, so it'll all be waiting ready for you.' So that's what happened; some time later we followed them. But while we were having our second cup of tea, I said to Meredydd, 'Somebody has written a press statement about this, haven't they?' and he said, 'Oh, I don't know, us three haven't. We'd better phone Cymdeithas.' 'Oh, no, nothing!' I remember then writing the press statement. Half the point of direct action and taking responsibility is that you explain why you're doing it! So just in time I scribbled the statement.

Then we headed off into the transmitter station and it was quite a labyrinth. There was more than one room, and there were lots of switches, and we started fiddling with them and nothing seemed to happen. There was a lot of humming, but at last we found something that looked like a master switch and we turned it off and the humming stopped.

Then in due course, a young constable arrives, and the first thing he said was, 'Oh, Meredydd, I'm so glad to meet you. You adjudicated in the local eisteddfod and you gave my daughter first prize the other week: do you remember?' 'Ah, yes, what a delightful girl,' said Meredydd. So after about ten minutes the constable said, 'Well, what are you doing here?' So we said, 'Well, we've come to switch off the transmitter. We expect to be arrested – we've got our pyjamas in a case and so on.' 'Well, I don't think I can do that. I'll have to phone back to the station.' So he phoned Lampeter and then I think a second constable came up and got talking to us, and said, 'We're waiting to hear from the sergeant in Lampeter.'

What was happening, as I discovered later, was the room we were in belonged to the BBC or they rented it. Anyway we were on BBC territory, and the police were not sure whether perhaps Meredydd Evans, whom they connected with his earlier career in the BBC, had a right to be there. They wanted to get confirmation from the BBC that we were trespassing. They phoned Cardiff, and whoever they got onto, it was evening now, certainly didn't want to take any responsibility and said, 'You'll have to speak to the head of BBC Wales,' who was Owen Edwards, grandson of the famous Owen Edwards of the nineteenth century and son of Sir Ifan ab Owen Edwards, and he was out to dinner. So he was probably having a good dinner, and at eleven o'clock or something like that, they decided to call us in to the police station, and ask us a few questions and then tell us to go home. This was not what we had expected at all.

It took them about eight or nine months to decide what to charge us with, and in the end it was burglary, because they couldn't prove breaking and entering because we hadn't done breaking and entering, and the definition of burglary, which I didn't know, was in the hours between dusk and dawn. But during that eight or nine months we addressed meetings everywhere, and got the maximum publicity, so that was our contribution to the Welsh channel campaign. Years later I met a crime correspondent who told me, 'You were lucky that night, because that transmitter not only broadcasts the television signal, but it provides the microwave link for military communications to Northern Ireland. You were really lucky that the SAS didn't come in, thinking it was the IRA who had done this.'

Cynog Dafis: Gwynfor was absolutely serious about his hunger strike. No doubt at all about that. No, no, it wasn't a bluff, oh no. I was the editor at that time of *Y Ddraig Goch*, the Plaid Cymru monthly newspaper, and I remember writing an extensive editorial about the decision and what it meant. It was a lengthy piece.

Ned Thomas: I wrote a weekly column on television for the *Times Educational Supplement*, for which I'd worked for a while. It was a time of many reports on the future of broadcasting. I can't remember all their names now, but they led up in the end to the establishment of the fourth channel. Television broadcasting in Britain in the 1970s was basically BBC1, BBC2, ITV and everybody watched those, and Welsh had a little slot in BBC1, and ITV, at hours which normal people wouldn't watch, or wouldn't be able to watch television.

Because I was a television correspondent and followed these things, I got a small grant, from Leverhulme I think it was, to go and look at Switzerland and Belgium and wrote a little bit about this in *Planet* – to see how they did it in small countries with more than one language. In Belgium, because they got on so badly with each other, they couldn't even share masts. It was the same with road signs. The Road Research Laboratory, which was considered the kind of authority in Britain on road safety, said, 'You can't possibly have two languages on road signs, because people will crash all over the place' – and then I obtained the figures from Finland in Finnish and Swedish – and they had a very good record, probably more to do with the fact that the fines for even one drink were lethally expensive. You had to argue those things. In the television context, people told you it's impossible, and people, including people within the BBC in Wales and Welsh-speakers, were saying, 'Wouldn't it be simpler to have a kind of sound channel for Welsh which when you turn your volume down on the English programme you put in a separate voice and do the same on radio . . .' Some of them were wild ideas, anything but facing the possibility of having a channel.

Ruth Stephens: We were horrified when Gwynfor said he was going to starve to death for the sake of the language. We had to admire him for doing that, and for threatening to do that, but, I mean, Willie Whitelaw and Thatcher and these had promised it to him, and then they went back on their word. So he was justified in what he wanted to do; it was desperate of him to threaten to do it, but we didn't want him to do such an awful thing. But the politics of it got through in the end: it made sense. Wales was well represented in Westminster. We'd got the history of the Labour Party in Wales; they came out strongly to support the S4C, and even Thatcher and Whitelaw and these people came to in the end. Then they threatened to turn back and not to let it go through and that was shameful after all the representations that had been made to them. We'd got it through to a point and then for them to turn around and say, 'Oh, no, we've changed our minds,' was too much.

Ned Thomas: We got a lot of support in Wales from people who perhaps previously wouldn't particularly have supported the idea of a channel for Wales. And in that atmosphere, Gwynfor made this announcement. I had people whom I knew in London television and the sort who came along to interview Gwynfor, and they would interview me and the people of the Pencarreg transmitter too, and off-camera they'd say to me, 'Gwynfor doesn't really mean it, does he?' And I had to say, 'Well, actually, I would never have argued for this course; he's taken me and many others by surprise, but knowing the man, what he says he'll do, he will do. He has many virtues, but he isn't a person of great imagination: I'm not sure he has thought it all through, but he will do it.' I regarded it as going beyond what I thought were the limits of direct action, because you were going into Bobby Sands' territory. He had been a lifelong constitutionalist; he had been criticised at the time of Tryweryn for refusing to go beyond constitutional means of protest, and some people think that that had left its mark on him, and that he was in a way compensating. I don't know. It has a kind of poetic likelihood.

Meri Huws: I came back to Wales from Oxford and took my first job as a social worker in Caernarfon in 1980, '81. I came back as decisions were being made on a political level. Gwynfor was doing what Gwynfor was doing in terms of threatening to take his life or starve himself to death and I was chair of Cymdeithas yr Iaith when the decision was made to establish S4C, but I also had sympathy with the debate about not taking the language away from BBC Wales, because you would isolate it, you'd create a ghetto, and possibly, possibly, there was an element of that that was right.

Ned Thomas: Ffred Ffransis, who was one of the long-term Cymdeithas campaigners – there was a turnover, but Ffred Ffransis has been there all along – he wanted to establish fasting centres throughout Wales, where we would all go and agree to fast, that if Gwynfor was fasting to death, we should all join him. I belonged to the section who thought this was absolutely mad and luckily – well, I say luckily – we won the argument within Cymdeithas.

I had worked in the old *Times* building and I knew most of the leader writers so when Gwynfor's fast was announced I thought, 'Gosh, I've got to try to do something,' so I arranged to go and see the then editor. And when the *Times* had its leading article, it was very measured in the way the *Times* tended to be in those pre-Murdoch days. It said, 'On the one hand, on the other hand,' but having said that, it came down firmly that the government should honour the pledge for a Welsh-language channel.

Dafydd Iwan: Gwynfor knew also that it was going to stir up all kinds of emotions, and he was going to put the government on the spot. Now some in Plaid Cymru, notably Dafydd Elis-Thomas, thought that this was a selfish act which we should have stopped, but I didn't see that. I saw it was Gwynfor Evans. He had decided that without television, without that potent medium of the future, the Welsh language wouldn't stand a chance at all, and he was probably right.

Ned Thomas: Cymdeithas had asked me to be on the Senedd, the ruling body, and they also got a prominent trade unionist, so they fortified the ruling body with people who were not students and people under twenty-five or something, because it was also, we were now in the early Thatcher period, and the great closing down of steel and coal, and the Miners' Strike so there was a feeling of a popular front against Thatcher.

My son Danny was in the fifth or sixth form at the time, and unknown to his parents, he went with two classmates and a minder from Cymdeithas and invaded William Whitelaw's constituency office in Carlisle. Now, Whitelaw was not the member for Carlisle City, he was the member for Penrith and the Borders, but he had his office in Carlisle, so they went in in daylight when there was perhaps one person there and there were three of them – they opened all the drawers and threw all the papers and disks and so on all over the place, and waited for the police, and the police took them straight to a magistrates' court that day, and my son was home in the evening, a little bit late from school, but not really late so as to worry us, and the magistrate said, 'Fine of £5 each and bound over to good behaviour, thank you very much, dismissed,' and Danny came home. The next morning, he received in a small brown envelope, with the postmark Carlisle, a cheque for £5 which some local had sent him, because Carlisle in those days was solid Labour, and the magistrates did no favours to Whitelaw, they just did the minimum fine.

So that cheered me, when people who are on your side and committed help you, that's the least you can expect. But when people across borders help as well that cheers me up. I know it's a small thing in its way, but I think that's very important.

Gruff Rhys: I went to Gwynfor's rally in Llangefni. I would have been nine or ten. I was into DIY, so I was making number 4s in wood with dovetail joints to take to the rally. I remember going on a bus that was totally overloaded, so the kids had to sit on the parents and I remember my head banging on the window all the way, it was so packed. And I got my number 4 signed by Gwynfor at the end of the night.

Dafydd Iwan: I chaired a few of Gwynfor's meetings and spoke in a few of them, as well, and of course, during that tour, it was announced that they were going to set up the channel, so it became a victory tour. All this he worked out. He was determined: he would have starved himself to death, there's no doubt about that.

Ruth Stephens: Such effort goes into these campaigns, and such good people are putting all their life into it really, their time and their energies. Labour and Plaid were united that they supported what had been promised. They could all see the point, that that was what Wales needed. And then for the Tories to do that was shameful. We supported Gwynfor but were relieved when he didn't have to do anything so drastic, because it was ridiculous to have to do that after all the work that had gone on for years before to reason sensibly with people to get them to a point. Oh, it was a terrible, terrible time. We were really worried about Gwynfor.

Menna Elfyn: I don't believe that people think, 'Oh, Gwynfor won the channel for us,' because prior to that, Cymdeithas yr Iaith had planned and executed a campaign of some form of action every week for three months, so I think it was an accumulated effect, but of course having Gwynfor saying that was really the crowning glory, no doubt about that, and to get someone like Margaret Thatcher to do a U-turn was something incredible, but she didn't want another Northern Ireland on her hands.

Ned Thomas: It's very interesting to read that the channel wouldn't have come about but for Gwynfor, and by that time I remember a friend of mine, John Osmond, telling me that he met the junior minister in the Welsh Office in the period. They were beginning to rethink, and he said something to the effect that they didn't want the different protest groups in Wales to come together in one. And there were some people on the far left in Wales, too, who thought that the government was giving in on the television in order to divide one section of the protest from the kind of reaction to what happened to the steel industry, the thousands of people who were overnight more or less put out of work, so that could have been the kind of background.

Then, when the government relented and agreed to fund S4C, they were in an interesting position. Along the way, every time they had said, 'It's impossible because it would cost so much' and the nearer we came to it, the more they raised the cost, to show that it was completely unreal. Now, when they did the U-turn, they themselves had set the costs far beyond what I would have thought was legitimate to expect, so S4C started off with a very good deal indeed.

Ffred Ffransis: That's the time, the beginning of the awakening. In that period in 1979 onwards, the beginning of seventeen years of Tory rule in Westminster, when there was no political power in nationalism in Wales at all, whereby the Tories saw it to their advantage to try to buy off parts of the Welsh establishment, exactly the same principle as somebody like Frantz Fanon testified to as *'la donné de la terre'* in Algeria, when he said 'Avoid the capital city like the plague. Neo-colonialism will try to take control over the country, especially economically, and take control of the ruling class.'

Max Perkins: In 1979, the newly elected Tory government appointed Wyn Roberts, from Anglesey, to a post in the Welsh Office. They recognised his worth as somebody who could reach out, and of course he was the architect of the Welsh Language Act and I think the Tories' attitude was, 'Well, throw that at them and keep them quiet, and we won't get so much language vandalism.'

Ffred Ffransis: In the same way – for sincere reasons by Wyn Roberts, a minister in the Welsh Office, who had an emotional attachment to the Welsh language – the Tories had made their audacious attempt to buy off the Welsh-language establishment. And in the end, after all the rows about protests, they said, 'Here's money for a Welsh-language channel,' 'OK, here's money to increase Welsh-speaking schools. We'll increase the grants for the Eisteddfod,' and so on. 'As long as you don't drop the vote politically and socio-economically, we'll support this. We'll try and take this over,' and so I'm not suggesting it was in any perverse way, I'm sure it happened as an accident, but it seemed so telling that the young Tory boy, William Hague, married the daughter of the director of the National Eisteddfod of Wales. It seemed as if that was the consummation of the Tory bid for Wales.

Menna Elfyn: We were always aware with Cymdeithas, and this is where, I think, we missed out. We tried, we were aware of the 80 per cent of people that didn't speak Welsh, and that we needed to win them over, and, of course, being non-violent was a good way of doing that, but it didn't really go far enough. There was always that belief that we needed an English television channel for Wales that was Wales-orientated, and as soon as we got S4C, well, everybody was tired, I suppose – you got drained – and then things moved on: 'Oh, we've won the channel,' but we didn't win the channel for those people who really needed to be on board with us.

NINE

MEIBION GLYNDŴR /
THE SONS OF GLYNDŴR

Voices

Iwan Bala	Dafydd Iwan	Max Perkins
Dewi 'Mav' Bowen	Ben Lake	Dewi Prysor
Richard Frame	Alun Llwyd	Terry Stevens
Gethin ap Gruffydd	Rhys Mwyn	Ned Thomas
Meri Huws		Angharad Tomos

———

Across rural Wales a series of arson attacks on empty properties commenced on 13 December 1979. The purpose of the fires was to draw attention to the increasing prevalence of second homes in the country. Within four weeks some eight English-owned holiday cottages had been destroyed. Over the course of the next fourteen years, during a campaign that had two distinct phases, this figure would, in the estimation of the arson squad established to investigate the burnings, rise to between 220 and 228 properties.

The many groups supportive of the idea of a campaign that highlighted the crisis of second homes were drawn together by the authorities under the unhelpful, catch-all rubric of Welsh Nationalists. Throughout the era, polls found a small majority in Wales to be in favour of the campaign; particular attention was given to the apparent policy of causing damage to unoccupied property, whilst avoiding harming members of the public. One group in particular, Meibion Glyndŵr, the Sons of Glyndŵr, became synonymous with the burnings

209

and their name both became familiar in the media and, due to their anonymity, grew into folklore.

Rhys Mwyn: Meibion Glyndŵr came around at the same time as the S4C campaign, but they're distinct movements. The issue of second homes was real and visible to everyone.

Meri Huws: In that period when I was chair of Cymdeithas there was a slogan, 'Deddf Eiddo' [Property Law] – houses and jobs to keep the language. And we tried. The natural thing to do at that time would have been to align ourselves with Shelter Cymru, which was being established around the same time. And yet, it seemed that creating that alignment was really difficult, because I think the language was the divider there, that we felt that we shouldn't be discussing these issues through the medium of English with other people who possibly didn't speak Welsh, and we kept the discussions within our language, as well. And we didn't bridge out. And that's why I think we did lose momentum to some extent in the 1980s, in that we weren't always prepared to create those bridges; we weren't prepared to communicate with others in another language, which was necessary if we were to create understanding.

Dafydd Iwan: There are many campaigns we could have been more efficient about, but in the end it's the question of changing minds. And the one factor which always makes it very, very difficult is the movement of people, people from across the border seeing Wales as their holiday destination and retirement home location. When people do campaign about second homes that never answers it. In the 1980s we were looking for answers and we were looking for policies, but we were coming up against the law all the time: you can't say this house is for Welsh-speakers only, you can't do that. In the end, money talks. Cymdeithas yr Iaith started the Deddf Eiddo campaign, demanding a property act.

Rhys Mwyn: That first night in December 1979 was coordinated, three or four cottages went up. There was somewhere near Fishguard, somewhere on the Llŷn and somewhere else. The first cottage that went up was called Tyddyn Gwêr; it was high up on Mynydd Nefyn in Gwynedd. I visited it for a book I was writing. I went down to the Bryncynan Arms then, which is a little pub just outside Nefyn. All the locals there knew who I was and said, 'Oh, Rhys Mwyn! What are you doing here?' and I said, 'I've been up to Tyddyn Gwêr, which is the first holiday home that was burnt by the Meibion Glyndŵr,' and all of the local lads laughed. And it was an interesting laugh, because it wasn't, 'Ooh, you shouldn't be writing about that!' It was a laugh of, 'Yeah, well, it was a second home.' And we all felt that. None of us lost any tears when cottages were burned. There was an element where you felt, 'Well, it's such an issue; it needs something that brings that issue to greater public awareness.' As long as there wasn't a loss of life, most of us could kind of live with it – which is dangerous, isn't it? Because had there been a loss of life, we'd have all been in a serious place.

During our gigging time I would quite often say from the stage, 'Some people have got two and three homes, and some people are homeless, and then occasionally someone burns one down' – and everyone would clap. But the point was most people coming to gigs might not have sympathised with Welsh nationalism, but they certainly sympathised with the fact that, how is it that people have got three – it's not second homes, third homes, fourth homes – and then other people have none? And I think on that level, people understood that argument.

Gethin ap Gruffydd: I was approached by Meibion Glyndŵr people and I said, 'Look, I'm known. I'm watched. It's in your own interest I stay well away, or I'll be a weak link and that would be the end of it.' They got away with a lot, Meibion Glyndŵr. They were very well organised and had things very well thought out. I've no doubt they asked other people as well. It was all Meibion Glyndŵr, the entire campaign. Those rumours of the security services being involved come up all the time and there's nothing to them, disinformation. What there was a lot of was people from England moving into rural areas of Wales for a short time and then moving away again and I have no doubt some of them were with the security services. And we must be the easiest society in the world to penetrate.

Ben Lake: If I was to try and personify your typical Meibion activist, heavily caveated of course, I think it's probably more likely to be the young people who had stayed in the local area, perhaps worked, were in professions, were struggling to get by and really resenting the fact that they weren't able to get a house in their home area. I think the objective was very similar between Adfer and Meibion Glyndŵr – but Adfer was perhaps in a better position to be able to take the longer view of coming together, of taking over houses, of renovating them, of taking that peaceful, orderly route; whereas with Meibion, you get more of the impression that this was one of frustration to the point of tears and desperation, and they didn't have the same amount of time to be able to embark on a more considered project and a more considered way of doing it.

Dewi Prysor: It all kicked off in December 1979 with the first attacks, which was three months after I started secondary school in Blaenau Ffestiniog. Blaenau Ffestiniog, a Welsh-speaking slate-quarry town, it had been Labour for decades but there was always a strong and growing Plaid Cymru contingent. In 1974 the town had turned Plaid, the working-class kids of quarrymen were militant nationalists at heart, sharing books like *To Dream of Freedom*, borrowed from older brothers and their mates. Tattoos of the White Eagle, Eryr Wen (the symbol of the Free Wales Army), were common – mostly home made with Indian ink. At my school the White Eagle, Free Wales Army and MAC [Mudiad Amddiffyn Cymru] slogans were copied on class walls and desks, a massive FWA was painted in white on the gym's stone wall, in sight of the street. It was never properly erased. Later a huge Meibion Glyndŵr slogan was painted on the same wall.

The attacks on holiday homes on 13 December 1979 were a catalyst. As schoolkids we were excited, and that excitement fuelled a further step towards militant nationalism among the youth in working-class towns. These first coordinated attacks weren't Cymdeithas-style, pacifist direct action. This was darker, clandestine and anonymous, with a profound sense of a movement that meant business. This appealed to us as young teenage boys.

Ben Lake: I say this as somebody from Lampeter, a rural background. The image of Meibion Glyndŵr that I had was of the friends of mine who would sometimes find greater release and satisfaction in drunkenly pushing over a cow, or what have you, to deal with their frustration, as opposed to sitting down and thinking, 'Right, how do we get through to the council?' Meibion Glyndŵr and Free Wales Army tended to be young individuals who were disillusioned and despairing at the constitutional state of affairs and were anxious to get things changed quicker than the churn of the democratic process would allow; these individual incidents were acts of almost recklessness, a youthful kind of frustration. However, that theory always came up against the fact that some of the devices used were incredibly sophisticated and spoke to a far greater coordination and planning than a couple of youngsters in the pub on a Friday night coming out to do it might be capable of.

Dewi Prysor: When the name 'Meibion Glyndŵr' was used first, the name chosen made it clear that this was a nationalist campaign. We all felt that this was what was needed, because pacifism doesn't work unless you have tens of thousands on the streets, which wasn't going to happen. Following the 1979 devolution referendum result, there was despondency in general among lifelong Plaid people. Although some of us remembered the shame of the vote, it wasn't a real concern for us. Devolution was just a word. Assembly or not, we supported a Free Wales whatever happened. There was no pacifist political campaign for Welsh independence, so in this vacuum Meibion Glyndŵr appeared, and supporting Meibion Glyndŵr was part of youth culture, as was ska, punk, reggae and football. A bus load went to the Abergele march every year. Slogans like 'MG' and the White Eagle were popping up everywhere. In one of the pubs in Blaenau there was a shelf in a corner of the bar where the television sat and the White Eagle and the letters MG were burnt into the log on which it rested with a poker. It was still there in the late 1990s.

Rhys Mwyn: Whether there were any connections with Irish Republicans, I don't know. Cayo and the Free Wales Army certainly seemed to suggest those links but I think the IRA would have spotted the Free Wales Army coming over the hill, probably gone for a drink session, not much more than that. Meibion Glyndŵr, I don't know how we get to the bottom of that, because if somebody's still alive, they're hardly going to say, 'Well, it was me all along.' That's basically the conclusion I've drawn.

During the first year of cottage-burning other buildings were attacked in more urban environments. Towards the end of 1981 a small explosion occurred at the Welsh Office in Cardiff. This was followed by similar incidents at an Army Recruitment Centre in Pontypridd, Conservative clubs in Cardiff, as well as British Steel offices in the capital. In what the authorities regarded as an escalation in intent, an explosive device was also discovered later that year at the home of Nicholas Edwards, the Welsh Secretary.

Iwan Bala: I was aware of the bombing campaign. It seemed to me that that was a South Wales Valleys thing more than it was a North Wales thing, although that wasn't the case, but at the time it seemed to me that these guys were coming up from the Valleys to do these things, the harder types. I was aware of that happening, and these links there seemed to be with Ireland.

Richard Frame: In 1980 I had a stall in Newport Market that manufactured badges, and someone came in and asked if we could produce a badge saying 'Strike a Light for Wales'. The design was the lettering of those words and a drawing of three matches and a cottage.

Dafydd Iwan: Bethan my wife, her auntie had a shop in a small village near where quite a few places were burnt. During the winter she kept the keys for all the summer homes and the second homes in the area; not once did anybody go and knock on her door to talk to her and one of the houses was actually burnt. So, putting everything together, I've never really understood it. I remember coming back one night, and I could actually see the dying embers of a house over in the Llŷn way. There wasn't a road – there was only a track, a path – and it had been raining for days. Anybody approaching that house would have left marks, you couldn't avoid it. And where would they have parked their getaway car? There were always so many questions.

On Sul y Blodau (Palm Sunday) 1980, which fell on 30 March, a mass arrest took place during Operation Tân (Fire), the first coordinated police response to the arson campaign. Fifty people, including actors, authors and known sympathisers of Meibion Glyndŵr, were subject to a series of dawn raids, carried out by the police under the Prevention of Terrorism Act 1976. The theatrical nature of the operation drew sharp criticism and was condemned as a gesture without substance. As no evidence was discovered and none of those arrested charged, Operation Tân was considered a failure, all the more so as it represented the first occasion on which the police had invoked the Prevention of Terrorism Act in Wales.

Ned Thomas: I think there was support in local communities, and of course this was increased when, on Palm Sunday 1980, there was a mass arrest of maybe about fifty, arrested in dawn raids, and it was completely on the grounds that they were thought to be sympathetic. Someone like Robat Gruffudd, who runs Y Lolfa publishing house in Tal-y-bont, no doubt he was sympathetic, but he had a business to run; he didn't do anything. And in the end, none of those people were charged, or if they were charged, they were found not guilty.

On the evening one holiday cottage near Tal-y-bont was burnt, a friend of mine was driving from Machynlleth to Aberystwyth, so technically he could have diverted his journey and burnt this cottage. Somewhere along the way, the police had got his car number and he took it all the way to the highest court he could and he was discharged, in Swansea, I think, at the Crown Court.

Alun Llwyd: As a boy, I distinctly remember that Palm Sunday morning on the radio, saying, 'Hang on, why have they been arrested?' I think, to me, at that point in time, my only reflection was thinking, 'This whole thing is absolutely mental,' which, even at that young age, made me think, 'So who is actually burning these holiday homes?' because there's no link here between what is happening. And it all became deeply sinister then for me, and the conspiracy theories started building in my head, because, well, you can't arrest these people, because those are obviously nothing to do with anything here. You could argue that was a brilliant own-goal by the security services. That was the first time ever I started questioning whether there wasn't a gang of people going out late at night and burning holiday homes, and was there something far more sinister going on here.

Ben Lake: When we think of what happened on that Palm Sunday, when they brought in the actors and publishers and people like that, I think it is very tempting to think that there was some form of state collusion. It's been fairly well documented.

Dewi Prysor: We all referred to Operation Tân as Sul y Blodau. Years later I got to know a few of the people who got pulled by the police in Blaenau Ffestiniog and Tanygrisiau. They were mostly around about ten to twenty years older than myself; they weren't even activists, they just happened to have been seen on the odd march.

Ben Lake: The one problem that I kept coming up against and I couldn't quite solve was how, certainly during the original initial few years of cottage burnings, nobody was ever caught. And I have to disclose a bit of a family interest in this, because both my grandfather and my father were policemen, and my father for a time towards the latter end of the campaign, the next generation, if you like, of Meibion Glyndŵr, was on Special Branch and so was in one of those unique scenarios: of being a Welsh-speaking Welshman from the area but also playing for the other side, if you could put it that way. The one thing my father keeps coming back to is how they would attend some of the burnings and the devices that had been used were of a level of technical expertise that you couldn't write it down to a bunch of locals in the pub having had a few, feeling angry, and then acting out in recklessness. And he mentioned that there were a few burnings in which the devices that were used and the time delays on the devices were seriously sophisticated, to the point that they would regard them as more sophisticated than some of the IRA devices.

My father, when speaking as a policeman, thinks that there could well have been an individual or individuals with that same degree of expertise and forethought that you saw earlier in John Barnard Jenkins and the MAC; that it wasn't necessarily just either a handful of reckless arsonists or youthful enthusiasts and then more of an MI5 job; that actually you could have had an individual or individuals who were behind Meibion Glyndŵr.

Dafydd Iwan: There's another aspect to this as well: if we were as efficient as that second stage of the bombing campaign, we'd have been self-governing years ago. There are questions – and I know for a fact that there has been quite a large-scale involvement of MI5 or the secret services, which came to light in a later case of sending somebody devices in Jiffy bags.

Dewi Prysor: This is a fantasy of Dafydd Iwan's. It's quite ridiculous. I greatly admire Dafydd, but I think he felt, as a pacifist, that the actions of Meibion Glyndŵr would damage Plaid Cymru and Welsh nationalism, so he came up with this notion that the arson campaign was planned and executed by the British state. He was high up in Plaid then. He felt he had to defend the pacifist honour of Plaid Cymru and he was probably genuinely worried that Meibion would turn public opinion against Plaid and constitutional nationalism. Even if that were true, it didn't work. The Meibion Glyndŵr campaign gave Welsh nationalism a boost, especially with young people. Plaid's problem wasn't secret services manufacturing false flags, but Plaid's policies and the drainage of its members.

Dafydd Iwan: It wasn't a good time in Plaid Cymru, being Chair at that time was difficult, because you had a lot of animosity, people setting into each other and we tend to do it in Wales. When times get bad, we pitch into each other. It was a bad time for Plaid Cymru, because we didn't show any unity of purpose, but thank God we came through it.

Ben Lake: It's perhaps interesting to note for some of the big issues of Wales in the 1980s, the voices that were leading political campaigns were Cymdeithas yr Iaith and it was the unions in South Wales, and, when it came to the extra-constitutional campaigning, people like Meibion Glyndŵr. It's an interesting decade that I don't think we've quite understood.

Dafydd Iwan: I used to get anonymous letters, referring to me not just as a singer but as a bomb-maker. They were usually in very bad Welsh or bad English, and in capital letters.

Angharad Tomos: Once the arson campaign was under way there was support for that. And during the arson campaign, we couldn't get any publicity for Cymdeithas. Meibion Glyndŵr were getting all the publicity, and so we were getting all the blame and none of the credit. I'd be out canvassing for Plaid Cymru and they'd chuck everything at us: it's Cymdeithas behind it all, it's arson, it's everything. People didn't differentiate between us at all – they're just the Welshies.

Dewi Prysor: The early Cymdeithas members would sometimes be charged with conspiracy for climbing television masts and received some hefty sentences. They knew they would get jail and it was very heroic of them. Now there were firebombers at large striking with ease, as well as nonviolent pacifist direct action continuing. The police were making no breakthroughs, so dirty tricks were employed by Special Branch or the secret services. They pulled in four individuals, including three actors – Bryn Fôn, actor and singer, was held for sixty hours. It's widely accepted that this was either a shot in the dark, or the work of a person with a grudge, or an orchestrated attempt to frame them. Late-night police roadblocks were set up. Telephone bugging was widespread. The police even placed a listening device in a public telephone in Talysarn, Nantlle Valley.

A variety of organisations claimed responsibility for the arson attacks. These included WAWR ('wawr' = 'dawn'), the 'Workers' Army of the Welsh Republic', Cadwyr Cymru (The Keepers of Wales) and Meibion Glyndŵr. During the early years of the arson campaign, all the above groups, with the exception of Meibion Glyndŵr, either ceased operations or were apprehended by the police. It is thought Mudiad Amddiffyn Cymru, the organisation led by John Jenkins in the 1960s, remained dormant during this period, but due to the fact that their previous activities had included the use of explosives, theories developed suggesting Mudiad Amddiffyn Cymru played a role in the arson attacks. These remained unproven. In media accounts, *Meibion Glyndŵr* increasingly emerged as the group most associated with the series of cottage arson attacks, ensuring the two Cymraeg words became synonymous with the arson campaign. In 1983, conspiracy and explosive charges were brought in Cardiff Crown Court against nine alleged members of WAWR, all of whom had been remanded in custody and denied bail prior to their trial. One defendant, Dafydd Ladd, a known anarchist, pleaded guilty to the possession of explosive charges and to holding a false passport and was imprisoned for ten years. John Jenkins, the former leader of Mudiad Amddiffyn Cymru, was sentenced to two years for assisting Ladd in resisting arrest.

After hearing allegations of fabrication of evidence and heavy-handed interviewing techniques, the jury rejected the cases against the four remaining defendants on the grounds of police conspiracy. The suspects were released at the conclusion of a ten-week trial that was rumoured to have cost half a million pounds. A fifth defendant, Jenny Smith, Ladd's partner, had been released earlier with all charges against her dropped. Another man, named Gareth Westacott, who had spent nine months in prison awaiting bail, disappeared before the court hearings began.

Despite the trial, arson attacks on holiday properties had continued unabated in the Welsh-speaking parts of North and West Wales during the winter months, when cottages were more likely to be unoccupied. In 1983 20,000 such properties were recorded in Wales, while the number of local people on council house waiting lists approached 50,000. In a statement, *Meibion Glyndŵr* claimed that the uninterrupted transformation of rural Wales constituted a form of ethnic cleansing and 'cultural genocide'.

Iwan Bala: There were always a few groups named. John Jenkins was quite effective with Mudiad Amddiffyn Cymru, but there weren't enough of them, and I don't think we had that fire in the belly that the Irish have – luckily in many ways, because otherwise there would have been a lot of deaths, and nobody would have wanted that type of scenario.

Dewi Prysor: WAWR, the Workers' Army of the Welsh Republic, were effective at targeting economic and political targets. A few members of the Welsh Socialist Republican Movement (WSRM) got framed and accused of being members of WAWR and eventually released after many months of awaiting trial, and acquitted. I wrote to John Jenkins in Albany Prison as a teenager, but the letter was sent back because fourteen-year-olds weren't allowed to write to inmates. The returned letter was addressed to Miss Dewi Williams!

Iwan Bala: I'm sure there was a lot of intervention by MI5, well, pretty sure. I was a member of the Welsh Nationalist Republicans, and that was carved up from the inside but it's hard to prove anything. But that's what people were talking about.

Ned Thomas: In the Welsh pub song movement, there was a song which I think, after it had risen to the top of the charts, the BBC was forced to ban. It translates as: 'Nobody remembers anything in the light of day', so it was as if some people may have had quite a good idea of who was responsible, but when the police came round said: 'Oh, I don't know.' I don't think anybody knew anything except for the one or two cases of copycats who were arrested and made examples of who hadn't perhaps even done anything, but might have been preparing to do something in a rather obvious way.

Dewi Prysor: The Meibion Glyndŵr campaign was never racist. It was nationalist but not in a right-wing way. It was anti-colonialist, anti-imperialist, anti-white settlers, anti-holiday homes – Meibion Glyndŵr stated so in their letters to the press following an attack. Ordinary English folk, whether local or newcomers, were never targeted, and not a single ethnic community or business was threatened. It was always about holiday-home buyers, or those who moved here and attacked Welsh-language policies or Welsh education, or sacked people for speaking Welsh at work. Those people's property could be targeted for damage.

There were a lot of gigs organised at the time, raising money for march organisers or the Covenanters (Y Cyfamodwyr). I sold hundreds and I mean hundreds of Meibion Glyndŵr T-shirts. Others did too. There was the odd Welsh lad in a Welsh regiment of the British Army buying dozens of T-shirts when home on leave to take back to base for his mates. There was one lad who was stationed in the north of Ireland, and every time he came home to Blaenau he'd have an order to take back with him! For all of its drama, the 1980s were very creative and quite colourful. There was a lot of fun, and friends made.

Dafydd Iwan: The Meibion Glyndŵr campaign still doesn't make sense to me. I can't see how it was physically possible. I should have been running as chief suspect, because I was travelling the length and breadth of Wales, doing concerts and going back late at night, and reading in the morning of a house burnt near where I sang. And I expected a knock on my door any time. I remember once being stopped by a police road block in the Llŷn and they asked me to wind down the window, and I did, and he went, 'Oh, oh, it's you, Dafydd, carry on.' He could have at least looked in the boot. I can't say I was disappointed, but it didn't make any sense. If this was a genuine road block looking for arsonists, they should stop every car and look in the boot.

Rhys Mwyn: The band Man were travelling back from a gig somewhere like Liverpool or Manchester through Wales, with a spare can of petrol. They were pulled up by the cops: 'What are you doing with a can of petrol?' and they were forced to take every bit of equipment out of the van in the middle of the night on some B-road in the Berwyn. Gorwel Owen, who later produced the Gorky's and Super Furry Animals early records, he was pulled up somewhere. A lot of us travelling late at night from gigs knew in that period there would be a cop stop. Dafydd Iwan got pulled over often, I think. It almost got to the point with some of them, 'It's us again.' You got friendly with them, you'd have a chat, you could see the cops were bored, but there was a point with Anhrefn that we had to get solicitors to complain to North Wales Police because we were stopped every single week: it got ridiculous. We couldn't leave Bangor before we'd be pulled up.

Ned Thomas: There was a lot of sympathy, I think, in Welsh-speaking circles. There were some cases within easy reach of Aberystwyth, but a lot were more in present-day Gwynedd, and some were further south, too. There was an early group and then there was a big gap, and a late, bigger group of cottage burnings.

Ben Lake: I think there's potentially another truth, and that is that there was at least an individual involved in the second part of the campaign who had real expertise and the means by which to do some of these timed devices.

The second phase of the Meibion Glyndŵr campaign began on 3 October 1988 when five or more estate agents in England that marketed holiday properties in Wales were firebombed. The targets covered a broad radius including Bristol, West Kirby, Neston, Worcester and Chipping Camden. Six weeks later, on 26 November 1988, several Central London estate agents were attacked by the same means. This new use of London as a target inevitably led to officers from Scotland Yard and the security services assisting the ongoing investigation into the identity of Meibion Glyndŵr.

Dewi Prysor: There were breaks here and there in the campaign. My guess about the escalation of 1988 is that it was a changing of the guard. Volunteers would do their bit for a while, then stand down, disappear. The cell system had its weakness; discipline slips over time; someone could work out who the others were. You may trust your mate, but how will he react if he's caught? Standing cells down before the cops got too close, or before the law of averages increased the threat of being spotted made sense. Establishing new cells took time and that time could also be spent making more sophisticated devices.

Ned Thomas: The late burnings were professional, with covering up of fingerprints and so on. The police supposed whoever was responsible, either they had had training, maybe from Ireland or something, who knows, or that possibly it was some arm of the police or MI-something.

Ben Lake: Another element of interest is there was a brief outbreak of cottage-burning on the Isle of Man. I was very interested in the Celtic League and how there was a potential network of cooperation between the Celtic nations, as it were. At least from what I could see there was a clear objection to the tactics of the IRA, especially after the Birmingham Bombing, and you could see it in the Celtic League documents and publications: they write against it. It's in the eighties at some point.

There's a very, very interesting sequence of events whereby things go quiet a little bit in Wales, and they kick off on the Isle of Man. The cottage-burning episodes on the Isle of Man disappeared almost as quickly as they arose, and then if you were to place it in a rough kind of chronological order, things quieten down in Wales, pipe up on the Isle of Man, and then emerge again in Wales. It may be nothing.

Dewi Prysor: In the late 1980s I was involved in the Covenanters [Y Cyfamodwyr]. It was a carry-on of the same faces and figures who were part of the militant nationalism and anti-investiture campaign of the 1960s. The movement wasn't inspirational at all, looking back, but it was a vehicle for increasing awareness, radicalising communities, and campaigning for independence. It was the only movement calling for independence at that time. They supported the Meibion Glyndŵr campaign but not in public. A motion to publicly support Meibion Glyndŵr was voted down in an AGM. The Covenanters was infiltrated, though what there was to infiltrate I can't imagine. There was a person from Llanelli who attended Covenanters meetings. He sold his sofa, and the buyers found a Dyfed Powys Police receipt down the back of it. He was being paid £30 for 'attending a Covenanters' meeting'. This is absolutely true, I have a photocopy. He was paid £30 each time he went to a meeting and reported back what was said and who attended. These days he calls himself the Snake Man, because he keeps snakes. I call him the Snake with Snakes. There were other plants during this time. One guy got thrown out of a meeting, there and then, when he'd been outed. I'm sure there were some *agent provocateurs* around in the eighties. It was a tactic that was used in the sixties and seventies too – two people were set up and got jail.

Dafydd Iwan: My friend Dewi, Dewi Jones, was imprisoned with another friend, ostensibly for placing a bomb on Holyhead harbour. I asked him once about it but he didn't want to talk a lot. This Dewi at the time was an architect, or at least a draughtsman, with Anglesey Council. Before going there to Holyhead, he met this chap who claimed he used to be a military expert. He asked Dewi, 'Are you experienced in electrical circuits and installing underfloor heating systems? Could you answer me how does that work?' and Dewi drew a plan, a scribble, of the circuit, and Dewi said, 'Well, they came across that in one of my drawers and used it and said, "Oh, this is obviously a plan for an explosive device."' They gave him two years, and Dewi said, 'I had nothing to do with it.' There are so many questions.

A lot of people came to see me during that period, always English, well-dressed and well-spoken, often charming, claiming to be researching a PhD or an article into Welsh nationalism. And it always came down to the arson attacks. Every time. I remember one even asking on the phone, 'Do you have a phone number for Meibion Glyndŵr?' And I said, 'No, but if you find it, I'm sure the police will be interested!' It's a very strange feeling, but I think there was a lot of suspicious activity by the security forces. It is difficult to understand, but I suppose something might come out one day.

Dewi Prysor: I remember being in a Covenanters meeting in a smoky room above the Cŵps pub in Aberystwyth with all these old guard characters, and outside there were two to five thousand people in the street joining together in a Cymdeithas march for a Property Act. I left the meeting and joined the march, during which people would volunteer to spray a slogan on public buildings on the route. I volunteered on a whim and sprayed a post box, got arrested and charged and released in the early hours. Luckily, I found an all-night party in a student house.

Rhys Mwyn: Coming from an anarcho-punk background, I've always had ideological clashes with Cymdeithas, but not serious ones, not serious issues. We supported them but were always outside the group. Cymdeithas have been absolutely instrumental; most of the changes have come down to their campaigns. It's interesting that Cymdeithas yr Iaith not only disassociated themselves from Meibion Glyndŵr but thought they were a real problem. Cymdeithas yr Iaith have always maintained a pacifist direct action stance, so they take responsibility for their own actions. They're happy to get arrested for damaging offices or a mast or a road sign, in different campaigns, but they take responsibility: 'It was me: arrest me, officer.' So they've always been quite clear. And in that sense they do deserve respect for the consistency of their campaigns.

Dewi Prysor: Along with the groundswell of feeling regarding housing and Welsh communities there was now an organised clandestine movement that some would describe as 'terrorist', which had ever more sophisticated devices. There was also the potential for mass non-violent direct action by Cymdeithas. These elements all created an atmosphere of potential social unrest that could evolve in time into something bigger. I absolutely believe that. There was definitely something in the air: young lads from council estates supporting the more militant elements while students were joining Cymdeithas, and Cymdeithas's non-violent direct action was getting more imaginative and militant, like they were in the sixties and seventies. Cymdeithas had got its mojo back with the Deddf Eiddo campaign. But I'd say it was Meibion Glyndŵr's campaign that got them moving again.

In around 1990 or 1991, the National Front published literature that stated its members were going to join the annual Abergele Martyrs march, which was an obvious dirty tricks tactic to slander Welsh nationalists and frame them as a bunch of right-wing nutters. A famous North Wales biker gang were prepared to attend the rally and send the National Front packing. The bikers turned up but the National Front didn't show. At that time, it was widely known that the NF had been infiltrated by the secret services, and our suspicion was that the secret services were behind the attempted black ops at Abergele.

In 1990 a letter bomb was sent to Land and Sea, a powerboat showroom based at Abersoch on the Llŷn peninsula, a business that was registered to a Manchester address. Further letter bombs were intercepted by postal workers destined for, among others, the head of North Wales CID, Detective Chief Superintendent Gwyn Williams and to Detective Chief Inspector Maldwyn Roberts, the senior detective in charge of investigating Meibion Glyndŵr.

Rhys Mwyn: On the periphery of Meibion Glyndŵr there was a whole bunch of people that we all knew. We all knew them. They'd come to gigs; they would be characters on the fringes of events or rallies or demos: you'd see them quite often with their flags. It then became a thing where some of them started wearing berets and things. They were called the Meibion Glyndŵr Colour Party. I used to call them St John's Ambulance.

Dewi Prysor: The first Colour Party appeared at the Abergele March in about 1989. Everyone who took part was arrested and had their houses raided. They were from strong working-class areas, they were the younger generation, sons and daughters of quarrymen. The following year I volunteered to show solidarity with those arrested the previous year. Some friends and I put on uniforms, berets and dark glasses, as a Colour Party troop, in defiance of what had happened to the previous Colour Party. It was also a visual statement of support for Meibion Glyndŵr, a propaganda stunt. We wanted to remind the authorities there was a clandestine organisation out there with a support network which was maybe getting bigger. It was bluff, propaganda, a publicity stunt, nothing more. Mind games.

I find it bizarre now, that I did that kind of thing. It's not me at all. But it was a different climate back then, and I was only twenty-three. We knew the police were watching us, filming and taking photos, bugging phones, watching movements, so there was no chance we'd be members of Meibion Glyndŵr. But propaganda and publicising was something we could do. People love carnivals. They dress up and march up and down their village, that's OK. But if you do it as a political stunt, you get ridiculed.

In 1993 21-year-old Sion Aubrey Roberts was arrested and stood trial with two other men, David Gareth Davies (known as Stwmp) and Dewi Prysor Williams, for offences relating to the letter-bomb campaign.

All three men admitted to being members of Y Cyfamodwyr, a group campaigning for Welsh independence. Roberts and Williams had taken part in a military-style parade organised by a group named Meibion Glyndŵr Colour Party to commemorate the two men, Alwyn Jones and George Taylor, who died when a device in their possession exploded shortly before the investiture of the Prince of Wales at Caernarfon Castle in 1969.

Dewi 'Mav' Bowen: I had a friend called John Michael and he was accused by a lot of people of being in the Welsh Covenant. And there were different factions, different names. The boy up in Anglesey, Sion, from Gwalchmai, he'd brag about doing stuff, but he got hit with the blame.

Dewi Prysor: I was arrested seven weeks after Stwmp and Sion. The MI5 weren't involved, just the Arson Squad. They'd gone through their video footage of Sion's flat, and thought maybe one of the people they'd seen was me. They got a policeman who had been stationed in Trawsfynydd back in the mid-eighties to view the footage, and although the footage was from half a mile away, and the policeman hadn't seen me for seven years when I had youthful, short punk hair, he came to the conclusion that I was the silhouetted figure on the video.

At the trial, my defence made contact with an Irishman who had been the foreman on a building site I was working on as a sparky, in Kinmel Bay. We had worked overtime, and the foreman noted my log-out time in his log-book. The log-book was presented at the trial. It was crucial as it showed that there was no chance of me being in Sion's flat at the time the video showed. The other bit of evidence they had was circumstantial.

At the trial at Caernarfon Crown Court, confusing and contradictory evidence from detectives and unidentified intelligence officers led to consternation in many of those watching the proceedings, including the presiding judge. Furthermore, the intelligence officers insisted that they appear hidden behind a screen and had sought an injunction to avoid discussing their methodology. This subterfuge was met with judicial orders to force the full disclosure of evidence, much of which was later found to have been fabricated. The trial lasted forty-one days and was estimated to have cost £3 million.

As had happened at the trial of WAWR a decade earlier, the defendants stood accused of targeting state or commercial buildings and their occupants with incendiary devices. In each case, under the category of 'conspiracy', the prosecutors attempted to link the alleged activities of the accused with the arson campaign against holiday homes. The cottage burnings endured throughout the fifteen months Roberts, Williams and Davies were awaiting trial. Sion Aubrey Roberts, who denied the accusations, was imprisoned on 26 March 1993 for twelve years. All charges were dropped against Dewi Prysor Williams and David Gareth Davies. Having been refused bail, both had spent fourteen months incarcerated while awaiting trial.

Ned Thomas: I remember being interviewed under caution by a detective from Gloucestershire. Because I was a member of the Welsh Language Society's ruling body, he came to the house with a Welsh-speaking, middle-aged policeman from Gloucestershire, who was a natural Welsh-speaker, if a little bit rusty, who didn't understand any of the terms which the detective had to say. He had to go through the usual performance: 'I must warn you that everything will be taken down and could be used in evidence,' and all I said throughout the interview was, 'I have no comment, I have no comment.' But the Welsh policeman had to translate this for me, and of course he couldn't do it, because he had only learnt these terms in English, so I had to help him out with translating.

And by the time the trial had happened, most of the campaign had ended anyway.

There was one coordinated attack, five attacks in one night, I think around November, maybe, or autumn anyway, in 1992, but apart from that, nothing else happened.

Dewi Prysor: The trial put a stop to any future plans Meibion Glyndŵr had, especially after Sion and Stwmp's legal team found that MI5 had been following both of them for some months. They had thirty-five operatives following Sion on a Cymdeithas yr Iaith march in Caernarfon. This was the end of the campaign, although there was a five-target hit in one night, from Llangefni to Bala to Caerfyrddin, while we were on remand, which we took as a solidarity message. It gave us a lift. It was in November 1992, Sion had joined us in HMP Walton from the YP Hindley prison following his twenty-first birthday in October. That was the last Meibion action. Meibion Glyndŵr has gone away.

The BBC satirical sketch show Not the Nine O'Clock News *ran from 1979 until 1982. An episode in its second series, broadcast in 1980, had concluded with a twenty-second feature. The piece mocked a then current British Coal Board advertising campaign that promoted the use of coal. The campaign's tag line, 'Come Home to a Real Fire', implied coal was a more authentic fuel than its rival gas. In the brief sketch, a coal fire is seen flickering, as a mellifluous voice speaks in a tone redolent of television advertising and states, 'Come Home to a Real Fire. Buy a Cottage in Wales.' The words are also shown on screen.*

The programme regularly achieved considerable audience figures and the inclusion of a joke satirising the Meibion Glyndŵr campaign indicated the extent to which the arson attacks had permeated public consciousness. At the same time another phrase had grown in popularity during the 1980s. Visitors to Wales would complain that they had entered a pub, apparently unaware that in parts of the country Cymraeg was the dominant tongue, and those present 'had all started speaking Welsh'. The same visitors were presumably equally taken aback, not to say horrified, by the locals speaking French when visiting Provence or the Dordogne. Both the Meibion Glyndŵr campaign and Cymraeg activism had altered the reputation of Wales and, it was alleged, had had a perceptible effect on the country's tourism industry.

Max Perkins: The other interesting debate during the 1980s was how the Welsh Tourist Board dealt with the second homes issue, the burning of second homes, and that didn't do them any favours. People felt slightly threatened. I know the arguments about whether there should be second homes or not and how much damage it did to the local economy and local housing. There were a lot of very interesting issues around all that. The thing I remember most clearly was that Wales didn't get a square deal from the British Tourist Authority.

Terry Stevens: I wrote the Labour Party's policy on tourism in the early eighties; I wrote Plaid's rural tourism strategy in the late eighties; I wrote the Tourism Community Development Manual for the Development Board for Rural Wales; and the fundamental issue was people thinking that tourism was an easy industry to enter and didn't have the wherewithal to make it happen.

Max Perkins: The British Tourist Authority never really made much attempt to market Wales. The Welsh Tourist Board probably had fewer resources, but they never really matched the identity of Scotland, with kilts and bagpipes and so on; they never actually quite put their finger on what they were trying to sell. Probably the only thing people were interested in at that time was going to Laugharne and Dylan Thomas. They didn't seem to latch on to the fact that there's so much more to Wales than a few mountains and Dylan Thomas.

The English attitude was a bit negative, it was said that 'you go into a pub and they all start speaking Welsh', and all that sort of thing. My younger son, who now lives in New Zealand, his parents-in-law came over to Wales once and I took them around Caerleon and they heard a party of school kids speaking Welsh. They thought that was marvellous. Wales is a different country from England. That's the type of thing that people can make more of. If you visit New Zealand they're trying to promote the Maori language and people take an interest.

Terry Stevens: That argument, 'We walked into a pub and they all started speaking Welsh,' I think that was totally fictitious. The classic example that you can point to for the opposite of that statement is

Butlin's in Pwllheli. It existed very, very happily side by side with a Welsh-speaking community for many years, caravan sites on Pen Braint in Anglesey existed with people coming out of Liverpool without any of those issues. Where it became an issue was people coming in and setting up their own tourism businesses and not doing particularly well, and it was another thing to add to the second home issues.

Ben Lake: Meibion Glyndŵr, for a host of reasons, it got out of control, and we know that these were criminal campaigns and I make no excuse for them, nor do I try to defend them at all, but when I did some of my research to try and understand the direction behind it, I drew the same conclusion time and time again, which was that the constitutional democratic process failed to give voice and true redress to these concerns: these real, genuine fears of loss of community, which was just as true of the South Wales coal belt and the mining areas as it was of rural Pen Llŷn, and it was a desperate lashing out: 'Come on, this is a problem, why aren't you taking it seriously?'

Rhys Mwyn: I think if you look historically, very few people were convicted of actually doing it, and you might have had the odd person with a jerrycan of petrol, maybe copycats, but I suspect that with the organised events, Meibion Glyndŵr got away with it. It's hard to know. I think it comes back to this thing that, within the broad spectrum, there's a whole range, isn't there? When people in their, well, let's say lack of knowledge, talk about Welsh nationalism they fail to realise that it's such a broad spectrum. It's not one thing, it's not one group, it's not one ideology.

The identity of the members of Meibion Glyndŵr has never been revealed and a sense of omertà *is permanently attached to the activities with which the group is associated.*

TEN

MENYWOD DROS FYWYD AR Y DDAEAR / WOMEN FOR LIFE ON EARTH

Voices

Rosemary Butler	Siân James	Ann Pettitt
Menna Elfyn	Sue Lent	Karmen Thomas
Meri Huws	Mary Millington	Angharad Tomos

———

On 27 August 1981 a group of around forty people congregated on the green outside City Hall, Cardiff. The location had been chosen as the starting point for a 120-mile march to RAF Greenham Common, Wiltshire, in protest at the decision to use the air force base as a site to house American nuclear-armed cruise missiles on British soil. The march had been arranged by Ann Pettitt and Karmen Thomas, both residents of rural Carmarthenshire who had moved to Wales during the late 1970s, and took place under the aegis of Women for Life on Earth, a women's anti-nuclear group founded by Pettitt, which opposed the dumping of nuclear waste and the proliferation of nuclear weaponry.

That afternoon the march made its way from the capital east towards Newport and reached its destination at the gates of the air force base nine days later. In a photograph of the march the group are walking the four-mile footpath of the Severn Bridge, their flags and banners blowing in the high winds; a handful of the group are pushing prams. The image captures the sense of optimism and determination with which the Greenham Common Women's Peace Camp became

*synonymous. This would be founded immediately following the
conclusion of the march, by a handful of protestors who chained
themselves to the base's perimeter gate.*

Karmen Thomas: I got involved with the local CND group, and
the local Chapel members and a couple of the ministers were very
involved. I was asked to be the secretary of the Trades Council by
this brilliant guy, Bryn Daniels. We used to go down to the Pick and
Shovel in Ammanford, a workmen's institute where there was this
room at the back that had a bust of Lenin and a bust of Keir Hardie.
All the old Communists used to sit and have a natter there, and Bryn
asked me if I'd take on the role of Trades Council secretary. I'd never
heard of trades councils; I had no idea what they were, so they had to
find me a union, which was quite funny, so I ended up being in the
T&G, the Transport & General, and Trostre was my base, which was
really bizarre, because it was just full of male steelmen.

Bryn Daniels was elderly, I think he was about eighty and he
was well known and very well respected. He wasn't a hothead. His
views and his comments were always very measured, with a lot of
understanding in the background, and he was a real political mentor
for me in many ways. I had to visit the library in Ammanford to read
up on the role of the Trades Council. I was obviously given advice by
the Wales TUC and things like that and was basically shoved into this
room. I'll never forget the first meeting where I was introduced, all
these guys. There were the miners, there were the firemen, a couple of
guys from the GMB who worked in small industrial units, and it was
like I was this young – and I looked a lot younger than I was – this
skinny young thing: 'What? She's going to be our secretary?'

Siân James: When I talk to young people about this now, they have no
conception of how afraid we were, a friend of mine was on that initial
march, but suddenly we were watching films like *The Three-Minute
Warning*. When I speak to people, I tell them: 'In three minutes, I was

to dip all the children's clothes in detergent, air dry them on the line, I was to find a room in my house which had no external walls – try that, that's not easy – you were to take the doors off the hinges, lean them up against the door, all crawl in, wearing your clothes that had been in detergent and air-line-dried – this is all in three minutes, mind you – and then I was going to have two weeks' food and water in this makeshift shed, water for two weeks, food for two weeks, batteries, a radio.'

Karmen Thomas: Some of the older women that were in our local CND group talked about things that happened years ago that were Welsh initiatives that I'd never, ever heard of. Like the Welsh Women's Peace Petition of 1923, a declaration that they wanted peace that went to almost every household in Wales, including all the little farms, and almost 400,000 women signed it. I never knew about these sort of things.

We used to have things like GWNG, Y Gynghrair Wrth-Niwclear Gymreig, the Welsh Anti-Nuclear Movement in Aberystwyth; I used to go with Gwynfor Evans. We had our own centralised group where we discussed things on very much a Welsh narrative, to the point, I think, that certain people in the more English communities in Carmarthenshire were a bit wary of it being used as a Welsh propaganda tool. But you couldn't deny the fact that there was an awful lot about making Wales a nuclear-free zone and the symbolism of that. It wasn't Britain being a nuclear-free zone, it was Wales being a nuclear-free zone. The fact that local authorities took that on board and were really sympathetic I think happened really quickly, in terms of all the counties in Wales going down that route of being symbolically a nuclear-free zone. I think that made it very, very different to the CND groups in England, who were very much part of British CND and what their priorities were.

Siân James: The man next door was in the Territorials, and his take on it was slightly different. I said, 'What are you going to do, then, when the three-minute warning goes off?' and he said, 'I've got to make my way to Brecon.' I said, 'What do you mean, you've got to make your way to Brecon?' 'Well, I've got a warrant.' I said, 'Let's have a look at this warrant, then.' Because I'm egging him on now, I've grown up with this person. 'So what's this warrant to do, then?' 'Well, I don't drive, so I'll be able to commandeer something to drive me to Brecon.' 'Why've you got to get to Brecon?' 'Well, that's where the bunker . . .' 'What bunker? What are you talking about?'

Karmen Thomas: I was working as a CND group member and Ann was the same. Ann came up with this idea. There were rumours coming round that they were going to site American cruise missiles on British soil and that the first place was this obscure little place in Greenham Common, near Newbury. Ann got the whole idea of doing a walk there like there had been in Copenhagen; there'd been a march there by women. Her partner Barry suggested we meet and have a chat – I'd not met Ann in Wales at that point – because she obviously felt she couldn't do it on her own.

Ann Pettitt: Karmen was from Betws, other people lived near Llandeilo, Llandybie, down there. We were resistant to the hierarchies and bureaucracy of CND. We used to have West Wales meetings, West Wales Anti-Nuclear, as it was called, gatherings at Easter time down in Tenby. Somebody would lend us the use of a hotel there. It was great. We'd have music and all kinds of things going on and very lively workshops, 150 people coming along.

And dancing on the beach: it was really, really good. But then, if you went down to the meetings in Swansea, they were so far-left dominated and so urban, which meant that they were much more structured, bureaucratic; it was a Labour Party approach. If you had an idea, you'd make a caucus and form it into a resolution and put it forward to a blah-blah, and we used to just go off and do things while they were having all their resolutions and getting bogged down in procedural stuff.

Karmen Thomas: Ann came over because I didn't drive and when she came over, we were chatting and she looked around the place and she said, 'Do you know, I'm sure I've met you before. I know this place; it's really strange,' and then we started talking about what we'd done, gossiping about the past and we had both been squatters in the East End of London. And then she said, 'I know who you are! I visited you one day,' and I vaguely remembered. It had been only two days after the birth of my son Ben, and Ann was pregnant and her midwife was this very amazing Jamaican lady, who was into all sorts of Jamaican remedies for childbirth and healthy eating and had told Ann to come and see me, because going to the local pregnancy group was a bit weird in the East End of London. So she came to visit me. And I still had the same big, heavy wooden furniture I'd had in London and there was a fire going and that's where we met. But she was moving to Wales and I was moving to the North so we didn't bother staying in touch. We suddenly realised that we'd actually met at a very important time in life, me as a very young mum with my first child, in this dream-world of baby and mother, and Ann was going to be in that world herself, and we talked about Madge our midwife; she was fantastic, absolutely brilliant.

Somehow, I think in both our heads, we thought, because of this background, I couldn't refuse to join Ann in organising this march. We were too practical to be superstitious about the idea we were meant to meet and all that: neither of us are like that, we're both incredibly practical, but I think there was a little romantic element going on. We've met in this weird sort of way, and here we are again, in the middle of Wales, of all places. I just threw myself into it and said, 'Yeah, fine, right, we'll do it: let's get on with it.'

Ann Pettitt: There's an idea that there's some kind of intrinsic link between Wales and me organising a march which kicks off the Greenham Common movement and the peace camps. And I tend to resist this, because I want to resist being dragged into a nationalist agenda. I always tend to sort of scotch that idea. But I have to be clear that I don't think I would have thought about organising a march myself about cruise missiles, focusing on the arms race. I wouldn't have thought that I would've taken that initiative if I'd not been living here in Wales, if I'd still been living in London.

Karmen Thomas: We decided, 'We're going to be a group of women,' and then we wondered, 'Well, what if men want to turn up?' and we didn't really address that. It wasn't, 'We are going to be women-only, we can do this without men.' We just thought, 'We're going to do this.' It was almost fuzzy in a way. We decided we wanted a cross-section of women, ages and backgrounds, and worked out what we thought was the best way to do this, so we wrote a calling card. I think we went to *Cosmopolitan*, *Woman's Own*, as well as other, more alternative sorts of magazines.

Ann Pettitt: I decided it would be a women's march; that put some people off, because our anti-nuclear group was very much a mixed group of men and women. And most people were fantastically busy on their own accounts: they couldn't spare ten days; it was hard enough for us.

Sue Lent: I was twenty-nine at the time of the Greenham march. I actually came to Cardiff as a student, so many people in South Wales always refer to how they got into politics and it's always 'my father and my grandfather', and all the rest of it. I didn't have any of that. I was one of that generation who university politicised. I can remember us setting up the women's section of Plasnewydd ward; that would have been mid-seventies, so I was definitely very much into women's politics and, for me, it was that that I'd been interested in before I'd decided I was a socialist. But I think at some point I realised that you're not going to get women's equality without socialism. I'd had my eldest son in July '80 and we were away that next academic year, because my husband was doing a course. He was doing a PGCE up in Keele, so I was very isolated that year. I didn't drive and we had this flat out in the country. I used to get the *Guardian*, and because we were stuck out in the countryside, this used to be the highlight of my day, and that's where I first heard about the march. It was in the *Guardian*, although for some reason, the women involved didn't like to say it was in the *Guardian*; they always used to refer to it as being in 'the newspaper'. But the *Guardian* used to have a women's page and it was printed in there.

Karmen Thomas: There were a couple of people locally. Ann knew these people, these two women, Liney Seward and Lynne Whittemore, who also came in and helped with the basics of the organising, and I mentioned it to a young friend of mine who was a Welsh-speaking girl from the Valleys. Her father was a coal miner and she decided, having never been out of Wales, that she was going to do this. But it worked. We couldn't have had a better cross-section of ages, from pretty old, I think Effie was our oldest, from Pembrokeshire, I think she was getting on for seventy. She was quite something. And then we had women from the north of England, London, Bristol, North Wales, and a couple of students, a teacher, doctor and then some of the mums were full-time mums, some had teenage daughters, some had little kids.

Sue Lent: I remember hearing about it, but I didn't apply to go or do anything. Then, because it started in Cardiff – we'd come back in the July, and of course the march was late August – and I had a friend in Newport, Mary Crofton – she was actually older than my parents but I was very close to her, I'd known her a few years, and she was an Irish woman, very active in Troops Out. We were talking on the phone the night before and she said, 'Are you going on the march? You know the march is starting tomorrow?' She was going to come and meet the march, because it was stopping in Newport.

Ann Pettitt: We didn't actually know women who came on the march: they weren't people we knew by and large. The night before, we had a meeting in the Quaker Meeting House in Cardiff, and they provided some accommodation there, and we had something like thirty-six who signed up to go on it. We didn't know them beforehand.

Sue Lent: We went down to City Hall – I remember hearing Ann on the radio that morning, talking about it and saying they were going to march to Greenham Common, and we thought, 'We must rush down there.' I think we just drove down, left the car there, and then were just intending really to walk the first day, maybe even just only the first morning, but we walked to Newport and I recorded in my diary that Ann came round in the afternoon, checking who was doing the whole march. The march was a lot smaller after the lunchtime; I think quite a few people from Cardiff did the walk as far as lunch. We were fed amazingly well all the way through, and we stopped at a church which has gone now in Llanrumney, where you get to the open green there, there was a little Methodist church, Llanrumney Methodists, and we had lunch there.

A lot of people went back, but in the afternoon Ann came round, and it was then that I started to think, well, maybe I could do it. I had a child with me – my son Chris was just over a year old – but there were two other women in particular who had babies very close to Chris's age. I think the girl, Becky, was about three months older and there was another little boy who was a few months older, so those three children did the whole march.

Karmen Thomas: We couldn't have had a better mixture of people and it's amazing we gelled as well as we did. I have seen archival evidence of people writing saying there were arguments and this, that and the other. There were odd arguments, but not many considering these people had been thrown together and they were going to have to walk miles. It worked incredibly smoothly, especially given the number of places we were going to, all those connections had been done through letter or telephone. Some of them had been done very last-minute because we had the letters of reply back so late.

Sue Lent: I didn't know anybody despite it starting in Cardiff. I think I assumed there would be women from Cardiff on the march, but the only other woman from Cardiff was actually Margery Lewis, who at that time was in her sixties and is not with us any more. I spoke to Margery just as we were walking through Dumfries Place, and she asked me if I was doing the whole march and how far I was going to go on, and I said, 'Oh, maybe Newport,' and I said to her, 'What about you?' and she said, 'Oh, I'm doing the whole thing.' She was very upright, very slim. She was about mid-sixties then, and she was used to doing a lot of walking. Into her nineties, I used to see her walking round the park: she lived not far from me. But she was the only other woman living in Cardiff who went on it, but everybody was very friendly and welcoming. Ann Pettitt and Karmen were lovely as the main organisers.

Ann Pettitt: There was Eunice Stallard from the Stallard family, who went on to be stalwarts of Welsh CND, and a young woman called Sips. There was Sue Lent, who is a Cardiff councillor now, from Splott, and there was Margery Lewis, who we stayed with in Cardiff, who did a lot of the Cardiff arranging. She didn't know who we were. She had recently been widowed and she spotted it in a little advert somewhere in *Peace News*, or I managed to get a free advert in a couple of women's magazines, because I wanted to reach out beyond the so-called peace movement and get women who weren't already self-identified with any kind of political movement, and it was successful in that way. And

242

Margery said, 'Oh, I had no idea who you were. I thought you maybe were some sort of religious outfit.'

Rosemary Butler: There was a group of women based in Eton Road Community Centre in Newport. Amazing people. And it just happened they wanted people to help these strange women who were going to come through and we had to look after them. We made sandwiches and all the rest of it and these people came with pushchairs, and they were sleeping on the floor in the community centre – some of them slept in people's houses, and mainly ended up on the floor – and they were gone the next morning.

Sue Lent: Paul Flynn, the MP, who got involved right in the beginning, had been there on the first day when we'd arrived in Newport. He'd come out in the car – I always remember that – he had this loudspeaker and he was saying, 'Welcome to nuclear-free Gwent.' I'm actually a delegate from Cardiff Council to the Nuclear-Free Local Authorities Forum: we had a celebration of forty years of the Nuclear-Free Local Authorities movement, that started in 1980. This was 1981, and I don't think South Glamorgan was. They all were eventually; I think all the Welsh counties were nuclear-free, but I think Gwent was possibly the first, or one of the first. I thought it was great, Paul doing that; I didn't know him at the time, but I know now it was Paul Flynn. But I've also recorded in my diary that some of the women didn't like that, that a man came and kind of welcomed us, although there were men on the march.

Karmen Thomas: It's a bit of a blur for me. I think it was just so intense for Ann and me with the responsibility of it all. I remember going on the train to Cardiff and I felt really quite sick with anticipation of having to meet people I hadn't met before and thinking, 'What if it goes wrong? Will they blame us?' and lots of stuff like that.

Sue Lent: There's a photograph of us crossing the Severn Bridge. The person that you can see the clearest with the long, dark hair is me, with the dress on. The one with her head slightly turned towards me is a Helen John. She had, I think, five children, I think the one in the picture was the youngest. I was twenty-nine, Helen was already about forty-three or something. That's the two of us that you can see from the back, crossing the Severn Bridge. I was always at the back. We didn't have very good cameras in those days. I had a camera with me and I've got some quite nice ones of Eunice chained to the railings, but I should have made sure I had one of me with her, chained there as well.

Obviously, having a camp like that, that's just women, it's going to attract women who don't want anything to do with men; I'm sure Ann and Karmen will have said, the original march was women-led, that was how it was always put: women-led, but the few men that did the whole march, they couldn't have been nicer and were less inclined to push themselves forward. I think there were only four men who did the whole thing, but there were lots of men who joined in for bits of it. There was this German lad who joined us in Bristol and did the rest of it, and he had this pole with the nuclear-free yellow daffodil symbol of No Nuclear Power. He'd heard about the march and had actually come to this country and met us when it was passing, so there were some males. I think what happened at Greenham once the camp was established was, as you would expect, you ended up with some women who didn't want anything to do with men. Probably for Ann and Karmen, they would have felt that that wasn't what the original march was.

Ann Pettitt: Well, that evolved, as it would, inevitably. That all took quite a long time. You're talking about eighteen months. Let's say there were different factions with different identities. I was never actually at Greenham. I think Orange Gate was identified as a kind of Welsh grandmothers' gate. That was where you went to get proper cake and a decent cup of tea! This is something very culturally significant: you got a proper welcome at Orange Gate! It wasn't exclusively Welsh, but it tended to be older women.

Karmen Thomas: All the flipping Welsh hospitality. There were always tins, large tins, full of Welsh cakes that would appear, wrapped in grease-proof paper to keep them moist. I remember that vividly, somebody would always bring out a battered tin of Welsh cakes.

Mary Millington: I arrived at the camp in August 1982. I was there just a bit less than a year after the camp started and I was very active for the first five years. When I first went, there was only one gate, what we later called Yellow Gate, the main gate of the base: there were only women there, and there was a big camp of New Age travellers at what we later called Green Gate, which was the construction gate. I had quite a nice time settling in: we had a caravan and I bought a little tent. Then in the October, they did a big, big eviction. There were only eleven of us at our camp and they completely managed to move on the New Age travellers from Green Gate. We'd already started working for Embrace the Base. We'd already started posting out invitations to people and asking them to send on to ten friends, but then with this eviction everything got taken away and we were reduced to just putting up a washing line between two poplar trees and all sleeping in a communal bender in the rain.

I think it was amazing that we survived. They took our caravans away and then they dumped rocks so that we couldn't put the caravans back, and then we wrote on the rocks and they dumped soil on top of the rocks, and we started making benders then and living on top of the rocks and in the woods in benders proper. And then some locals formed RAGE – Rate-payers Against Greenham Encampment – they threw pigs' blood, pig shit, maggots all over us, and they would come and slash tents and benders with knives; they threw firecrackers. They really tried very hard to get rid of us. And then the authorities changed the law so that they could come and evict us at any time at all, with a muncher truck. People gave us little red tents, they were amazing, they were like concertinas, they were tents for one, but you put a stone at one end and a stone at the other end, and they had sort of triangular poles inside, and you could just concertina them up, and if someone called 'Bailiffs!' all you had to do was throw on your clothes, pack your bags, and just pick up the tent, kick the stones away, pick up the tent and put it over your shoulder. They couldn't actually drag property off us; they could only take property that was lying around, so we managed to stay on there.

In the meantime, Green Gate was set up as a rest camp, and women used to go there for a rest, because there were no evictions there. Then, bit by bit, Blue Gate, a lot of the anarchist women went to Blue Gate, and the local people who lived on the other side of the road absolutely hated them; they had a terrible time. They were threatened with violence, but they were so anarchistic and so averse to washing that they just sort of managed to hang on. I thought they were amazing. I couldn't have lived there. Bit by bit, we were circling the whole base. At one time, they had police on the outside all the way round, keeping an eye on us and they were burning green wood, some of them, to keep warm and then inside the base they had British soldiers present all the time; it was costing them a fortune. They still had this idea that they would get rid of us. The Americans must have been putting pressure on them.

Sue Lent: The original camp was just at the main gate, which later became called Yellow Gate. When we went up for Embrace the Base, the Orange Gate was definitely there by then; it was the Welsh gate, and they dropped us all at the Welsh gate.

I know, certainly, Welsh women went up a lot and they went up every week and took food and would cook a big pot of something and would go up. Margery Lewis from the original march used to go up a lot; there were women from the Rhondda who used to go up. There were an awful lot of women who ended up in politics in Wales who used to regularly go up and take stuff.

Karmen Thomas: The support in Ammanford I received was extraordinary. Maybe people thought it, but nobody actually came up to me and said, 'You're wasting your time. Who do you think you are? What the hell? It's the defence of the country that you're messing up.' There was a local café by the railway which took you into Betws, the main railway that used to take all the coal trains down. There used to be a little caff there, and whenever I went in there from Greenham, I never paid. I got to the point where I just didn't go in there, because I felt really guilty: he'd just say, 'No, not taking it.' He used to call me the Red, this little guy, and he would never accept my payment. I remember turning up one night on New Year's Eve and went in, and it was just brilliant, the spirit. He said to me, 'I haven't seen you for a long time,' but I thought, 'I can't keep coming in here and not paying.'

The miners' community gave loads of money and they really were supportive of what was going on at Greenham. I found that really amazing. They organised a dinnertime collection for the camp. I didn't go down that often to the Greenham camp, I had other stuff to do, and I had two children by then and I remember being very cross; these guys had been through such a lot, this is pre the '84–'85 strike obviously, this is '81, but still, there had been a lot of problems and they still gave the money and then when I took it down I really lost my temper. People there were going, 'We're not having men here, we're not having anything from men here,' and I said, 'I understand that, but we're not part of a one-dimensional world: there's not all these good, wonderful women and all these horrible, nasty men, it doesn't work like that.' I said, 'I've just got all this money from these hairy guys who probably ogle Page Three of the *Sun*, so I'll take it back, shall I, because it's tainted?' And I got myself really worked up and very angry about that sort of patronising attitude. And that's when I felt, to some extent, 'I can't keep coming down here, because I don't fit in, in many ways.' What I saw was a takeover, to some extent, of that sort of middle-class liberalism. It wasn't there all the time, but there was a specific type of woman who thought: 'These men,' and I thought, 'You don't know people.'

Sue Lent: I know Ann used to say about taking food up there, and then somebody would come out and say, 'Oh, is it vegan?' and she'd intimate that some of it had got a bit precious and of course Ann has kept her own pigs!

Meri Huws: My mother had been brought up in the church but was atheist by the time I came along. She was slightly unusual in that she had been to Aberystwyth, she worked in the Ministry of Agriculture – she was a dairy advisory officer – and became quite bloody-minded as she got older. She went to Greenham and she was arrested for sitting outside RAF Brawdy in her sixties, so that was her trajectory. One of the things which really challenged our traditional way of thinking was Greenham and the Women's March. Things started. It shook people. Because you had what were perceived as being nice middle-class women suddenly deciding that they were going to walk.

Sue Lent: I think Greenham probably did inspire a certain number of women, and older women as well, who had maybe just retired and had the time. We were at that point of the change in a way, where women could still be at home and look after their kids, which gave you time, if you had an understanding partner, to go off and do stuff. I couldn't have done all that and given all that time if I'd been working full-time.

Rosemary Butler: We went to Greenham quite often. There was a feeling of camaraderie that was fantastic. You'd turn up, the bus would stop at the motorway service stations and of course there's no men around, so we're all using the men's toilets, stupid stuff, but that kind of thing, and to hold hands with nuns while singing songs like 'There's a hole in your fence, dear Margaret, dear Margaret!' And those are the moments when you learn to be aware of the police. You're there, you're right by the fence, and suddenly hear 'Stand back! There's an ambulance coming through!' and we all stand back and right behind the ambulance are all these police on horses coming towards us.

Mary Millington: They were practising on us before the Miners' Strike. They had this thing of six police onto one. I witnessed it. 1983 was very busy. It was while they were still building the silos – I think it was another cutting of the fence by Blue Gate, Violet Gate – we all went. We cut the fence down and thirteen of us were in court in Reading. But at that time, they had six policemen onto one. I happened to be standing near someone called Sarah Green and her baby, Jay, who'd been born in the May. He was only very young, and six of these police came towards her, so we sat down. I put my arm around her, and we were protecting the baby, and they said, 'You needn't think you'll get treated any different because you've got a baby.' I thought, 'Oh, my God,' but then a policewoman came up and said, 'Hey, give these women space.' But that was the way it was. I think they got hold of quite a lot of butch-looking women that way, six police onto one, and just sort of beat people up. And also riding along with a cosh and hitting people; they did quite a lot of practice on us before the Miners' Strike.

And then, of course, when the Miners' Strike started, we got a lot of support. The Kentish miners' wives got in touch with us very early on; we got coal from the NUM, and Arthur Scargill was very supportive of us.

Rosemary Butler: We were very cruel to the young soldiers who were sat the other side of the fence, and we stood and stared at them, these poor little eighteen-year-olds, just in the army, with these hordes of women the other side of the fence. And that was amazing, because you'd go back to your bus, and you'd be walking this way along the road, and the buses would be coming that way, and for an hour, walking, with buses going that way, you can imagine the number of buses there were. Incredible, absolutely incredible.

Angharad Tomos: In the Eisteddfod, I met people from South Wales and other places, but they would be Welsh-speakers, so there was nothing else like the Eisteddfod, and the music scene itself was in Welsh; if you went to discos in other parts of Wales, they'd be Welsh-speakers once again. For myself, there was no forum. And maybe Greenham was the first place, or the anti-nuclear campaign was the first place, locally, for me to come across English-speakers that came from the same perspective as I did.

Sue Lent: It's interesting with Cymdeithas, because there then became quite a lot of links between how people learnt about direct action. There were women who got involved in Greenham who had already been involved in the Welsh-language struggle and had taken direct action. I didn't realise until fairly recently that the miners also said that they had learnt from the Greenham women, whereas you tend to think it's more the kind of other way round, but they said they'd learnt from the Greenham women, through their experiences of direct action and how they'd been treated by the police.

Despite being regularly treated with physical and psychological violence throughout its existence, the Greenham Common Women's Peace Camp suffered only one casualty. Helen Thomas, aged twenty-two, of Newcastle Emlyn, was tragically killed by a horse box, which some eyewitness accounts state was in the service of the police, at the Camp's Yellow Gate on 5 August 1989. Helen Thomas is the only named individual in the Greenham Common Peace Garden memorial, which includes a sculpture partly fabricated from Welsh Pennant sandstone. The commemorative sign that marks her life is written in Cymraeg and English.

Menna Elfyn: I didn't spend a lot of time at Greenham, but I went there a few times and I wrote a poem, and I helped Helen Thomas' mother take out a judicial review through Emyr Lewis and we didn't succeed.

Sue Lent: When Mary Millington left Greenham, she came to Wales; she hadn't been before, but one of the reasons was because she was close to Helen Thomas, who was killed at Greenham.

Mary Millington: Helen came to the camp early 1989, when we had two Zimbabwean women over – we had a Greenham–Zimbabwe exchange. 1988 was when I met Helen Thomas, and when we weren't so busy I was going to talk to her about Wales and the Welsh language, but of course she was killed before that time came. She was killed on 5 August 1989 by a police horsebox, and we were very sad after that. There was a lot of quarrelling; we were just hanging on and not really able to comfort each other. The family were wonderful, but it was awful for them. We thought they'd hate us, but they didn't: they were very fair. Helen was Welsh-speaking, the family is Welsh-speaking, they still own an electrical shop in Newcastle Emlyn.

I always wanted to learn Welsh; when I left Greenham, I got a job in London, primary school teaching, and I was able to go to the City Lit classes in Holborn to learn Welsh in London, so I'd go there every Friday. Then I started going to Llangrannog, an organisation called CEED arranged family and adult classes every autumn and every spring, at Easter and the autumn half-terms, and I'd go there and it was fantastic, meeting Dafydd Iwan. I just started wanting to be in Wales and I just thought, 'Well, why not move to Wales, where you'll get proper tuition, you'll be able to proceed?' so I went there pretty soon, and eventually took the A level.

Siân James: The politicisation of us during the Thatcher years and our awareness of Wales and of what little value Wales was to government, and the whole issue of the Welsh Office and us being ruled by mandarins who sat in Cardiff or London, we were becoming more and more aware of this. And then we had 1982, with the Falklands War, and there was this growing awareness that whatever we called it, when the word 'British' appeared, you could rub out 'British' and put in

'English', and that was a big step forward. We were active in CND, and we'd been on marches. We are now at this point, there's the whole growing awareness of Greenham, of things that have been done or decisions that have been made, Ronald Reagan and Margaret Thatcher. And by this point, we're very actively supporting Cuban solidarity, Nicaraguan solidarity; we're supporting Free Nelson Mandela. So your consciousness and your awareness of things, you're starting to realise that these things do have a direct effect on us in the Upper Swansea Valley, and we did our bit.

My biggest moment of disappointment was writing letters for years to Robben Island, and when I actually did get to visit Robben Island, discovering from an ex-inmate that they were only allowed one letter a month. Who'd you choose? Would you choose a letter from some unknown woman in the Upper Swansea Valley or would you choose a letter from your loved ones? Well, you did. 'Oh,' they said, 'never underestimate what that letter-writing campaign did. Because they would stagger up. We didn't know what was going on, but the guards would speak amongst themselves and we'd be listening, and the guards would be saying, "Six sackfuls of letters today, all these letters from people all over the world, they weigh a ton! What are we going to do with them. Where are we going to store them?"' and the letters kept coming and kept coming and the bags got more numerous and heavier, and the guards were talking amongst themselves and they were saying that they were realising that perhaps South Africa was pretty isolated in what they believed; it contributed to their own awareness. I remember this guy saying, 'Please, please don't ever feel that your letter didn't help. It may not have been read, but those guards staggering up from the jetty on Robben Island, those letters having to be processed' – i.e. whatever, bunged in a shed – they were starting to realise that things were not quite what the government was telling them, so those letters were really important. Robben Island, Nicaragua, Anti-apartheid, Greenham, it was the same struggle and it pre-dated the Strike.

A noteworthy consequence of both the march and of the Greenham Common Women's Peace Camp was the number of people, the great majority of whom were women, who participated at or visited the camp and later went on to hold office in Welsh public life. At a time when women were poorly represented in Wales, several members of the generation who forced a break with this orthodoxy had experienced the political energies of Greenham. The Women's Peace Camp also empowered the Welsh-language movement and was invoked as an influence on several of the community support groups established during the Miners' Strike.

ELEVEN

STREIC Y GLOWYR /
THE MINERS' STRIKE, 1984–1985

Voices

James Dean Bradfield	Kim Howells	Ken Smith
Bob Croydon	Siân James	Lesley Smith
Phil Cullen	Tecwyn Vaughan	Karmen Thomas
Ron Davies	Jones	Phil White
Steve Eaves	Neil Kinnock	Rowan Williams
Menna Elfyn	Tom Marston	Mary Winter
Arfon Evans	Eluned Morgan	Tony Winter
Ffred Ffransis	Christine Powell	Nicky Wire
Richard Frame	Adam Price	Leanne Wood
Edwina Hart		

———

Part 1: The South Wales Coalfield, 1981–1983

In February 1981 the National Coal Board announced a set of measures that had been agreed with the president of the National Union of Mineworkers, Joe Gormley. These included the proposed closure of twenty-three collieries, five of which were located in the South Wales coalfield, including the highly symbolic Tymawr Lewis Merthyr pit in the heart of the Rhondda. At that year's NUM South Wales Area conference Emlyn Williams, president of the SWA, gave a speech in which he declared to his members: 'We have

*a social responsibility to take extra-parliamentary action against
Mrs Thatcher's government.'*

*The result was a series of wildcat strikes, led by the South Wales
miners, who sought support across the UK coalfield, ensuring that
the industrial action evolved into a national dispute. In response,
the Conservative government, then in its first term, withdrew their
proposed programme of pit closures. The miners had won the opening
battle of the new decade's war.*

Phil Cullen: If you really want to grasp what happened in the Miners'
Strike in South Wales, you have to understand the basic infrastructure
of the NUM. I think that's key to it. And you cannot look at South
Wales in isolation compared to the rest of the country. Once you've
understood the structure of the NUM you can understand the strike.
The NUM was formed in 1945, out of the Miners' Federation, and
the Federation lived on. You had the National Union of Mineworkers
president, general secretary, vice-president, and they were a bit like film
stars to the ordinary miner, who never had anything to do with them;
they only used to see them on television. I remember the president of
the NUM visiting my pit, Cynheidre, twice when I was chairman, and
that's the only time that the men ever got to actually meet him and to
have a joke with him. They were totally removed.

You had an area structure, then you had an area, say the Yorkshire
Area, South Wales Area, Scottish Area, Kent, Nottingham and so
on, and each area also had a president, a general secretary and a vice-
president, and an executive to go with it. They were actually registered
trade unions in their own right. The areas would then have National
Executive members selected from that committee: it would normally
be the president and the general secretary, maybe a third, depending on
its size. The men in the pits had very little to do with the area general
secretaries and presidents, unless they knew them personally; they had
virtually nothing to do with them whatsoever.

Underneath that, you had the lodge set-up, which had an awful lot of autonomy in itself. We had our own bank accounts, we had our own funds, we had our own officials, we had our own committee. And the area officials were not allowed into the pit unless we invited them into the pit; or requested them to come into the pit. They couldn't just turn up. It was that tight. It was a very military type of command going right back to the time it was formed after the war.

Men's allegiances were normally to their lodge officials. If they had a problem, it was the likes of me they'd come to, not only in my own pit, right the way across the coalfield. The men looked for guidance from the lodge officials, and the lodge officials, if the problem required it, would get the area officials involved, and it would work on that type of structure. The men would have to go through the lodge, through people like myself, to get to the area officials. Nothing that I'm aware of ever went to the National Executive. It just didn't. They seemed to spend most of their time on strategic issues with government. You couldn't get near Joe Gormley or Arthur Scargill: they were right up on a different plane.

Neil Kinnock: The Miners' Strike was much more to do with class than geography. I wouldn't say this about all the Tories elected in '79, or even in '83, but certainly the leadership of the Conservative Party then were, first of all ideologues, which means the dehumanisation of people, because everything is subject to the thesis, the doctrine, the dogma. That's the first thing, but secondly, Margaret Thatcher's whole attitude may be related to her background and upbringing, which she shared with a few others in the leadership of the Tory Party. Norman Tebbit, for instance, held the mass of the working class in utter contempt, because these were people who hadn't had the wit or the earnestness, or the hard work or whatever they thought it took, or Thatcher thought it took, to escape from being part of the mass; or what you and I would call the community. In all respects, therefore – she never articulated this and probably never used the term – they were *Untermensch* and they could be used to convenience and then discarded.

Maybe I'm over-stating what could be called the psychological weakness that beset the leadership of the Tory Party and the government then, but I don't think it's a million miles away from an accurate appraisal of their conscious attitudes, that were then expanded through the prism of ideology, and when applied to countless communities, which just happened to include industrial South Wales, were ruinous. Totally destructive.

Phil Cullen: The areas had their own politics, and this is key to the whole thing. In areas, in a mine where things are difficult, difficult geology, difficult conditions, things are not going right, then the management aren't happy, the owners, i.e. the Coal Board, aren't happy and the men aren't happy. And it's very easy to encourage a left-wing, progressive, anti-management line in that type of pit. In a pit where the coal is spewing out, if somebody knocks on the manager's door: 'Listen, I need time for a funeral.' 'Ah, aye, you go along.' Somebody comes in, 'We need new rugby posts for the rugby club.' 'Yes, yes, go and see the welders' – if you've got that type of pit, it's very difficult to organise any form of left-wing agenda, because people are not motivated by it.

Kim Howells: I went down the pits in the early 1970s, that's how I got tangled back up in the coal industry. I worked in a mine called Thornhill Colliery near Dewsbury, and I did my first training in Allerton Bywater and I was up there for the best part of a year, and then a guy who had taught me at Hornsey Art College wrote me a very stiff letter, saying, 'You're wasting your time and talent. Why don't you come to Cambridge and do a degree?' so I went to the art college in Cambridge. I'd also had a letter off my brother Adrian, my middle brother, the next one down from me, who wrote to me saying if I didn't jack in working in the mines, he would tell my mother and father, and I could just see my mother turning up at the bloody pithead, saying, 'You, out of there!' I went back to live in London with my first wife and I was very much involved in politics. In the 1972 Miners' Strike, the pickets came and stayed in our tiny little flat; it was absolute bloody mayhem. We went and picketed what was then the Bankside Power Station and the next time I went anywhere near the old Bankside Power Station, I was the Arts Minister going to visit it as the Tate Modern.

I got offered a job at Swansea University in '79 where I'd been helping to teach on the miners' day release courses which the NUM was running. The NUM offered me a job when my contract came to an end at Swansea University, then we were on bloody strike and I didn't earn anything for a few months.

Neil Kinnock: You can't separate out Thatcher from the rapid and violent reduction of so many industries and services in Wales. British manufacturing lost about 25 per cent of its capacity in the Thatcher years due to begin with to a combination of monetary policies. When the oil was coming onshore the pound that was falsely strengthened by the oil was made even stronger, ruinously stronger, by the interest rates that she and another Welshman, Geoffrey Howe, were operating, which devastated British manufacturing.

Wales, with a larger proportion of its economy being more manufacturing-dependent than the rest of the United Kingdom, or nearly the whole of the rest of the United Kingdom, suffered disproportionately because of the devastation of manufacturing, especially in foreign markets.

Kim Howells: I'd always been interested in economics and always looked very carefully at the energy industries. The demise, the huge contraction in the steel industry, was quite obviously a signal to any coalfield that produced coke and coal that they were in trouble, that there would be a big drop in demand for coke and coal, and Llanwern and Port Talbot continued to do pretty well, they were big, efficient units. All these other steelworks and foundries, especially the stuff in the Midlands and Stoke, they were all in a bad way and being closed down, and we could see, it was quite obvious in especially those Gwent pits that were producing coke and coal, that there was a big shadow over them, and when that first hit list came out in '81, they figured very, very strongly on there.

Phil Cullen: That brought us to 1981 and this is when the Coal Board in South Wales tried to close Lewis Merthyr, it was known as the Tymawr pit, Tymawr was part of the pit that was already closed years ago; it was only the Lewis Merthyr bit of the mine that was still open and is now the Rhondda Heritage Park. There was a big hoo-hah about it, partly because it was right slap-bang in the Rhondda and it was seen as being very symbolic.

At that time, back in 1981, we'd heard people banging on about Thatcher and what she was going to do to the miners and all the rest of it, but she didn't come for the miners early, because she didn't feel ready. There's no doubt that it was a grim day for us when she was elected in 1979; we all knew that. But she wasn't strong enough to take on the miners then. Sometimes, in hindsight, we give the right of British politics too much credit. We look at it and we say, 'Oh, they knew this, they knew that': they didn't know that. The closure of Tymawr Lewis Merthyr was nothing more than the Coal Board looking to shed an uneconomic pit.

Kim Howells: These massively inflated hopes for the coal industry, which had been based on the demise of the oil industry as far as bulk fuel for power stations was concerned, really were false dreams, and I wrote papers for the NUM executive pointing out that we were in big trouble and that the demand, even for power station coal, was going to start declining very quickly, and so it proved to be true.

Arfon Evans: In the 1920s, 1930s, Maerdy was a village in the Rhondda of about 3,000 and the Young Communist League was over 250 strong.

The Young Communists met in the Maerdy Working Men's Hall. The party was strong, you had leadership that was engaged, not just in the pit, but within that community, going through the struggles. They would never sell out.

During the 1920s and 1930s the party gave people hope; it gave people an alternative at a very difficult time, one of starvation, unemployment. It organised the unemployment marches, the party did. Right up until 1984 I was the only Communist left on the NUM Executive; I was the last one, even though the party was very small numerically, in influence it was absolutely incredible. The party would influence the resolutions to the NUM Conference, would always consider attacking the government's economic policies, and propose resolutions with meat on them: about wages, about pit closures. They would organise around at Conference and get a national response.

Phil White: My village, Maesteg, was built on coal. It was a very small rural hamlet at one stage, many moons ago; it was iron and coal. The community hospital was built from the pennies of the miners. Llynfi Valley, Maesteg, Caerau in particular was a very staunch Communist area, very staunch, through the twenties and thirties, and really formed the backbone of the Fed, the Miners' Federation, at that time, in this area. The lockouts from 1921 were always remembered across this valley. The older men still had those memories of their own families suffering through that time.

Phil Cullen: You had, within the National Executive of the NUM, areas which were traditionally militant because mining conditions were difficult and you'd got other areas where they weren't. If you look at Leicestershire, Nottinghamshire, Staffs, Derbyshire, North Wales, they didn't tend to be very militant, historically. That doesn't mean that every miner working there was a nodding dog. It was those sort of areas that formed, they would say the moderate – I would say right-wing – parts of the NUM.

Then areas where things were traditionally tough, and things were hard, and the coal owners had been particularly brutal, would have been South Wales and Kent, Scotland, Durham. Those were the left-wing parts of the NUM.

Although nationalised, the entire British coalfield had previously been subject to changes in Coal Board policy that encouraged incentivisation and resulted in unequal pay structures between the regions. These measures had been introduced in agreement with the NUM and its leader Joe Gormley, who retired in 1982. The result was a system in which wage levels varied greatly depending on the working conditions at each region's coal seam and the nature of the coal mined there.

Adam Price: The anthracite coalfield in many ways is the bridge of Wales: it looks both ways geographically, culturally, historically. It's a kind of internal border country, and there's a fantastic fusion going on there. Gwyn Alf Williams writes about this; there was room for Karl Marx and Methodism, all intermingled, in that area. You had Jim Griffiths from Betws, who isn't as celebrated as Aneurin Bevan, but who created the system of national insurance in the 1945 government.

Philip Weekes, who was the head of the NCB in South Wales during the strike, wrote afterwards in a BBC lecture that there was always a difference with the NUM officials from the anthracite coalfield. You could feel the biblical language, even as they were negotiating as union reps; there was a different kind of tone, because they were drawing upon some fairly deep cultural veins.

Phil Cullen: In this area of Wales, we mined the finest anthracite in the world. The nature of the coal in Nottingham is, well, to put it bluntly, shit. It's soft, steam coal. The coal of the anthracite coalfield is entirely different. The chomp of the mechanical equipment and the electrical equipment, in order to get anthracite out, was not comparable with the stuff they were mining in Nottinghamshire. Of course, in Nottingham their wages went through the roof and people there were earning twice or three times what we were then earning in South Wales.

And there was always this power struggle going on, between left and right on the National Executive, for control. The situation was that the NUM was agitating for higher income, but the government – a Labour government – had to watch that it didn't upset other workers, like the power workers, the steel workers and the dockers. This is what destroyed the NUM, and this was as early as 1978, something like that. It was tied in with the more coal you produced, the more money you got paid, it was called the Incentive Bonus Scheme. That immediately favoured the Nottinghamshire miners, who were taking something like ten cuts a shift. If we had the shearer up and down twice in Cynheidre, we were very pleased.

Siân James: Two feet 10 inch seams, my husband Martin sometimes worked in. Martin worked in the 3 feet 6 inch and the 2 feet 10 inch seams. That's 34-inch high seams, 40-inch high seams. The anthracite is so valuable, it's worth cutting it. But to repair the cutting machines, my husband had to have a pair of knee-pads on and crawl in at the side of the face. He wasn't walking through these big, airy caverns that you could drive a lorry through, but the coal was so valuable. It's geologically difficult to mine it, there are faults and the face can drop. You can be coaling for a really good length, 100 feet, and then boof, the face drops. Down it drops and everything has to be readjusted.

Phil Cullen: It would take us half a shift to get the coal shearers, the machines that used to cut the coal, ready again. Heads had to be changed and the whole thing had to be overhauled.

Siân James: That's the reality of working in the anthracite coalfield. My father-in-law benefited from the bonuses when they were working the Peacock Vein at Abernant. Martin didn't see those glory days of the anthracite coalfield, but that production-related scheme really divided miners. I didn't hear bloody Nottingham say a lot about it then. And in 1982, when we'd had local pits close, there'd not been a peep from up there in Nottingham.

Phil White: The Incentive Bonus Scheme was the remnants of Joe Gormley and it was a thank you to his bosses that he left that legacy. And he divided the union in that way and made sure that the likes of Nottingham could earn very good money through an incentive bonus, whereas within Wales, we were very far from ever going to make any money from an incentive bonus. Many's the time I saw on the board up in St John's Colliery a penny: your bonus this week was a penny. But then you did hear of £20, £30, £40 being paid out on a weekly basis across the industry. During the '81 campaign I actually spent some time up in Nottingham and Derbyshire, making sure that we could get them out and making sure they were supportive.

Siân James: I met apprentices in Nottingham who were on £495 a week, apprentices, sixteen-, seventeen-, eighteen-year-old kids, because they were coaling and it was a bonus related to coal production, which, I hasten to add, the NU bloody M had agreed.

Phil Cullen: Even in South Wales, you had a perverse situation where you had the ladies in the Betws canteen earning more money than face-workers at Cynheidre. This is what, in my view, was the start of the undoing of the unity of the so-called NUM, because they introduced market forces in the sense that it became every pit for itself and every man for himself. It even divided pits up. Some of the leadership in South Wales, and the other, more militant areas, like South Yorkshire, did point out that it would have a destabilising effect, but nobody wanted to know. Once you put £20 or £30 extra in someone's pay packet a week, you're not going to get a result out of it.

The National Coal Board was under the new leadership of Ian MacGregor, a man much admired by Margaret Thatcher and members of her cabinet for his management techniques, who had transferred to coal from the steel industry where, as chairman of British Steel, he had overseen a significant decrease in workforce numbers. In 1980 166,000 were employed within the steel industry; within three years MacGregor had reduced the figure to 71,000. MacGregor's appointment as president of the National Coal Board was viewed by the NUM as a clear indication that the already declining mining industry would undergo a similar process of rationalisation and job losses.

Tom Marston: I think it was Callaghan who brought over Ian MacGregor to the car industry, to British Leyland, and we saw what was happening there, to people like Derek Robinson of the Transport and General Union, how he was ostracised. I was in management in the steel industry and MacGregor became leader of the steel industry, and I saw his methods in real life. We had the steel strike early in 1980 and as soon as the strike was over, my immediate boss was offered early retirement and I was promoted, but my position wasn't replaced beneath me. And then within a few months, I could see the MacGregor process working, rationalisation: my whole department disappeared underneath me.

Ken Smith: What some people didn't get – especially the Labour leadership – was the existential threat that was there with the Tory government and with Ian MacGregor, and that was the bit that really was the catalyst of it. It went contrary to what people like Norman Willis, Neil Kinnock, Eric Hobsbawm were saying at the time, promoting New Realism and compromise. The Tories were not out for compromise, and that emboldened Thatcher and the Tories. The Labour and trade union leaders – with some exceptions – were caught like rabbits in the headlights, because on the one side, they were not able to disown their past, particularly Neil Kinnock in South Wales, but on the other hand, it didn't fit in with their world view.

Siân James: My daughter is truly a child of Thatcher. I think Margaret Thatcher was elected on 6 May '79 and Marina was born on 4 June. She grew up in this atmosphere of 'Greed is good; competition is healthy.' Even the nature of going to school changed from when I was a child. At school I don't remember asking anybody what their fathers did; we assumed they all worked in the colliery or the factory. Local. My children were up against things like, 'You haven't got a car. Why haven't you got a car?' 'What does your daddy do? Oh, he works in a factory?' It was really quite strange how we saw people's aspirations change.

We knew Thatcher was gunning for us. There was no doubt in our mind. And Thatcher coincided with my husband Martin going underground. He had got an apprenticeship at a very young age in the local watch-making factory, the Tick-Tock, and I think that was his parents' attempt for him to better himself.

Martin came home from work one day and the staff had all been lined up in the canteen, the largest place that they could congregate, and they'd been told that digital watches were a flash in the pan and not to be worried by them, that they were a craze. Famous last words. The Japanese had bought the watch factory, then it started to change under them. My dad said to Martin, 'Go underground, Martin: it's a job with a future.'

Kim Howells: I remember at the time, certainly in the late seventies and early eighties, talking to people in the Coal Board who were clearly up to something, even people who were regarded as benign characters, like Philip Weekes who ran the South Wales coalfield; they seemed to me to have accepted, really, that the boom years were over and that, one way or another, they were going to have to start closing pits.

In February 1983 a now more determined National Coal Board
renewed its programme of pit closures. As in 1981, the Tymawr Lewis
Merthyr colliery in the Rhondda was included on the list of mines
being considered for pit closure, along with Blaengwrach in Neath.
The presence of these two mines on the NCB 'hit list' prompted a
stay-down strike by the miners of Lewis Merthyr, who remained
underground for several days.

By the end of February 1983 all 23,500 miners of the South Wales
coalfield were out on strike and the area's NUM sent delegates to pits
across Britain, including to Nottinghamshire and Yorkshire, in order
to persuade them to strike in support. However, in March, a national
ballot was held that decisively rejected industrial action. For many
members of the South Wales coalfield this lack of national support
led to a scepticism about the unity of the coalfield and the prospective
success of any future national ballot. In July 1983 Tymawr Lewis
Merthyr was duly closed.

Neil Kinnock: I consistently put, I say rightly, the case for coal, and I thought that the approach being taken by the Thatcher government, even before I thought of it as vengeful and vicious, was being stupid in gambling with our indigenous energy resources. I was against it on entirely rational grounds of UK economic and energy security, even before I got round to despising her as a vengeful and extremely reactionary politician.

Phil White: There were more closures under Labour governments in the sixties than in any one decade or any one time. And probably better pits were closed in the sixties than were kept open in the seventies. Some of those pits towards the end of the seventies, through lack of investment, were in pretty poor shape, and if we were never going to get investment back into those mines, then they were never going to become viable or economic. I think we were fighting for at least the opportunity to prove the case of viability, and the only pretence we had of that was a thing called the Colliery Review Procedure, which my colliery, St John's, Maesteg, went through at the time. Good mines, decent mines that had investment, closed prematurely; all the mines that didn't have the investment were left open, all pointing towards what? The case against. Not the case for.

Phil Cullen: There was a thing called the Colliery Review Procedure, which was absolutely meaningless. The Coal Board would put your pit into it, and once they put you into it, everyone knew you were going to close: it was a paper exercise. There was no spontaneous action to be taken; you had to follow the process. It's got to be followed to its ultimate end, wherever that may take you and how long it may take you; you must follow the process. With Tymawr Lewis Merthyr, the Coal Board decided that they could just shut it without that, and that's what put a lot of the area officials' backs up, because they'd gone into the closure without observing and respecting the NUM's involvement.

In 1983 the South Wales miners went into other areas to seek support for what we saw was about to happen. They were going for about five pits then, including Lewis Merthyr, and men were sent into the areas and the only areas that supported South Wales at that time were Scotland and Kent. The only English coalfield that supported South Wales was Kent. And the history of Kent, if you know anything about it, is that they are the cream of the militant miners. That's all we had in terms of support. It left the miners in South Wales with a very, very bitter taste in their mouths, and we knew that it was the Incentive Bonus Scheme that had done this. It destroyed all unity and that is the key to it all.

Kim Howells: During the dispute over the '83 hit list, which Lewis Merthyr had been placed on, we'd sent what we called delegates – some people called them pickets, we called them delegates – to every coalfield in Britain. Peter Evans from Deep Duffryn Colliery, who was by then working in Merthyr Vale, came back and he was a very bright guy, Pete. I remember him saying to me, 'They were great to us in Nottingham and in Mansfield. They gave us everything we asked for except their vote.' We also sent boys to have a look at the stockpiles at the power stations, boys who were surveyors, who knew the score, who were coming back to tell us they had got unprecedented stockpile levels. At the same time Scargill was saying that it was just a show, that they'd bulldozed the stockpiled coal up to the edges of their stocking areas and that they would be short of stock.

Arfon Evans: I was very fortunate – as chairman of Maerdy Lodge and being a member of the South Wales Executive, I probably went down every pit before the strike, because I had to conduct various investigations and give reports. I think I went down about twenty-eight pits. And what I would have to concede is if you're going to fight a pit closure programme, then you have to fight it on the basis that you're fighting for pits that you really want to keep open. I certainly wouldn't want to fight for a pit that was starved of investment, that was archaic, was dangerous, was dirty, was a hazard to the workmen. I think partly the Tymawr Lewis Merthyr situation came into that category, unfortunately.

Kim Howells: The boys in Lewis Merthyr were led by Des Dutfield and had stayed down in that colliery, occupied it. They were hoping that the British coalfields would have come out in support of them, but no they didn't. It hadn't happened when Deep Duffryn had closed in '79, either.

There were pits where we had support. You'd get terrific NUM lodges and branches who were prepared to come out, but you've got to get everybody out if you're going to win a dispute; you're not going to do it piecemeal, with pits here and there on their own.

Tom Marston: My feeling before the 1984 Miners' Strike took place was that the mines around Neath were being deliberately run down: expensive equipment was being left underground and buried.

In October 1983 Neil Kinnock, MP for Islwyn, replaced Michael Foot as leader of the Labour Party. Until standing down, Foot had represented the constituency of Ebbw Vale, a seat, like Kinnock's, located in the heart of the South Wales coalfield. After the conclusion of the Thatcher government's first term, it was evident that the modified version of post-war social democracy represented by Labourism was in a much weaker position as a political programme than the new Conservative ideology of monetarism. The party also faced the threat of the recently founded Social Democratic Party, which positioned itself on what it considered to be the centre ground of British politics. The new party was achieving some success: in the previous parliament three Welsh Labour MPs had defected to the SDP. From the left wing, the Labour leadership also faced opposition from the members of Militant, which had become entrenched within the party.

This situation ensured that any likely strike by the NUM, which was now under the combative leadership of Arthur Scargill, a man who held sympathies for Militant, placed Kinnock in a position of difficulty. The new Labour leader's instincts were to move his party towards a position of middle-ground political consensus with, in his view, broad rather than factional appeal. At the same time, mining communities and the NUM were instinctively loyal to Labour, to the point of the two becoming synonymous; months before his election, the NUM South Wales Area had publicly endorsed Neil Kinnock as leader.

Ron Davies: 1983. The great debacle, the organised Labour movement had lost its way. 1983 came along, Michael Foot was leader of the party, a lovely man, and the irony is, that if anybody was asked to describe what kind of person they would like to see as a political

269

leader, they would talk about generosity, a liberal attitude, kindness and empathy with your fellow man and so on – and Michael Foot had those qualities absolutely by the bucketful. What he didn't have was the ruthlessness which politicians need but the public wouldn't necessarily admire.

James Dean Bradfield: Neil Kinnock is writ large in my history. He was lovely to everybody; he was brilliant. The election results would always come in at Pontllanfraith Leisure Centre and it was surreal to have him come and speak. He would always say, 'Jimmy Bradfield', and he was really nice. He used to be walking down the Oakdale Road, from the colliery, with Glenys and stuff, so I have only good memories of him, and a massively strange sense of pride, when election results were coming in.

Ron Davies: The 1983 election was subsequently a complete and utter shambles and then shortly afterwards, in the autumn of that year, at Party Conference down in Brighton, where he famously did an imitation of King Canute trying to hold back the sea. Neil fell over in the sand and then emerged as leader of the Labour Party. Nobody is universally popular and Neil did have a capacity for making enemies because he wasn't that inclusive type of individual, but he set about bravely taking on the Militant tendency. Looking back, the big argument at the time was, 'Militant should be taken on through political argument,' which is fine, but it wasn't a political argument, it was an organisational argument.

James Dean Bradfield: I was getting *Militant* magazine delivered to my door, once every month, so I was getting a bit into that and then I remember seeing him fall on Brighton Beach, when the tide came in and I remember feeling really conflicted, because I really did care about him. I thought his alliteration was a good fucking thing. I thought he had good flow, but then other people would say that he's a windbag of a man, and that really hurt me, because he lived on my street, and I thought he was a good person. Then I saw him on my street in a news report when the Colliery Miners' Lodge went past my house marching and there was a bit of footage of him coming down my street as well. Suddenly, my part of Wales, South Wales, is home to the Leader of the Opposition and the man that's taking on Derek Hatton. I've actually seen my street on TV, and I don't see Wales much on TV.

Ron Davies: Neil recognised, to his great credit, that you have to take things on organisation by organisation, and he set about dismantling the Militant tendency and trying to create a broader swathe of centre-left dominance within the Labour Party. At that time I was a contemporary of Tony Blair and Gordon Brown and a number of others, but those two particularly were the rising stars.

Ken Smith: If you look at the political development at the time, particularly around the election and Neil Kinnock as Labour leader, it was the advent of New Labour. New Realism was the phrase that was used, I remember the examples being given to justify that thinking and saying about how miners would never go on strike again because they all had videos, they all had nice cars, they had foreign holidays, and they were too cosy and comfy.

Neil Kinnock: Thatcher's ostensible reason for the attack on the miners, was the fact that the National Coal Board, the nationalised coal industry, was every year a major financial loser – just like the coal industry of every other country in the world. Nonetheless, it gave her a superficial excuse for cutting back the coal industry and bringing about closures in an attempt, which would never, ever be small-scale, to so-called balance the books. She had that ostensible excuse, but the real reason, of course, was a visceral detestation of the most organised section of the British working class.

Part 2: The Start of the 1984 Strike

On 6 March 1984, in a demonstration of its fortified sense of purpose, the National Coal Board once more announced a set of measures intended to rationalise the mining industry. The process would commence with the closure of twenty pits, including Cortonwood Colliery in South Yorkshire and Polmaise Colliery in Scotland, both of which were told to shut with immediate effect. The National Union of Mineworkers had long anticipated the Board's decision, following as it did a protracted period of closure threats, localised strike action and fraught negotiations that dated back to the start of the decade during the Conservative government's first term in office.

Two days later, the NUM leadership endorsed the stoppages already under way in Yorkshire and Scotland and urged the other coalfields to support them. Almost 50 per cent of the Scottish coalfield was already engaged in industrial dispute with their area management prior to the beginning of the strike.

A further four days later, the president of the National Union of Mineworkers, Arthur Scargill, called a national strike in opposition to the pit closures. The strike was instigated without a national ballot, a situation that was debated throughout the dispute and exploited by its opponents, who regularly argued that the lack of a national ballot undermined the strike's legality; Scargill instead informed the NUM regions they had the authority to make unilateral individual decisions on whether or not to undertake strike action, a procedure with historic precedent within the union and its federal structure. The absence of a national ballot also contributed to disunity across the coalfield: the majority of Nottingham Area miners used it as a justification to continue working throughout the strike.

The South Wales coalfield, a region within the NUM with a long-standing reputation for communal radicalism, had supported strike action in the previous three ballots taken by its lodges earlier in the decade. On 12 March the South Wales Executive Committee decided

to call the South Wales region out on strike without recourse to a ballot
and within two days, in a demonstration of the miners' unanimity
and commitment to the union, a complete stoppage occurred across the
coalfield's twenty-eight pits. It is estimated that, at its commencement,
99.6 per cent of the South Wales miners participated in the strike.

Phil Cullen: Come forward now a year to 1984. It was the spring. I've heard all sorts of rubbish from people, things like, 'Well, you shouldn't have gone on strike: you should have waited until the winter.' What were we supposed to tell the men of Cortonwood, whose pit was slated for closure? We're supposed to tell the men of Cortonwood, 'Well, look, we'll allow them to close your pit, but we will go on strike for you in the winter, after they've closed the pit.' It doesn't make any sense whatsoever. The employer in any industry holds the cards. The unions always have to respond to things the employers inflict on them.

When they came for that strike in the spring of 1984, they were very tactical in the way they did it. They didn't close a single pit in South Wales, and I find that very strange, because they could have gone for plenty of uneconomic pits in South Wales. They didn't go for one. They went for pits in some of the most militant areas, but they didn't go for any in South Wales. I've always had the opinion that that was done deliberately to try and put a wedge between the traditional left-wing areas of the NUM and anyone else. And it nearly worked.

Arfon Evans: Many Communist Party members held the view that there would need to be a more conciliatory approach by Arthur Scargill to bring together the wider sections of the labour and trade union movement, along with the broader movements, if we were going to have any chance of winning the '84 Miners' Strike. Scargill modelled himself on A. J. Cook [General Secretary of the Miners' Federation of Great Britain 1924–31], and Cook's main theme was no compromise. And sadly, the right wing of the union, Joe Gormley, by the rule book had prevented Mick McGahey from becoming president. And McGahey would have handled this in a much different way. He would have made life much more difficult for MacGregor and for Thatcher.

Mary Winter: I stood in a by-election as a candidate for the Communist Party when the 1984 Miners' Strike was on, and at the time it felt like here was a battle against the Thatcher government. Here were the miners who were the backbone of Welsh industry and we had to support them. Certainly in the early days, that was the feeling. And during the by-election Mick McGahey came down as part of my election campaign. In his speech, which was in the Urdd Centre in Aberdare, he said, 'The problem with the Labour Party is that it's a resolutionary party not a revolutionary party.' And at that time, at that point in the strike, it was very much, yes, the miners are right, we've got to support them 100 per cent; there was no pulling back from it.

Edwina Hart: I blame the Labour Party for their not wanting Mick McGahey to become president of the National Union of Mineworkers because he was in the Communist Party, which ensured you had a very fraught figure leading the NUM, in Arthur Scargill, rather than a canny Communist Scot. It would have made quite a difference. The hatred the party had for the Communist Party meant they were blinded on certain things. I think with Mick McGahey we'd have still seen coal mining go, but I think we'd have seen a different way of resolving that dispute.

Tony Winter: During the strike, the worst thing that happened was that Scargill enforced that he was going to keep the NUM within his arms. He fought tooth and nail not to involve the wider trade union movement in his struggle, with the exception of the print workers in London, who spent a fortune and collected tens of thousands of pounds and sent it down to the Valleys. A few other trade unions nationally did sterling work for the miners, but Scargill wanted to keep this as a miners' strike, which was fatal.

Phil Cullen: Arthur Scargill was Arthur Scargill. And his personality didn't endear himself to a lot of people and there's no doubt about that. I believe that Arthur believed in what he was saying; whether he went about it in the correct manner is open to debate. You've got to get back to the fundamental basics that all the intelligentsia have forgotten: the men elected Arthur Scargill on a platform of opposing pit closures. If you are going to elect someone who doesn't hide the fact that he's a Marxist or claims to be a Marxist – a millionaire Marxist, maybe, but he's still a Marxist – there's not much point in crying about it when he asks you to take strike action to do what he said he wanted to do.

Siân James: When Arthur Scargill was elected, my father voted for him; my father-in-law voted for him; my husband Martin voted for him; my cousins voted for him; my brother voted for him. What was the first thing they said? 'This man will not go on his knees. This man won't sell us down the river.' And that's the Arthur Scargill we expected, so when you get the crap from the union and the academics, well, they didn't rely on miners' pay. We'd already been cut to the bone.

Christine Powell: Scargill was elected by the rank and file, and he did, within his ability, within his skill set, do what he said he was going to do: he fought for the NUM, and there are those people who believe that he killed the NUM. I think perhaps Scargill still saw himself as the person who had led the '74 strike in the north of England. But things were different, and the thing that was different was Thatcher. It didn't matter who was the head of the NUM, Thatcher was going to kill the coal industry whether it was by strike, or by stealth, or privatisation: it was going.

Phil Cullen: The strike in South Wales was very slow to take off because of this bad taste in the mouth. The miners weren't happy about what had happened to Wales the year before because the English coalfields, with the exception of Kent, had not backed us at all. Cleverly, they didn't put a Welsh pit in the frame for closure, so they took the area executive's fire out of it, they'd left South Wales alone, deliberately. Master plan, I've got to say.

Kim Howells: We knew what the score was and that's why so many lodges voted against taking strike action in South Wales. They'd been through it already, during '81 and '83.

Phil Cullen: What are you going to do? You're in a situation where the men expect the leadership to take some form of action, to fight for their jobs, that's why you're there, that's your purpose in life, to represent your members. The Coal Board came along with a big axe and said, 'Right, we're cutting these down,' at the worst possible time, in the spring. Miners have never taken strike action in the spring, and the employer went for it in the spring. The trap was set. And unfortunately, we had to walk into it: there wasn't an alternative.

The strike was then given permission to kick off on an area basis under Rule 41, and the Coal Board challenged it in the courts, and it was held to be a legal strike. The strike in the areas that were on strike was lawful: that's what the courts decided.

Ken Smith: There were sharp differences in many ways between the approach and tactics that were being employed in Yorkshire and the approach and tactics in South Wales. Ultimately, they wanted the same thing; there was no divergence in what the objective was. This was a fight; the gauntlet had been laid down by Thatcher. It was a fight to the finish and, particularly in Wales, but as it turned out, everywhere, it was for the preservation of an industry and communities.

Phil Cullen: The idea that we could have a rolling picket that was going to have a domino effect failed drastically. I blame the Yorkshire miners a lot for that, because they went into Nottingham instead of leaving the Nottingham leadership to talk to their own men, but once the Yorkshire miners went into Nottingham, you had immediate conflict and they put their backs up and basically were never going to get them out. My own opinion is, to be perfectly blunt about it, we wouldn't have got them out anyway, but I have no evidence to support that; it's pure presumption on my part. I do genuinely believe that we wouldn't have got them out in Nottingham. They were earning too much money and their pits weren't at stake.

Christine Powell: I always remember my dad saying, 'The problem with people not being that interested in unions any more is you're having your fortnight in Benidorm every year and then somebody stands up and says, "Let me save you," and you say, "Why?"' Everything became too comfortable. People didn't realise they were comfortable because of the unions, not despite them.

Arfon Evans: Mick McGahey, who I was quite close to, due to my Communist Party involvement, would say, 'It's not right that another coalfield, or another miner, should have the decision to close another man's pit.' The Yorkshire coalfield went in really so aggressively to the Nottinghamshire coalfield. If anybody should have gone into the Nottinghamshire coalfield, it should have been the Welsh miners, with our political skills and with less of an aggressive attack on their past. Simultaneously, I believed as well, there were possibilities that we could win a national ballot, if it was put to the Nottinghamshire coalfield as well. I think there were tremendous failures.

Ken Smith: The thing about a national ballot became a huge fetish during the strike, but the fact was that the NUM as a federal organisation didn't need a national ballot. It used to have national ballots on pay, but

277

where jobs were threatened at a local level they didn't need a national ballot, and the emphasis on solidarity and not crossing picket lines to support others whose jobs were under threat overcame that.

Having said that, as the momentum of the strike went on, it became an issue. I think it was about 19 April, during the strike, that they thought they could go for and could win a national ballot. There would have still been problems in Nottingham and maybe one or two other areas, but it would have turned the tap off on that whole fetish of that argument. I don't think it would have fundamentally changed the course of the strike; it would have just been a monkey off the back and then the NUM executive never called it, and a lot of us on the Left felt that was a mistake. It was definitely used by the Labour leader and right-wing trade union leaders to avoid supporting the miners unequivocally.

Phil Cullen: The fact that we didn't go for a ballot – people say, oh, that was a mistake. OK, maybe it was a mistake, but we didn't know the size of the mistake we were making at the time, and I must admit I'm very sceptical that we could have won a ballot anyway, because of the Incentive Bonus Scheme and because there was no threat to the collieries in the English Midlands, and that's where the strike was lost, in the English Midlands. That's my opinion and nobody will change that.

Arfon Evans: We all knew that the Thatcher government were going to have their reprisal over '72 and '74. They had planned the state machine, the Army, the police, the private hauliers. I spent time in Holland, in Rotterdam, which was the main spot market for coal in the world, and I was trying to negotiate with the union there an embargo on imports into the UK, and at every level – I went to the top of the tree, I came down to the branches – everywhere I went, the response was, 'When you have a national ballot, when you are unified in the Labour Party, and when the TUC supports you, that's when we will put an embargo on British coal.' That could be an easy cop-out, but nevertheless, it was fact: we hadn't got the support of the TUC; we hadn't got the Labour Party. Every meeting I attended, right across the length and breadth of this country, those were the main issues: the ballot, the lack of Labour Party support, the lack of TUC support, and that was a major impediment.

Kim Howells: Even now, I still meet guys who say to me, 'If we'd had a national ballot it would have been fucking lost,' and my reply is 'Yes, but it's called democracy, bud!' There we are. Quite a sizeable majority of NUM lodges in our coalfield voted not to take strike action. On the Sunday when we realised that we'd lost that vote in South Wales, the lodges met in the ambulance room in Hirwaun and we organised to picket every pit in South Wales the following morning and that's what we did. It was certainly not constitutional, but Emlyn Williams and George Rees and the rest knew damn well that we weren't going to look too hot if we suddenly had bloody pickets from other coalfields coming on to the South Wales coalfield; we'd been the most militant of all of the coalfields, for most of our existence, in the NUM.

Siân James: By this point we've got this background of 'Don't support the miners, they should go back to work, the lack of a vote is undemocratic,' and if I hear those words once again ... I don't care. My husband didn't care that he hadn't had a national bloody ballot.

Kim Howells: That was a terrible, terrible burden that we had to carry all the way through the strike. It was always the most difficult subject. I became the spokesman for South Wales, and on television and radio interviews it was always the most difficult one to try and defend, the lack of a ballot.

Phil White: As far as we were concerned in Wales, there wasn't a need of a national ballot because it was already set from '81. Other areas, Nottingham in the main, felt differently and wanted a national ballot. At the time I was one of many that felt quite strongly that we already had the mandate, so it wasn't unconstitutional. I don't think we discussed that if we had a national ballot that we would lose it. Don't get me wrong: it wouldn't be a huge majority, but I think it would have been a majority of a reputable size to give us that confidence, as a union, that we have got the membership with us.

At my pit, Maesteg St John's, we didn't vote to go out in the first general meeting. We made sure that our friends from Tower Colliery were at the gate when we turned up on the Monday, and immediately following that, we had our next meeting and we voted to come out.

By '84 we had already lost Crynant Colliery just literally as the crow flies a mile up the road, and before that Caerau Colliery. A lot of the men transferred down. A number of the men were tired: '80, '81, '82, were years of conflict. I think men were just a bit worn down by it all. And here it comes in '84, 'Guys, this is now an onslaught that could wipe out the whole industry in South Wales,' as we were trying to explain. But there you are, I think the men were just generally tired of it.

Phil Cullen: Some people will tell you that they thought the strike was doomed from day one; I can't say. I don't know. I don't think anybody actually knew how it was going to pan out. I don't think the government did, either. I think there'd never been a dispute in the modern era that went on like this. This was nothing normal, or usual. For people to say, 'Oh, the government planned it': they didn't. They planned to win a normal, short strike so that they could close the most uneconomic pits. When we went into it, the Tories, the Coal Board, the NUM, the men, no one knew where it was going to take us. And it progressed from there.

Christine Powell: At the start of the strike I thought, 'How long is this one going to last?' Two or three days, a week perhaps, and then you begin to get serious. In the middle of it, you didn't think about whether or not you could win or you couldn't win, you were in the middle of it and you got on with it. On reflection, there was absolutely no way on God's Earth we were going to win. Margaret Thatcher would have blown us up before we'd have won. And I exaggerate not.

Ron Davies: Neil Kinnock agonised over the Miners' Strike. It was really, really difficult for him. There was no love lost between him and Scargill and, I think genuinely with Neil, the issue was that there was a lack of a ballot; so many people had said it. Just down the road from where I live in Bedwas, there was a pit that I knew very well. They had a ballot which they'd organised amongst themselves; I think there were probably 600 plus men working there at the time, and the ballot was 90 per cent against strike action, because they knew what was going to happen, and, paradoxically, shortly afterwards, when the strike was called, pickets were put out and Bedwas men were absolutely solid in the strike, even though everybody knew that what was happening was unfair in terms of process. Neil knew that and he was agonising on it, partly because of the way in which the democratic traditions of the union had been traduced, but I think he could have accepted that, if it was for a morally defensible and believable cause. We all knew that it wasn't. These men were going to be thrown on the scrapheap and it was part of both the generational change in terms of politics, but also in terms of the industry itself. The tide was ebbing on the mining industry.

Arfon Evans: In the NUM we had backed Neil Kinnock as an MP, before he became leader; we'd introduced him at meetings and given him our support.

Phil White: I remember Kinnock coming here to Maesteg Town Hall in 1978, the big left-wing Member of Parliament who was going to change everything, 'I'm going to become the leader. I want your support, right. We're going to build this for the next two years.' A little bit impressive, to be honest, but it didn't take long to start seeing through him, and really his role during the strike, I make no apologies for: it wasn't anything. National ballot, national ballot, and of course him and Arthur were at loggerheads. There were good Members of Parliament who were very supportive of us during the seventies strikes, but you couldn't call on them outside of that, other than their own individual actions. That support certainly wasn't there in the eighties, and we knew it wasn't going to be there.

Part 3: Community Resilience, Summer 1984

By August 1984, almost six months into the strike, it was rumoured that only one miner had returned to work across the entire South Wales coalfield. The evident solidarity across the area and dedication to the strike was sustained by the support groups established in mining communities, the women's support groups in particular, which were responsible for the organisation of feeding and clothing their communities. This proved an essential task, as the decision to brand the strike illegal ensured that the unpaid miners were ineligible for any form of social security. The South Wales miners also participated in collective NUM action, both at a national UK level and within Wales, such as the demonstrations and picketing of the Port Talbot steelworks at Margam, one of many locations where tactics used by the police proved confrontational.

Ken Smith: I think the experience of the South Wales NUM was a lot more grounded in the experience of the twenties and the thirties, and the hardships of that period, and building community support and action, whereas the Yorkshire approach was much more grounded in the flying pickets of the 1970s. In terms of things like support groups in South Wales the general feeling was that the approach should be really democratic, as inclusive as possible, and also understanding that it was political motivation that inspired people to keep them going to find the stamina and resilience. I think a lot of us saw from the start it was going to be a fairly long strike.

Arfon Evans: There were fantastic solidarities, food and money and all the rest, and you could never question that, but if you're going to win against a right-wing Conservative government, you need to have the full support of the Labour and trade union movement combined. And it was insufficient, the NUM on its own; we couldn't even get good agreements with the steel workers.

Mary Winter: Part of that, I think, was down to the macho approach of the NUM. It wasn't that the other unions weren't jumping on board; I think it was also that the NUM itself was being purist.

I was a member of the National and Local Government Officers' Association at the time: I was working in social services. We were doing the collection of food parcels or collection of money for families in our valley and you had a number of women's groups that were doing a similar sort of work. But we weren't as a whole community involved in the politics of the strike. There was a division between that kind of altruistic assistance, that social kind of help, and the politics of the strike. There was no real pulling in of all the other unions; there wasn't that kind of atmosphere.

Phil White: I think the only risk the TUC ever took was whether they'd have another sugar in their tea: that help was never forthcoming. This was about us, only us, in the end. We had seen our colleagues fallen in the other industries so easily. And I mean the word 'easily'; it looked to me easily. We were there for them, the triple alliance, rail, steel and coal. ASLEF and the NUR were very supportive.

Mary Winter: There was a big rally held in Port Talbot, in Aberavon, in the swimming pool, a big mass meeting, and during that meeting,

283

members of the NUM crawled up in the gantry and lowered a noose down, very quietly, over the head of the general secretary of the TUC, who was addressing that meeting, and I felt ashamed. Ashamed. And that was the position.

Karmen Thomas: We had the soup kitchen in the Miners' Welfare in Ammanford. I thought, 'I'm not just going to be a union official. I'll come in and help. I have skills of cooking and, to begin with, there was, not resentment, almost a mistrust. Why would I want to be working with all these guys, did I fancy them? Was I having affairs? No, this is my politics, this is what I'm doing.' And the women were also bearing the brunt of the lack of money during the strike. In a sense it was as though they thought, 'Why aren't you at home with your children? Your husband's lucky, he's got a job at the moment, and he's looking after the children; what sort of bloke is he?'

Tony Winter: The women fought to keep the families fed, and I was actively involved in that, because I chaired the committee that organised the distribution of food in our valley. I had the pleasure of attending a meeting every Friday night in Aberavon Institute with 90 per cent of the audience made up of women all wanting to know whose turn was it to have the next batch of grub.

Mary Winter: You see, what happened there? The women's role was to sort the food. It was the men who were the committee men, but the women were the ones who did the actual sorting out; it was the women's role. The other thing you'd get there was the Penywaun women would be arguing for Penywaun food, Abercynon women would be arguing for Abercynon food, and Cwmpennar for theirs. Things were very, very parochial, very divided.

Ken Smith: I was on the National Committee of the Labour Party Young Socialists (LPYS). I'd been involved with St John's NUM organising joint LPYS/NUM schools and things like that. So we already had the connections to get the support groups going very early in the strike. We started food parcels within about three weeks: people went collecting in different areas and we even organised international solidarity and fundraising trips from April. There were sometimes a few turf wars over who should be fundraising in which areas.

I've still got friendships with people who just wanted to help, and were politicised for the rest of their life. People who will never forget that experience, people who were completely transformed by the experience as well, particularly the miners' wives.

Phil Cullen: The Coal Board were constantly whining about the state of the coalfaces. After all, we were on strike to save the mines, to save our jobs, not shut them down, but yet they were constantly playing on men's senses that we wouldn't have faces to go back to anyway, that the faces were under great pressure, that the faces had moved, they were deteriorating, the roadways were deteriorating, the pits were deteriorating, and basically, we wouldn't have mines to go back to, and that was worrying, as well, for a lot of the people.

The men that went back to work, did they actually go back to work? No. They went into the colliery, but they didn't do any work. Those men sat playing cards in the washery, as far away from us as they could possibly put them, and that's where they stayed all day.

Karmen Thomas: Our pit, Betws, looked quite impressive, the big, huge road going all the way up to the main buildings at the top. There were guys coming into work and the reaction on the picket line was, 'We need to take them out and we need to beat the crap out of these people.' Sometimes that was intimidating, because I was the only woman on the picket line as an official. At a later picket line, we had some of the wives turn up as well. I said, 'Why don't you come along? Come on, we need everybody. If I can be on there so can you.' So we had quite a few women on other occasions. But there were intense moments and I'd have to deal with talking to the police about, 'This is where we're going to be. We're not having any discussion, this is where it's going to be,' and I think they were quite bemused at talking to a woman. My role in this was a bit strange to them. These were local police. At one particular picket line, it didn't get so intense because they all knew each other, a lot of them at the time, and there was always quite a healthy mistrust of the police as well, to a certain degree, even if your brother was a policeman.

Phil Cullen: I knew people well from Penrhiwceiber pit, a bloke called Dai Davis was the Area Executive member and the police in the strike were frightened to go up near Penrhiwceiber. There were trains with the coal going in there and they would be derailed, and there were men of sixty-odd who would be out on the track, clearing tons of coal by the side of the track. The train drivers' union were told, 'You don't get out of the cab, you stay in the cab and lock the door. They'll leave you alone as long as you stay in the cab.' Women as well would be on the side of the tracks and the coal was spewing out and they were coming in droves to get it. There's still this community there now.

Karmen Thomas: I've always liked that, where I've lived in Wales, that slightly anarchic attitude towards the police: 'Don't you push me around. Don't you tell me what to do. Who the hell are you? Just because you're wearing a uniform,' that sort of thing. You sorted things out yourself, to a certain degree.

Phil Cullen: There were things that were then going on in South Wales which put people's backs up. There was a licensed mine up in Tumble which was allowed to work. There was a briquette, smokeless fuel, plant down in Bynea which was allowed to work. And the NUM had done a deal that those men could go in to work; we wouldn't picket them, we would allow them to work, we wouldn't stop the lorries going in or anything, provided they gave us some coal, and we would then give that coal to the old in our communities, and to the aged.

Now, that sounds very compassionate, but if you're a miner who's on strike and you don't understand the deal that's been made – because it wasn't explained to people, it was all hush-hush and all the rest of it – and you're going there and you can see somebody who's working in a licensed mine, it becomes frustration, and it allows cynical views to develop within the area.

Ron Davies: There was a horrible rally, meeting, whatever it was, down in Port Talbot, when Neil Kinnock was shouted down and booed. It was a difficult time for him, but I think he realised that the strike and Militant would be defining issues for him.

Siân James: We got to about the August of the strike and that's when we started to realise that the strike was going to be on for a lot longer, because here we were now. We'd been on strike five months and it was a glorious summer, and I remember walking the children up to my grandmother's and walking back, and seeing a lot of the young miners sitting on the fence, on the wall of our estate, 'How's it going, what's happening?' and saying, 'What do you think's going to happen next, then? God, it's been a long time, hasn't it,' you know. And MacGregor would be making noises by this point about the enemy within, which Margaret Thatcher had called us, so there was a great sense of uncertainty at this point, 'What happens next?' And one of the lads, Carl, turned round and said, 'I think we'll be out on strike at Christmas.' I can remember going home and thinking, 'Christmas? That's another four months, isn't it?'

I walked into the house and I said to Martin, 'Carl Owen thinks we're going to be on strike at Christmas,' and Martin said, 'I think he's right,' and that was the moment where I think mentally, I thought, 'We're digging in now.' We've had the attacks. And I remember thinking, 'If I'm the enemy within, I'm going to be the best enemy that she's ever had. I'm going to show her what enmity means. She'll be sorry she called us the enemy within.' And I think that was the moment where I stepped up a gear and I accepted that we would have to do more. Whatever we'd done previously, we'd have to do more. And whatever it took. I think that was a very crystallising moment for us as a family. If it meant breaking the law, we would break it, you know. We'd just gone through to a war.

Christine Powell: I was teaching, so once the August came, I could now do what I wanted to do, which was to take a greater part in the actual fundraising. During that time, I went on the women's mass picket to the steelworks at Margam. We were in this now for the duration. In our local area we were lucky, because we'd been very successful in fund-raising: there were a thousand food parcels going out a week. We'd have a meeting every Sunday, lodge officials would come and perhaps there'd be somebody with a particular hardship, who we were able to help. We were really lucky in this area and we were solid. My telephone developed some rather weird clicking noises.

Ken Smith: Men from St John's went to Margam to picket and then went to court over it and were acquitted eventually. Picketing was seen as a very legitimate tactic and it was about one workforce to another workforce, as opposed to things like dropping bricks, which don't rely on collective solidarity and strength. I was down at the picket lines and we mobilised women to come on the picket line. There were a lot of people who said, 'You can't do this, you can't do that,' at the time: we said, 'Well, we're all part of the strike now, the women won't be on the front line, but if you get a mass picket with lots of women there that will work.'

In the Llynfi Afan group we didn't have a division of labour in that sense; we had miners going out delivering food parcels every week and collecting the money. We all did it, but we all went on picket lines and marches together as well.

Phil White: Men from St John's were on the Margam cranes, as were men from the other pits. I took a minibus full of the boys down, and the only reason why I didn't get there was because I was already charged under the Riot Act so I had to keep in the background.

Christine Powell: We had one person going back to work into Treforgan, but that didn't last very long, as far as I recall. I can't remember anybody going into Blaenant. But emotions were high because the men who were out were sacrificing a lot. And although it's always been my gut feeling to never forgive a scab, I never understood why I felt like that until I was on a panel speaking in Pontardawe Arts Centre. Somebody from the floor asked about the term 'scabs' and another panellist, I think he was from Cynheidre, said, 'When you're working underground, you're depending upon each other. Everybody's got to look out for everybody else because of the hostile environment in which you're working.' And he said, 'If somebody's let you down that badly, how the hell can you ever trust them again?'

Arfon Evans: People talk about how there were pickets on the line in Maerdy; I was never aware of any pickets on the line in Maerdy because we didn't need them. We didn't need them at all. We came out unified and, when we went back to work in 1985, we went back unified.

We had people from Maerdy who had fought in the Spanish Civil War – a miner called Franky Owen died out there at the Battle of Brunete. As a lodge we were committed internationalists.

Phil Cullen: South Wales was not the same right the way across the coalfield. At Cynheidre, we had a massive problem with men returning to work. It must be realised that these men, the worst of these scabs, had already been on strike for nine months. Since then, I've worked in other industries: before I went back to university, I worked in the engineering industry, and you couldn't have got them out for eight hours, never mind eight months. Some of those men, not all of them, were really suffering financial hardship when they went back to work. The bottom line was that we had a big problem in Cynheidre; why did we have a problem in Cynheidre? Because if you're living in a village like Penrhiwceiber or Maesteg St John's in the Valleys, you would have to be suicidal to go back to work. You would have to be a bit of a nutcase. You've got to think of your family, your kids in school – they were all in the same schools, they were all doing the shopping in the same shops, they were going to the same pubs – the whole social infrastructure of Penrhiwceiber Colliery was within a mile and a half of the village of Penrhiwceiber.

You had this unity that you were never going to get in a pit like Cynheidre. In Cynheidre, we had men from Carmarthen who were working there, we had men from Swansea, men from the Gower and men coming from Llanpumsaint. They didn't all even speak the same language. Totally split. People would go to work and they'd go home and they'd go to their shopping, they'd go out socially with their friends, and they wouldn't see another miner, or only one or two that they were on nodding terms with.

Karmen Thomas: Our location in Ammanford played a part in the fact that things didn't get too hairy, because the Betws pit was on the edge of the coalfield, though different miners did go at different times in the night and travelled; whenever there was talk of massive police presence building up at a particular mine, men would get together and travel up to those mines to support those areas. That happened a lot. The actual networking was very good, considering it was pre-computers, pre-mobile phones. It's amazing how quickly information got back. Many people didn't have their own phones. Lots of things were phoned in to the Miners' Welfare Hall. I didn't have a phone at home. I used to get messages from a phone box; the kids used to hang out by the phone box and I used to give the phone box number as my phone, and they'd then take the message, that was my phone. It was paid for by BT.

Phil Cullen: Our phones were being tapped. When I picked up the receiver, you'd hear beep-beep-beep, you'd hear a pipping noise. We had a little bit of fun with the authorities. We found out that there was a group of scabs meeting at a pub just outside Swansea in Morriston and we were talking on the phone, saying that we were organising a real ruck down there and we would give them a right kicking, and organising five or six buses, we were going to have them today. Two of us went down in the car, and we sat there, having a cup of coffee, and the police all turned up in their riot vans and there was no one there. We'd sold them a pup. We did lots of things to them which would make you laugh. There was a funny side to it as well. Some say people like myself had lost the plot. We were working harder in the strike than we ever did in work. It was that we didn't want to be beaten.

Siân James: I kept saying to my husband, 'Martin, is there anything you need me to do?' 'No, nothing I need you to do,' and then one day, I'd bumped into somebody I knew from the local village, in Abercraf, and she said, 'Where've you been?' and I said, 'What do you mean, where've I been? What am I supposed to have done?' and she said, 'Well, we're getting ourselves sorted out and there's a support group and we need people to come out and help in Abercraf.' I said, 'Alright.' I came home and I said to Martin, 'Why didn't you tell me?' and he said, 'Well, I didn't think you'd be interested.' And I said, 'That's not fair!' That's how I got involved with the bigger support group then, through the local set-up, and I think the really interesting thing about our support group was that there were three valleys that got together, the top ends of three smaller valleys.

Suddenly you get this opportunity to go to the main meeting, and that was really liberating, because there were three rules. The first rule was all monies were to be pooled. If you had a very wealthy cousin who lived in X and he was sending money down for your local support group, thank you, but it's got to go into the main pot.

Second rule was everybody gets the same out, regardless of circumstances. We're not means-testing anybody, which is really important for those people who had parents and grandparents who had very bad memories of the 1926 strike: soup kitchens and being on the parish register. The third rule was – and this was the exciting one for the women – if you turned up for a meeting, you got a vote. There was none of this you've got to be elected and you've got to be on the lodge and you've got to be a representative, or you're there in your capacity as such and such. You were there in your capacity as you.

Karmen Thomas: It was a lot of work, because there was a lot of stress, but there were some really good highlights, as well. We had people coming down from London, this bunch of Jamaicans coming down in a van with loads of vegetables. British Jamaicans, they were so stoned, it was untrue. It was like almost a caricature image. They brought down all these amazing amounts of vegetables, a vanload, vegetables people hadn't seen before, like plantain, 'What the hell do you do with these?' 'They're bananas but they don't taste like bananas.' And they came down a few times.

That was good, such different cultures meeting up for an evening: there were no ethnic minorities in Ammanford. We'd give them food; they'd receive the local Welsh hospitality, 'Before you go back to London, you've got to have some food and a couple of pints.' This was before drink-driving was at the point of being enforced. There was one guy, a friend of mine, who lived nearby who had moved in, who used to refer to himself as the only black man in the Valleys. Even the Indian restaurant, the guys who worked there came from Swansea and used to come up on the bus and then go back on the last bus, which is why they shut at the time they did. So those evenings when we had these big vanloads of veg and other foodstuffs were really quite strange highlights.

Christine Powell: There was definitely a community. And it wasn't just the community of us within the support group: it was the people who supported the support group. We had a lot of people who loved coming down to visit us, the Lesbians and Gays Support the Miners were a case in point, and then we had situations where people from other coalfields were really having a bad time of it, and we'd fund them to come down to us for a weekend. The Durham Colliery Mechanics' Association came down once, and, boy, what a weekend that was.

Adam Price: During the strike there were incredibly articulate leaders, that autodidact culture still had more than vestiges, but I can remember going to the Miners' Welfare in Ammanford; the library had long gone but there was a book rack as you went into the bar, which had 'Knowledge is Power' on it, but it lay empty, and there were no books there. What an incredibly evocative image.

I think the strike had its own dynamic and its own reality, which was about that particular time, but it also did reconnect with earlier generations of struggle and tradition. I was fourteen at the time, and I was active in the strike, but also then and in the years subsequently getting interested in all this: during that period in the mid-1920s a workers' soviet was created for a few weeks in Ammanford. The forces of the state were repulsed from the Amman Valley for several weeks, and it became very tense to say the least and was known as the Battle of Pontamman. It's disappeared from wider consciousness. I met people during the strike, some of whom were my neighbours, who were members of the Communist Party, who actually were there as boys in Pontamman as the battle was happening: the Battle of Pontamman.

Steve Eaves: When the Miners' Strike started, week one was this kind of state of shock for everybody. Week two, a group of us, me and other members of Cymdeithas, organised and made sure that there were door-to-door collections of food from the second week of the strike to

293

the end of the strike. That was a huge undertaking, because we were all young parents, we had little children, so it was a hell of a thing, coming home from work and playing a little bit with the kids and then off out to collect, knocking on doors and asking for food for the miners. During the daytime I was working in the centre of Bangor. We had a stall by the clock on Bangor high street, collecting for the miners, asking people coming from the Tesco, which was in the centre of Bangor at the time, 'Oh, could you spare a tin or two for the miners?'

We kind of instigated from the North and then it was wholeheartedly embraced by Cymdeithas across Wales. Ffred Ffransis was arranging holidays for the miners' kids, and we had miners' kids coming up from the Valleys, and what a little bunch of buggers they were. They came up in a minibus, all the way from Abernant in the Rhondda, throwing stuff out of the windows and putting fingers up to everybody. They'd never been to Llanberis and Caernarfon. Throughout the strike, we had, every second week, a bus that would come up from the coalfield to fill up with the food we'd collected. I had a room in the house that was full, from the door to the back wall and floor to ceiling, with food for the miners. There are some nice photos of the miners who stayed here overnight with us, before driving back.

Siân James was the wife of one of the guys who came here every other week to collect food, and she was a housewife at the time, and the strike galvanised her, and she became another person: she became emancipated by the strike.

Siân James: At this point we're fundraising, very traditional stuff, selling raffle tickets, selling door-to-door, collecting donations, organising a jumble sale up in Abercraf, because we were very proud. Our little support group in Abercraf wanted to send money every week, because we were one of the smallest. Neath, Ystradgynlais and Brynwith, these places had 200, 300 miners on strike in each one of those places. In Ynyswen they had about thirty-six. They were small numbers, but we wanted to do our bit. I remember going to the local doctor and his wife giving us a sackful of clothes, and me eying her up and down – she was a lovely lady, but she was very, very thin, very, very slender. I picked the sack up from her home, I thought, 'Cor, there'll be nothing here to scavenge for us,' because she was tiny. Immaculately tailored, immaculately, and it was the whole idea that somebody living in our community could actually shop in the shops in London. She was very, very supportive: 'I've got a bag full of clothes here, would you like them?' 'Oh, yes, please!' They'd been giving every week, and they'd been giving food and they'd been giving money.

It was very disparate people who were supporting us. You never had to remind old age pensioners. As you'd go up the path, the door would open and they would say, 'Ah, Siân, my mother, when I was a girl, used to tell us about what it was like, so we're not going back there again.' They were great and they gave weekly what they could. They'd have a little bag with four Welsh cakes in, and they'd say, 'These are for you, Martin and the children,' or 'I've made some tarts this week,' or 'I got an extra quarter-pound of tea, Siân, would you like it?' They were very, very aware in that way. You never had to remind those older members of the community. Even the English people who'd come to live there, they were quite bemused by it but they would donate and they would buy.

James Dean Bradfield: I remember a box being put down outside Oakdale School, and the children that were part of striking families, of which there were many, were allowed to pick up cans from the box and take them home. That would be a political statement now, wouldn't it? You wouldn't be allowed to do that, I think. The *Mail* or the *Express* would say, 'Why are they giving food parcels out at this school? You're paid to teach, not to preach.' Kids would pick up cans and take them home to striking families that weren't getting wages. So suddenly, it's like, 'Fuck, they're taking a can of Campbell's Chunky Chicken back home with them for tea.'

Steve Eaves: In Cymdeithas we were in constant conflict with the Labour Party, because they wouldn't join us: they wouldn't join us in the food collection because someone had said it's run by nationalists. I was working in the council at Bangor. I knew all the Labour councillors; they were my employers. I knew the Labour mentality, I'd grown up with people with the Labour mentality, but they wouldn't join in with the Cymdeithas support for the strike.

We organised a speaking tour for miners and the NUM leaders from South Wales to come; the Labour councillors wouldn't support it because we'd organised it. Totally, totally tribal. But they weren't doing anything themselves. I was constantly arguing with these people, 'Why don't you join in? It doesn't matter. It doesn't matter who comes to collect, getting the food is the thing. We can talk about ideas after.'

Ffred Ffransis: In Cymdeithas this was perceived by us as a strike, not so much for wages, not so much for living conditions, but for communities, for the survival of communities. And we were all kind of saying, 'Hang on, that's what we're doing as well. We're fighting for the survival of communities as well.'

We had all sorts of meetings, down in the South Wales Valleys, people who'd never been together in the same meetings. Members of the Labour Party in the Valleys and members of Cymdeithas came up to me, 'Who are these people?' looking at each other and so on. I remember one chat with Kim Howells and he gave the impression that he was very supportive at the time.

Menna Elfyn: I remember being part of the work we did in Cymdeithas during the Miners' Strike, in getting food, in giving holidays to miners' children. We had two to stay in my home; it was a time of generosity and people opening their homes. I was also on the picket line in Abernant and the bus was coming with people going to work and people were so angry, and I felt for both sides.

Ffred Ffransis: Cymdeithas yr Iaith did all sorts of things for the miners and people criticised it: 'What's this got to do with the language?' We went back to that basis of building alliances. There was the big other radical issue of 1984, the milk quotas which were destroying the agricultural communities, so we facilitated many milk producers going from the rural Welsh-speaking areas to the Valleys to give out free milk to support the miners and they were all up for this.

Down in Carmarthenshire, members of families who supported Cymdeithas yr Iaith paid for a fifty-seater coach to bring children of miners from the Valleys over to this area for their holidays. They wouldn't have any other holiday, and we spent the week taking them around the area and they had great holidays. The families were so grateful and kept in contact afterwards.

Part 4: Policing the Strike

National media coverage grew increasingly unsympathetic to the strike. A historical and continual criticism of Wales is its lack of robust domestic media, a position that the social conditions of the strike brought into acute focus. The tabloid press depicted Scargill as an out-of-control caricature, while television news reports concentrated on the difficulties the police experienced in their attempts to maintain order. The one-sided nature of the coverage left many in mining communities exasperated, as their experience of the strike, and the manner in which it was policed in particular, was absent from the conventional media narrative.

Leanne Wood: The strike was all you knew, so there was nothing to compare it to. It was just normal, and it's only looking back now, years later, that you can see how abnormal a time it was, and how weird the whole thing was. I think it was as if there were two stories going on: there were the stories that people were telling you in the community about the kind of strength of the miners and the unions and how we

297

were going to defeat this and the whole network of people that were organising food distribution and having to take in tins and vegetables for other people in your class, because it was all well organised. And then the news and the TV, which was like a completely different story. It was the opposite; it was like looking at things in a photographic negative. You were seeing Thatcher triumphant and how the police were going to smash the miners and all of that kind of rhetoric.

Bob Croydon: I can remember being involved in an exercise which analysed the language that was used in the reporting on television, where the bias against the miners was, where the BBC would give very negative coverage of disturbances on the picket line. I remember sitting there with a ring thing, counting the number of times, where it was always implied that the violence was coming from the miners. That subtle use of language which implied that the miners had kicked off, not the police. And a more balanced view was taken on independent television – ITN.

Leanne Wood: Being eleven, as I was at the time, I remember being confused and also experiencing a big kind of awakening moment around the role of the police. When you're a child, you're taught that the police are there to keep order and keep everybody safe, and if you were in trouble, you could end up being in trouble with the police, but generally, they were a force for good and they were looking after us all. And then the Miners' Strike happened and there they were on TV, beating up people who were my fellow community people. To try and make sense of what the truth was in that situation, my instinct was to believe the people in my community, obviously, but it was confusing for a child.

Eluned Morgan: I was about sixteen, seventeen at the time. I assumed that everybody in South Wales was pro-miners, and I remember going into a shop in the centre of Cardiff with my little Coal Not Dole badge on and being shoved out of the shop, which was a really strange experience, because I assumed that everyone was on the miners' side. You knew that something fundamental was going on and there was a fight for survival of an industry and a sector.

Lesley Smith: There was definitely a very strong movement in the Dulais valley to support the Miners' Strike, and to support the miners' families, not the strike itself, but there was also resentment around about it. One of my neighbours moaned because the miners were going round collecting money and then they'd go and have a pint in the club once a week.

Mary Winter: Our neighbours became quite resentful of the strike and of people like myself who were supporting the strike. They were of an age where they were able to take redundancy and they were actually reasonably well-off. But there was a growing feeling at this time, as we said in our communities, 'Come on, boys, we can do something here.'

Lesley Smith: There are sometimes rose-coloured glasses about the past and there definitely was camaraderie in the mining industry – there had to be, you were down in a hole with somebody for hours – but there wer also the normal things you'd see in any other place,. One family would hate another family; one family would be jealous of another family; somebody would have a car. There were the Chapel-goers versus the Church-goers versus the non-religious. All these things are perhaps highlighted more because we're in small Valleys communities.

Christine Powell: Our codeword for picketing was 'We're going on a sponsored swim.' We had the phone calls: we're going on a sponsored swim. A bus picked me up, we went down to the Margam steelworks at Port Talbot and a coachload of us got off. There were a couple of pickets that were there permanently, so we went over and said hiya to them, and then a load of police turned up. I think they were surprised about how many women were there. The things that stand out in my mind that day are that we were wandering around, and as we walked up towards the houses, this chap came out of his house and he said, 'Oi!' and I thought we were going to take a pile of abuse, and he said, 'Oh, if any of you ladies want to use the loo. There we are, just go round the corner there, and there, you can use my loo, no problem.' That was lovely.

Then, as we walked back towards the steelworks gates, there were two women police officers walking in the opposite direction, and that was the summer that PC Yvonne Fletcher was killed, and as they walked past us, there was myself, Hefina Headon and Edwina Roberts, both of whom are no longer with us and, as we walked past them, one of the WPCs said, 'Oh, they're no better than those people that killed Yvonne Fletcher.' Thank God Edwina was between Hefina and myself because we had one arm each to hold her down. But that was the attitude.

We were lining the road coming out of the steelworks, so there was our line and the police facing us and there was a certain amount of laughing and joking going on, then suddenly the atmosphere changed and the lorries came out. There was a lot of fruity language being heard, and all I could manage was, 'I hope your bloody transmission fails on the motorway.' The policeman that was looking straight at me, I could see him laughing, because amongst all the language that was going on around that counted as humour.

Some of the men had gone further down the road and set fire to the gorse, so there was smoke blown across the motorway. We milled around a bit and then a lot of us women crossed the road onto a roundabout and a pile of police followed us. I can remember standing on the roundabout and there was this young policeman in front of me. Either a policeman or from the Army and he was standing there with his fists clenched by his side and his knuckles were white, and his jaw was gritted. I remember thinking to myself, 'I'm glad the policemen in this country aren't armed.'

Then everybody wandered back off the roundabout, and then the cars started going around it and I hadn't got across the road, so I was stuck there on my own with thirteen police officers – and I know it was thirteen because I counted them. So at one point in the strike, I had thirteen police officers looking after me.

Phil Cullen: They were paying people that had gone back to work in cheque form, because they couldn't do anything else. Then, at Cynheidre they told the men they would pay them in cash, provided they held the notes against the windows of the buses as they drove out through the picket lines: 'Look at me, I've got money to take home to my family.'

The police overtime was rubbed in our faces all the time. I saw buses driving past us on the picket line out of that mine with £10 notes being held against the windows of the bus. We knew who they were, because the Coal Board were telling us who they were. They were providing us with a list every morning of the men who had gone back to work. It was that bad. Let there be no ambiguity about it: it was vicious. They used every dirty tactic in the book.

Bob Croydon: At that time I was involved with a residential estate agency and the chief inspector of the Vale of Glamorgan wanted to buy a house, literally across the road. He came into the office and he looked at a house on Cyncoed Road, and I said, 'Oh, funnily enough, one of your guys looked at it yesterday; it was a constable.' This guy was having an angst about buying a house and a constable was thinking about buying one further up the road, because they were on such ridiculous overtime, and they were sleeping on the buses and eating chips and trousering all the money.

Phil Cullen: They bought houses out of it. And there was no doubt that that didn't go down very well in the communities around.

301

Bob Croydon: The rank and file coppers couldn't have enough of it and the government was shovelling the money towards them. They were dressing troops as policemen as well, but that's always part of the great myth: you could never actually prove that. But there seemed to be a hell of a lot more policemen on the picket lines up in the Valleys with no signs of any diminution in their badge numbers than were giving me speeding tickets in Cowbridge.

Christine Powell: It's a myth I subscribe to. Somebody that was known locally had gone off to the Army and there he was, in a Met uniform, facing one of the striking miners.

James Dean Bradfield: That's when the myth-making starts getting a bit too heavy. Some people were in Cardiff and they saw exactly the same police officers, dressed up in Army uniform in Cardiff.

Phil White: A friend of mine who worked at St John's Colliery went into the police force; his brother was on strike. He said, 'Beware of the ones wearing no badges on their lapels.' It became very commonly known, and if you look at any old archive photographs, look at the no lapel numberings. There's no doubt about it whatsoever: of course they were soldiers.

You don't become [a policeman] overnight; one policeman turned into five. It had to be four others besides our one policeman.

Phil Cullen: There were Army elements being used – there were people on the picket lines without numbers on their lapels. There were things going on we have no idea about. And they played a really dirty game.

James Dean Bradfield: During the strike we knew that there was something bigger at play, when you have lots of police officers being drafted in from the West Country and you can actually hear it, the burr in their voices. You know that something bigger is happening; they're actually drafting in police from over the border. You won't find it in any records, but they were bussed down. I heard it; I heard the West Country policemen walking round. I don't know if that's fine in terms of resources, but you know that your small part of the country is being dragged into something bigger.

Phil Cullen: They brought the Met in. At the time, our plod had blue shirts; the Met had white shirts, and we knew straight away that the Met was there and they had the Met in Cynheidre, and they had them down in this holiday park at St Ishmael; they hired the whole place. When we'd come in in the morning to picket we'd hear them. They'd have their riot shields and it was dark – it was very intimidating. You'd hear them, they'd bang their batons against the shields, boom-boom-boom-boom, and it was very, very frightening. It's unbelievable what went on, unbelievable. It was war.

Richard Frame: I got to know some of the police afterwards and of course they had a really great time. A lot of them paid for their extensions and their holidays and new cars. The police enjoyed it. And people, they remember that sort of thing, especially up in the Valleys in those small communities. It was terrible, what they were expected to go through.

Bob Croydon: The trauma that it wrought in the Valleys communities and the mining communities was very, very long-lasting. 'Scab' is an emotive term, but there were certainly very deep-rooted divisions.

Phil Cullen: There was one guy that had gone back to work and he would stand by a bridge in Llanelli, Union Bridge, and this guy used to stand in a phone box and be collected in a minibus and then ferried in to a certain part of town with a police escort which would bring him up to the colliery; it was like a military campaign. They'd have outriders bringing them up in the convoy. The cost must have been astronomical.

This was going on in every pit with men who were going back to work, and one particular morning the pickets found out where he was hiding. They went into the phone box at about four o'clock in the morning, snipped the cable, so that he couldn't make a phone call, put a chain outside on the floor with a wedge and a lock, and as he went in, the door was closed, and he was chained in the phone box and a wedge put down. The guy couldn't get out so he didn't go into work that day. He was let out later in the afternoon by having a lady wanting to use the phone, and she went up and phoned the police, and that's how they got him out.

There were lots of things that went on like that. One particular morning, the pickets obtained forty gallons of waste oil from the washery and poured it all down on the main road. You came down a very steep up and down hill on the one way to Cynheidre. They poured the oil on one side of the road entrance. Then at the other entrance they took some telegraph posts which had been left by BT on the side of the road and they built a barricade. The buses couldn't get up the hill on one side and then they couldn't bring the buses in on the other side, so they had to physically march these boys into work, but they wouldn't come in; they refused to get off the buses. It was a shambles.

Some men were wasters before the strike and they were wasters after the strike. One of the things that I found rather distasteful is that if you're going to treat people badly, you treat them all badly. There was somebody who had gone back to work who played rugby for Tumble, and he was a bit of a hero before the strike; he'd be left alone. But other people would get a dog's life, and I've always found that distasteful. Either you treat them all the same or you don't bother at all.

Siân James: We had various run-ins with the school about school dinner money, making the children stand up because they hadn't paid their school dinner money. We were a little bit at war now, I was saying, 'Powys County Council can stuff it; I'm not paying school dinner money,' and my kids were quite happy to say it: 'Haven't got the money, Miss!' But they got really, really shitty about this. Our local councillor was a farmer, Gwyn Gwilym, and he was Mayor of Powys and sat on various committees. And he was on strike: he worked as a miner, because farming was different in our valley.

Adam Price: There were incredible scenes with the Dyfed Farmers' Action Group, which were another dimension. John Howard was one of Wales's leading Marxist farmers, an incredibly electrifying speaker, making this connection between the struggle of the farmers and the struggle of the miners, with an almost Latin American sense of the politics of the peasantry. In Welsh, 'y werin' doesn't have any of that residue of snobbishness that the term 'peasant' has in English; *'paysan'* doesn't have that in any other language, but in English it does. There was a class politics to farming; farmers and miners have had a chequered past in terms of their political relationships in times past, as had the language movement, the national movement and the union movement. History accelerates when these currents come together and suddenly you're in a fast-flowing stream and it's difficult quite fully to describe it if you're not in it.

Siân James: Possibly the only thing I've ever agreed with Emlyn Williams on, and he took a lot of flak for this, but Emlyn used to describe the miners in the Swansea area and up towards Garnant as peasantry, and he didn't mean that in any derogatory term, come shearing, come lambing and come the harvest, half the collieries were empty. Nobody thought it was odd that these men all worked in mines, because they had to supplement the farming, and at that point, even the farmers we grew up with were pretty supportive of the strike.

I was appearing on TV and had a couple of what I call cosmic experiences. We'd been on Gay Pride, which is covered in the film *Pride* and we'd spent a lot of time with our gay friends in London, and my children adored the friends that we had there and they adored our children; they were very, very good to our children. We'd been up on this march and, on the following Monday, the children were asked to say in school, where they had been. My son Rhodri said, 'Oh, Miss, we was on Gay Pride, and we made banners and we marched and we waved our banners!' and one kid said, 'What's Gay Pride?' and I was called into the headmaster's office and I was told that my child had embarrassed the teacher, because the teacher did not know how to explain this to the class. We'd had a couple of incidents where my father was supposed to be picking the children up and then remembering very late, and the headmaster had had to stay behind because we 'had been so inconsiderate', so my dad had gone, 'Oh, I'm ever so sorry, they'd made arrangements for me to pick the children up,' and then, when I went down to the school the next time, I was called into the office and I was told, and these were the immortal words, 'When is this nonsense going to stop, Mrs James?' I said, 'What nonsense is that, then?' There was a massive slanging match which resulted in me telling him what I thought of him as a teacher, and then him making excuses to me. The children are still friends with the children that they knew there, where there were wonderful teachers who taught my children that we have very fond memories of, but I think they couldn't cope with the changes in us.

Adam Price: People were having these incredibly intense conversations and saying, 'Oh, right, that happened to you as well,' and seeing things in each other's experience and then re-translating them back to their own.

All of that was happening and it was like a mass open-air political workshop at times. I was a fourteen-year-old going down to London, sleeping on the floors of SWP members and anarchists in London and being immersed in it all. I was quite tall, so they thought I was a miner and I'd often have a pint bought for me. It was the best of times, it was the worst of times. In so many ways.

Siân James: I was in a gay club in London, talking to people about politics and their politics and how they felt and how they've been belittled in their lives and demeaned, passed over, told that they will never amount to anything because of their sexuality; and you're thinking, 'Why are we treating people like this? This is not human beings showing support.' Then when you're talking to mothers on estates in Brixton and they're telling you about Sus and they're telling you about their children and how they feel the Metropolitan Police is being utilised against them. How they'd only ever known cuts, cuts and more cuts in their community.

Christine Powell: AIDS was obviously prevalent in '84 when LGSM [Lesbians and Gays Support the Miners] came down to support us, and people who were suffering were being treated terribly.

Adam Price: My parents went to stay up near Blaenau Ffestiniog during the strike, as a bit of respite, and experienced that strong connection between the slate-quarrying areas and those who worked in the nuclear industry in the north-west as well, that was a really strong bond, and that felt new. That was a new dimension as well.

Tecwyn Vaughan Jones: I was living in Cardiff during the strike, but I'd go home every month to Blaenau and there was a tremendous effort there. The community was so supportive of the miners, and my mother was taking food every week, and because I was earning a good salary in Cardiff, she thought that I could give £5 to them, and she made me give money every time I went home. My mother was no supporter of the Labour Party, but it wasn't done in the name of the Labour Party; it was done in the name of the community, and that made a difference. I was quite happy to do that and on a Saturday morning help fill up boxes. The enthusiasm was extraordinary. Thatcher was absolutely and utterly reviled in a place like Blaenau Ffestiniog.

Kim Howells: In the NUM we sent people up to picket the nuclear power stations in North Wales, and the links that we created with Blaenau Ffestiniog and Anglesey were very important. We had these discussions and joint initiatives, which certainly had not happened in my lifetime, between young workers in South Wales and North Wales. We worked bloody hard at that. And there were some great people, especially in Blaenau Ffestiniog, men and women who sustained those links for a very long time. I used to go up there a lot, partly because I was trying to keep a grip on the way that we were picketing some of these places, especially the nuclear power stations, which were continuing to churn out electricity when it seemed to me the only way of gaining any concessions, let alone winning the strike, was to stop the power stations since they were the great big market for coal. Going up there and meeting people who were involved in all sorts of other political activities was a real eye-opener for me.

Neil Kinnock: Strength, confidence, integrity, the identity of people related to their work, the places of work and the nature of the work; nothing produces stronger identity or stronger men and women than coal mining, both because of its physical demands but also because of its dangers and its total dependence on cooperation and teamwork, and that produces a culture of community which is very, very strong. It was shattered by the way in which, first of all, the strike itself drove thousands of families deep into poverty, and then indeed into destitution, so that whole families were dependent on charity food, because there was no other source of feeding themselves.

Part 5: The Autumn and Winter of 1984

Siân James: We're getting now into the September, October, and this is where we're starting to hear the people saying, 'I can't cope any more, I've got to go back. The bills are huge. I'm going to have the house repossessed,' and you're starting to see the cracks, and that's when we had to put in additional support.

We'd had an awful incident in Ystradgynlais where a shopkeeper – a woman – had put a sign up saying, 'Miners' wives need not ask for credit, as it will not be given.' That didn't last for long; not after she'd had two dozen women picketing outside, and when the elderly people were coming along and being told what she'd done and turning straight around and refusing to go into the shop. She soon pulled that down, and said it was a joke.

Phil Cullen: At Cynheidre there was a mass picket there and lots of people were picketing from all over the place, who'd have seen us being a big Achilles' heel. But interestingly, it wasn't the only Achilles' heel. There was another one over in East Wales and that had a big movement back to work. Abernant, they had about nineteen men going in. They tried to have this big thing across South Wales where they all went back at the same time on this particular morning – it had all been planned – it was the South Wales Back to Work Group that did it. It was planned by various individuals representing the Coal Board.

Siân James: You were starting to see the fracturing; you were starting to gently see it. This is where I also start to diverge from the rosy-tinted spectacle view of the strike, where everybody was united. I lost my best friend, the very best friend I had, during the strike. I announced that I was going to Greenham Common in this period and she'd come up for a cup of coffee, and they were quite a wealthy couple and she said, 'What you doing on the weekend?' 'Oh,' I said, 'I'm really excited: I'm going to Greenham Common! Going up to Greenham again. It's great when you go to Greenham, loads of energy and you see loads of people and you meet really interesting people!' 'Greenham Common? What you go to Greenham Common for?' and then she said, 'You're not one of those Ban the Bombs are you?' and I said, 'Yeah!' and we'd never talked about that; we'd never talked about me being a member of CND, because that's not what we talked about. We picked the boys up from rugby, that sort of thing. And she said, 'I think Mrs Thatcher's right about that lot.' Bang! I thought, 'Wow, I didn't know this fundamental thing about this person. I really thought I knew this person, and I don't! Does this person know so little about me?' and then you realise that you didn't have that sort of relationship. After that, I gave up, I wasn't that person any more, and I wasn't that person who was prepared to not talk about those things.

Phil Cullen: People were worn down, people were weak. It didn't happen for eight months. It was fracturing. They could see other people drifting back to work in England, every news bulletin that came on, for the whole year. I've never seen anything like it before. It was as though the rule of law had been put aside. The police were actually stopping us on the road, on our lawful business. I've seen it with my own eyes; it was perverse. Lorries taken from quarries and open-cast coalmines which weren't taxed, which weren't insured, had bald tyres, and police were giving them an escort from Port Talbot's deep-water harbour at Margam, all the way to Llanwern steelworks to keep it going and giving them a police escort up the M4.

Christine Powell: I didn't know this till years later, the NUT rep at the school I taught, the deputy head was NUT through and through and she said, people were coming up to her in schools saying: 'Do you realise Christine Powell's husband's a striking miner?' I didn't give a damn. A lot of people would surreptitiously give me a bit of money as they passed me in the corridor as they didn't want to be seen to be supporting me.

Tom Marston: Lorries of coal would be passing; they would actually force us off the road. The police escort would push you off the road. It's hard to believe when you saw the deprivation that some miners went through. I saw the Electricity Board breaking into my brother-in-law's house. And they were getting away with it; they weren't prosecuted. Oh, it was terrible.

Phil Cullen: Once you were convicted of a criminal offence, the Coal Board would immediately sack you. We had this huge residue of people who had been charged with a crime. Luckily, I wasn't charged; they couldn't prove what I did. It would have been assault at Margam steelworks and criminal damage at Cynheidre. And there were forty of us in there, the cells were full. We were packed in and they arrested us in the evening. They entered our homes without a warrant, and I was arm-locked against my fireplace with two policemen with my wife screaming the place down, then dragged out of that house in handcuffs, as if I'd murdered somebody. They had us in all night, and the NUM arranged solicitors to come down and within half an hour of the solicitors being there, we were all released without charge and without bail. They used the system in order to ensure that the rule of law only worked on their side, and they suspended it for everybody else.

Christine Powell: There were families that were practically living under martial law and people think you're exaggerating now, because they couldn't imagine it.

Phil Cullen: I'm not going to say that I've got a halo; I did very bad things to some of the scabs because I was out on strike and I was young, in my twenties, and I felt, 'If I can do it, they can do it.' I felt that some of the older ones were selling my job down the river, because they wanted us all to go back to work, so they could have a pay-off and then leave, which was exactly what happened.

Siân James: This is the point where the interest in the miners started to change and this is the point where the union had to change its attitude to the women, because now people were realising what was keeping the strike going was the women. There'd been this huge focus on picket lines, violence, action, men, go back to work, arguing, shouting on picket lines, and then all of a sudden, it was like, 'Hey-ho, what about these women who are raising money, cooking food, packing food parcels?' Suddenly, there were requests for women to be on platforms. This is where you're starting to see now, the stories starting to drift; the union's control of the story, and the management of the story, is now starting to drift. People are going off-message.

The kids carried on being friends, that didn't affect them, but there would be people in your village saying things like, 'That *Sun*'s got the right view of it: why doesn't that Arthur Scargill go back to work?' 'What? You read the *Sun*? Really?'

Karmen Thomas: People still read the papers, and they believed what they read in the papers. By then I'd been through the Greenham experience and I knew very well how much the papers lie through their teeth because they have their own agenda, so people started reading the stuff in their daily papers and there was a real push against Scargill – although I'm not a fan of Scargill, I can't imagine the pressure he was under, but he was also a glory man, and that was his downfall, to a certain degree.

The Thatcher propaganda machine worked very well on what they focused on to disrupt people and it's always the petty things that people pick up on and start deciding where they're being betrayed: the car he was driving, the holiday he was taking, what he'd bought in the supermarket – 'He can afford to buy this,' these sort of things which people pick up on and decide it becomes a major problem for them. The Thatcher government was very clever at that, at dividing the population.

According to documents released under the thirty-year rule,
the Conservative cabinet, and Margaret Thatcher in particular,
experienced one of their 'darkest moments' of the strike during
the month of October. The members of the mining officials' union,

NACODS, were balloted for strike action. The government assessed that a vote in favour of taking strike action would result in the introduction of a three-day week due to power shortages.

Phil Cullen: NACODS was the National Association of Colliery Overmen, Deputies and Shotfirers: they were the officials at the mine, who at one time had been NUM members, but had gone on a course to become firemen, deputies, and some of them had gone on to be overmen and some stayed as shotmen; they had their own union.

Phil White: We were stopping NACODS in their cars up at the pit, and they would listen to our reasoning. A number of them, more than one or two, were crying, because they knew themselves they should be out. Those NACODS were once NUM. It's very rare you went from a boy to a NACODS: you went from a boy as an NUM as a trainee to a NACODS. But that was the key. That, really, would have been the turning point if they had come out. It would have been, no doubt.

Ken Smith: A lot has come out that the Thatcher government was having a real wobble around that time, and if NACODS had come out, the strike could have been ended quite quickly and on generally favourable terms. There was a big tactical question at the time about the TUC and how far the TUC could have been pushed as well.

Phil White: We had a number of skirmishes up in St John's when the NACODS took the vote to strike and then the NACODS leadership went against their membership. We spent a number of weeks up in St John's when it got quite hostile, trying to convince the NACODS, who were our colleagues: 'Look, boys, you have had a national ballot; you have voted to come on strike; you could save this situation,' and then a lot of hostility grew. An increased police presence incited that hostility, not us; the police incited that hostility.

The NACODS vote was September, but before that we had no involvement with the police other than our picketing as a lodge at Margam steelworks and any coal movement across the Bridgend and Neath–Port Talbot area.

Phil Cullen: Before you can go underground, it is a legal requirement that NACODS have got to inspect it and the deputies wouldn't cross the picket line. Even after the injunction, the High Court said we could have six pickets and I think we chose to have three. We would stop their bus coming in every morning; we'd say, 'Good morning, gents, this is an official picket line of the National Union of Mineworkers. We ask you to respect the picket line, please get going, so you can get back to bed as soon as possible,' and they'd jump off at the picket line; the driver would go and turn his bus round with our OK, thumbs up. He'd turn his bus round and they'd all get back on and we'd wave them off to go home to bed and all on full pay.

The scabs would all go in with a police escort and all the rest of it in the morning and then the NACODS boys would turn up on their bus, we'd turn that round, and then the people we were allowing into work would go in after, because they wouldn't have anything to do with the scabs.

Arfon Evans: We came to an agreement that the pit closure programme was presented by a hostile right-wing government, and above all, our main objective would be to keep the pits open, and therefore it would need NACODS and NUM safetymen to keep pits open. Let's say NACODS joined the strike, all their function, really, was to look at ventilation, roof and sides, which meant that the air was pure, no gas found, and that any falls in the ground would not block the ventilation.

They had a function under the Coal Mines Act, which was there by law, but could they be replaced? I think so. In fact, we had men ourselves; I used to inspect mines, we had people qualified to carry out the same function.

By Christmas 1984 the strain on mining communities living in deprivation was severe, despite which, of the twenty-six pits in Britain that remained free of strike breakers, twenty-one were located among the twenty-eight collieries of the South Wales coalfield. Incentives offered by the National Coal Board to return to work and a sustained media campaign of vilification towards the NUM leadership had led to an erosion in the integrity of the strike, which ended on the eve of its anniversary. On 3 March 1985, a year from the start of industrial action, the NUM's National Executive voted 98–91 in favour of a formal return to work. A year after the bitterest of protracted conflicts, it was estimated that 93 per cent of Wales' miners had remained on strike for its duration.

Phil Cullen: We thought if we could get the men over Christmas we would be laughing. We really thought that that was the hardest time, particularly with men with families and children, and they were relying on the support of friends, neighbours and other extended family to help out. We thought, 'Once we get them over that, we'll be right. It'll stem the tide back to work.' But it didn't. Once they came back to work, I think people had had that time to relax a bit, enjoy the normal things of life, and I think that destabilised the strike still further. And this drift continued: we started to get people going back to work who didn't want to go back at all, they weren't part of this Back to Work movement. They hadn't taken the union to court; they thought the strike had become a pointless exercise.

Christine Powell: I remember at Christmas we had a huge drive for presents: no child went without a present, no family went without a turkey. We'd had a visit in the summer from a journalist from Denmark and he stayed with my husband Stuart and me. He put an appeal in, he was a journalist for a Communist newspaper, and for a couple of weeks I'd come home every night, open my front door, and the postman had delivered boxes of toys for our kids from Denmark. It was absolutely overwhelming.

We were supported, over the Christmas period we went over to Parc and Dare Hall and the Flying Pickets did a concert for us. Afterwards we were all in the bar with the Flying Pickets; there was this feeling of belonging, of feeling safe, it really was a lovely feeling of solidarity and community.

Phil White: Families were still being supported by families; those families on strike were being supported by families, the support group, our monies were still coming in up to Christmas, it seemed. We had a bit of a 'Whoo' and let me say a lot of support for the Christmas appeal came from abroad, overseas, a lot of it did. We had a lot of that going on. My children, of course, they didn't get everything probably they would have had under normal circumstances of Christmas, but they didn't go without, either. Our families made sure of that, but don't get me wrong: it was bad, it was really bad for some. Not for everyone, but it was bad for quite – 'some' is maybe the wrong word – for a good number.

Arfon Evans: If Maerdy was the barometer for the British coalfield, I knew within weeks I was going to have trouble. Because families were starving; families were in debt; families were breaking up, marriages were being damaged. A twelvemonth strike: what more could you ask of anyone, when you knew that, around the corner, you weren't going to win? Around the corner, power stations had plenty of coal to go on another twelvemonth, and you knew you had a situation where your leadership weren't going to negotiate, and neither were the government, because it wasn't about the price of coal, it wasn't about an efficient coal industry; it was about smashing the strength of the NUM as the bastion of the trade union movement. Once they could smash the NUM, then anything that came behind – as we've seen – would be chickenfeed for them.

Phil Cullen: On the National Executive you had union leaders whose members were back in work full time. They weren't on strike, they were all back in work, except one or two, the Naughty Forty or the Dirty Thirty, but the Executive were voting to prolong the strike, while areas like South Wales and Scotland were asking the National Executive, 'What happens if we can't reach a negotiated settlement?' Sometimes the right wing tend to blame Arthur Scargill, that he didn't want to talk to the Coal Board. Rubbish. You can only negotiate with someone that wants to negotiate with you. It can't be a unilateral process. And they didn't. The Coal Board knew they had us by the short and curlies by this time and they weren't going to let us off the hook with any form of negotiated settlement.

Kim Howells: We bloody struggled to the end, but I think we certainly knew that the likelihood of winning was zilch. Had there been another government, then it would have been different, but that's nonsense. When I was in Parliament – I was there for twenty-one years – I used to meet people who had been sworn and mortal enemies through the strike, especially people like Heseltine, Norman Lamont, Ken Clarke. I talked a lot with Ken Clarke about what the government's position was exactly, and they never, never said, 'We were desperately worried we were going to lose out.' There was a determination that they were going to win this one.

Phil Cullen: Our people were going to the National Executive expressing legitimately that things are bad, people are really suffering, people are losing their homes, marriages are breaking down, people are divorced, communities are being split, and yet these people who are sitting pretty, whose members weren't on strike at all, were voting to prolong the strike. How can that be right?

Things got from bad to worse. We were accepting – I'm convinced, I've read the barrister's report – financial assistance from Libya to prolong the strike, because Gaddafi saw the British state as a problem, and anything he could do to cause problems for the British state, he would do it. There's no doubt in my mind that we were accepting money from places like Libya and this is in Hansard. Dennis Skinner pointed out: 'What is the difference between the British government importing Libyan oil to burn in our power stations on base load to defeat the miners, and the miners accepting Libyan cash in order to feed their families and prolong the strike? There is no difference: why be critical of it?' And the government were doing that: they were importing oil. But it went down quite badly with some of the men. Some of them didn't like it.

I remember then being in the Lodge office at Cynheidre as a picket, and it came on the news that a man had been killed, David Wilkie, a taxi driver, on the Heads of the Valleys road.

Richard Frame: I remember that business with the blokes chucking the bloody concrete slab onto the road; that was terrible. The other thing that was bad in Newport was someone who had a haulage company was breaking the strike and shipping coal in, or taking coal out via the river, and these were the lorries that the pickets were attacking. He then became chairman of the Newport Rugby Club, and even now, people still hold that against him; they remember that. Scargill was the wrong sort of bloke. He had a way of antagonising everybody; I met him a couple of times and he was very nice in person. Kim Howells was softly spoken, Welsh. It's all about bloody personalities unfortunately, and Scargill was the wrong sort.

Nicky Wire: The Miners' Strike was really fraught, because there was no escape from it. I remember, besides actually living in it, I'd always watch the news, and you'd have *Wales Today* on and Kim Howells would be interviewed. Kinnock was trying to dance around it all and it was so divisive, a really heavy atmosphere, imbued with violence. It wasn't social media violence; it was real violence: the dropping of the breeze block. It was fucking heavy and much as we all agreed and wanted the miners to win, it really felt like it was going down a hole that it was not going to get out of.

Phil Cullen: Two boys, Hancock and Shankland, had picked up a concrete post. It was just lying there, it was one of these concrete posts you see in the garden, I don't know why it was there, but it was and they flung it over the top and onto the dual carriageway and it killed the taxi driver who was taking the scab into work in Merthyr Vale. And the Home Secretary was on TV that morning, he said, 'This isn't strike action, this isn't picketing, this is murder.' They had the boys by the afternoon. Later on, I did a degree in law, and Hancock and Shankland is one of the cases that you do when it comes to the *mens rea* of murder: you've got the *actus reus* and the *mens rea* of murder, and it's one of the lead cases. You must understand Hancock and Shankland. That gave me a head start, on that course, because I could recite it better than the lecturers!

The jury found them guilty of murder; they were charged with murder, found guilty of murder, and they appealed. The House of Lords reduced the sentence to one of manslaughter, because of the simple element of *mens rea*, the guilt aforethought. The planning of it wasn't there. If they had planned to kill him, they would have killed him, not the taxi driver. They didn't have any intention to kill the taxi driver, but they clearly acted in a reckless way that could cause death, and that's unfortunately what happened.

That was the start of December. There were things like that towards the end of the strike. We had something like ten or twelve people, I believe, who were killed on picket lines during the strike. They were run over by lorries, some of them. And there were some that were run over by a police van; there were all sorts of things that went on. There's two sides of the coin: it wasn't just their side that died, people on our side died.

Part 6: The End of the Strike

Phil White: During the entire length of the strike at St John's we only had one scab return. He'd arranged to meet four of us to talk about not going back to work any more; we met with him, myself, the lodge secretary, the vice-secretary, and the secretary of COSA [Colliery Officials and Staffs Area]. Within two days the four of us received letters from the Coal Board stating that we had been part of an intimidation process against a returning miner, and we were sacked. Sacked within days, the four of us.

And we were very wary about going to this meeting, and we kept asking ourselves, 'But wouldn't it be great if we could have him back, wouldn't that be,' but what a set-up it was. And we were always wary of a set-up, and it was horrendous for the family, because at that time, when we were sacked, there was no chance, no talk of our reinstatement or anything, I'd given it all. To be on strike for a twelvemonth and then not having a job to go back to was very frightening.

Phil Cullen: The strike started to crumble really badly in places like Cynheidre. It was getting to be a bit intimidating, almost as many men in as there were out. The last week was just a shambles. By that time it was obvious even to people described as extremists, like myself: the strike was lost.

Phil White: Then St John's went back to work as one, under the banner.

The majority of the men didn't want to go back to work that first day under that banner without us, but by then Emlyn Williams had done a deal with the South Wales director, Philip Weekes, that he would reinstate all sacked miners, except for the two boys that killed the taxi driver, but he would reinstate everyone else, and he did. For two weeks the four of us were still out until we had our reinstatement back.

Ken Smith: Maerdy had nobody who crossed the picket line. There were very few who crossed the picket line in our area, and behind every one of those cases was a tragedy, a personal tragedy in some cases. It was people who had stuck out for eleven months, and you're never going to put them in the bracket of people like the UDM [Union of Democratic Mineworkers, a breakaway miners' union established in 1985] people in Nottinghamshire. The workforce went back as one at Maesteg St John's.

Phil White: But then we all went back as one. We genuinely didn't want to; we had the banner out, and we marched back. A very dark hour, half past six in the morning, just starting to break light and we walked through the gates. Very solemn it was, when we walked through. We stood back from having a brass band. Up in Maesteg that didn't quite fit the bill. We'd always come last in playing brass. It was a solemn affair, the way we seen it.

Siân James: We had very dear friends in Durham and, when they actually went back to work, the pecking order was if you had '52' painted on your helmet, you'd made the year of the strike. You only spoke to people who'd done fifty-two weeks. The fifty-one-weekers, couldn't speak to the fifty-two-weekers; they didn't dare. On your helmet was painted what week of the strike you gave in. And the hierarchy of the colliery was the longer you stayed out, the better your position in those collieries. And I don't think that the people who are busily rewriting the history of the strike actually understand what that did to people, how they had to hold out.

Twenty years after its conclusion the policing of the strike was revealed to have cost in the region of £200 million; the demonstrable use of force during the dispute resulted in one of the most divisive and hostile episodes in the history of post-war Britain. Some of the techniques used in the policing of the strike were assessed to have been illegal, a situation which places the continual emphasis on the lack of a national ballot in context. Cabinet papers released under the thirty-year rule revealed Margaret Thatcher considered calling a state of emergency during 1984 and plans were in place to use the Army in a logistical capacity. These measures were accompanied by offers from the military of further increase in their capacity if required.

Long after the conclusion of the strike, the enduring impression was of a government for whom defeat of the miners represented the defeat of organised labour, a defeat that was deemed successful only if it were total.

For an area such as South Wales, the forces arrayed against the strike signified a threat to its communities, where mining embodied not only a way of life, but a shared consciousness; a once indefatigable moral economy, one forged in resilience and fellowship, had duly been tested to destruction.

Arfon Evans: Arthur Horner, a founder member of the Communist Party, said that sometimes it's more important to protect and defend the union than to negotiate a wage settlement or a dispute, because the union needs protection. I supported a return to work without a negotiated settlement, in the Executive, but I took that decision because I wanted to protect the union, because there were indications that the union could have been dismantled and smashed, and, secondly, I took it because I didn't feel it was right that miners and miners' families should experience any further hardship. They had given enough. And that's where my sentiment lay. Because I was regarded as a tanky, or a Eurocommunist, I was accused of selling out.

I held a quick general meeting, probably one of the first in the coal-fields, knowing that it would reverberate right back from South Wales into the rest of the British coalfield and back to Scargill, because they recognised that Maerdy was one of the key fighting lodges in the British coalfield. That was a very conscious decision; it was for the preservation of our community. It would have been absolutely horrific if men in Maerdy had gone back to work without the decision of the lodge.

Neil Kinnock: When the great closure programme came from '85 on, there was no effort whatsoever at reinvestment, retraining, transition; within months, maybe weeks, certainly within months, what had been confident communities with real vitality and strength had become drug-dependent, subject to family break-up, divorce, delinquency of various kinds, rootlessness and social fragmentation. And that had happened almost overnight.

Ken Smith: I think miners themselves were very conscious – none of them wanted to work in those conditions indefinitely. They were all very political about the environment in those days, and I don't think they saw it as being a totem that you had to produce coal and you had to burn coal; it was more about if you weren't going to be employed in the mines, where were you going to be employed? Because there was nothing else, and if you were going to be employed in coal mining, then what's the best way to make that environmentally friendly, efficient and economic. Anybody who works in an industry at the end of the day will want that to happen, because it secures their employment.

Kim Howells: All the pits didn't close immediately after the strike. It stretched out to '89. I remember horrendous weekends where we would lose 4,000 jobs in one particular area, and those were terrible times. Hywel Francis and I went to Oakdale when the men were coming to pick up their redundancy, and neither the NUM nor the Coal Board, let alone the government, had done anything about advising the men on how it might be possible to get retraining for some other industry or to advance their education. It was a disgrace; it was a terrible failure. I was concerned with the absolute unwillingness of Scargill and the NUM to contemplate doing that. They saw that as another kind of symbol of defeat, instead of saying, 'We must reopen all these pits,' we were arguing that we really had to take seriously the fact that chances are that these pits were never going to reopen and that we should think very seriously about making sure that people had the ways and means financially, and in terms of opportunity, to retrain and be educated.

Ken Smith: I think what you saw is that that generation survived – just. But I think the lasting legacy of the strike was for future generations in those communities. It was the same whether in Wales or Yorkshire, if you look at the sort of growth of drug abuse and social problems that began to kick in in some of those community areas with the level of unemployment, the levels of deprivation.

Phil Cullen: The men who went back to work were never forgiven. One of them died recently and had to have a private funeral; they didn't tell anybody the times. They were never spoken to again. There were men in this village that never spoke to their best friends again.

The people in Cynheidre that had gone back to work and signed the court injunction, to stop the picketing, those people, they never came back to work. They were paid off by the Coal Board, handsomely. Some of these boys weren't young; some of these guys were on about £30,000 a year, a lot of money back then.

We knew Cynheidre was finished, we had no illusions that the Colliery Modified Review Procedure was going to save the place.

Kim Howells: They were a resourceful, pretty youthful workforce in the coal industry at the time and a lot of them did it off their own backs. Months afterwards, I bumped into people who were saying, 'I'm training to be a nurse.' Many of the older boys, said, 'Fuck it, I've had enough, and I'm never going to get another job,' and there was a terrible feeling of pessimism in some areas.

Ken Smith: I think the miners and their communities were abandoned in two senses. One was the strike itself, when they were abandoned by people like the Labour leaders and leaders of the TUC, with some honourable exceptions; but they were abandoned afterwards, as well. I think if at that stage Plaid had been a more capable force, they might have gained ground in a much more substantial way, earlier than the SNP did in Scotland.

It's always been that tension between the rural community culture and the language compared to the industrial heartlands of South Wales, which are equally proud Welsh people, but don't consider themselves nationalistic. The South Wales miners were always proudly internationalist in their outlook.

Christine Powell: A lot of people suffered through what happened. I don't know if my view was coloured by the fact that my family came out of it in one piece, but I feel bloody proud that I was part of that. Nearly every miner I know agrees there are better ways to earn a living than digging deep underground developing health problems, but it wasn't about that. Without a shadow of a doubt, this all goes back to Thatcher and Thatcherism, and what better group to hit than the miners, because it's not just the industry and the history the miners have got of standing up for themselves, but it's the community based around those things. It will be the last ever great industrial dispute. It's a shame that the legacy is the society we now live in.

Phil Cullen: I always said, it wasn't the miners that lost the strike; it was the whole working class of this country lost the strike. Look at it now, with zero-hour contracts and people with about five or six jobs, trying to make ends meet. I believe it more than ever that the miners did not lose the strike: everybody, the working class, society lost that strike. It was the last great working-class stand.

Siân James: We saw a great industry brought to its knees; we understood why it couldn't carry on. But I always say to people, we could have done what Germany did, which is plan. We could have planned. We could have invested in cleaner technology, we could have invested in alternative sources, clean coal technology, adding scrubbers, and we could have eked out that commodity for us and shored it up with other things. But no, we had a government that was hell-bent on saving money and bringing a union to its knees. And it was so hard.

Neil Kinnock: In stable industrial development, I'm not being workerist or harking back, the fact of the matter is, it is the insecurity of employment that is largely responsible for the lack of self-confidence in people. Even people who are working for relatively larger firms, mainly in the service and tertiary sectors in Wales now, are not absolutely certain that that's going to be their employer for the next twenty years. That certainly doesn't encourage the self-confidence of investment in the place where they live, the community in which they live. I'd be doing you a real disservice if I suggested there wasn't a spirit of community in Wales. There certainly is. I see it in Port Talbot and in Aberavon, which goes up into the Valleys and has been devastated over the last fifty years and is a shell of its former self. The lack of confidence must derive from a degree of uncertainty about the coming years. Until we get it back, then getting the confidence from which comes creativity, imagination, enterprise, initiative, that's going to be in abeyance: in abeyance, not abolished, but in abeyance for as long as that insecurity lasts.

Phil White: I'm very proud of our community resilience and spirit, and just as proud of all those smaller valleys. I went over to Tower Colliery and within a twelvemonth was the lodge chairman and it lasted right up to its buy-out, in 1994. The last remaining pit in Wales. I knew all the boys there, from the Aberdare and the Rhymney Valleys, and the

Rhondda Valley. You're born into it and it's built into you, and it's born into you as well.

Look what they had in Tredegar with Nye at the time when Nye Bevan was in the industry: an early version of the NHS. What was set up in the Valleys in South Wales was on another parallel universe, when you think of other places just in the UK. But we made it happen, we made it happen through our pennies, through the miners' weekly pennies. Sometimes we'd squeeze a couple of bob off the coal owners, but it virtually all came from the miners' coffers and our pennies.

Rowan Williams: During the eighties I'd been back a lot to Wales to visit family and friends and was aware of how things were dissolving; certainly, the Miners' Strike was a moment when I was very conscious of connections and keeping an eye on what was going on and feeling actually this is a moment of real dissolution here. There was a little group of us in Cambridge, members of the Cambridge Labour Party at the time, who had a fund for Welsh miners.

There were several different issues overlapping during the strike. There was what you might call the targeted movement against the unions; there's the uncomfortable economic clock ticking about the viability of certain industries, especially mining; and those interlock, and certainly by the time I was back in Wales in the early nineties, those two are virtually indistinguishable, but the financial issue was probably uppermost. It did seem to me that absolutely nobody had thought about what former mining communities would then look like, and there'd been no attempt at any strategy about investment.

But it's not just that, and this is the difficult thing; this is why it's not just a black-and-white story. You can't simply replace jobs in that sort of setting, because the old industrial patterns were not only about jobs, and that's something which people didn't entirely grasp. They were about community patterns; they were about common culture; they were about expectations of literacy and involvement and a level of political agency which unions provided. If you take away, not just employment, but a whole cultural expectation, an agency, then you have, well, you have what happened in the eighties and nineties. You have the wilderness of post-industrial society.

Mary Winter: I found it very difficult afterwards. It was hard to articulate: 'It shouldn't have gone the way it did go; there should have been some kind of reconciliation; there should have been some kind of arrangement and agreement; it's so sad.' One of the saddest images I have is of Arfon leading the Maerdy miners back to work. And how he managed to do that I do not know.

Arfon Evans: When I took the boys out at the start of the strike, my main message was, 'Whenever we come back to work, whatever situation or condition, we will come back in unity.' We met five thirty in the morning at the Maerdy Hall, the Maerdy Miners' Institute. I was absolutely overwhelmed. We had all the miners lining up in Maerdy Square and what followed was absolutely incredible. The Maerdy Women's Support Group, all the support groups throughout the UK, along with the support groups we had in Italy, Denmark, all joined the miners of Maerdy. I thought only Maerdy was going back to work, because all the British press were there, all of the media. We had the Tylorstown Colliery Band, which we had sponsored over the years, because it was going to close and we rescued it by agreeing that the miners would contribute.

Then at that time of the morning – half past five, six o'clock – as we walked from the Maerdy Miners' Institute, all of the population of Maerdy were alongside the roads, all the doors were opening and people were coming out and clapping. I could see the faces of the older generation in Maerdy on the doorsteps, in tears. We walked that two miles, the band playing in front, and even though, even though our boys – I call them the boys – knew we had lost the strike, we had achieved our main goal of maintaining solidarity. Sometimes people talk about solidarity and I think that was one of the best examples I've seen: after twelve months of strike, miners and their families coming together with the community, with all the supporters throughout. We reached the pit and then I spoke to everyone from the baths roof, but no words were needed.

TWELVE

CÂN I GYMRY / A SONG FOR THE WELSH

Voices

Nici Beech
Cian Ciarán
Steve Eaves
David R.
   Edwards
Meri Huws
Rhys Ifans
Dafydd Iwan
Siôn Jobbins

Tecwyn Vaughan
   Jones
Gaynor Legall
Alun Llwyd
Eluned Morgan
Pat Morgan
Rhys Mwyn
Branwen Niclas
Gorwel Owen

Helen Prosser
Guto Pryce
Dewi Prysor
Gruff Rhys
Mark Roberts
Angharad Tomos
Bedwyr Williams
Charlotte Williams
David Wrench

———

Several hitherto unlikely alliances had been formed by the conclusion of the Miners' Strike. Cymdeithas yr Iaith, which had organised food parcels, holidays and other supportive measures in solidarity with mining communities during the strike, continued to be a spirited campaigning presence. In tandem with their Cymraeg-centred activities the society was active in the women's, Nicaragua and LGBT movements, and was also on occasion in dialogue with Sinn Féin throughout the 1980s, the decade in which the society elected its first female chairperson.

The society's campaigning energy was directed towards equal status for the Welsh language and for Deddf Eiddo – a property act to legislate solutions to mitigate the housing crisis in Wales. Many of Cymdeithas yr Iaith's activities and rallies were held in tandem

*with concerts by the youthful punk and post-punk-influenced bands
developing into a Cymraeg music movement.*

Meri Huws: Cymdeithas was definitely a safe place. If you look at
the activists of that period, in many ways at times I think the young
women outnumbered the young men. I became the first female Chair
of Cymdeithas and after that, there have been a succession of women,
including Angharad Tomos and Helen Prosser, who've taken that
role on. So that gender divide did not exist within Cymdeithas, and
I suppose that was quite unusual in Welsh life at that stage, because
to see a woman sitting in the sêt fawr in a chapel would be incredibly
unusual at that time, and certainly within politics in Wales, we were
still talking about how rare it was to have young women as candidates.
It was unusual to have an organisation which had no gender bias.

One of the things which really challenged our traditional way of
thinking, which I found difficult, was Greenham and the Women's
March, which really shook people. The other thing which did change
attitudes in Wales was the Miners' Strike. They didn't quite overlap, but
in a way they did as well. The Miners' Strike really brought together a
strange alliance of people.

At an action in Bangor we locked the Secretary of State for
Wales, Wyn Roberts, in his surgery just before Christmas. You had
Cymdeithas yr Iaith, people from Bangor who were not even socialists,
alongside the international socialist group, all together, being arrested,
having decided to lock ourselves in together with Wyn Roberts. He
was refusing to meet the miners.

Rhys Mwyn: People like Meri Huws were radical at the time, Helen
Greenwood, Siân Howys, who was at Greenham, and lots of those
characters were Welsh-language campaigners and feminists and they
crossed over to Greenham, they crossed over to the peace movement.
Ffred Ffransis, a Welsh-learner from Rhyl, crystallises the Welsh
Language Society, a full-on activist permanently, but from a part of

Wales that isn't very Welsh-speaking and that's something that's interesting. Tony Schiavone, another leading activist, was of Italian heritage: I think his father was a prisoner of war.

You do get people within Cymdeithas historically that are really radical. I think my relationship with them is good and bad: I've certainly argued with most of them. But you cannot take part in the debate about Wales and just agree with everybody, but that debate in the 1980s wasn't easy. Jesus, it wasn't easy: it was hard work. You lost friends, you got tarred for your views, and I always say to them, 'You want an independent Wales, but I can't have independent thought.'

David R. Edwards: The only thing I've got in common with Welsh-speakers is that I speak the language; it's my mother tongue. But culturally, to use that word, which I don't particularly like, I've got nothing in common with them. That's why I started Datblygu, because there was nothing I could identify with, whether it was Welsh books, films, radio, television; it was all beyond me and a nonsense, and it still is, to be honest. There's a mental proliferation of always looking back rather than looking forward or looking at what's under your nose. Welsh people keep going on about what the English did to them 700 years ago; that was 700 years ago.

Meri Huws: The early 1980s was an interesting period in Wales, because Rhys and his brother Siôn in Anhrefn and various other groups introduced us to a new type of music, but also a new type of thinking, which was anarchic. It challenged the state in very, very definite ways. That, for me, felt quite comfortable, because I think one thing which defined me as being slightly different as well was the fact that I did not see myself as being a nationalist. I perceived myself as being a socialist. I didn't like the nationalist focus on preservation of culture and preservation of heritage, no change, not moving forward, essentially setting Wales in aspic, and I was far more interested in the civil rights movement and changes which could occur through people power, which essentially was what punk was about.

I think that those early eighties years really shook us in Wales and started to move us on. It's not been a linear path: there's been a back and forward, back and forward since that time. We lost momentum. After the Miners' Strike, there was a strike in Blaenau Ffestiniog where you saw a similar alliance of people coming together. But I think the Miners' Strike also broke people's hearts in Wales, and their spirits, so people resorted to traditional trade unions and more traditional nationalism as well in that period.

Branwen Niclas: My mum took me to Greenham in December 1983, when cruise was arriving. The Miners' Strike, Thatcherism, the Tories saying no at first to S4C, Gwynfor Evans threatening to go on hunger strike: it was a very, very political environment I was growing up in, in my head. The relevance of Cymdeithas for me was the fact that it wasn't only questioning the status quo, but actively campaigning for positive things for Wales. I joined Cymdeithas when I was about thirteen but wasn't actively involved until later on. I went to a Welsh-medium school where I was encouraged by certain teachers during my A levels to take a subject such as French through the medium of English. I was quite angry and disappointed at the time and Cymdeithas was a positive way to channel your anger and feelings of injustice, so I became involved through Siân Howys, the local organiser for Cymdeithas, in education matters in Wales, then became involved in various campaigns in North Wales, came to know people like Alun Llwyd, Rhys Ifans and others, then went to university in Aberystwyth, where Alun and I became very involved in the campaign for a Welsh Language Act, and we ran that campaign more or less for three years.

Rhys Ifans: I was brought up in a Welsh-speaking family in north-east Wales. Ruthin is in Clwyd in Denbighshire now, which is very much a rural, agricultural area, but on its doorstep, over the mountain, was industrial north-east Wales. I went to school in Mold, and the majority of the kids in my school were from the Deeside, Shotton catchments. My experience was very different to someone from say Caernarfon, growing up. I was growing up as a Welsh-speaker, being called a Nat with great regularity, from my own people, and being called a Nat before I even had a sense of what Nat meant. When I was called a Nat as a kid, I actually thought Welsh Nat was some kind of insect, and it turns out, given the insults, that it was meant in that spirit. It always stuns me when I think that, in my living memory, there was such antagonism in my rural, largely Welsh-speaking town, towards the Welsh language and Welsh-speakers. I was acutely aware of being on some kind of cultural, linguistic front line, a place where the cultural plates were in constant flux, and I was aware of that, even as a teenager.

Branwen Niclas: We established a little group within Cymdeithas called Merched Peryglus which came from a Waldo Williams poem, 'Merched Peryglus', 'Dangerous Women'. I wanted to explore about the role of women within Cymdeithas more, the way that we would campaign and what we brought into the dynamics of the struggle. It was definitely a formative experience for me, going to Greenham. That's where I was arrested for the first time. Not with Cymdeithas, but by cutting the fence and going through the fence in Greenham before I went to college. We were arrested but nothing came from it. But in 1983, going to Greenham had a very deep impact on me. I remember during the Miners' Strike there was a stall in Bangor where you could take food items on a Saturday, and supporting that, but I felt more in tune with the women who had given up everything and had gone to live in Greenham.

Rhys Ifans: Both my parents, my father particularly, were activists. By the time I was born, he'd largely mellowed and was a Plaid Cymru activist, although his direct action genes were fully intact. Near us in Ruthin there's a mountain called Moel Famau, which is the biggest mountain in the mountain range. By now it's a ruin but a structure was built there on the mountain top to commemorate Queen Victoria's Jubilee – I think it was Queen Victoria's Jubilee, something to do with the royal family. Hundreds of them were built across the UK and became beacons at some point. I grew up thinking that was built by Owain Glyndŵr, and that it was a look-out post, because you could see Chester and the flats of Cheshire from that mountain, so that gives you a sense of where I was growing up. My first sense of personal outrage, aside from the fact that I felt often mocked and bullied for speaking Welsh and being from a Welsh-speaking home, even in a Welsh school, was when Mrs Thatcher took away our free milk. That touched me directly, immediately. I thought, 'Why would someone do that?' And then the other two great events that enraged and radicalised me were the Falklands War in 1982 and then the Miners' Strike.

Siôn Jobbins: The British Army's very clever: when I was writing a book about the Welsh flag it became obvious that one of the main propagators of the Welsh flag is the British Army. They had flag days during the First World War to try and raise money, I'm not sure what the actual flags were, but the records state they were selling Welsh flags, and there is a dragon flown in the Boer War at a Welsh military hospital, and the same happened in the Second World War. The Army was obviously seeing the need to get these Welsh working-class blokes in, and appealing to their Welshness worked, which it does. It's a peculiar type of Welshness, very big on rugby and also peculiarly proud of Glyndŵr; they think he's a good fighter.

Rhys Ifans: I had family who worked in Shotton, and Point of Ayr. We were not directly affected, I wasn't from a mining community by any stretch of the imagination, but I had family and school friends, very good friends, who had parents and family working in Point of Ayr Colliery. The Miners' Strike was something that, in a strange way, was unifying in Welsh terms. I remember going with Cymdeithas yr Iaith, on picket lines at Point of Ayr many, many times, and being warmly welcomed. Bridges were built and bridges were crossed during that time. Not so much in the Falklands War: I think the Falklands War had an opposite effect. The Union Jack became a powerful object again in Welsh culture.

Alun Llwyd: I do a lot of birdwatching, and I used to go birdwatching to the Point of Ayr, you used to have to get a train and go through Flint and Shotton, and these places were kind of insane places, slaughtered, absolutely slaughtered. I connected with that more than I did anything else, suddenly realising that the language is part of all this.

Rhys Mwyn: I think the relationship with gay rights, the gay liberation movement, the feminist movement, coming back to things like Cymdeithas matured during the eighties; people began to open up, that was positive.

Tecwyn Vaughan Jones: I was very much in the closet at that particular time, even though I knew members of the Welsh Language Society and had relationships with them. We were all in the same boat and we trusted each other not to out each other.

I remember reading articles in *Barn* [*Opinion*] in the early eighties which vilified homosexuality. Frank Price Jones, who taught at Bangor University, was one of the people who wrote very freely about that, and he was of the mind that the National Eisteddfod was a den of iniquity: the toilets in the National Eisteddfod were terrible places, and he saw that as a tsunami, part of the effect of what he called a tsunami – ton fawr – that came over from England and was flooding even the remotest part of Wales with this iniquity. I don't know how many people believed that but we read it to each other and we were rolling about laughing at this.

Charlotte Williams: I first fully understood the racialisation of the Welsh when I went to university in Bangor during the early eighties. I went to university a bit later in life – I had two children already – and it was bang on at that moment of Cymdeithas yr Iaith actions, the holiday cottage burnings in North Wales, the student protests. You'd be sitting in a class and the lecture would begin, and then the Welsh-speaking students would start beating on the desks; there would be daubing on the windows; there was always loads of graffiti. This was a young people's movement, and it was coming from this student group. The difficulty I had with it at the time was that it was very exclusive. I had thought of myself as Welsh up to then, and I remember there being a line-up to take photographs of our year group, and these student activists said, 'Well, the Welsh ones are having their photograph separately, and the rest of you will have your photograph separately,' and I remember thinking, 'This is just a total nonsense!' I couldn't assume I was Welsh, and yet I'd grown up in a bilingual home and my mother's Welsh and I'd never lived anywhere else. And all of that came from a strong feeling of being pushed out of that space by this political movement in its time. The assumption was, black people only lived in Cardiff, and of course there is a huge distance – a psychological distance – between North and South Wales.

Gaynor Legall: In the eighties I worked for Barnardo's for ten years, during which time I travelled around Wales. In areas like Powys and Flintshire they saw me as something different. There was no overt racism: I was no threat to them; I was just a novelty. Whereas if I went into other parts of Wales, you sensed the antagonism. It wasn't just curiosity. My view is that most people who are brought up in Britain are racist, because that's what you're taught, without even knowing that it's what you're being taught; books, television programmes, there was never any representation of anything other than the Anglo-Saxon white person. In order to understand racism, you had to educate yourself about the world, and, in parts of rural Wales, they saw absolutely no need to educate themselves about South Wales, never mind the rest of Wales; it was all a foreign country.

Charlotte Williams: During the eighties there were attempts to define what we might call rural racism: what did it involve? And was it worthy of government attention and intervention? That kind of thing. There were racist incidents in rural places, particularly for small businesses such as Indian restaurants, derogatory comments, but it didn't impinge on people in the same way that it would have done to people living in more urban areas. Instead, there was a feeling of being a curiosity, of having to constantly explain yourself; people asking, 'Is that your mother?' from an assumption that you're adopted, or the assumption that you've migrated; being exoticised or treated as a curio; or being stared at; being asked 'What are you doing on the beach?'

Gaynor Legall: My personal experience of working in a variety of arenas was that there was what is now described as the Welsh crachach, which was very protective and had an elitist view of the language. I remember being in a room with people where they went into a group and spoke Welsh, knowing that I couldn't speak Welsh. If a group of black people did that, they would be worried because they'd think we were conspiring in some sort of way. I think that view of the Welsh language, whether it belonged to the ignorant rural types, or the very self-important elitist types, existed for quite a long time. I think it put people off and made them antagonistic towards the language and the use of the language, which was unfortunate.

Tecwyn Vaughan Jones: After university my first job was in the Welsh Folk Museum in St Fagans, I worked there for about eight years, and my job was to go round Wales, collecting information regarding the folk life of people when they were growing up in different parts of Wales. I was talking to people who had their childhood in the 1890s, even 1880s, some of the older ones, I was being sent to Welsh-language areas all the time, because there was an idea that as I came from Blaenau Ffestiniog, I would be able to speak to all the rural Welsh-speaking people.

Blaenau Ffestiniog is an industrial area, and I had nothing at all in common, I decided, with the farmers and the rural population of the Llŷn Peninsula in West Wales. My most successful interviews were held in the South Wales Valleys, in the Rhondda, in Treorchy, in the Rhymney Valley, and I gelled with these people. The language wasn't there, but I thought these people were ten times more Welsh than I could ever be. Being like them was my ambition: socialist, Welsh – and therefore I didn't need the language. Fortunately the language was part of my identity, and I included that as well.

Angharad Tomos: I was scared to be the first chair of Cymdeithas. They asked me and I said, 'I don't want to be a failure, being the first woman,' so Meri Huws, who later became the head of the Welsh Language Board, was the first, and then after a year, I thought, 'Oh, I'll take it on.' I remember being on the Senedd when the Miners' Strike was beginning, and we were discussing why this is relevant to us, because they were not generally Welsh-speaking areas, and Ffred Ffransis said, 'It's for Welsh communities,' and gradually understanding that the Welsh language was only a badge. We were taking it as a symbol, but the main thrust of Cymdeithas was trying to achieve equality for communities throughout Wales. We were always saying, 'Oh, why can't we break through to the English-speaking parts of Wales,' but most of our literature was in Welsh. And we were reluctant to use English or bilingual leaflets at the beginning. We had the new manifesto in 1982, and that was much more community-based, and gradually, during the Miners' Strike, what we did was to make personal contacts and that made a change, because for the first time we were discussing through the medium of English with Welsh people, and for me, that was new. English was just a language of the oppressor before, discussing Welsh politics through the medium of English with Welsh people was something that had an effect on me.

Helen Prosser: A big step for me was coming home for Christmas holidays and joining Ffred Ffransis at a protest in the Welsh Joint Education Committee, the exams board. We were campaigning for a Welsh-language committee to look after the whole of the Welsh language, to have an overview. We didn't deface anything – it was just plastering posters onto the WJEC building – and I'll never forget how Ffred handled the caretaker. He was so polite. I think that made a huge impression on me, I don't like conflict, and didn't find these things easy. At the time, the WJEC was run by the local authorities in Wales and I think the local authorities were probably blocking any development. That year we walked from the Eisteddfod in Llangenny to Cardiff and Rhys Ifans was one of the three people who walked every step.

The biggest action I participated in was when we went to the City and Guilds in London and rushed into their offices as they were packing up for the day and threw all their things on the floor. I imagined, years later, people coming to my office and throwing everything everywhere. But something really interesting happened that day: the police lady came and said she was arresting us, and later on, she could see we were tidy people and she said to me, 'I can't imagine doing what you've just done unless it was for my family,' and I've always remembered that. She could imagine it. It's that her only strong emotional connection would be to her family.

The youthful membership of Cymdeithas promoted the burgeoning Cymraeg punk and post-punk scene with great energy. The movement was initiated by Anhrefn, a band formed in Llanfair Caereinion, Powys, by Rhys Mwyn and his brother Siôn. Other distinctive groups included Y Cyrff, Ffa Coffi Pawb, Fflaps, Llwybr Llaethog, whose single 'Dull Di-Drais' included the voice of Ffred Ffransis, made reference to his imprisonment and contained a bilingual statement printed by Cymdeithas, and Datblygu, the last led by the iconoclastic David R. Edwards. Although they were not always formally associated with Cymdeithas, a symbiotic relationship developed between the bands and their contemporaries in the society. By singing in Cymraeg the groups took an inherently political approach to their music that led to an examination of the contemporary role of the language and a fierce and necessary re-evaluation of what constituted 'Welsh Language Culture'. This approach revealed the conservatism and isolation of certain aspects of Welsh society. Many of the songs written in this new and unflinching spirit liberated Cymraeg from sentimental and nostalgic definitions of Welsh identity and proved that the language flourished in a context that was fearless and vital.

Gruff Rhys: By the time I was in my mid-teens, I was buying Anhrefn cassettes and their outlook was completely different, and they were from Powys and putting on Crass gigs and touring Europe and saying provocative things like 'We love the English.' That seemed very exciting and the emphasis by Anhrefn on inclusion seemed more realistic; there was, I think, a change of emphasis and a will to seek other parts of Wales. The difference between pre-Anhrefn gigs and post-Anhrefn was that as anarchists they stopped singing 'Hen Wlad Fy Nhadau' at the end of gigs. Singing the anthem had become the norm and the whole rock scene had become too chauvinistic and self-congratulatory. In some respects, it was year zero, but with the evergreen Cymdeithas yr Iaith still involved as a continuation. I remember punk kids being thrown out of Clwb Ifor Bach for refusing to stand for the anthem at a seated Heather Jones folk gig in the downstairs bar. It was a fantastic culture war and I think those lessons regarding the rigour and lack of complacency of the movement have been forgotten.

Rhys Mwyn: We did a gig for Red Wedge, which was a funny thing to do. It was one of the most interesting experiences we had with Labour. It was in Brecon market hall, and somebody from Brecon thought it would be a good idea to get Anhrefn and Datblygu on the bill, to have Welsh-language content; for us we thought it's a way of reaching people in Brecon.

At the end of the night, when the gig finished, there was the inevitable, 'Right, who pays us now, where do we get the expenses from?' and there was no one at the market hall from the local Labour Party. Oh, right. 'Well, we've been promised expenses' or whatever it was. And were told 'Oh, they've gone to the pub somewhere.' After we packed up, we drove down to this pub in the middle of Brecon and it was full of old boys – proper old boys, round the table, with pints in hand – with the money. And it was like, 'Hi, it's Rhys from Anhrefn, we did the gig for you.' 'What do you want?' I've never seen such a dismissive attitude. And it was '[Sigh] here's your money.' They couldn't have given a shit about what we'd done. Our contact with the older generation throughout Anhrefn was relatively zero, because the audience were mainly younger than us. It was a new generation of Welsh and there was obviously anybody and everybody in the audience, but in a Welsh context, people only came to our gigs if they shared a vision for the future, a varied vision for the future, but they were there because they would be anti-racist, pro-gay rights, pro-feminists, pro-peace, anti-apartheid – you didn't have these discussions, everybody got it. Animal rights, everybody got it. You could argue that once things took off for all of us as bands, we were preaching to the converted most of the time, because it's the young people who say, 'We want a new Wales,' not the old ones.

We did that gig in the Brecon market hall and John Peel came along to the gig and reviewed it for the *Observer*. You had the great David R. Edwards and John Peel in discussion, and I would have sat there, giggling, listening, I couldn't get a word in anyway, so I was listening to those two going on.

David R. Edwards: I grew up in a Welsh-speaking household, I spoke Welsh to my parents, it was as natural as breathing. When I was growing up in Cardigan, we'd travel up to see my mother's parents near Lampeter, and the Welsh Language Society had been spray-painting these road signs and my dad would take the piss out of it all, saying it was a pile of shit, and I'd agree with him. They didn't go to Chapel and their politics and religion were outward-looking rather than inward-looking. They were Labour supporters in an area where it wasn't very common to be a Labour supporter. Both of my parents' parents grew up on smallholdings.

My dad grew up on a farm near Gwbert, Cardigan, but my grand-father packed in farming in 1947 and moved to a council house for the comforts of life. He used to work all week on the farm, and then on the Saturday – this is back in the 1930s – he used to get on the cart and take the horse to the Black Lion in Cardigan and the horse knew the way. He'd get hammered on whiskey and chain-smoke, and he'd be so drunk, he couldn't guide the horse, but the horse knew the way to go back to the farm. The name Datblygu [meaning 'develop'] came before Pat joined the band, it was me and Wyn, Wyn Davies, who formed the band. We did demos and Wyn left and my mother was asking me what I'd been up to, so I played her some tapes, she said, 'Oh, that's a development from what I've heard before; how about calling the band Datblygu?'

Pat Morgan: I started listening to Radio Cymru and buying *Y Cymro*. I was living in Llangorse at the time and I'd done my pre-reg year in university, in Aberystwyth. It was totally unfashionable to speak Welsh. I picked up then on the Welsh music scene. It was during the punk era, so I was a big fan of Treiglad Pherffaith, that was Ifor ap Glyn's punk group. Ifor introduced me to Datblygu, and from there on there was no turning back. I thought, 'This is really speaking to me, in Welsh, and it's not embarrassing, it's perfect.' I joined in 1984, after going to one of their gigs in Neuadd Blaendyffryn at Llandysul, and within no time I was playing bass – I'd already been in a punk bondage band in Brecon called Slugbait. We started writing to each other and I said that I played bass, and he wanted me to join the band.

David R. Edwards: We were very much as Datblygu out on a limb, it was basically me and Pat, we were very much out there on our own. People have always said we were anti-English but I've always been anti-bloody-Welsh.

Pat Morgan: We always alienated most of the audience. They hated the rawness, the unprofessional sound. It was very low-fi and it was a bit of a mess. We did have bottles thrown at us in one gig but soon Rhys Mwyn would be on the phone to David nearly every week. I'd always been a bit of a Welsh nationalist from a young age – I'm talking teens, when Gwynfor Evans went on hunger strike and we got the Welsh channel. I was very much in favour of all of that going on. David never seemed to champion Cymdeithas yr Iaith very much, although we were pro-Welsh-language: we did the gigs for Cymdeithas yr Iaith and were very happy to do that. David was a bit of a provocateur so anything he was expected to like or follow, he'd do the opposite. That was in his nature. We would do the gigs for Cymdeithas yr Iaith and raise money for them, but at the same time be not quite their willing followers.

David R. Edwards: Now and again, they'd ask us to play at the gigs, so we'd go out and do it, but Cymdeithas yr Iaith I think were misguided, I think it's a Welsh middle-class Establishment thing. It may have started off radical, just like Plaid Cymru did, but it's been tempered over the years: it's an outlet for middle-class students. They've got to protest about something, and so in the end they protest about nothing very much – Welsh culture, the National Eisteddfod. All that never appealed to me. The way Wales was portrayed on Radio Cymru, you'd think everybody was a farmer.

Pat Morgan: I coined the phrase 'We're the Baader–Meinhof of Welsh pop,' but it was to show the other musicians up, to stop them being folky and embarrassing, singing Welsh with an American accent and trying to be Bruce Springsteen. The Eisteddfod would have no problem with us appearing, so we'd find out where the gigs were, turn up and play. That's how songs like 'Dafydd Iwan yn y Glaw' were formed: David saying to me, 'Play something,' I'd play three notes on the bass, looking as if I'd done it all my life and then he'd start ranting about Dafydd Iwan. Just get in there and do it. We're here now; let rip! Here's our chance!

Dafydd Iwan: I had a letter from David of Datblygu a few years ago. He'd heard me speak on Radio 4 about the royal family and my beliefs and he wrote me a very supportive letter, saying there were more things in common between us than people realised. He's a very clever chap, but he went through some difficult times. I think he was thrown out of one of my concerts once; I didn't know it was him, but he stood there, shouting rude things about Dafydd Iwan and he was ejected, but I like some of his songs now, they're really good satire and very clever. My daughter Elliw was friendly with him for a while in Aberystwyth.

The songs and energy of Datblygu and Anhrefn had touched a nerve within a younger cohort of music fans comprised of a generation whose cultural references included the weekly music papers and the late-night John Peel show on Radio 1. The bands would on occasion play concerts promoted by Cymdeithas at the Eisteddfod, an institution whose values they would interrogate from the stage.

Alun Llwyd: Towards the tail-end of the age of me staying in the caravan with my parents at the Eisteddfod I would go out to gigs. I would go to a pub, drink under-age and watch Datblygu.

David Wrench: I grew up in Bryngwran, which is a little village, and I was taught in Welsh at school. My dad was first-language Welsh; he's from Amlwch, off a farm outside Porth Llechog in the north of Anglesey, and my mum was from Kenfig Hill in South Wales, so she didn't speak Welsh. I felt very separated from the Welsh-language culture. And I looked down upon it. I really felt ostracised from it: I felt like these people were against me and I felt pushed away. Which is ridiculous, because I was a Welsh-speaker anyway. As soon as I became a teenager, I hated the Eisteddfod culture; I really loathed it, and it put me off. I almost stopped speaking Welsh as a protest at this, even though I could speak it fluently. They were so didactic about it, so it put me off. My music teacher told me I had absolutely no future in music and she wouldn't even teach me A level, so I moved to Holyhead School, which was an English-language, rough school. My dad was a PE teacher there, he was a weight-lifter who won medals for Wales in the Commonwealth Games and I was so much happier. My form tutor and my physics teacher was Gorwel Owen. Obviously, quite an amazing person. He took me to my first gig, which was Sonic Youth in Manchester. We were talking about music, and he said, 'Have you heard Datblygu?' and I hadn't, and then I listened to them and Datblygu completely changed how I thought about the language, how I thought about my own culture; it was a complete change. Someone's actually speaking about what it's like to live in Wales. What it's like to deal with all the fucking harp-playing stiffs. That's who David was having a go at, everything I'd been fighting against and hating myself at school in Bodedern.

Gorwel Owen: It was an interesting school. Imagine taking a little bit of Liverpool and plonking it at the end of Anglesey. It was a very underfunded area, not that different from Valleys schools in the amenities during that era. I was a pupil there as well. It was an interesting mix of town kids and rural kids, like me and Dave. Anglesey is the strange mix where all the political parties have held the seat; there are parts which are strongly small c conservative.

Gruff Rhys: I was in a band in school, Machlud, a soft rock band, and we accidentally ended up on Anhrefn's post-punk compilation, *Cam O'r Tywyllwch*, because my brother had let them stay in the house when they were touring. Two of the band then left school at fifteen to work in the quarry. Cymdeithas yr Iaith was always a young organisation; there was a girl in school, Menna Charles Morris, who was two years older than me and she arranged buses to all the Welsh-language gigs and ran the Cymdeithas yr Iaith cell in school. She'd get at least one, sometimes two, sometimes three buses going to gigs. Then, during the Miners' Strike, she was going around the houses, collecting food and donations.

When I was about thirteen, a teacher in the school called Arwel Jones had a mobile disco. There was a craze of charismatic DJs in the seventies – Mici Plwm was the champion DJ – and they'd play Welsh-language music and instrumental music and French hits; the key was that there was no English. The sports teacher in our school was a DJ as well, and he arranged a rock school and he got all the local bands to set up their gear, all the drummers in one classroom, all the guitar players in another classroom, and then he got all the kids to be taught by the members of these local bands.

I was put in a drum room with four drummers and we'd all have to play exactly the same thing, and Dafydd Ieuan was one of the other drummers. It was the first time I met Daf, and then at the end of the day, everyone was put into bands, so they'd take a member from the drum room, a member from the guitar room: it was a band-making machine. By the end of the night, there was a gig with these newly formed bands. I remember it being around the same month as S4C starting, which was hugely exciting at the beginning, programming wild stuff. By the time I was sixteen, I had my own band, Ffa Coffi Pawb, with my mate Rhodri; there were a lot of young bands starting and they were inspired by this new movement.

Gorwel Owen: I first met Gruff Rhys at a record fair organised by Rhys Mwyn that had talks as well, one of those brilliant ideas that don't always work. Paul Davies was there, an artist, building on the floor a map of Wales out of junk. Gruff was helping him, I didn't know who he was but I bought a Ffa Coffi tape from him, then we then did a radio session together; they were really open and excited.

Branwen Niclas: My mother spent quite a lot of time in hospital when I was growing up, so we would go to Gruff's house and that's where we would stay. We spent every Christmas Eve with Gruff and the family. When Gruff was starting to play the drums and be part of these groups like Machlud, I was part of that little world and Dafydd, Gruff's brother, seemed very cool to us at the time. He was organising Pesda Roc and it was like a fantasy world at that time as well, growing up as a young teenager.

Nici Beech: I would go on a bus on an hour's journey away from home and be like any teenager attending a gig. I remember seeing Y Ficar and thinking that some of their music was a bit of a rip off. But that was followed by gigs in the small venue in Corwen that were organised by Cymdeithas and the Urdd and smaller gigs in Llanrwst that probably Tony Schiavone organised. I quite quickly transferred interest into more underground bands. All the vibrant culture was new to me: I hadn't experienced Welsh-language culture; I wasn't a member of the young farmers or the Urdd. I was different to the society in my village. I was one of four from my year who went to a new school and then going to the National Eisteddfod at Rhyl, staying with my nana in the caravan. I was meeting up with friends I'd met at gigs to go out and see if we could get into gigs at the town.

I think Datblygu appealed to teenage angst, as did Y Cyrff who came from down the road from me. They were really competent; they were really tight on stage.

Mark Roberts: Llanrwst is a market town. On a Saturday, when the pubs were still going strong, it could be quite a dangerous place when the pubs were chucking out, not unlike anywhere else. We were messing about and jamming and trying to come up with songs, running before we could walk, and basically it was a teacher, my geography teacher in school, Tony Schiavone, who said, 'If you can translate the songs into Welsh, I'll get you a gig in two weeks' time.' We were playing Clash cover versions and we just then translated them into Welsh to do our first couple of gigs. Tony doesn't blow his own trumpet, but he was an important figure at the time, putting on gigs in all the surrounding areas: he came from outside the town I grew up in, but he was always trying to organise gigs in community halls and just getting stuff happening.

Bedwyr Williams: I really liked Y Cyrff. They had a real presence on stage and looked like they knew how to handle themselves. They came from not too far away from where I lived as well.

David Wrench: Y Cyrff were a bit rougher and he was such a good vocalist, Mark, and look how those people went on to be so massively successful. Watching Ffa Coffi, Gruff was a star from the beginning; he had this presence.

Branwen Niclas: It was part of life, going up to Llanrwst with a minibus to collect Y Cyrff from Llanrwst and down to Cardiff for a gig. The amount of miles we did in those years. We didn't think about it, either. The music and the campaigning was one and the same in many instances. The campaigning and the cultural side intertwined. On a weekend, you could travel to somewhere on the Saturday morning, there would be a political meeting in the afternoon, a Cymdeithas rally, then another meeting, post-rally, and in the evening, followed by a Cymdeithas gig, so it seemed like a grass-roots way of life, but in reality, it was a small group of people organising these rallies and events were attended by lots of the same people.

Siôn Jobbins: I was born in 1968, so Datblygu happened exactly at the right time for me; I wrote letters to Dave Datblygu, who was living in Brecon at the time and to Rhys Mwyn.

And you'd get these letters written in green Berol pen and cassettes through the post back from David and it was absolutely fantastic to get in touch with these people. I was a bit edgy, I was in the sixth form, and his music sort of changed my life. He was saying it's very boring living here, it can be very cloying and make you feel like you're really trapped and bored and can't get away from it. He interrogated the Chapel-going conformity, the pressure that you wanted to get away from.

Bedwyr Williams: I grew up in Colwyn Bay, a Victorian seaside resort like Llandudno, and that means that you have a big chunk of an English-speaking population there that has been there a long time, and also the Ministry of Food was there during the war, so some people stayed on and retired and that meant that it was predominantly English-speaking. Old Colwyn, where I actually grew up, is slightly more Welsh-speaking, closer to the limestone quarry. As somebody who went to school there, my experience of Welsh-speaking was the Chapel, which was more inland. My family were farmers and the people in the town that spoke Welsh were from Gwynedd, but they were middle-class people that had moved there to teach Welsh in the school, or to teach in Welsh schools.

Rhys Mwyn: John Peel was pretty instrumental. The thing with John Peel that people don't realise today is, if you got played, or especially if you did a session, if you then went up to Sunderland or Birmingham people knew your songs because they listened to John Peel. We did a gig in Harlow in Essex, which Attila the Stockbroker curated, it was Y Cyrff – the boys who would form Catatonia – Anhrefn and Datblygu, doing a night in Harlow. And it was full.

Pat Morgan: Cymdeithas followed us to Harlow, to our first gig in England, to check that we weren't going to sing in English. Honestly. Ffred Ffransis was there as a sort of spy.

Rhys Mwyn: Throughout the eighties and that period of Datblygu, Y Cyrff, Fflaps and Anhrefn recording Peel sessions, we all felt strongly that it was important that we sang in Welsh on those sessions. I remember talking with Fflaps about this, because Fflaps were from a more bilingual background, saying, 'Look, it is important, because John Peel's picked up on the Welsh-language records that I've put out and that's what we're trying to do.' It would have been a shame for them to do an English-language session, in terms of the mission of getting the Welsh language out there.

Gruff Rhys: Datblygu were a bit ahead of the curve, so the generation of Geraint Davies who had been in Hergest, the kind of Welsh Eagles – he'd actually made some mad records pre-Hergest, but was by then a producer at the BBC in Bangor, doing the pop shows – was horrified by Datblygu. Datblygu were revered but there was still that rejection from mainstream Radio Cymru.

In '87 or '88 Cymdeithas arranged to do a musical revue, a touring concert around Wales, and got a load of musicians and young actors together for a campaign to have late-night pop shows on Radio Cymru that reflected the age. There was only a two-hour show on Saturday mornings and the gatekeepers were fairly conservative, people like Geraint Davies, and I got roped into writing songs and playing guitar, Dafydd Ieuan was on drums, and they got Rhys Ifans, Alun Llwyd in it, among others as well.

Rhys Ifans: I was switched on musically through English bands. But then I remember getting one of Datblygu's very early cassettes. I had to go on this Welsh TV show to review it, and I thought it was fucking brilliant, and I went on and reviewed it and gave it a glowing review – didn't know who they were, and the people on the TV show were drop-jawed; they couldn't understand why this was good. That's what we were dealing with then. But then again, that created another network, that had its own motor, but it was fed and sustained by Cymdeithas yr Iaith.

Cymdeithas yr Iaith didn't radicalise me: Cymdeithas yr Iaith was a finishing school. It was a way of connecting with like-minded young people across Wales. Whereas now you would connect with people in Cardiff and Swansea and Port Talbot on your computer, back then you had to drive there or hitch there or get in the back of Ffred Ffransis' van and get there. Geographically, I really got a sense of Wales and what being Welsh was. My mother's from South Wales. I knew South Wales anyway, it was part of my kind of dreamscape, growing up, as was the Llŷn Peninsula where my father's from. So I had a map of Wales inside me that was intact and I think that's something still to this day that's lacking for many Welsh people, North Wales and South Wales alike: they don't have a map of Wales inside them that they belong to and that belongs to them.

Bedwyr Williams: My dad still goes to the club in Colwyn Bay called Clwb yr Efail, which means Smithy Club. It was set up after the Eisteddfod in Colwyn Bay in the 1950s. People like Lewis Valentine would go there, clever older guys – the guy who designed the Cymdeithas logo was one of them. He judged the art prize in their annual competition and my dad used to enter that all the time. My dad did a cartoon of the gold for Princess Diana's ring being driven out of Wales and the nuclear waste being driven into a quarry, and also one of the fire-bombing campaign. I learnt about history through that competition.

Nici Beech: The North Wales organiser of Cymdeithas at that time was Siân Howys who was a very inspiring person. I went to Carmarthen probably for the first time for her court case. I would have also been to

Wrexham and Mold for the first time through Cymdeithas, but I think it's the Eisteddfod that broadens your knowledge of the geography of Wales and the only reason I would have gone to the Eisteddfod was for the gigs organised by Cymdeithas. I didn't have the experience of growing up as a child going to the Eisteddfod like a lot of people I met through music. There weren't many women artists involved. There was Pat Morgan from Datblygu and Ann Matthews from Fflaps. I didn't get to see Datblygu live that much because of where I lived, and it was definitely a male-orientated scene, but having said that, we started organising our own gigs at sixteen or seventeen. We had to have someone in Corwen to accompany us as an adult to sign in our names for the venue hire. We did three quite big gigs at Pafiliwn Corwen for Cymdeithas; we had an unofficial branch in our school and produced fanzines in the sixth form. The proceeds from the gigs all went to Cymdeithas.

I think the first time I met Alun Llwyd was at a regional Cymdeithas meeting. I was a member and believed in what they were doing but never took direct action. My mum had an issue about Cymdeithas meeting Sinn Féin and in the fanzine we did there was a page that had a picture of Bobby Sands and the lyrics of a Meic Stevens song. She didn't like that connection, and because of the IRA she thought it best not to join any group or party until you were eighteen.

Alun Llwyd: Growing up as part of Cymdeithas I met a Sinn Féin delegation when I was in school, and that was crazy at that point in time. That was insane. I met them in this village hall in Betws-y-Coed. There was so much media furore over Cymdeithas actually talking to Sinn Féin. But at the time, I felt, 'OK, I've got a massive problem with you because you are part of something that is killing people and I cannot comprehend or agree with any of that, but at the same time, what I can see is that your policies towards the Irish language are probably just as, if not more, progressive than the policies we have here for the Welsh language.'

Steve Eaves: There was a controversy when we from Gwynedd, on behalf of Cymdeithas yr Iaith, organised a visit from Sinn Féin, and Irish Republicans and language activists. We organised a tour of different Welsh-language activities, like Nant Gwrtheyrn, Welsh shops and Recordiau Sain, introducing them to different aspects of the language struggle in Wales. Because Sinn Féin was a proscribed organisation at the time, we were demonised in Wales. Dafydd Elis-Thomas condemned us: there was a headline in the *Daily Post* saying that the trip was being organised by Communists and anarchists within Cymdeithas yr Iaith. That was me and my mates. There were all these kind of things which you wouldn't think were central to the Welsh-language movement, but we saw them as important.

Alun Llwyd: It's part of a wider cultural, social, political battle and you see areas where you can cooperate, where you can discuss, regardless of people's agendas and means, and things like Animal Aid were the same. Animal Aid were doing direct violent action at this point in time. There were all these radical movements around me that were operating in different ways, but you could see that it was part of a wider battle. The gig circuit was crazy, and it was opening up in all kinds of places, and I would argue that there was a heavy political slant. All these events were being put on by either miners' support groups or Cymdeithas or CND or Anti-Apartheid, and they were probably all recognising a young audience and wanting to gain the support of that young audience, but all the gigs would have a political angle at that point in time.

Bedwyr Williams: Because my family were farmers, whenever they saw Cymdeithas smashing things up, they'd be embarrassed about it. But my mum worked in a technical college – she didn't do A levels or go to college but she did Open University and worked in amusement arcades, all sorts of stuff, to get money to further herself, to improve herself. And she got some work teaching in the technical college in

354

Llandrillo-yn-Rhos, near Colwyn Bay, She called Cymdeithas secretly once, because somebody had told her not to speak Welsh in the staff room, or had made a remark or something, and I remember being really shocked that she did that. I think in her generation, even though she didn't go to college, she would have heard people like Dafydd Iwan sing and her response was 'OK, well now I've got an education, I may have got it later,' but it was her saying, 'Well, fuck this,' and living where we were living, she would have had an equal measure of English- and Welsh-speaking friends, so it wasn't like she was a hothead, but I remember afterwards being really proud that she did that.

Branwen Niclas: 1987 till 1990, we ran the campaign for equal status for the Welsh language in Wales, so therefore our campaigning had different targets every week, and it was a way of life from the time we were eighteen till twenty-two really. It was the way of life for campaigning, the organising, the gigs, the travelling: it was a package. The Eisteddfod was such a fantastic platform for Cymdeithas to be campaigning on a daily basis, not only on the field, where we would be sharing petitions, distributing leaflets, organising rallies or protests, or following politicians around. But in the evening, you were organising a gig each night and sometimes not only one gig, but three gigs a night. We were part of the Eisteddfod establishment as well, because it was such a prominent platform for us to engage with the public, the media and also a fantastic fundraiser. Money from the gigs during the Eisteddfod week would carry us through almost the whole year. We needed that cash.

Alun Llwyd: Cymdeithas used to run three or four venues all week long at the Eisteddfod. There were gigs every single night and a massive bussing operation taking you right, left and centre. When I was chairman of Cymdeithas those gigs would fund Cymdeithas for a whole year.

Rhys Ifans: The Clwyd cell of Cymdeithas yr Iaith particularly were very left-wing. We even had a block vote in the annual conference. There were a lot of members of Cymdeithas yr Iaith in that period who were ultimately left-wingers before they were nationalists. I count myself as one of them. I still find the title nationalist a difficult one on my lips, for obvious reasons. I responded to the injustices of the world not as a Welsh nationalist but as a socialist at the time.

Ffred Ffransis and Tony Schiavone were instrumental, and the main thrust of our activism was creative. There were many incidents of direct action – I was arrested in Mold, during a Cymdeithas rally and then Mrs Thatcher came to visit our school during the Miners' Strike to open the first computer classroom in the UK. It was the only classroom that had a lock on the door and carpets on the floor, only the top cream of mathematics students were allowed to go in there and play with these computers. Mrs Thatcher came to our school to open this new kind of Tory vanguard, and it was bang in the middle of the Miners' Strike and the headmaster had got wind that I had a welcoming committee planned for her visit, and I was locked in a classroom with a teacher, while she was visiting. He locked the door and sat there, and for the two hours of her visit I was incarcerated. My father went fucking bananas.

Gruff Rhys: Ffred Ffransis turned up in the house that I was renting rooms with Dafydd Ieuan in Bangor and the other tenants were sports science students. We were having wild parties and not being popular with the rest of the house, and they complained to the landlord who was a really heavy thug, and he turned up with two other heavies to throw us out. At that very moment when we were getting threatened with violence if we didn't move our stuff, Ffred Ffransis rang the doorbell and it turned out that he was in jail with the guy who was throwing us out of the house. He turned to us and went, 'Are you a friend of Ffred's?' and Ffred came in and said, 'Yeah, these are wonderful boys, they're really helping me out,' and he said, 'If you're a friend of Ffred's, you're a friend of mine'. We got to keep our rooms in the house.

Then Ffred drove us in a minivan that he used to ship crafts around from Africa to Wales and drove us to Ganllwyd just outside Dolgellau, where they'd rented a village hall for a few days and we stayed in the hall as well, on the floor, and we put together a musical revue, to criticise the pop output of Radio Cymru, and then we toured it around Wales, around the Welsh-speaking clubs like all over Wales. I think we played Crymych rugby club.

Eluned Morgan: I thought Cymdeithas was a really attractive organisation and I was a member for a short while when I was about fifteen because it was one of the very few places a Welsh-speaker in Cardiff could go to actually speak Welsh. At the time it was only at the pop concerts that Cymdeithas put on that you could actually communicate in the medium of Welsh and enjoy yourself communicating in Welsh. There was no other platform. In that sense, Cymdeithas was one of the things that changed me from being a passive Welsh-speaker to being an active Welsh-speaker, which has made me very different from my cohort in school. I was always very clear in my politics, in terms of society, but in terms of language politics, I was very sympathetic to the language issue. And later, within the Labour Party, as somebody who was a Welsh-speaker, there was probably quite a lot of insecurity about to what extent you had been brought in. If you were a Welsh-speaker, you couldn't automatically be put into a box; it was very difficult to be a Welsh-speaker and to be Labour at that time.

Guto Pryce: I saw Ffa Coffi Pawb play at my school, Glantaf in Cardiff, when they did a tour of schools, which was something Ffred Ffransis and Tony Schiavone would have organised to make the Welsh language hip with the kids. Music was something that people could grasp on to quite easily, underage drinking was probably attractive to non-Welsh-speaking people as well. Go and see a band, get some ciders, jump about, have a weakened lager piss-up; when you're only fifteen that will do.

Siôn Jobbins: A lot of kids who came from bilingual backgrounds would get into Welsh music pop. I'm not saying they turned into Welsh nationalists but it made Welsh a more normal language for a lot of people. Obviously, a lot of people didn't like it at all. There was good stuff before then, like Geraint Jarman, but I remember going to a house party, someone's eighteenth, and we brought Y Cyrff's first single, 'Yr Haint', with us, and you could stick that on the record player and it felt fine, it didn't feel awkward. That was a big thing for us, and it was quite liberating. Even in a Welsh-speaking school like Glantaf, there was some tension between people who were more Welsh than others. I think some people who came from non-Welsh-speaking backgrounds felt that people who could speak Welsh at home were more fluent and looked down on them, and I don't think that's true; I think I felt that people looked down at us because we spoke Welsh. It's quite complex!

Rhys Ifans: We did two very successful – well, some would say successful – revues with Cymdeithas yr Iaith: the first one led up to the launch of S4C. They were pornographic, they were anarchic, hell-raising happenings. We took them around Wales. They were a nursery for me, just on a personal level, and a lot of characters were created then and of course those characters, you know, in the great tradition of Punch and Judy, were vessels where I could really shine a critical light on Cymraegness without getting my head kicked in. And then later, the 'Two Franks' series was created for S4C, which featured two Welsh learners from the north of England and they were vessels to basically look at Welsh culture and tear it to shreds.

Cymdeithas yr Iaith was fantastic in the sense that it unified not only in terms of activism but culturally as well; it unified a lot of disenfranchised Welsh-speaking young people who were sick and fucking tired of clog dancing and the like, hymn-singing. This was not our experience. We were confident enough to be influenced by the good things that were happening over the border and in America and in the rest of Europe, and to embrace them, and we felt part of a wider, radicalised community that was in some ways without borders.

Bedwyr Williams: Because we're quite close to the border in north-east Wales, the farmers properly look up to that Cheshire set; I remember my dad told me about someone in the village I live in now that would make mince pies and take them to the hunt that happened on Boxing Day, and I thought, 'There's nothing in this for you. These aren't even your people.' It's tugging the forelock to hell. And this isn't to do with the language; it's more to do with Wales. It's not a second-class version of England, but it's a lower-class version.

Alun Llwyd: Whatever the linguistic nature of a community, the situations and the threats that those communities face are the same: mainly social, economic threats. And those threats applied to Caernarfon and to Cwmbran. And that's what was interesting for me about growing up in Wrexham, because obviously I was part of Cymdeithas and the majority of Cymdeithas were coming from the stronger Welsh-language areas. But for me, that was never an issue, because it was, 'Well, I'm from Wrexham and the issues I face here are still the same issues that you face, in terms of community life.'

The newer generation of Cymdeithas activists revived the society's principle of direct action. If there were echoes of earlier campaigns from the preceding decades, these new protests took place in the context of deindustrialisation, the increased financialisation of the social housing system that followed the government's Right to Buy policy and a more draconian legal system.

Branwen Niclas: Alun Llwyd and I had been arrested for direct action, where we had taken full responsibility for our actions, before 1990. We'd been very active since we turned eighteen, and we'd refused to pay fines, so we had been in prison for non-payment of fines before we decided to take direct action for the Property Act. We knew what we were facing. It was a time of big change in communities in Wales; 1987 to 1990, during our college years, there was tremendous change in the communities, where the prices of property went haywire. In Aberystwyth, I remember the estate agents were even open on a Sunday to sell properties. The local people couldn't afford to stay or to buy properties – or to rent properties – in their own communities. That became a big campaign as well for us at the time. Cymdeithas more or less wrote a bill called the Property Act for Wales. We had campaigned for 'nid yw Cymru ar werth', 'Wales is not for sale', but a Property Act was a resolution or answer, an offer to resolve the situation. People like Ffred Ffransis would always say that our actions would reflect the seriousness of the situation, and usually we would campaign by writing letters, by petitioning, and maybe direct action would come as a last resort, or at the end of a campaign, but we thought we'd reverse it this time because the situation was so serious.

Me and Angharad Tomos did the research and the plan was to break into David Hunt, the Welsh Secretary's constituency office, on the Wirral. I'd gone to Ireland between Christmas and the New Year, and the New Year was going to start off with this big action, but Alun had gone home to Wrexham and he went to see the office himself and decided that, because the office was on the first floor, he wouldn't be able to do it, because he was afraid of heights.

When I was in Ireland, I remember phoning from a kiosk, and all I heard was, 'The party is still on, but the venue has been changed.' So when I came back from Ireland, I had no idea where we would be breaking into, but in the end, it was Llandrillo-yn-Rhos, the government buildings there, so not quite maybe the splash that we'd hoped for. But anyway we broke into the offices and, you know, I can't remember, I think the original claim was something like £64,000 worth of damage; it wasn't quite as bad as that. We phoned the police before cutting the phone line and waited then till the police arrived.

Alun Llwyd: I think part of the strength of what Cymdeithas were doing at the time was that any kind of non-violent direct action is not just non-violent in the way that it's conducted, but it's also non-violent in the way that it's accepted. The key part is, 'Yes, I broke into a Tory government office, and yes, I wrecked a Tory government office, and yes, we poured lemonade down the back of £50,000 worth of computers, but more importantly, we rang the police after that and said, we're here, we've done this, come and get us.'

Branwen Niclas: Our aim was to be imprisoned, and I at the time was working for Cymdeithas, and Alun was the chair of Cymdeithas, and the idea was that two prominent members of Cymdeithas were taking part and taking responsibility for quite a big act.

At the beginning, they refused us bail, but then we got bail in about two days, and it was quite a long nine months of waiting till our trial in Mold Crown Court. There was a lot of waiting and a bit of messing around, and I think they were fearful of a lot of campaigning and protests around our court case, so the dates would always change, and it was quite stressful on one level.

We were imprisoned the beginning of September, 4 September 1990, something like that, and we were released 2 or 3 or 4 December, and then Dewi Prysor and the other two people accused of the letter bomb campaign were arrested soon afterwards. It was all a little . . . funny.

Dewi Prysor: I was picked up on 22 January. Branwen's was the first letter I received in prison. I'd only just got to HMP Walton and, the following morning, there was a letter, and it was from Branwen.

Branwen Niclas: It had all been planned by the authorities. There was a rally when Alun and I were in prison in Carmarthen – obviously we weren't there. But there were something like thirty spooks in that rally. Those facts didn't come out till Dewi Prysor's trial, but there was a lot of infiltration during those years, there's no doubt about it.

Dewi Prysor: That was the Deddf Eiddo, a rally for the property act. They were following Sion Jenkins during that rally in Caernarfon. There were thirty spooks watching Sion.

Branwen Niclas: I think Alun and I were knackered. For both of us, I think, there was a kind of burn-out. It was almost as if we were on a hamster wheel for years, and we received the last long imprisonment. And there hadn't been a long imprisonment in Cymdeithas anyway since about I think 1985, 1986, which was Ffred Ffransis, so there hadn't been a long imprisonment, and that was part of our aim, was to be imprisoned to show the seriousness of the political situation.

It was twelve months with six months suspended, so we were in for three. And that was probably what we were expecting. We knew we were going for a definite period of imprisonment, and that was our aim: we knew it wouldn't be something like two weeks or fourteen days, twenty-eight days, and we'd done fourteen days before for non-payment of fines. But in a way, it helped both of us, because I think the shock is the first time when you go into prison, but if you know you can handle it, 'Well, I can hack it,' we could hack it for a few months, and we were happy and ready to do that at that time in our lives.

In the eighties and early nineties, we had the Tory government in Westminster. But now there's more political lobbying in Wales, rather than direct-action campaigning.

In 1990 Datblygu released Pyst, *the record recognised as their masterpiece. The album was recorded by Gorwel Owen in his home studio, in a flat above a post office in Anglesey.*

David R. Edwards' lyrics were equally piercing in their appraisal of Wales and of their author, who was by now living an increasingly dissolute life. At the same time as the album's release the profile of Datblygu and their contemporaries was increased by a new S4C programme, Fideo 9, *dedicated to contemporary Cymraeg music.*

Bedwyr Williams: I never joined Cymdeithas yr Iaith. I'm always a bit reticent about agreeing with loads of people. And growing up in Wales, the thing that I don't like was that Wales is a big team place: you're either in a choir, or you're in a band, or a rugby team and even though I loved all those Welsh bands it was cliquey as well, and at a certain point, I knew 'I'm not like this. I can't be just somebody going like that – it's not me. I've got my own thing going on; I need to get away from this.' I guess I think that's why I always liked Datblygu; David was doing it in Welsh but aiming his Sten gun at everyone.

David R. Edwards: When we released an album called *Pyst* John Peel played the first three tracks and he said, on the radio, at eleven o'clock on a Sunday night, the first songs on the show, he said, 'If you've never bought a Welsh-language record before, go out and buy this one.'

Pat Morgan: I had a Morris 1000, very slow on the road, and I used to tell David, 'There's a crocodile behind me because I can't get more than 35 miles an hour,' and that gets put into a song about going to the bottle bank, and a plodding piano that goes with that. 'Dwylo Olew' ['Oily Hands'], that was the garage in Bronllys. It's life in a country village where you're sort of stuck with what you see out of your window. When we were living together, he couldn't get a job, so there was one going in the petrol station, serving petrol, and I thought, 'God, you must get something better than this.' He got a job in Brecon Tourist Information where the bus from Llangorse got in to Brecon about an hour before the office opened, so he'd go to the supermarket, drink a bottle of sherry and then go to work. I ended up saying, 'Why don't you write to the chairman of Powys Health Board and say you've been applying for all these jobs and not even got an interview, why can't you give me a chance?' He got a job in the Finance department in Bronllys Hospital. He worked there for a couple of years and then lived in the nurses' home. I very much associate *Pyst* with Bronllys Hospital, and David living in the nurses' home.

David Wrench: Gorwel played me *Pyst* just before it came out, and still it's one of my top ten records by anyone. It's insanely good. I don't understand: if an English-language audience can get *L'Histoire de Melodie Nelson* by Serge Gainsbourg why they can't get *Pyst*.

Gorwel Owen: There's a song on another Datblygu album, *Wyau*, that talks about driving through places that aren't on the map. It captures what it was like then, travelling through Wales. The studio was above a post office in my old bedroom. What I remember was how much fun it was and how quick it was to record *Pyst*: there were two or three songs they had recorded for *Fideo 9*; the rest were done over two weekends, and that involved going to Holyhead, where I taught, to record the piano. They were very fast. Dave's one of the few people I've worked with when you say, 'Do you want to hear how that sounded?' he says, 'No, next.' It was winter, and Dave was teaching then.

Siôn Jobbins: The good thing which Rhys Mwyn and Datblygu did was they criticised Welsh-language culture, but in Welsh, saying 'Cymru crummy' and 'Plaid Cymru are crap,' and with Datblygu, for the first time, they actually managed and I'm still not sure how – to reach out to people who didn't speak Welsh. It's quite peculiar, especially with Datblygu, where the words are so important, and the beauty of the words is what makes it so special.

Rhys Ifans: There was a real desire in that radicalised alternative music scene back then to reach out beyond the strongholds of the Welsh language. I've always grown up with this conflict about being a Welsh-speaker: there's a frustration and an anger naturally at people who are antagonistic and oppressive towards the Welsh language, particularly Welsh people, sometimes good Welsh socialists, which was astounding. There was a real antagonism in the seventies towards the Welsh language, Neil Kinnock particularly, which is very sad. I think you have to understand they grew up in households where the international language of socialism was English, and they were coming from that point as opposed to some form of imperialism. It's a difficult one, that part, and I'm glad it's gone.

David Wrench: I would get annoyed with the constant fact that there was an element in Wales who would be happy just that stuff was happening, and not about the quality of it. You'd see stuff on S4C and think the production values were so bad. A major change was a programme on S4C called *Fideo 9*. I'd tune in every week to see it because it was always good, and the production values were good, and they were doing something. Even if they had a lower budget, it was about ideas. You could watch it and see people were passionate about what they were doing, and they were doing it as well as they possibly could do. Geraint Jarman was a producer and it was hosted by Eddie Ladd.

Cian Ciarán: I was a fourteen-year-old drummer, playing every week-end, fifty quid in your pocket, then with Welsh-language TV there were eventually three or four music-led programmes; you'd be doing three, four, five videos a year and doing interviews. It was a great education that got lost in the nineties, and is pretty much non-existent now.

Pat Morgan: When Geraint Jarman started doing *Fideo 9* was when everything really took off. But in the period of '84 to '89 it was hard work, letter writing, and phones. It was quite expensive to phone in those days, so it tended to be letter writing. I sort of had to manage

David when we used to appear on TV. He was a little bit of a homebird, difficult to galvanise into getting out of the house. I would be the driver and the instigator of pushing us to go places and do it. But once he was there, that was it: he was in a zone, be-all and end-all.

Alun Llwyd: I first got to know Dave when I was working at a local radio station called Marcher Sound in Wrexham, and I was doing a Welsh-language rock bulletin every Friday night. I always loved doing it because it allowed me the licence to actually ring up Dave Datblygu and have a chat to him about the new Datblygu EP.

I first talked to him then, but when I moved to university in Aberystwyth, Dave turned up one evening at a pub I was working in – but then he turned up at the pub every night after that. And suddenly there was a gang of people around Dave and you could see it sapping away his energy, and whether there was a weakness there from his point of view, there was a lot of attention, a lot of drink, a lot of drugs, and you kind of felt something had got away, because Datblygu, to me, were always this kind of mysterious thing that were based in Brecon, or that were based in Cardigan, and suddenly he was hanging around in Aberystwyth. 'Hang on, this isn't right, this isn't what it was meant to be.'

Pat Morgan: I think he was looking for friends then, mixing with the drug-taking people, and he went off the rails, unfortunately. For a while he was living rough in the shelter near the pier in Aberystwyth. He put his address as the Shelter in Aberystwyth, The Esplanade. He was a bit wild.

Gorwel Owen: I only remember really exciting gigs, sometimes the technology was hit and miss but Dave was very reactive, in often humorous ways, to audiences.

Alun Llwyd: There were amazing Datblygu shows, which were basically huge raves with a thousand people. But it was a very short window. It culminated when me and Bran came out of prison and Cymdeithas put on a massive all-day event in Pafiliwn Pontrhyd-fendigaid and Datblygu performed there. That was towards the tail-end when it happened, and then Dave disappeared for a while after that.

Bedwyr Williams: I saw Datblygu when I was sixteen in the Tivoli in Buckley. David played a tape on a shit cassette player that he put on the stage with a mike to it, and there was somebody playing a swannee whistle in time to the music; it looked so sophisticated. It was a different level of experience and that was my first time of seeing them live. People in Caernarfon that were working class, that hated the middle-class Welsh-speakers, really liked him, because he was so scathing. There's that song, 'Cân i Gymry', he machine-guns the Welsh Establishment and it's relentless, it's amazing. I've come to really love it properly in my forties, and I think a lot of people have, people finally appreciate the value of that band.

Gruff Rhys: Datblygu broke into the psyche of Welsh-speakers in a mainstream way with 'Cân i Gymry'. It's a forensic takedown in list form of the Welsh-speaking middle class. It's so uncanny and accurate, it's a work of genius. There had been other moments of genius on their other records, but this was made to measure for Welsh-speakers in particular. It was a weirdly radio-friendly, uplifting track and got played a lot on Radio Cymru.

Nici Beech: It was spot-on as an analysis of a kind of society that existed and perhaps still exists. It's an accusation that people have all those badges but almost don't understand Wales enough. At the time David named names and mentioned a presenter on S4C who was young and the daughter of an actor and had the background of

367

the privileged middle class who seem to find themselves on TV, but it's about everyone really, apart from Dave. When I was growing up, I hated the cyfryngis [media types] in the late eighties, the people who earned a lot of money on a gravy train and then I became one of them, I worked for S4C and put Gorky's and Catatonia on kids' TV, although I missed the proper gravy train.

Cân i Gymry

Gradd da yn y Gymraeg
Ar y Volvo bathodyn Tafod y Ddraig
Hoff o fynychu pwyllgorau blinedig
Am ddyfodol yr iaith yn enwedig,
Meistrioli iaith lleifrifol fel hobi
Platiau dwyiethog i helpu y gyrru
Agwedd cwbl addas
Ar gyfer cynllun cartre
Syth mas o set 'Dinas'.
Wastod yn mynd i Lydaw
Byth yn mynd i Ffrainc,
Wastod yn mynd i Wlad y Basg
Byth yn mynd i Sbaen.
Fin nos yn mynychu bwytai
Wedi dydd ar y prosesydd geiriau,
Mewn swydd sy'n talu'r morgais
I'ch gwyneb person cwbl cwrtais,
O'r ysgol feithrin i Brifysgol Cymru
Tocyn oes ar y trên grefi,
Byddai'n well da fi fod yn jynci
Na bod mor wyrdd â phoster Plaid Cymru.

[*Translation*]

A Song for the Welsh

A good degree in Welsh
On the Volvo a Tafod y Ddraig sticker,
Fond of attending tiresome committee meetings
About the future of the language in particular,
Mastering a minority language as a hobby
Bilingual plates to help the driving,
A perfectly appropriate attitude
For a home plan straight out of the 'Dinas' set.
Always going to Brittany,
Never going to France,
Always going to the Basque country
Never going to Spain.
At night going to restaurants
After a day on the word processor,
in a job that pays your mortgage
To your face a perfectly courteous person
From nursery school to the University of Wales
A lifetime ticket on the gravy train,
I would rather be a junkie
Than be as green as a Plaid Cymru poster.

Rhys Mwyn: There was a time in the early eighties onwards where slowly but surely Welsh culture was redefined by a very small group of people, and in a way, it ends up with, it doesn't really matter who, it could be Catatonia, playing at a place like TJ's in Newport, and there's none of this: 'Oh, they're singing in Welsh,' or 'They're not singing in Welsh.' No one gives a shit. They're just saying it's a good band. In a very short period of time, in less than ten years, there was a huge change.

THIRTEEN

CAU PWLL, LLADD CYMUNED / CLOSE A PIT, KILL A COMMUNITY

Voices

Dewi 'Mav' Bowen
James Dean Bradfield
Ian Courtney
Bob Croydon
Phil Cullen
Andrew Davies
Ron Davies
Arfon Evans
Richard Frame

Peter Hain
Kim Howells
David Hurn
Patrick Jones
Neil Kinnock
Eluned Morgan
Richard Parfitt
Ann Pettitt
Christine Powell

Adam Price
Michael Sheen
Lesley Smith
Terry Stevens
Rachel Trezise
Phil White
Rowan Williams
Nicky Wire
Leanne Wood

———

The urban communities of South Wales endured a series of societal problems throughout the 1980s. The divestment of nationalised industry, introduced by the monetarist policies of the Conservative government, which saw a fundamental redrawing of the relationship between the state and the citizen, had a profound effect on the working lives of the population. Prior to the Miners' Strike, the recession at the start of the decade had had a disproportionate impact on employment levels in Wales and was manifested by a sense of shock present in everyday life. Contemporary Westminster briefing notes from the Secretary of State for Wales to the rest of the Cabinet referred to the possibility of a return to the conditions of the Great Depression within the country. These anxieties were sustained by the symbolism

*of the mass job losses that occurred with increasing regularity and
vehemence; in March 1980, over the course of an afternoon, British
Steel terminated 6,500 jobs at its Shotton plant on Deeside, north-east
Wales. At the time this was the largest industrial redundancy to occur
on a single day in Western Europe. The resonance of an area's largest
employer taking such drastic measures was felt across the country and
accelerated a loss of confidence in the future. Within a year, the official
number of unemployed in Wales stood at around 150,000; the figure of
available vacancies was little more than 5,000.*

*Half a decade later, by which time growth had returned to the
United Kingdom and to the south-east of England in particular,
Wales's unemployment count reached a record post-war high of
170,500. In the wake of the strike, mining redundancies added to
the already significant losses in the manufacturing, steel and other
energy sectors. In some parts of South Wales, notably the Valleys,
the employment rate among the working-age population had fallen
far below 70 per cent. Instead of offers of alternative long- or mid-
term employment, communities were treated to a successive series
of schemes and initiatives intended to address the developing crises
caused by the loss of jobs and social cohesion.*

Arfon Evans: You close a pit and you kill a community. The village
of Maerdy on its own had a rateable value going back to the Rhondda
Council that was something like £2 or £3 million a year. The wages spent
in the local community were unbelievable, and once you withdrew that
it was there, graphically, in front of you. You could see the demise of
the community from Maerdy down to Porth.

The Rhondda has been so faithful to the Labour Party, returning
MPs by majorities of over 30,000, and it really breaks my heart when
you consider the sacrifices made, how our dry steam-coal fuelled the
British Navy in the First World War. In Maerdy in 1885, eighty-one
miners were killed on Christmas Eve. Elfed Davies was the one MP
I can remember who was a miner; he worked in Tylorstown pit. But

there was nothing to show for that 30,000 majority. If I was an MP with a 30,000 majority, I would have built infrastructure into the Rhondda, I think I would have attracted industrialists to come in, because there's no finer employees, who are prepared to work hard, be retrained. I would have turned Parliament upside-down, inside-out.

Peter Hain: After the strike, virtually all the pits in Neath had been closed; there were still a number of smaller pits, including one with a pit pony still operating. But what really struck me was that if I talked to a school or went into the working men's club in Neath, the mining glue that bound these communities together was still very strong. Even if the numbers had withered dramatically, virtually everybody's father or grandfather and certainly great-grandfather had worked down the pit.

Leanne Wood: In the aftermath of the Miners' Strike there was a definite sense of defeat, and prior to the defeat there was a lot of hope; we believed we could do this. They wouldn't have embarked on it if they didn't think they could win the strike, I'm sure of that. Because the pain that you have to go through to do something like that is huge. It ruined families, and split communities. I remember campaigns about twenty or twenty-five years later to try and save the Burberry factory in the Rhondda, and that fighting spirit had gone. The belief at the start of that campaign to save the factory was that we weren't going to win. It was a completely different vibe. And I think that was because of our defeat during the Miners' Strike. Once you've suffered a defeat like that, it is hard to get back up.

Phil Cullen: There are statistics that show that Merthyr became the sick man of the country overnight; people are going to do what they have to do. Fifteen people from my pit, Cynheidre, a massive colliery, went into teaching. I went into the law, but the vast majority of people never worked again. When Cynheidre was in its death throes and we'd given up the fight to save the pit, the Coal Board had quite a few people from its training department seconded there and there was money available for people to set up small business, to retrain, and all of a sudden we had an enormous amount of prospective photographers. Everyone was going to be a David Bailey, with huge lenses walking about, taking photos of this, that and the other, and I thought, 'This will end in tears.' Within six months of the pit closing and the redundancy money being spent there wasn't one of them that made it.

Phil White: After the strike those who took redundancy lived the life of Riley for a short period of time, which was never a life that they were going to be able to sustain, and there were those who made a success of their redundancy as well. Some of them did start their own little employment business. I remember two friends, they started a business changing tyres.

Neil Kinnock: Although the pits were closing around us and Ebbw Vale was losing workers, and BP were shutting down, Ford was coming in to Bridgend, even as the radiator plant in Llanelli was shutting. Hoover's was cutting back on employment, but that was because of improved technology, so we were told. I was aware of this very fragile economic condition that was worsening, and nevertheless, in the early eighties, the custom and practice, the expectations, the habits of the previous thirty years were still very, very substantial.

Rachel Trezise: After the strike there was a real sense of 'We've lost. There's nothing.' Talk about being encouraged with writing: everyone told me, 'No, don't do that, don't write. Go and work in a factory.' There was that real sense of everyone being scared that you were trying too hard. There was no confidence; everybody was on their knees. Employment was either Sony or Ford in Bridgend. My brother was a car sprayer – he's not now, he's a tattooist – but he had a really good job in Ford, it was £400 a week, but that was unknown, really. And he was there for a while: he was there for seven, eight years.

Christine Powell: After the mine closed my husband was on the dole for a total of two days. He managed to get into Ford's in Bridgend. They'd already desolated this valley. Of all the pits, we only had Treforgan and Blaenant left. The damage had been done here; the Miners' Strike was just finishing us off.

The greatest responsibility for the economic future of Wales remained with the Welsh Development Agency, run by a board appointed by the Westminster government. In parallel with its responsibilities for land reclamation and redevelopment, the latter often taking the form of factory construction, as well as financial support for Welsh businesses, the WDA energetically pursued a policy of inward investment. The policy's goal was to attract overseas companies to establish a manufacturing base in Wales, which was achieved by the offer of generous fiscal incentives. The success of inward investment was measured by the single criterion of job creation. This basic metric hindered the chances of another of the policy's stated aims: self-sustaining growth. The products assembled by companies courted by inward investment rewards were frequently at the end of their life cycles; the skills required for their production were basic and non-transferable; and pay levels were consequently moderate, particularly in comparison to the wages earned in the skilled industrial work that these new jobs sought to replace. Despite the incentives of grants, premises and access to further funding, businesses were hesitant to relocate head office or research and development departments, reinforcing the sense that Wales and its labour force, however skilled, was cheap to hire and best left to assembly-line categories of employment.

Andrew Davies: The Welsh Development Agency was set up and it was a one-club golfer. The strategy was basically, 'How do you make up for those job losses?' It was build it and they will come.

Ian Courtney: The WDA was dominated by property people, several of whom had come in from Cwmbran New Town and they saw these inward investment projects purely as how much money was doled out per job created, and what square footage of factory space they could build. There was absolutely zero fucking subtlety.

Bob Croydon: The WDA was there to generate employment because it was clear that industries were going into decline, and one of their policies was what we used to refer to as the Red Shed programme. It was their panacea – a colliery would close, the local MP would kick up a stink, the WDA would put the bulldozers in, flatten it into a plateau, put up a load of tin sheds and then put To Let boards on them, and the miners who had been made redundant would plough their redundancy money into making dartboards, or fibreglass chess sets and then go banko in a year. And of course, that deterred outside investment, because a London industrial property investor would say, 'It's not worth investing or buying a factory in South Wales because the WDA will come along and undercut us.'

Christine Powell: There was Ford's and they were employing in the steelworks at Margam where a lot of the boys from the pit went. I know one person who worked in Hitachi. There were no skills to develop. The people employed there were the precursors of robots, grab a couple of integrated circuits, stick that one in there, solder that joint, pass it on to the next person.

James Dean Bradfield: You had a lot of Japanese factories in the Valleys. There were some friends, a few relatives, working in the Hitachi factory. I didn't hear much moaning; if new jobs came in, people just went, 'Thank fuck for that. I've got a job.' There wasn't much questioning of the job that was there. I think it was classic divide-and-conquer. If you've got no job and your wife has lost her job, or your husband has lost his job, or son or daughter, then these other new jobs come in and they're very much unskilled jobs. There's no union to speak of and there's less of a residual pay structure and there's not as much insurance.

Patrick Jones: People were really struggling and ended up having to battle on, which is what they wanted, the powers that be. They wanted everyone to have their little tunnel and not care. The community started fragmenting. It was divide and rule. The further you got up into Rhymney and Tredegar and Ebbw Vale and Blaenavon, there was a huge sense of loss and abandonment.

Andrew Davies: There was an opportunity to adopt a Scandinavian route, to invest in people, to create a high-skill, high-value-added economy, and it was wasted. What we had instead was inward investment; Bob's Croydon's phrase was 'renting jobs from the Japanese'. They were also known as screwdriver jobs. They were light assembly and to a large extent, more often than not, they employed women rather than men. Former miners, for all sorts of reasons, didn't see those jobs as attractive or masculine, or for them. While these job schemes made up for it in the short term, they were not sustainable. It's difficult to think of many of those Japanese companies that came during the 1980s, the Panasonics, the Sonys, the Hitachis, Sharp, which became permanent or had any longevity. They were footloose, and when economic conditions changed, they were always the first to go. If you look at it now, there's hardly any of that investment still here.

Bob Croydon: Renting jobs from the Japanese was another policy of the Welsh Development Agency. We used to do a huge amount of work for them. It was all semi-skilled, in the sense that it took the workforce a week to learn how to use a soldering iron, put the red wire to the yellow wire and all the rest of it. And you had situations in some places where there were more women employed than men.

It wasn't perceived as man's work: it wasn't heavy industrial work, nor was it, indeed, skilled work. It partly led to the housing crisis and the labour crisis, because from the 1980s onwards you didn't have fifty bricklayers being trained by a British Steel works. People don't think about the bricklayers employed by British Steel, but they used to have to line those furnaces and reline the furnaces, so they trained brick-layers. There were carpenters and blacksmiths graduating from the Coal Board, fitters and turners, guys who worked in Ford. BP would train fifty apprentices and keep five; forty-five of those guys who'd trained as fitters on the apprenticeship would end up working in garages. Even if they ended up working in Kwik Fit, they actually had an HNC [Higher National Certificate] or whatever the qualification was at the time. The spread-out benefits of that heavy industry were everywhere in Wales's past and once that had gone, how do you replace it? Rent a shed off the Welsh Development Agency and start a business making coffee tables and call yourself an entrepreneur? It was irreplaceable.

Peter Hain: 'Here's a lump of money towards using your lump sum to start up your own business,' but your own business is only going to work if there's a local economy for you to work in. Unless it's making chip butties, there isn't a local economy for your business to thrive in.

Phil White: No one asked what could we be doing in terms of seed, what can we actually grow here? If we can't take the men to the factories, can we bring the factories to the workforce?

Lesley Smith: Roles in the family changed, because women started working, some would have called that pin money in the early days, but it became a necessity. Once those grants disappeared, so did those factories. We've always found it difficult to attract investment in the Valleys, and very much because of the transport issues.

The work in the factories was designed for women's hands; the pay, even though it wasn't awful pay, it wasn't good pay like the miners had.

Lives did change, and not just lives. Communities changed, people left their valley to work – to get buses going down to the DVLA, all these call-centre places. There was nothing in our valley. At one point the organisation I work for, a charity and a social enterprise, was one of the biggest employers in the valley, and we only had about twelve people working for us.

Neil Kinnock: I had the first Japanese factory in my constituency in Trethomas, Takiron, which was a Mitsubishi subsidiary. It made extruded plastic goods. The boys came straight out of the pits and went to the perfectly designed and very well managed Takiron factory and thought they were in wonderland: the wages were almost as good as in the pit, not that they were brilliant in the pit, and people went to work at eight o'clock in the morning and went home at four o'clock in the afternoon and they were clean, they weren't knackered, there was no danger; it was bloody wonderful. As it happened, Takiron had a stroke of accidental genius, they appointed Ken Jones, who I'd played rugby with at university, as their personnel manager. British Lion Ken Jones, Welsh centre, wonderful man. He was appointed by the union and Ken understood the boys immediately. And there was never any trouble of any kind in a very, very productive Takiron factory which was thriving for twenty-five, thirty years. I was very lucky.

Peter Hain: I invited the chairman and a number of other WDA luminaries to visit me and took them to the Blaenant Colliery site in the Dulais Valley, and other areas, and said, 'Look, we ought to establish industrial parks here, and attract new technology businesses and train local people to work in them.' And essentially, they went with an alternative vision of using the Valleys as human supply chains for the M4 corridor.

Adam Price: It strikes me that we don't have a sense, culturally and historically, of what it is to be a progressive economy, because of our experiences both of pre-nationalisation and then of nationalisation; nationalisation didn't turn out so well for us, either. We don't have a stock of stories about what it would be to set up an enterprise – a socially-owned enterprise or a cooperatively-owned enterprise, or one owned by a private individual with progressive values. We don't have stories that present us with different ways of organising our economy that we can point to.

Peter Hain: Most European countries are a hell of a lot better at it than we were, because especially under the Tories we had this free market, neoliberal dogma that said: 'Public investment, you don't back winners.' My view was, look at all the successful economies in the modern era – and I exclude Britain from these, I don't think it is a successful economy – South Korea, for example, Germany, and a number of others, South Korea being important because it was a post-war start-up economy, where the government decided they wanted to build a ship-building industry, so they built one.

Andrew Davies: Later, when I was Economic Development Minister, I was at an economic forum, which premised 'The biggest public policy disaster in the UK in Wales was xyz,' and I said, 'No, I don't agree: the biggest missed opportunity and failure was the failure to use North Sea oil during the 1980s,' and that was a once-in-a-lifetime opportunity to invest in infrastructure, skills, to really put Britain onto a different trajectory, and for all sorts of reasons it was not used. We're left with Victorian rail infrastructure and all the other social and economic infrastructure; I think it's an absolute crime, that investment from North Sea oil was used instead for tax cuts primarily, but also for maintaining levels of social security.

Phil Cullen: I worked for a couple of years in the aircraft industry in Llanelli. We were building internal galleys for commercial airlines, C. F. Taylor was the name of the company. They had a factory in

Wokingham which had been there for years; they were a leading company. They had an opportunity of two free factory units given to them by the WDA. They had loads of incentives, they were paid by the British government, indirectly through the WDA, for every member of staff they took off the dole and people thought this would be the new future of Llanelli. C. F. Taylor took as much money as they could, they employed as few people as they possibly could get away with, and then they went back to Wokingham. They were clever enough – they stayed for nearly ten years – but once all the incentives went, they went. They wouldn't recognise trade unions, although Wokingham was heavily unionised. I used to talk to the conveners in Wokingham and they disliked us intensely in Llanelli, because they felt we were being used as a stick to beat them with. A galley for a Boeing 747 built in South Wales was about a third of the cost of one being built in Wokingham.

Adam Price: What has survived in places like the anthracite coalfield and Llanelli, for example, is a locally owned, locally rooted manufacturing sector, companies which sometimes are sneeringly referred to as metal-bashers, the engineering equivalent of 'trade', but working with metal, because that was the other industry that was dominant and survived. In modern metallurgy industrial south-west Wales is certainly one of the leading centres in the UK, and probably in Europe. It's a story that we don't tell very well, because it somehow doesn't fit with the prevailing notion of who we are. If we were in the Black Forest or in Swabia in Germany, this would be a defining piece of our identity. The way that they see their culture partly as *Maschinenbauer*: people who take things apart and put them together, even as kids. This is part of our culture, companies have survived: we still make things, and working with metal has very, very deep roots, economically and socially but also culturally as well, and yet we haven't been able to locate it within the story that we tell about ourselves.

*In the absence of industry or trade apprenticeships, the Youth
Training Scheme, or YTS, had been established in 1983 as a means
of introducing the principles of free enterprise to school leavers or the
youthful unemployed. The scheme was operated by the Manpower
Services Commission, a Westminster quango. That same year the
government adopted a new policy towards mental health following the
publication of a report, 'Making a Reality of Community Care', and
passed a Mental Health Act. In the aftermath of the Miners' Strike,
both these areas of policy – opportunities for young people and mental
health provision – would have ramifications within communities that
were attempting to recover from the effects of a year of bitter dispute
and lost livelihoods. The influence of Right to Buy, a policy of the
Thatcher administration introduced early in its first term that allowed
council tenants to buy their homes, would also endure.*

Ron Davies: There's a great Chinese saying, 'No line is so thin it
doesn't have two sides,' and there were two sides to Thatcher. She
was admired and loathed in equal measure. She was loathed because
of her style and because of what had happened to the mining industry,
the steel industry and the other heavy industries and the subsequent
mass unemployment, but I can recall chatting to guys who had lost
their jobs but were very pleased and they were going to vote Tory
because they'd been able to buy their council house, which they'd
wanted to do for twenty years. She was able to ride that out and then
emerged with a huge majority in 1987, even though Labour had done
reasonably well.

The Welsh group in Parliament would meet on a very regular basis
and was always bubbling away at some issue. I was becoming very
conscious, and it was part of my own epiphany, partly through the
work that I was doing on the front bench, and partly through my
constituency work, of the Welsh dimension. When you get to Welsh
questions, you start to question: What's the Secretary of State doing?
What's the Welsh budget? What scale of unemployment is happening?

And I spoke on the then Welsh Secretary Peter Walker's bill, called the Valleys Initiative, which was just nonsense.

Kim Howells: All those Valleys Initiatives were rubbish, absolute bloody rubbish. They were the worst kind of job creation schemes because they had no strategy; they had no idea about what might be possible. I used to get into terrible arguments by reminding people that in the heart of the coalfield, take somewhere like Aberdare or Treorchy or almost anywhere round there, they're 160 miles from the centre of London, 150 miles from what was then the busiest airport in the world, a stone's throw from the M4 corridor; we ought to have been booming.

Phil Cullen: If you remove 36,000 jobs from the coalfield you have to be seen to mitigate that mess somehow. It's all very well talking about retraining, but that amount of people can't all become entrepreneurs. It's not possible to split the atom in everyone's garden shed. You had a huge number of men who, bluntly, were not suitable to any form of work other than coal mining, then, because they were threatened with their unemployment benefit being stopped, they would trot along to these schemes, but the reality is if you look at people living in Aberdare, Maesteg or the Rhondda, they were not on the M4 corridor. The geographical sums didn't add up, the work simply wasn't in the Valleys. You can train people and send them on all the courses you like, but if there wasn't a major employer like Ford or Bosch in the area, by the time they've bought their train tickets to Cardiff, people were marginally worse off than if they'd made a claim for benefit.

Peter Hain: I think the gross failure of the Thatcher government and the Tories was not to provide investment in new jobs and new skills, instead of which, as a deliberate policy, redundant miners were put on what was called Invalidity Benefit, which subsequently became Disability Living Allowance, which to a lot of people was attractive because it was tax-free, but it meant that instead of whole lives focused around work, people were subsidised into a workless culture which was later reproduced in their kids through the 1990s and still into the 2000s; this led to the fragmentation and decline of a culture.

Andrew Davies: In the South Wales Valleys people were moved off the unemployment register. I don't know how many times the definition of unemployment was changed by the Tory government, maybe as many as twenty times. People weren't counted as unemployed; they were economically inactive and that's why you've still got high levels of deprivation there, people weren't helped in any meaningful way, they were kept unemployed, but in a way that was not defined as unemployed.

Ron Davies: The Tory Welsh Office treated Wales by repackaging what was already there. You take money from this budget and money from that budget and there was never any additional money. They'd bundle it all together and say, 'Here, there's an initiative.' It was a difficult time for us in Labour, because we knew what was happening: the Welsh industrial base was disappearing and it was being replaced by people that we knew were going to be here today and eventually gone next year, if not tomorrow. If you criticised the process when a car factory or a Panasonic came along, if we said, 'Can't we stop and think about this?' you were told you were selling down Welsh workers, you were depriving Welsh men and women of the opportunity of work. 'Why don't you welcome the fact that unemployment's going to go down?' We were hamstrung by that process, because inward investment was the big mover, that and the appalling Youth Training Schemes.

Leanne Wood: In my teenage years, the later eighties, I remember seeing my peers not being able to get any work and being forced into YTS schemes, which were massive at the time, and they were getting paid £28 a week for really hard manual labour. Manpower Services were running the YTS schemes. I remember speaking to some of those young lads, and then, later on, becoming a probation officer, and seeing some of them coming in through the court system. And because there was no secure employment, they were finding other ways of making money, in the informal economy, which was rife, and occasionally some of them would end up before the courts. There's a thread that connects right through. My work as a probation officer ended up with me going into politics, because I realised there was a limit to the problems you could solve in that kind of job.

Richard Frame: Those Manpower and YTS schemes were starting up all over the place. They did the Fourteen Locks scheme between Newport and Cwmbran, clearing the disused locks to turn it into a footpath. It was a bloody crap job they did; years later, they had to do it again. There were tons of senseless things being done to keep people like unemployed steelworkers entertained. It was a form of occupational therapy, half-hearted. There really wasn't much to it.

Rachel Trezise: My husband did a YTS scheme; they were so poorly paid. The Miners' Strike always seemed to be there in my life. It never ended. It was like a war that we were losing, from the time that I was born. Much to my annoyance everybody accepted it.

Terry Stevens: Across Wales, Manpower was welcomed as an Elastoplast. Many, many things were done to develop the infrastructure of tourism, parks, footpaths, stabilising buildings that were crumbling but were of heritage interest. After three years, you couldn't go back to those projects, and nobody was prepared to pick them up. It kept an awful lot of youngsters in some sort of employment for a little while, undoubtedly it helped them develop some skills, but it was Elastoplast and with no commitment to any long-term thought of keeping them on.

Phil White: I remember some pathetic attempt with those training schemes, all that taking you off the unemployment register, Manpower, all talk, 'This could be the opportunity,' but there really were no opportunities: you were only there to keep you off the unemployment benefit register. The YTS, what a heap. And they were literally, a heap. A heap of children at that time, and for those whose parents had been on strike for a twelvemonth, it was doubly hard.

Rachel Trezise: It happened so quickly to other people. There was the mining generation, and then there was virtually nothing. Kids in my comp, there would always be one person working in the family. My mother was an alcoholic, so that seemed normal to me, there were lots of drinkers around. Then I was about sixteen, seventeen when the heroin started coming in and lost lots of friends.

Dewi 'Mav' Bowen: My brother worked for TEDS for years, which is Taff Ely Drugs Support, and he said in court, 'Having a drug problem is almost a substitute for having a job, because you get up in the morning, you've got something you've got to do. And the real solution to drug addiction in the Valleys is give them a fucking proper job, because that's what they're missing.' And he was right.

Nicky Wire: It was definitely around, hard drugs, not so much that we ever came across it, but you knew it was happening. Because at that age I lived, I wouldn't say it was a sheltered life, but we had a really good group of people around us all. When we started YTS a couple of times, you would see miners in there with these huge, disfigured hands, trying to type out a CV and shit like that, and that was heart-breaking. I had to do a YTS, everyone did.

Dewi 'Mav' Bowen: I've really got to blame Thatcher for all this, because how did a town like Maerdy, a hard-working heavy industry place, turn into a hard drugs kind of community almost overnight?

385

Where the fuck did they come from? I still had my finger on the pulse of drug-dealing, even though I'd distanced myself from it all and had only ever been lightly involved in psychedelics – by then I'd become an aspiring prehistorian. But where did all that hard stuff come from? People said, 'I'll have a pack of that, I'll try it,' and they were smoking heroin. Now, brown heroin was a scourge, because it was an easy step from rolling a joint to putting a bit of brown in and smoking that, and it was awful. All over. Places like Skewen, Briton Ferry, all these people turning into junkies. A lot of younger redundant miners had lots of money and no families; some of them bought amphetamine sulphate and big motorbikes, taking lots of speed, and another bunch were taking brown. A fair bit of the redundancy money went into that, which oiled the wheels of where we are now, indeed.

Rowan Williams: Encountering it on the ground, and especially in the Valley communities, was a bit of a rude shock: the sheer physical dereliction of the towns, the obviously increased profile of the drug problem, and, once or twice, picking up first-hand from people the insight into that system. One of our clergy had a grandson, I think it was, who had a massive drug problem. I used to hear from him occasionally. I remember confirming a young man in Sirhowy Valley who had been a very active drug dealer. I'd pick up a little bit from the coalface on that. It was a bit of a shock to see how much the centre had been hollowed out and the image in my mind is of grandmothers bringing their grandchildren to church on a Sunday, because the intervening generation were neither very keen on church nor very keen on parenting sometimes, in some of these very battered communities.

Richard Frame: Newport was a roughty-toughty sort of place, beer-drinking, lots of pubs, docks and men who'd been used to working in the steelworks.

I worked in St Cadoc's, the asylum in Newport, for about seven or eight years. St Cadoc's was an old, gothic-looking Victorian asylum but it was also a true asylum – a place of safety. It was a huge place. When I got there it had once been a complete unit which was self-sufficient. There were no drugs used in treatment. The patients did everything. The nurse would get them up in the morning and get them out. The patients would feed themselves, they'd make their own clothes, they'd wash everything: it was a complete cycle of activity. Legislation had previously been brought in where they did away with all that, because it was regarded as being exploitative, and then the patients did bugger-all, they just sat around. And of course, they were going nuts.

Then the pharmaceuticals started coming into business and they introduced chlorpromazine. I remember talking to one of the charge nurses: he told me that a couple of days after they introduced chlorpromazine, he walked round the building and it went quiet. The drug absolutely knocked them out and it didn't take long for the side effects to start kicking in, all the shaking and the tremors, and then another drug, benzhexol, was introduced to cut out the side effects. The pharmaceutical companies had a great time; they were doing presentations to the consultants down in the front of the building, they'd be examining patients and experimenting on them. I now do mental health tribunals and I look at some of the medication that people are on and it's as long as my arm. And it's a vested interest. You had Valium in the sixties, but that whole raft of psychiatric drugs in particular was introduced in the early 1980s. As staff, we knew, we had been trained, that a lot of psychiatric disorders were treatable through different types of therapy, but the health service was no longer given the capacity to do it.

When Care in the Community came in, I even went to see the man who wrote the policy give a talk in Cwmbran in County Hall and as part of Care in the Community they stated they were going to discharge people into the community. What they were doing was, they were forcing these long-stay patients into almost becoming homeless and they ended up with me. I started working in homelessness in 1983. I ran a homeless hostel in Clarence Place in Newport, just above the TJ's music venue, and turned part of the hostel into a ward of former long-stay patients from St Cadoc's. There was a big problem in Newport of social deprivation.

Richard Parfitt: Many of my friends were outpatients at St Cadoc's. There were so many problems in the 1980s. Newport was a tough place. I had friends who had worked at Llanwern who took redundancy before they were forty. Really young.

Richard Frame: I was aware to a certain extent of the deprived areas in the town and how people were falling through the gaps. Services weren't there to meet their needs, and at the hostel we were soaking up lots of people who had nowhere else to turn to. It was an odd situation. The council wouldn't have accepted them as technically homeless unless we'd have been there, but because we were there, as a homeless hostel, they would accept them as homeless and we could then help them. Then at the end of their stay, we would have to send them back to another council estate where the whole thing would start again. It wasn't very cleverly thought out by the politicians. It's still there, a twenty-six-bed hostel. I was the first manager of it and then eventually became the director of the organisation. We started with about seven staff and ended up with about 700 staying with us, including several former steel workers. They were all homeless people that the local authority had accepted under the Statutory Homelessness Act.

A lot of those men – it was mostly men who came to live with us – sadly killed themselves eventually. They stayed with us for ages. I knew they weren't going to succeed once they were discharged from our hostel; it was cruel. It was part of this new government strategy in the 1980s. We put them in council flats on their own. So sad. I can think of two of them I knew who jumped into the river.

David Hurn: When I was photographing in Wales there was a great deal to photograph. Thatcher decimated what was basically the base of Welsh work; she decimated the coal industry, totally and utterly, but also steel and also slate, and the three major workforces in Wales were those three things. The only thing that she couldn't really decimate was agriculture. It's difficult to be a farmer in Wales; all you can really do is be a bloody sheep-farmer.

My feeling is that we don't ever make progress. The humanistic idea that, somehow, you're ploughing towards a better life, I don't actually believe that. I think we kind of stumble on, making the best of what we have at the moment. Nobody ever quite tells you what progress is. Is progress covering up the country with factories? Is it better to work in a Sony factory in a long line, putting something into the back of a television set? Is that progress from working down in a mine, with that extraordinary sense of community? It's uncivilised to work in a mine on your knees, shifting seven tons of coal a day – imagine what that's like. Is that progress? You go from at least something where there was a sense of community and everybody relying on everybody else for their lives.

Richard Frame: I was one of the founders of Newport Local History Society, and the first thing that I wanted to do was find out where John Frost, the Chartist, was buried, because nobody knew. I did find it in Bristol and got Neil Kinnock to unveil it. He gave a fantastic speech. Afterwards I went to a reception with him at the Mansion House and as we were driving there, I said to him, 'That was fantastic, have you got notes for that?' and he showed me a card with three bullet points on it. That was it. A great orator. I don't know whether he was the last of that breed, but there weren't many that you could put into a little group that were like that. He told me that it was reading *Rape of the Fair Country* that pushed him along into politics and a number of Welsh MPs that I've spoken to over the years have all said the same thing, that it was that book. I think it was a big attitudinal change. Thatcher's Britain was

Me–Me–Me and I think that when we were brought up in the fifties, sixties, just after the war, everything was about the community. I was in the Boy Scouts and the Cubs and it was all about public service and duty, not necessarily duty to the King or Queen, more about public service. We had to go and do shopping for the elderly; we had to do stuff involving the community, and I think it was Thatcher that finally put the lid on all of that. She turned everything into Me.

The Welsh Development Agency and Manpower Services Commission were only two among eight organisations mandated with addressing the socio-economic decline of South Wales. The other bodies included British Steel, local authorities, the Industry department of the Welsh Office, the Development Board for Rural Wales and the Land Authority for Wales. The result of this diversification was a persistent absence of a truly integrated economic development strategy and, given the prolonged rates of high unemployment in the country, only a limited degree of success. The contract between declining industries and the communities that had once been their workforce had frayed. Industry that still survived elsewhere was threadbare.

A WDA report prepared shortly before the Miners' Strike stated that nearly 400 factory sites in Wales remained unoccupied, a figure that tested the resilience of inward investment as a strategy. Within a decade many of these empty sites would temporarily flourish, although a criticism of factories and light industrial sites purpose-built for inward investment was that they were often located along the M4 corridor, some distance from the uplands of the Heads of the Valleys, where job creation had been identified as an economic necessity.

Michael Sheen: In South Wales a lot of the communities grew up around the industry and were left like boats on a muddy floor once the industry left, or as the industry died. It's a very complex relationship. I thought about it a lot when I was doing the Passion project in Port Talbot. The relationship reminded me of those folk tales, of the dragon that lives on the outskirts of the community and protects the village, protects the town and allows it to survive, but at the same time demands a sacrifice from the town. There's this understanding that you have to give a blood price in order to keep going.

Andrew Davies: If you just take the Swansea Bay area, in 1981 Port Talbot steelworks had 20,000 people working there; Llandarcy oil refinery and BP's Baglan Bay nearby petrochemical works both employed several thousand people; you had heavy industry, manufacturing, all around there, as well as the mining industry. Those jobs have all gone, and of course most of them were UK if not European pay rates. The Welsh economy, particularly the mining industry, reached its apogee of confidence in the early part of the twentieth century: working men's institutes, the very strong commitment to education and community, all that vibrancy, and there was a long decline through the twentieth century. Absolutely. As Economic Development Minister it struck me forcefully that social and human capital had been hollowed out.

Eluned Morgan: It always struck me, the way lots of people in the Valleys talked about those values and the importance of education and the understanding of education being seen as a way out, in a sense, for them and for their communities. And it was striking for me that that was certainly not the approach and attitude of working-class people in Ely. There was a cultural difference in terms of the working class from cities to those from mining communities, then, once those pits were closing, that was then eroded and that resulted in despair.

Despite these hardships, the links in communities that shared an institutional memory of resilience and mutual support survived. The traditions of music, drama and sport, rugby in particular, which had provided the mainstay of social cohesion outside work, endured.

391

Michael Sheen: The Sandfields Estate, which is the dominant estate of Port Talbot, was built to house the steelworkers, and when I was growing up the comprehensive school, Sandfields Comp, was somewhere that we used to go and play rugby and had to fight our way home from essentially; it was quite a frightening place to go and play. There was a feeling that the estate was rough and you were in for a tough time if you went there. It was quite surprising to me when I realised quite recently that when Sandfields Comprehensive School was first opened, it was this bright, shiny flagship state school and that a man called Godfrey Evans, who came from the area, had gone to London, to Central School of Speech and Drama to train as a drama teacher, and had then chosen to come back. He was an incredibly talented man and could have had any kind of career, really, within the arts, as a director or as a teacher, but he came back to take up a position at the new flagship school, Sandfields Comprehensive.

This is within the context of Port Talbot having already produced Richard Burton and Tony Hopkins; there was a relationship between the area and acting that was probably different to a lot of similar communities with a relationship to heavy industry. It wasn't seen as being a poncey thing to do; there was a respect for it. That probably helps to explain partly why Godfrey Evans was able to set up an incredibly progressive arts ecosystem that grew out of Sandfields Comp. You wouldn't think that in the heart of this town, and in that school, something like this would start growing, but it did, because of him, and this goes along with something more common, which is that amateur dramatic, amateur operatic society infrastructure as well. There's a lot fewer now, but there used to be at one time ten or twelve amateur operatic societies in the Neath–Port Talbot area. What Godfrey started to do in Sandfields Comp was something that wasn't to do with musical theatre or that kind of tradition: it was very much to do with a very cutting-edge, very progressive theatre programme, and that eventually grew into him becoming the County Advisor for Dance and Drama. He then created throughout the whole of West Glamorgan this extraordinary youth arts network and infrastructure coming out of the education system. It was very connected to the schools; the money was there for it. He created the West Glamorgan Youth Theatre, which I was a product of, and which Russell T. Davies was a product of; he created the County Youth Dance Company, which Catherine Zeta-Jones came through; he created the County Youth Orchestra; there were all these county youth arts organisations that grew out of this one man. He created this network funded through the education system.

As I came through school, I didn't know any of this. I didn't understand any of this; I took it for granted that my teacher at Glan Afan Comprehensive School when I was thirteen, said, 'You should audition for the Youth Theatre,' so I did, didn't get in, and the next year, he said, 'You should do it again,' and I did it, I got in, and then I went to Youth Theatre and my brain exploded and my life changed. We were going to residential courses in Swansea at this big building and we would stay in these dormitories and rehearse, cut off from the world in this bubble; that was mind-blowing for me. I was there as a fourteen-year-old, with 21-year-olds and working on Brecht and Shakespeare. The first play I did was *The Insect Play*, by a Czechoslovakian writer, and it changed my life; it was an artistic awakening and a social awakening.

I came through that and went off to drama school, to RADA, because that was what you did. In the Youth Theatre, when they got to a certain age, they auditioned for drama schools and they got in. I never questioned this: it was only later that I realised, 'Hang on, this was one little town that was every year pumping people out into the top drama schools in the country.' I remember being at RADA and them saying, 'Oh, you're one of Godfrey's lads, are you?' It's only in retrospect I realised, 'Oh, it was because of the steelworks having the comprehensive school that drew Godfrey there, to start that system in a context of respect for performance, with an education system that was funding it, that led to this ecosystem that I am a product of.' Whenever anyone says, 'Well, to come from an area like you do, you're such a self-made person, you've had this experience.' Oh, no. No. No.

No. My career and my life are totally dependent on all these different factors. And I have watched all of them disappear, like footsteps in the sand, washed away.

Ann Pettitt: I loved teaching in Port Talbot. The last place I taught was in Port Talbot, and I thought it would be absolutely ghastly and it was great, lovely kids. Port Talbot was also the best school I taught at. I was there the best part of a year, and it was a split-site school. You'd have thought it would be awful, all sorts of problems: it wasn't. The split site was perfect, because you had two smaller units, and I could teach. I didn't have to firefight, I didn't have to yell and shout, I could actually go in and teach. I was teaching French, which isn't that easy: I could go in and I could have a lesson plan, I could deliver my lesson plan, I could teach bloody French.

And how was it so, how come I could deal so easily with the one or two little troublemakers in each class? Why was it so easy, and in the end, I was looking dreamily out across the landscape of the steelworks and the cracker plant, and I thought, 'That's it.' I talked to the deputy head there. I said, 'Why is it so easy for me here? Where's the banana skin? What's round the corner?' He said, 'Most of the kids come from two-parent families and at least one is in work and earning. It's that.' And it really turned round the way I see industry. I had looked at this great big polluting steel plant and seen nothing but the negative: pollution and industrial grind and all the rest of it, and here I was, down in that Sandfields estate. It wasn't Sandfields School, but a lot of the kids were on that estate that you see from the motorway as you look down between there and the steel plant, and they were secure and happy and motivated to learn and well-behaved.

Rachel Trezise: I got some encouragement to write at school, once I'd shown an aptitude for it. Other than that, I didn't feel like I was part of it; I felt like I was a lower class than that. I write stuff for the theatre now, but I remember as a kid thinking I wasn't allowed to, that that wasn't part of my life. My parents were unemployed. My father left when I was three and my mam cleaned the library. She used to take me to the library, to work with her now and again, and that was where I discovered books. We had reading at school obviously, but I was never encouraged.

Michael Sheen: I remember playing football on pitches at the foot of the BP Baglan plant with the cooling towers. It was more of a fixture on the landscape growing up, or at least equal to that of the steelworks. There was the steelworks to the left from where we lived, and then to the right was the BP plant and those cooling towers and across the Western Avenue a football pitch where I used to play a lot of games. The sky would literally be orange or purple because of the stuff that was coming out of the plant, and that was a very strange, alien kind of landscape to be living in. I didn't think at the time about what was actually happening. It was a slightly weird thing that you accepted, waking up in the mornings and seeing these little acidic deposits on the cars or the same thing on people's washing lines. It took a long time before it dawned on me how many people there were in wheelchairs and with illnesses down at the beach; eventually, you realise and then you start to see figures about the highest levels of leukaemia in Europe are in the Port Talbot area.

Leanne Wood: We still had an immense community spirit, certainly in the community that I lived in. I live in the street that I grew up on and I know most of the people there – they're long-term residents. There's not a very regular turnover of people, and that is a tight-knit community. There'd been a defeat and, yes, that had changed things, and it changed people's outlooks, but I also think that there's still something there, because people feel a sense of civic pride in pulling together and making things happen for each other. Which is incredible, considering everything people have been through.

James Dean Bradfield: I used to go to Oakdale Workmen's Institute, which is now in St Fagans, and just look at the plethora of newspapers there. They would have *Socialist Worker*, periodicals, papers from different parts of the world in there. I would have tea and cake in there with my grandfather, who is from Sunderland, but was a miner in Wales. I had the privilege of being in all these beautiful, faded rooms with beautiful tiling and periodicals and newspapers and tea and cake and jazz and beer and music.

I think there's the modern tendency to point the finger at some communities, whether it be dockers in Liverpool, or whether it be South Wales mining communities, whether it be Nottingham miners, whether it be the South Shields miners, I think there's a modern tendency to point the finger and say, 'Rose-tinted spectacles, emotionally incontinent. You're weaving mythic tales of not-so-distant history which really wasn't that glorious.' No. Some of it was glorious, actually. I worked in all the places and benefited from the places that grew out of those industries in South Wales. People told us, 'Oh, don't be so corny and stop trying to direct your own mini period drama.'

No, it was real. We recorded our first single in a miners' institute, in the swimming pool that was built in Cwmfelinfach Miners' Institute. It was still there when we recorded our first, self-financed single. I was a barman for four, five years in the Newbridge Institute which was built by miners from Oakdale Colliery and I received a massive education there. I got to meet Steve Marriott there and the DJ played our single there; they gave me lots of tips. And I learned how to defend myself there; I learned how to sing some songs there; and I made lots of friends there. Sean played in Oakdale Colliery band: he started playing cornet, then he played trumpet. These men, who were miners playing trombone and euphonium, started showing Sean stuff like Charlie Parker and started playing him John Coltrane. Sean started coming home with old jazz cassettes given to him by miners that played in Oakdale Colliery band that were trying to teach him and he started influencing me, because he was playing me jazz as well. All the benefits of all those institutions, I was there for that. I don't want to sound like Max Boyce, but I was there, in those places. Sean was taught about American bebop jazz by some big, hulking ex-miners that were playing trombone and euphonium and trumpet in the colliery band. Sean got to travel and had a major education from those guys, and they took him under their wing. They taught him about American jazz, they taught him about Birdland. And Sean taught me about it. What a fucking amazing place.

Kim Howells: When I was a boy the headmaster of my school was told by somebody from the Aberdare Library that I was reading Jack Kerouac. He said, 'Well, why are you reading this beatnik nonsense, you should be concentrating on your set books for A-level,' and Jack Kerouac had just been published, and there it was in Aberdare Library. I've always had a lifelong love of climbing and mountaineering, and part of it stems from the fact that in Aberdare Library there were glossy, huge, very expensive copies of the Alpine Yearbooks. Who the hell in Aberdare was booking out the Alpine Yearbook?

My Uncle Glen, who was a Labour councillor in Aberdare, said to me, just before I went off to what was then the most glamorous art college in Britain, Hornsey College of Art in north London, 'Now remember, boy, don't be overawed by what people say when you get there. You come from the Athens of the coalfield,' that's what they called Aberdare.

Rowan Williams: One of the things that gave me some hope was that some of these communities still had active rugby clubs. They hadn't completely disappeared, but as a national, iconic marker, it wasn't what it had been in the seventies. A rugby team, where you are very literally watching each other's backs, as you were if you worked in industry.

Rachel Trezise: Rugby was still part of the life in the Valleys, massively. Nobody I knew well played it, but all the boys in comp played rugby. The rugby club in Treorchy was run by the guy who was also the PE teacher in the school. People were still looking after each other. They were still neighbourly. Even now, when you hear about people saying how they don't know their next-door neighbour, you always know, everyone in my street always knows. So that was there. But that can be a bad thing, as well, when you're twelve, thirteen. I always felt like there was a safety net with the NHS and social security, so however bad things were with my family, I knew, by looking around at other people, that once I was sixteen, I could get a flat. The safety net was there. It's hard, in my day-to-day life. I think of the Valleys as its own place rather than being part of the rest of Wales, South Wales makes me think of that working-class solidarity.

Adam Price: I remember my parents coming down to visit me in London, when I was an MP, and they brought their sense of social being with them. I'd been living in this flat for a few years; by the end of the week, they knew everyone on the street. It was like something out of an Ealing comedy. People were opening their windows in second-floor flats and, 'Hi, Rufus and Angela!' because my parents didn't know any other way to be. It would take us two hours to get from there to the Tube station, because they'd say hello to everyone. But that's normal, isn't it?

Kim Howells: I've been in the Rockies in America and seen towns which were huge boom towns during the time when they mined silver and gold and uranium and lead in those areas, and now nobody lives there. I was standing on what we call the Barry Sidings, just to the north of Pontypridd by Trehafod. The Barry Sidings were where all of the old coal wagons used to be lined up before they were sent on the trains to Barry Docks, and it's very beautiful there now. If you look a little bit north there's the winding gear of the old Lewis Merthyr

Colliery, which is now of course a museum. You look literally across the valley at the Hetty pithead gear and you wonder how is there still a thriving community there? I mean, it's a bloody miracle.

FOURTEEN

BAE CAERDYDD / CARDIFF BAY

Voices

Hanif Bhamjee
Ian Courtney
Bob Croydon
Jane Davidson
Andrew Davies
Ron Davies

Edwina Hart
Adrian Jones
Neil Kinnock
Gaynor Legall
Sue Lent

Mary Millington
Max Perkins
Gwenno Saunders
Davinder Singh
Rowan Williams
Leanne Wood

———

In the spring of 1987 the Cardiff Bay Development Corporation was formally established by the Westminster government at the behest of the Secretary of State for Wales, Nicholas Edwards, who had held the office since 1979, an unusually long period for what was traditionally perceived to be a minor office of state. In part, Edwards had used his tenure to demonstrate an economic orthodoxy that contrasted with the market fundamentalism of his own Westminster government.

The principal goal of the Cardiff Bay Development Corporation was the construction of a barrage across the mouth of the bay that would lead to an increase in land values in the city's partially abandoned docks area and the subsequent regeneration of Cardiff's waterfront. This would be achieved via the recently established development templates of new housing, retail schemes and their attendant job creation. The corporation was launched with a mission statement which spoke of putting 'Cardiff on the international map as a superlative maritime city which will stand comparison with any such city in the world, thereby enhancing the image and economic well-being of Cardiff and Wales as a whole.'

At a time when areas such as the Valleys were suffering from a lack of investment this final clause was disputable. The newly named Cardiff Bay abutted the district of Butetown, a multicultural area that had historically been under-resourced and where attitudes towards the development within the community were mixed, if not sceptical. In its governance and constitution, the Development Corporation resembled the London Docklands Development Corporation, which had been established in 1981; both schemes had used the mechanism of a bespoke quango and the powers of compulsory purchase orders to justify, manage and achieve their aims. The creation of the Cardiff Bay Development Corporation furthered the perception that Wales was being governed at the whim of whichever Conservative held the position of Secretary of State for Wales. This was despite the fact that most of the country's serving MPs, by 1987 as many as 80 per cent, represented other parties.

Bob Croydon: In the later Thatcher years, the notion of economic intervention went out the window. Prior to that there were two more-interventionist secretaries of state, notably Nick Edwards, or Nick Crickhowell as he became, who did a huge amount for Wales. His successor, Peter Walker, was banished to Wales and was determined to prove that there was a different type of Conservativism at the time of Margaret Thatcher. They still behaved like bloody Roman proconsuls, though, Tory Welsh Secretaries, who with the stroke of a pen could alter the destiny of a place in the way colonial governors had previously.

Andrew Davies: The Tories ran Wales through quangos, and of course the only political opposition was local government. That well-known Swansea boy and profound socialist Michael Heseltine was Secretary of State for the Environment in the eighties, when the Conservative government developed enterprise zones. Heseltine initially argued that enterprise zones should not include retail; they were specifically to be about manufacturing and other light industrial use. Then Heseltine changed the rules to allow retail, and that was the first occasion in say, Swansea, where you started to get out-of-town retail development, which helped destroy part of the economic rationale for city centres.

The only city that didn't decline as a consequence is Cardiff, but the reason Cardiff has thrived is partly because it's the capital, partly because it has a lot of national institutions, but also, if you look at all the transport, because of its industrial heritage as the major coal-exporting centre. All the railways go to Cardiff.

Bob Croydon: I was actually writing the particulars for some buildings we were selling, after yet another local government reorganisation, when we were disposing of the assets of Mid-Glamorgan County Council. I was writing the equivalent of estate agents' particulars, a souped-up version of house details. If you looked at the building we were selling, you had a major retail centre 100 yards away, you had an international-quality art collection if you looked out of the back window, you had a castle and Roman remains at the other end of the road and, just around the corner, international sports. I was thinking, 'Hang on a minute, you'd be pushed to write a spec like that on an office block in Bristol, certainly not in Swindon or anywhere else.' The concentration of amenity in Cardiff is extraordinary, all the more so given it has a population not much more than Walsall's.

In 1950-odd Cardiff was declared capital by ministerial aside. Aberystwyth and Machynlleth and other places thought, 'How the fuck did that happen?' because there was no consultation, it was just from a question put to the Minister for Welsh Affairs: 'What should be the capital?' 'Well, obviously Cardiff,' because it was the largest single settlement. A hundred years earlier, it had been smaller; it was the twenty-fifth-largest settlement in Wales. Historically, it had no claim to being a capital, tucked away in the corner of Wales; it just happened.

There was a certain amount of resentment, which lingered and was crystallised in something like the Cardiff Bay Barrage development, the cost of which would have paid for a motorway across the top of Glamorgan. They're still working on the Heads of the Valleys road forty years later.

Adrian Jones: I think Cardiff Bay Development was the second biggest of the Heseltine regeneration programmes after London Docklands. It was seen very much as the flagship for Wales and the trickle-down was supposed to help the Valleys as well; it wasn't just for Cardiff in theory, although how that was really going to happen in practice was never explained.

Bob Croydon: The Cardiff Bay Development. An astronomical figure, millions and millions of pounds, was put into a swamp to transform it and then, of course, over the span of its construction there were a couple of property recessions. They really, really struggled to get it going. They achieved bugger all in the first five years. Cardiff Bay Development Corporation was led by a couple of people sucking up to Edwards, all obsessed with this notion of the barrage, which could have been the white elephant to end them all. The amount of money that went into the barrage, for what it achieved, was astonishing and the principal beneficiaries of it were Associated British Ports, who were the major landowner around the Bay.

Max Perkins: Nick Edwards was very gung-ho about this initiative, the Cardiff Bay Barrage, one of the greatest spin exercises going. The late Michael Roberts, who was then a junior Welsh Office minister, told me, 'Oh, we've got this great project coming up,' getting very excited about it, and I interviewed Thatcher when she came down to open it, and I said, 'Should there have been more public money put into it?' and she hit the roof. 'What do you mean? Don't you want it?' because I think it was almost entirely privately funded.

Nick Edwards said afterwards he got quite annoyed with me for asking that question and I never quite understood why, until the thirty-year rule was up. Apparently, he was also asking her for more public money. Nick Edwards was fairly liberal, I think, economically, compared with her. He and Wyn Roberts were the only two Welsh Secretaries from the Tory Party who really understood Wales. He was very committed to Wales, in a way that I don't think any other Welsh Secretary had been, not from the Tory Party, anyway.

Bob Croydon: Cardiff Bay was initiated by Nick Edwards, who fought Wales's corner as the Secretary of State far harder than anyone we've had since. Peter Walker was his successor; they were both really pro-interventionist.

Edwina Hart: The trade union movement was never kept out of discussions in anything the WDA did that required its involvement; you could approach the Welsh Office, make an appointment with Peter Walker and go and discuss things.

Gaynor Legall: Before Butetown became a separate ward, it was part of Cardiff South, which encompassed Grangetown, and there were three city councillors and three county councillors that serviced the ward. All of the city councillors and the county councillors lived in Grangetown. Butetown had been, in my view, neglected in terms of the challenges it faced for a long time. One of the previous city councillors was someone called Phil Dunleavy, and Phil had done youth work and worked with a lot of the kids from Butetown, based in this building in Grangetown. The wards were changed, and I became a councillor, but it was a single council ward, and because I was black and because of my professional background – I was a social worker – the expectations were huge, absolutely huge, not just within Butetown: people came to see me from all over Cardiff, because they thought I would understand.

We did surgeries on a Thursday, usually they were two hours; mine were always four or five hours long and I had to say to people, 'You'll have to come back next week,' there were these big queues. Regarding the sorts of challenges that were around, there was, I think, in the city council, a lack of understanding of what was going on and what was needed. It was a very traditional council. The Labour Party was quite right-wing in my view and there were some rivalries between the city and the county council.

When I was a councillor, Butetown was also part of my patch as a social worker, so I lived there, I was a social worker and I was the councillor. Trying to get the council to recognise what they could do in terms of employment was quite hard because the city council doesn't deal with things like that. The majority of the issues were around housing and the planning department. That coincided with the county council beginning the development of South Cardiff and what became Cardiff Bay.

Adrian Jones: The connection was so poor between Cardiff Bay and the city centre proper; there was no thought. There was no plan, no concept of any of this whatsoever, and no regard of the geographic location in this exposed position next to the Bristol Channel.

Bob Croydon: It's still not really connected to the rest of the city. There's still a sense of separation about it, not as acute as when it was Tiger Bay, but places like Mount Stuart Square are pretty sad remnants now. The benefits of Mermaid Quay, the eating and drinking jewel of Cardiff Bay, don't really extend more than two streets away into Butetown.

Hanif Bhamjee: There was an assumption about Butetown that was entirely incorrect, that it was somewhere with a high prevalence of crime, which was not the case. It had a high rate of unemployment during the second half of the 1980s, when there was an increase in the number of racist incidents reported throughout Wales.

Davinder Singh: There was a period in the mid-eighties when racism was right in your face. My relations were brought up in much larger groupings of Asians; we had people in Birmingham and in London and they grew up together, facing it together. But because they lived in conurbations where there were high numbers of people from that ethnicity, their perspective was very different to mine.

I went straight into broadcasting after college. There was a radio station in Cardiff that came out of Chapter Arts Centre, where I worked during vacation time and every weekend when I'd come home. I ended up getting an Equity Card, and because S4C needed black faces on a whole raft of programmes they were making, from *Pobol y Cwm* to *Pam Fi Duw?*, *Tair Chwaer*, *Glanhafren*, *Dinas*, *Bowen a'i Bartner* – I did them all. I was more often than not cast as a stereotypical black person; I would be a thug, a shopkeeper, a waiter, a doctor. I played those roles across all the shows.

HTV West used to film scenes in Indian restaurants or shops and they'd say, 'Oh, get that Asian feller.' I used to read the scripts and think they were rubbish, and then I started writing my own.

Hanif Bhamjee: Butetown was regularly described as a place where there were prostitutes marrying black people. Cardiff University published information leaflets instructing its students not to visit places like the Caribbean Club, which had always been popular with students. And this was at a time when the National Front were gaining significant support in places like Merthyr.

Gaynor Legall: As long as I can remember there were clubs where there was music and dancing in Butetown and one of the nice things about Butetown is that it was always a mixture of black and white. During the seventies, eighties era of reggae there were a couple of clubs and black and white went, locals and black people who lived else-where: a lot of toing and froing between Newport and Bristol. And then there's always been this student population that were looking for something else.

When I was a councillor, a lot of the clubs had closed and then there started to be this exclusivity and a culture where, in quite dilapidated buildings, there was quite a lot of after-hours drinking. And I wanted to stop that; I wanted to develop the area in a positive way. And I got into a real conflict, because one of these places was owned by somebody who was local, and I opposed the application – naïve as hell, not long appointed and I was looking for council official support. I was on my own. Didn't have a clue. They adjourned the thing and they explained to me that as I had opposed it, it was my job to build the evidence. What was funny about that was, the mother, who I called Aunty Violet, came and gave me a clip across the ear and said, 'You want to deprive my son of his livelihood?' That was typical of what went on.

You went to the Docks – it wasn't called Butetown before – to listen to music. There was the Quebec, where you listened to jazz, there was the Blue Moon, where you got off your face and listened to many different musics, and there were the reggae clubs and there were the ordinary clubs that played soul. It's always been a mixture, and there's always been a mixture of people attending them. Very different to London, very different.

Adrian Jones: Tiger Bay was a yellow press thing. It was called the Docks. The trolleybus used to say 'Pierhead Docks' and nobody called it Tiger Bay; they certainly didn't call it Cardiff Bay.

Gaynor Legall: The perception of Butetown by people who didn't live in Butetown, particularly what I generally call the Establishment, was totally different to the perception of Butetown from the people who lived there. The crime rate within Butetown was one of the lowest in Cardiff. There might have been a lot of thieves and crooks living in Butetown, but within the area there was not a lot of crime. The perception of Butetown then was, and is, it was a strong, positive, cohesive place to live and to grow up.

I dealt with complaints about never seeing a police officer there, and the lack of policing. My view is that the policing was inappropriate, so there were lots of issues around. It wasn't even called stop and search then, but [there were] kids being pulled over, people being beaten up by the police, the police not responding properly to issues around domestic violence, not turning up at all. The policing – if they had a strategy, it was not apparent. What I saw was the police coming in only on their terms and coming in in a very aggressive way when they came into the area, and oddly enough, it was at the police liaison meetings where the police brought the stats about Butetown and the perception showed that things like car theft were not much higher in Butetown than in other parts of the city. In Cardiff during the 1980s there was a spate of joy-riding, it was called, take and drive away; that didn't happen in Butetown. But unemployment had always been a problem in Butetown. Even in the sixties, when employment was at its height, it was hard to get a job if you lived in Butetown, and in the eighties it was dreadful: 85 per cent unemployment rate in the area.

Jane Davidson: I joined Labour in 1983 and there were two very different kinds of politics going on. We still had a City and a County structure in Cardiff; the person who was leading the County was a man called Russell Goodway, who was all about economic development and that agenda, very strongly in favour of the Cardiff Bay barrage. On the City side, we felt closer to constituents in the sense that we were the people who had to pick up the housing problems, the environmental problems. I was given the opportunity to be the Cardiff Council representative for the Coalfield Communities campaign, and in one notable meeting I was faced with a group of men, all above a certain age, all with kind of union ties on, and I appear in a dress and I'm asked if I've got the wrong room and that was the Labour Party model at the time.

I became a councillor in '87, but the Cardiff Bay Development Corporation was established earlier than that. It was another deep shock that people felt they could just ride roughshod over elected communities. Taking a certain approach because Wales was inconvenient is a model that, of course, Wales has experienced forever, since the Industrial Revolution: the idea that you don't have to return anything to Wales. That's always the view of a government of a different political persuasion, slamming its ideology onto Wales.

I was really lucky because of where I lived in Cardiff, Riverside Ward. At the time, the ward that was most interested in feminism, in girls' work, in creating safe spaces and being supportive of the twenty languages spoken because of the amount of immigration that we had. There was very strong support for multiculturalism.

Gwenno Saunders: My mum's socialist street choir, Côr Cochion, started in Riverside the year before I was born, in 1980, and it was a real mixture of people from all walks of life. The thing that held it all together was human rights, internationalism, socialism. Things like Nicaragua – what was going on in a lot of South America fed into campaigning – the anti-apartheid movement was massive. And the Welsh language fed into that, with Cymdeithas yr Iaith, and then my mum would be with Côr Cochion and she would be doing Cymdeithas stuff with people from Côr Cochion as well.

Mary Millington: I was a member of Côr Cochion in Cardiff. I arrived having supported the people who stayed at the Greenham Common camp from there, and the choir used to visit Greenham quite often. I can remember Lynne, Gwenno's mother, telling me she'd bought some eggs and she had these two babies in the pram and found herself throwing these eggs at Margaret Thatcher. I got arrested with Côr Cochion up at Faslane and ended up in Cornton Vale Prison, and having to go to and fro to Scotland for court and then prison, I thought, 'This is ridiculous, I should move to Scotland!' So I did.

Gwenno Saunders: When I was growing up my Welsh-language experiences were always in the context of the south of Cardiff, multicultural, how our stories weaved with other people's stories.

Because I lived in a multicultural area, everyone had other languages, so my view of Welsh was, I felt, related a lot to Bangladeshi kids that I hung out with, or the Somali kids. It felt that was my context for the Welsh language because I hated school, so school didn't mean Welsh to me, school was just an inconvenience and it didn't inform my Welsh-language identity.

Because I came from Riverside everyone was into gangsta rap and I started hanging out with girls from Butetown who I thought were just amazing because they knew who they were and where they were from.

Sue Lent: When I first joined Côr Cochion they used to sing the 'Internationale' in Welsh and English and they would alternate it at concerts. They didn't have a very democratic system at all; they didn't have an AGM or anything or notices of motions where you had to tell people what was coming up, they just had this meeting every six months, and when I first joined, I heard how terrible these meetings were, because there were always these awful rows. I missed the rows and some people left because there'd been a proposal that the 'Internationale' should only be sung in Welsh at each concert, and they didn't agree with that, they thought it should be the two languages, so I think six of them left. I certainly wasn't going to leave, because I'd only just joined, and in those days, you had to wait quite a while to join, which seems quite a ludicrous idea now, but the conductor was very precious, so he'd write these names in the little book. I think I'd put my name down once, a couple of years before, and it had never come to anything, and then I put it down again and the second time, after about six months, I got a call to go along, so I certainly wasn't going to leave.

Gwenno Saunders: I was constantly being dragged on pickets and marches and being really bored and cold, and not being allowed to stay home because no one was going to look after us, and then Mum went to prison a couple of times, which was quite exciting, especially because the first time was over Christmas, and she wasn't particularly keen, Mum. She was like, 'God, this is a bit of a hassle,' so we were all quite glad about it and everyone felt sorry for us because we weren't going to see our mum for two weeks, but we were quite pleased. It's such a normal thing in Wales for your mum to have been to prison. It's so often that you meet someone else with the same experience; it's only when you go outside of Wales that you say, 'Oh, yeah, my mum's been to prison a couple of times,' that it's not normal. But it was for effect as well: imprisoning women and mothers was a really good way of getting the message across that it mattered to their children. It was really clever campaigning, I think.

This is an international struggle going on, that's my memory of my childhood, that everyone knew where to stand, and it's really easy to over-simplify and over-romanticise it, but it was just a lot of people with shared principles that wanted things to change. And obviously there was the backdrop of the Soviet Union: my mum's a Communist and was obsessed with the Soviet Union, for good and for bad – we had a samovar in our house! I think a lot of the Communists perhaps over-looked the atrocities to a larger extent than they should have done, but it was something to believe in, this theory that there was an alternative. Someone was trying to do things differently to capitalism, that was a big thing.

Sue Lent: I became a councillor in 1989, and it was still going on then, the debate over Cardiff Bay Development Corporation: we didn't like them. Myself, Mark Drakeford, Julie Morgan, there was a little group of us that were constantly asking questions, although we weren't supposed to, and making a fuss in the council chamber about it. In terms of the Labour Party, you felt the more conservative old guard were very undemocratic and they were in the majority, and then there was this smaller left faction. There were people who had particular interests or concerns, but in the main, if you were on the right of the party, you thought it was great and that you had to have it to bring jobs, and, without it, Cardiff would just collapse and we'd have no economic development. And then you'd got the left who just thought it was a terrible waste of money and was going to destroy the feeding grounds and just wasn't necessary. A lot of the day-to-day protesting came from people who were living in Riverside, such as Gwenno's parents.

Gaynor Legall: When the development started, we had a big meeting, at the Butetown community centre. One of the initiatives put forward was that if you were local and from Butetown, the houses would be sold to you at a cheaper rate. The houses were on sale for £40,000, and people in the audience said, '£40,000? Oh, that's for the rich ones, you're selling to your cronies and all the rest of it.' Although there was quite a lot of consultation, I don't know whether the consultation hit the mark.

Bob Croydon: Everybody involved in the Cardiff Bay Development Corporation was given the chance to go to Baltimore for a week. That came from Edwards and that team around him. Baltimore, that was the great model, Baltimore. You heard 'Baltimore, Baltimore, Baltimore,' all the bloody time.

Gaynor Legall: We went twice, my interest was about community integration and employment: what happened there to improve employment. In fairness to the council, in their awarding of contracts, they tried to ensure that local people got jobs, but what happened in reality was they were sub-contracted, and the sub-contractors brought their own people in. The biggest criticism – and that continues – is that there's been no employment for people from Butetown in that area, and that's still the same now.

Adrian Jones: Baltimore was one of the first places that took their derelict or declined harbour area and then used the water as the focus for creating a new urban form. But it was an implant. It wasn't for the people of Baltimore; it wasn't for their benefit, it was to gentrify the place, and gentrification was then meant to have the trickle-down benefits.

When you went to one of the regeneration consultants they'd do you a presentation and say, 'Here's Baltimore, look at the ships, look at the cafés, look at the glass,' so there became a whole industry of illusion, based around that.

And it was all very new. All these dockland redevelopments were quite a stab in the dark, and they're actually quite hostile places. Salford Quays or Docklands in London are harsh in reality: new development right up against docksides and then there is the water there, fine, but you can't actually relate to it. And that's what happened in Cardiff.

Swansea did it a lot better, going back quite a long time and that was because Swansea City bought the docks in the seventies, and then they had a much more friendly, small-scale development which works quite well. What they tried to do in Cardiff, Mumbles did it organically. All this money spent on Cardiff Bay resulted in an inferior version of Mumbles.

Jane Davidson: We ran a campaign which was continually asking the corporation to justify its actions. We were allied with the Royal Society for the Protection of Birds: their key issue at the time was protecting the dunlin and the bird species at risk on the estuary. One of the outcomes from the Cardiff Bay Development Corporation is what is now the Gwent Wetlands Area, because that was the compensatory habitat.

Adrian Jones: There was huge fuss over this, because it was a Site of Special Scientific Interest. If you go to Newport you can see these enormous mudflats and it was the richest possible ground for birds and it was really interesting: like in the way that Dickens evokes the Thames, you'd see the tide creeping in over the mud. It was very atmospheric, and I don't think it was just what a few aesthetes thought, a lot of people thought that. There was a huge argument about it in Cardiff at the time, but it got overruled by this steamroller. You've got to have this prestige scheme. It's what I call the banality of the big idea. It goes back to the Roman consul. There was no stopping it, despite all the arguments that were made against it. But from the very start the big idea had nothing to it. Nothing was really thought through; you create this enclosed bay and you create images of people water-skiing and sipping cocktails overlooking it. But there was nothing about how it relates to the actual place at all; it was an artificial thing.

The community in Butetown was ignored and literally ghettoised and it was an absurd way to carry on. There was masses of development that could have happened there, which would have worked with the topography, the architectural relevance and the Butetown and Grangetown and Splott communities, but that didn't happen. It was really quite obscene to see the amount of money that was spent on Cardiff Bay and they didn't sort out the conservation of the key historical assets and I don't think they did anything really to improve the life chances of people in Butetown. It was just like an alien presence, the whole thing.

Gaynor Legall: There was every type of myth, misinformation, ignorance, confusion. It was quite a difficult time. Every time a house became vacant, there was a rumour. Cardiff Bay have bought the house: they were apparently going to set up their headquarters there, in a three-bedroom council house. And I used to say, 'Why would they move in there? Look at the size of it.' 'Yeah, but I've been told.' Once the Development Corporation was set up, the powers were taken away from the local council.

Bob Croydon: There was always that tension between Cardiff City Council and the Development Corporation, because they felt that their thunder had been stolen. That said, the amount of resources that were given to the Development Corporation far exceeded those available to Cardiff City Council. Nick Edwards allowed ABP – the privatised British Transport Docks Board had become Associated British Ports – to keep all their land, so the principal beneficiaries in terms of private land ownership were ABP. And Nick Edwards became non-executive director as soon as he packed in being Secretary of State for Wales. It was run in the same way as any of those other development corporations at the time. It happened later in Manchester with the Trafford Centre and various other places. If you look at another city with 350,000 people, the same population as Cardiff, it was a disproportionate amount of investment.

The gestation and eventual development of Cardiff Bay lasted over a decade, throughout which the government delivered its policy of attracting inward investment to Wales via the energetic activities of the Welsh Development Agency. The organisation attracted overseas firms with lively marketing and public relations campaigns. These were given impetus by a continual round of trade missions that built on the agency's previous successes in the motor and technology sectors; its distinguished client list included Sony, Panasonic, Bosch, Hitachi, Toyota, Ford, BMW, Mercedes, Rover and Jaguar, although only a handful of the firms established long-term positions in the country. A much-cited statistic claimed that Wales attracted a fifth of the total of UK foreign investment, despite the fact the country consisted of only a twentieth of the population. The figure was disputed with almost equal regularity.

In 1992 the House of Commons Public Accounts Committee criticised the WDA for numerous financial anomalies and was scathing in its assessments of the agency's management culture, accusing the quango of 'a catalogue of serious and inexcusable breaches of expected

standards of control and accountability'. The agency's chairman,
Gwyn Jones, a Swansea businessman, had been appointed in 1988 by
the then Welsh Secretary, Peter Walker. Jones and Walker had met at
a Conservative Party fundraising lunch, held at a Gower hotel; Jones'
appointment was proposed later on the same day. Jones had previously
donated to the party and had apparently made it clear to the Secretary
of State that he was a millionaire. The Public Accounts Committee
report claimed that under Jones' tenure the agency was beset with
'scandal after scandal'. Among other incidents were the misuse of
a company car fleet; the operation of an unapproved redundancy
scheme that regularly incurred excessive expenditure; a substantial
golden handshake payment that also included a gagging clause;
and the appointment of a director of marketing who had previously
been convicted of fraud. This particular member of staff was again
made the subject of a criminal investigation and received a custodial
sentence following his departure from the agency.

Jones resigned without contrition and in doing so highlighted the
extent to which quangos in Wales were rarely subject either to scrutiny
or accountability and operated a form of governance by the backdoor.
The committee made clear that standards at the agency had fallen
short of what the House deemed acceptable and proved notably robust
in its criticism, stating: 'We regard it as unacceptable that the Welsh
Office took no action.'

In his response in Parliament to the committee's conclusions, the
then Secretary of State for Wales, John Redwood, admitted: 'There
were irregularities in the behaviour and conduct of the agency in its
internal affairs. I believe that, when things have gone wrong, the
important thing is to find out why, to identify the problems, and to put
them right as quickly as possible.'

In an interview given to the Independent *newspaper Redwood had*
alluded to his desire to see 'Wales being as successful as Wokingham',
his Berkshire constituency. Such remarks by Redwood, his rumoured
refusal to sign red box papers printed in Cymraeg or to stay overnight

in Wales, and his derisory attempt at miming the words to 'Hen Wlad Fy Nhadau' while it was being sung at a Welsh Conservative Conference, an embarrassing incident that was widely broadcast, all accentuated the perception that, outside networks of those sympathetic to the Conservative Party, Wales struggled to be taken seriously by the Westminster government.

Max Perkins: It was always pretty obvious that the Tories were appointing what they used to call the Raglan Set to key positions in Wales, Geoffrey Inkin and people like that. There was that network of well-off people living particularly in the south-east of Wales. They were placemen, basically. They were useful. And there was this strong network of landowners who, for example, later put the kibosh on the Newport Barrage. That was all part of the Raglan huntin', fishin', shootin' set, going all the way up the Usk.

Jane Davidson: I think having the Cardiff Bay Development Corporation chaired by Sir Geoffrey Inkin, a very strong Conservative, rubbed it in. It was the dropping in of a new model and a bypassing of local democracy; that was very much at the heart of it.

Ron Davies: I don't want to be unkind, but the Welsh Labour Party as an organisation was weak. Transport House was useless. Barry Jones [Shadow Secretary of State] – he was from North Wales – he was weak, he wasn't going to have a fight with anybody, and so the stage was being set by Peter Walker. What then became the devolution movement was being fed by that, because there was an unease: 'Why have we got an English Secretary of State; this guy is coming down. We know that it's just flim-flam. He doesn't mean it and meanwhile our jobs have gone, our communities are rotting, our schools are underfunded, the health service isn't working properly, the environment is being destroyed and we in Wales are voiceless about this.' I thought that was feeding the devolution discussion by about 1990.

Max Perkins: The Tory Welsh secretaries certainly saw the WDA as a useful arm to do the work for them, with the right appointees. There were the scandals about how Peter Walker met Gwyn Jones at a lunch and, within about an hour, decided he would appoint him as chairman of the WDA. There was a whole series of further scandals then about the way they were recruiting people and trips abroad, a lot of noise around expenses and interviewing young women in hotel bedrooms, something strange was going on there. A lot of the senior managers were milking the system.

Ian Courtney: In the late 1980s I got a job in Cardiff with the WDA. And, after about twelve months, I realised that this was a total non-job. There was this tension between a bloke called David Waterstone, the chief executive, who was the brother of the founder of Waterstones Books, and the civil service, who were always interfering, I suppose, as he would see it, in his little empire.

Waterstone had a notable enmity with the Secretary of State Peter Walker, who had replaced Nicholas Edwards and had been sent off down to Wales to practise his alternative economic strategy. So out goes David Waterstone, who was a very impressive man, and in comes even more foreign direct investment and renting jobs from the Japanese.

All of a sudden, the attraction of foreign direct investment goes into overdrive. Ironically, part of the boost to this was the creation of the 1992 single market, so companies that were located outside of the EU had now a need to have facilities within the EU, and Wales positioned itself as an ideal place to locate factories. So, for many years, the WDA had great pleasure in saying Wales was 5 per cent of the population but received 20 per cent of foreign direct investment into the UK, or whatever the figures were. It was, largely speaking, consumer electronics, of which Japan was at the time the leading proponent. It's about the same time the Berlin Wall came down, and you had highly educated cheap labour forces in places like Czechoslovakia. Over a very short, intense period of time, from maybe 1989, 1990 through the next two or three years, investment was then followed in the mid-nineties by a flood of disinvestment; technological obsolescence combined with the Wall coming down put the mockers on it.

Rowan Williams: In the ten, eleven years I was Bishop of Monmouth, I remember watching a procession of industries in Cwmcarn, a big industrial plant, and different kinds of small-scale tech companies coming in for a couple of years, finding it was a bit cheaper in Venezuela or whatever and that was part of the story. And the work done was not, I suppose, the kind of tough lifetime's cumulative experience that you might get in coal or steel in the old days, with the union involvements, the hierarches that went with that, the social leverage that went with all that, the whole package.

Neil Kinnock: The departures were very, very abrupt. I had a large plant from the late eighties, just above Newbridge in what was then my constituency, a large plant, good pay, very satisfactory performance in all respects, and that was great. They sponsored Newbridge Rugby Football Club; it was all very sweet, and then they buggered off within three months. And that happened with TV and semiconductors and telephones and God knows what else.

Ian Courtney: After Peter Walker, there was a chap called David Hunt. Then John Major sent John Redwood down the M4 and William Hague after him. And John Redwood, one of his first tasks was to decide that the WDA had grown too large. I got made redundant and I got a job with Coopers & Lybrand, management consultants, who had made a shedful of money advising companies on how to maximise the take from the state and from inward investment.

And along came LG, Lucky-Goldstar, and Lucky-Goldstar had this mammoth operation. The office that I ran in Cardiff had secured the mandate to advise on two of its projects. There was a semi-conductor plant and there was a plant for consumer electronics, televisions.

Andrew Davies: When William Hague was Secretary of State for Wales, LG was going to save the Welsh economy. This was the swansong of investment by Asian tech companies. At the time the accusation was that the Tories, specifically William Hague, had raided every item of the Welsh Office budget, including health, further education – everything, every last penny – to induce LG to come, and of course once they came, they never created the jobs that were promised.

Ian Courtney: Several months and a quarter of a billion quid later LG decides that Wales and a facility in Newport are the place for them. Prime Minister John Major, William Hague, David Rowe-Beddoe, the chairman of the WDA, all turned up for this grand ceremony that's reported on the BBC national news: they dig the first sod.

Edwina Hart: I attended the LG opening which featured John Major cutting the sod. I then had a lecture about the development of the Korean language at the table I sat on for lunch. How the language had originated. It was one of the most boring lunches I've ever been to.

Ian Courtney: I said to my boss, 'Do you know anything about this LG deal?' and he said, 'No, not really,' I said, 'Look, someone owes me a favour, do you want me to make a call and get any info and background information on this?'

Sure enough, I was set up to have a call with a big American, San José-based technology consultancy. Someone there owed me a favour. The call lasted about five minutes. It went something like: 'Well, I'm enquiring about an inward investment project from South-East Asia into South Wales.' 'Well, it's got to be Taiwanese or South Korean.' 'Yes, it's South Korean.' 'OK. It's probably LG.' 'It is LG.' These guys were on top of everything. 'LG are dead in the water.' 'What do you mean?' 'They're at 16 microns, everybody's going to 32 microns, their technology is redundant even before the factory opens.' 'Thank you very much indeed.'

What really shocked me were two things. The Department of Trade and Industry had various specialist divisions including an electronics and semi-conductors one. It seemed to me that they either didn't know this, or at no time did the Welsh Office or the WDA choose to engage with these people. And the other point that struck me about this whole story was how pathetically hopelessly equipped the civil service was to deal with these kinds of industries.

Andrew Davies: Later on, when I was minister, the WDA was still in existence and I was left to deal with the legacy of LG. The chief executive of the WDA came to see me to say, 'Look, LG have never created the number of jobs they said they would. We need to negotiate with LG, but they are a bunch of bastards and they don't see the need to repay the grant.' I can't remember how much William Hague gave to LG, but that was indicative of the approach, these huge capital programmes, which never, ever, delivered what they promised. I instructed the WDA that we had to play hardball with LG. If we hadn't then it would be open season for any company to walk away from any commitments they had made. In the end we negotiated a £75 million repayment – in cash and land and property – the largest-ever grant repayment in the UK.

John Redwood's successor, David Hunt, refused to apply for European Union funding for Wales. One EU Structural Fund Programme in particular, titled Objective One, allowed the poorest areas in the region to apply for regeneration or development funding. In 2004 a report published by Plaid Cymru estimated the loss of these funds to Wales between 1994 and 2000 to be worth as much as £1 billion, a sum that would have greatly helped to alleviate the economic difficulties that beset areas such as the Valleys, which by 1994 had little discernible change to their material conditions to show for a decade and a half's worth of initiatives and growth schemes.

Andrew Davies: It's indicative of Wales's relative economic decline that two-thirds of Wales qualified for EU assistance. It was defined as an Assisted Area and the EU funding it qualified for was called Objective One. Ron Davies basically made the case for Objective One funding, the Tories could have got it, but John Redwood and his successor David Hunt refused to apply for European funding.

Leanne Wood: The Tories have never seen Wales as fertile ground for votes for them and so they've just not cared. I remember the Objective One fiasco. It was around the way the map was drawn, I think Adam Price was involved in Cardiff University at the time, when they were working on the West Wales and the Valleys bit of the map and the Tories were resisting the redrawing of the map; it was no skin off their nose at all. Why they would have wanted to do that, I don't know. It can't just have been purely from spite, surely?

Andrew Davies: A very large majority of the councils in Wales were Labour. The Conservatives under David Hunt and then Redwood reorganised local government and created twenty-two local authorities. They were very small, unitary authorities. Previously, you had eight counties and thirty-seven districts, so the reorganisation struck me as a classic case of divide and rule.

Ron Davies: The Tories had also reorganised local government. You had the eight county councils and then the thirty-six district councils and both sets were Labour-controlled. These had two umbrella organisations, the Association of County Councils and Association of District Councils, who were arguing against reorganisation. Harry Jones was the leader of Newport District Council, and Graham Powell was the leader of Gwent County Council. Not only that. Harry Jones was leader of the Welsh Association of District Councils, so he was the district council leader for Wales, and Graham Powell was the leader of the Welsh County Councils Association, and they were next-door neighbours in Newport, and they absolutely detested each other.

It was a classic case of Tory divide and rule. The new councils were a shadow of what had previously existed, and I suspect the Tories designed it so they would be too small to be effective opposition.

Rowan Williams: I can remember some rather frustrating conversations with the Welsh Office in those days and although I didn't have to negotiate with John Redwood, I did with one of his successors and that was a profoundly dispiriting experience. That really was the point at which Wales felt like a knocked-about country.

They wanted to say to us, 'Look, you're really not trying, are you,' or worse than that.

FIFTEEN

AR SAIL GYFARTAL /
ON THE BASIS OF EQUALITY

Voices

Kirsti Bohata	Mari James	Guto Pryce
James Dean Bradfield	Siôn Jobbins	Gruff Rhys
Cian Ciarán	Patrick Jones	Gwenno Saunders
Carl Iwan Clowes	Alun Llwyd	Michael Sheen
Ron Davies	Eluned Morgan	Huw Stephens
Steve Eaves	Rhys Mwyn	Angharad Tomos
Edwina Hart	Gorwel Owen	Rachel Trezise
Meri Huws	Richard Parfitt	Nicky Wire
Rhys Ifans	Helen Prosser	David Wrench

———

Three decades after the founding of Cymdeithas yr Iaith Gymraeg, the Welsh Language Act, ostensibly a progressive and consequential piece of legislation, was passed by Parliament in 1993. The act determined that all public-sector organisations in Wales treat Cymraeg and English 'on the basis of equality'. In the life of Wales's institutions, administrations and other public bodies, Cymraeg had finally achieved parity with English. A Welsh Language Board was created to ensure compliance with the act and to formalise the language's promotion.

Fifty years had passed since the Beasleys had begun their campaign of direct action by refusing summonses to appear in court, unless asked to do so in Cymraeg. The act gave the right to speak Welsh during court proceedings. And over two decades since the decision of

Cymdeithas yr Iaith Gymraeg to either paint or destroy them, it was compulsory in Wales for road signs to be bilingual. Together with the founding of S4C a decade earlier and recent legislation that made Cymraeg a compulsory school subject up to the age of fourteen, it might have been reasonably concluded that, by 1993, several of the key demands of Welsh language activism had been met. The society's major goal of campaigning for a Property Act, Deddf Eiddo, remained unfulfilled.

In marked contrast to a decade earlier, for the first time since the debacle of the 1979 referendum, the issue of devolution was once again debated among members of the Labour Party.

Ron Davies: By 1987, within the Labour Party, largely thanks to the Wales TUC, they were committed to devolution. It was largely the trade union block vote in the Welsh Labour Party Conference which kept devolution on the table and there was a bit of stirring amongst the grass-roots, not because they wanted to see a parliament or an assembly in Wales, but to do something about local government. So that kept it bubbling. The Wales TUC was led by people who turned out to be good pals, Derek Gregory from NUPE, which became Unison, and George Wright, living in Caerphilly. Ironically the two of them were Englishmen with very strong English accents, but they were both absolutely solid and clear on the need for Welsh devolution. Between them, they virtually controlled the trade union block vote which dominated the Labour Party Conference.

The Labour Party set up something called the Wales Commission to try to resolve what was now going to happen. The unwritten policy was, 'Well, we're in favour of it but we're not going to do anything about it.'

Edwina Hart: From the trade union side of it, devolution was something really quite natural to discuss, because we thought we could win quite a lot of good for the economy and for the people of Wales out of it. We were having the devolution discussions in the trade unions for a long time.

I was national president of the banking union and the first woman and the youngest to hold the position when I was elected in 1992.

Ron Davies: There was a bit of a groundswell in the party, being pushed by all sorts of influences, not only the TUC, but a growing realisation that something needed to be done in terms of developing a separate Welsh agenda, trying to do something about the Welsh economy. We needed to create 10,000 jobs in every constituency, that was the measure of the pressure we had.

Meri Huws: The 1993 Welsh Language Act, and, ironically, S4C, were both products of Conservative governments. It was definitely blood from a stone from those Westminster politicians, but it was ironic that we've seen those steps being taken by Conservative regimes. That old traditional Labourism really did not die a death until the end of the twentieth century.

Helen Prosser: I was chair of Cymdeithas at the time of the Welsh Language Act. I was working as a lecturer in Swansea University and we had so much media coverage, Angharad and myself were being interviewed all the time. We didn't think because we'd been in jail and broken the law, we wouldn't be employed. I was later employed by the Welsh Joint Education Committee whose offices I had previously broken into. I was there for about five years. It wasn't a problem. Then we had a bit of a time after that when unemployment became more of an issue, and young people were more concerned about not having a criminal record that would go against them. I feel lucky to have been politicised in that era. I really do.

Angharad Tomos: The Welsh Language Act was so weak: you had to prove that there was a demand for it and it didn't cover private bodies.

I'd always felt that, once you reach some kind of so-called victory, you were disappointed, because you were expecting so much more. Ron Davies actually came to speak in one of our meetings at the Eisteddfod and we thought, 'We can't believe it: he's Labour.'

Meri Huws: When I was chair of Cymdeithas in the early eighties, whenever we were trying to talk to Labour politicians Ron Davies was an exception, because he would talk to us. The others, the Cardiff crowd, did not see the language movement as being of relevance; if anything, it was dangerous in that it was subverting their socialism, or their Labour Party-ism. And that's where it really emerged, and some of the discussions at that time were like hitting your head against a brick wall, it was a case of being told: 'Go away, young woman, and grow up.'

Carl Iwan Clowes: From 1988 to '93 I chaired what's called the National Language Forum, where I convened most of the major Welsh-medium language bodies together on a regular basis for most of that period. So that involved everyone from the Eisteddfod, teachers' unions, the Welsh Teachers' Union, the students' union Welsh societies. The Language Act of '93 was pretty well accepted by most organisations that operated through the Welsh medium. It felt like a battle that had been won – wrongly, perhaps, with hindsight – but it felt a significant moment in terms of moving the agenda forward.

Steve Eaves: What the 1993 act set in motion was the process of depoliticising the language because, prior to that, Labour was against the Welsh language, Plaid was for the Welsh language, and it was, to use the term of the period, a political football. Suddenly people saw there was nothing political about having bilingual signage at the hospital in Bangor. We all speak Welsh here, so it should be in Welsh. There's nothing political about that. I could see how, in a way, that started to loosen, very, very slightly, the hegemony of English in Wales.

Everybody previously thought the common-sense way, the sensible approach to everything, is English-only but that changed after the Welsh Language Act 1993.

Helen Prosser: To stop using the Welsh language as a political football, that's what people aspired to and that was the slogan. It hasn't disappeared completely. I think the fear was particularly about schools; that if you were opening Welsh schools, they'd all become Plaid Cymru voters. I think Labour genuinely felt that.

Siôn Jobbins: After the Welsh Language Act in '93, Dafydd Elis-Thomas said, 'Look, we're not going to make the language an issue now.' He was the Plaid Cymru leader at the time and to some extent, after '93, people were tired. People had given a lot of time to the language; there's a natural inclination then for people to get on with their lives. I think by '97, the Welsh language had been depoliticised to some extent, so Wyn Roberts, a Tory Secretary of State, had made Welsh compulsory in school, I don't think a lot of people registered this. The act said 'OK, the language is part of what Wales is,' and then Cymdeithas decided, 'OK, we're taking time off' and they didn't make big demands.

Richard Parfitt: I've worked in universities. I know people – I won't name them, there's nothing wrong with them – who are English, still nothing wrong with them, who are in senior positions in management in universities in Wales who are going to night school to learn Welsh simply to get promoted. And it's like, 'Alright, so here we go, again,' some guy who lives up in Ebbw Vale, his family have lived here for hundreds of years, but he's going to stay cleaning the toilets in the university, while that guy gets promoted to the top. It's like A. A. Gill said: the only time someone's going to put a hood on and terrorise you in Wales is if they're a druid.

Rachel Trezise: In the mid-nineties I was looking for a job, and I was getting really resentful that you had to speak Welsh for the jobs advertised in Cardiff. I thought, 'Well, that automatically excludes me. I can't even get a job in Cardiff, let alone anywhere in England.' I was stuck in a really hard place, because outside of Wales, you're too Welsh, and then in Wales, you're not Welsh enough.

Steve Eaves: More or less as soon as it started being implemented, people started shooting holes in the act and rightly so. The Welsh Language Act was the first time in the history of Wales that there was legislation legitimising the use of Welsh. The wording of the act was 'On the basis of equality' – not 'equally' but 'On the basis of equality' – and that was so woolly and open to interpretation.

Siôn Jobbins: There's a school of thought that basically the big difference between Gwynfor Evans and Saunders Lewis was that Saunders felt that Wales was a heroic country, and Gwynfor said, 'No, it's not. You have to take these incremental wins and that's what creates the polity.' I think the '93 act said, 'Welsh is part of Wales, this is the political geography of Wales, so whether you live in Gwent or in Gwynedd, this is the same thing,' and I think to some extent, it put an end to the argument, 'Does Welsh belong to all of Wales?'

As well as a resurgent interest in devolution, the Welsh Language Act coincided with a popularity in Welsh music that was reflected in the mainstream UK Top Forty. Whereas individual Welsh bands or artists had always achieved commercial success, this moment represented the flourishing of a group of pan-Wales musicians who sang in both Cymraeg and English. The success of these bands was not only a source of national confidence, but also engendered the feeling that the country was emerging from its bleak immediate past due to the energy of its younger people.

Nicky Wire: I feel a vacancy that Welsh wasn't on the curriculum, full stop. There was nothing of it. I don't think I could have learned it, because I'm shit at languages. When we were starting the band, the position of the language in Wales felt completely different.

Gruff Rhys: Richey Manic did an amazing interview, with one of the Welsh-language pop magazines. They asked: 'What do you think of the Welsh language?' and he said, 'The Welsh language is for people who eat coal.' Ffa Coffi Pawb played Tredegar but it was in the context of the Eisteddfod in 1990; there were people turning up, but we were frustrated with Ffa Coffi Pawb. We toured Wales for seven years and did a handful of gigs in England; we played a pub with Datblygu in London, a few gigs in parts of Europe that spoke minority languages, but we'd been playing in ever-decreasing circles around Wales within the Welsh-language community and we were really keen to play in places like the Valleys and Newport.

Patrick Jones: Me and Nick would watch a thing on HTV called *Stîd*. I don't know what it means in Welsh. Anhrefn would play on it and we'd be mesmerised.

James Dean Bradfield: Anhrefn were important to me. At that point, I was listening to John Peel and he played them a lot. I remember there was one song called 'Cornel' which I really liked, and when I heard where they came from, they were my in for Welsh-language music. I always thought language isn't the only definer of culture, obviously. I think as I got older – I've seen a lot more to it now – I think it is a huge part of the culture. When I was younger, it was more a mindset of where we were coming from, that working-class community. So much Welsh culture to me was literally drummed in, it was doing the flag, learning the anthem and nothing else, and someone like Richard Parfitt gave voice to another part of Welsh culture.

Richard Parfitt: The bilingual signs, I don't think they started appearing until '93. I was an adult, but we were always very suspicious, that's the truth. I know it's true that people were stopped from learning the language, but it gets mixed up with the fact that the huge immigration into south-east Wales during the Industrial Revolution would have diluted the Welsh language anyway. You'd accidentally tune in to a Welsh TV programme, and that would be cause for hilarity. Living where we lived in Newport, you picked the TV tracking from Bristol and watched BBC and HTV West.

James Dean Bradfield: I think I was almost quite relieved when those bilingual signs came in. I felt there was an equality that I could actually start decoding. I think I felt quite envious of the Eisteddfod, because I felt like I couldn't go there and couldn't participate; it's different now.

Patrick Jones: Probably we thought North Wales people were farmers, and they probably thought we lived having tin baths. There was that divide, a quite primeval divide over Welshness. I don't know what brought us together. Maybe it was education and music.

Steve Eaves: I'd been involved in delivering Welsh-language awareness training, which means talking to people from all over Wales, Welsh-speakers and non-Welsh-speakers, people from different ethnic origins who work for hospitals, police forces, councils, environmental organisations, talking to them about the Welsh language, about attitudes and behaviours towards language.

A lot of the training was in Gwent, the old Gwent, or in Newport, or Cardiff or Carmarthen. In every session I've ever had, I've had people saying, 'It's all a load of rubbish. Why are you forcing the language on us? I didn't want to go to this session,' and 'You've got a nationalist agenda.'

James Dean Bradfield: Richey was a bit dismissive about the Welsh language. And Richey did say one or two things about the Welsh language which didn't sit easy with me. I was in a choir until I was sixteen, and I sang lots in Welsh, and it's that old self-reproaching quote, I can't remember exactly, 'Oh, yes, the language. Beautiful to hear it sung, but never to be uttered' – that sarcastic saying, which sums it up. I was singing it lots in choir and then not speaking it. But I wanted to learn it. It wasn't a burning issue, but I definitely wanted to, because I realised that in music, it could really work. That was my in – when you're young, your ins are whether you like something, and I realised it rolled, it worked, it was musical.

Rachel Trezise: I loved the Manics, absolutely. I loved Richey. They were saying all the things I couldn't say about the Valleys and sent me on to read lots of books I wouldn't ever have discovered. Orwell, Plath, all of it. I bought *NME* every Wednesday and before that, *Kerrang!* I was a big metal head and you'd see adverts and they'd say, 'World Tour', I used to think, 'Well, why aren't they playing Cwmparc, then? That's not the world. What about my world?'

Nicky Wire: Our big thing was always that ambition is critical. That really resonated with me and Richey. More so in music than anything else, because it wasn't so in sport, it wasn't so in acting, or art, Wales was successful at all those things. It felt like music was secondary. There were so many shit bands in Cardiff who'd wear yellow jeans. They'd look like Timmy Mallett; they were fucking dreadful beyond belief.

We were from the Valleys, but it didn't feel like we were. Our identity was to be passed off as Welsh; our identity wasn't associated with a city or a place. And it did give us an immense amount of will and steel. Me and Richey would be watching rugby sometimes. Scott Gibbs could be tackling someone and we would be like, 'Break his fucking back!' We were having our talks in our bedrooms, which would go on for days, and turn into these insane arguments about McCarthy versus Guns N' Roses and politics, everything, we were formulating our manifestos then. Once we'd clicked into the zone of being in a band, when we realised all our depths, where that was coming from, we never needed to back down. Unfortunately, I couldn't switch it off till I was about fucking thirty-five.

Rachel Trezise: I loved Guns N' Roses, as well, and it seemed to me that the Manics were quite like Guns N' Roses, even if they were poles apart. I think a few of my friends liked the Manics because they were Welsh, but I liked them because they were almost metal in the beginning.

Nicky Wire: Working-class rage is one of my great theories of what makes music so important and vital and why it's probably never going to happen again. No band had more rage than us. Internally, externally, it didn't stop. In about '90, '91 we got chucked out of TJ's; we got banned. We went on stage and went, 'You're all anarcho-punk old shit, with your shit haircuts.' We did a cover of 'Just Like Honey' and some of our own stuff, and shouted, 'You're all fucking wankers'.

James Dean Bradfield: We had that strange dichotomy of being furiously confident and cocky, and moving forward and being slightly unhinged – because I think we were a bit unhinged. I don't really under-stand where we got our confidence from. I really don't. The more and more I think about it it startles me, especially me and Nick at the start, when we started writing songs. We just never questioned that it wasn't going to happen. It was going to happen, even before we put an album out, sending out letters, saying, 'No, motherfuckers, listen up, we've come for what's ours.'

Michael Sheen: I went to drama school in '89, somewhere around then, so that period through the eighties, from the mid-eighties to when I left to go to drama school, I was experiencing that kind of life-changing, world-changing situation of being taught by incredible drama teachers; my surroundings I totally accepted. I didn't know any different. I barely went anywhere other than Port Talbot. I barely went to Neath, let alone Port Talbot; going to Neath was exotic. The idea of seeing decay or impoverishment, I didn't see it like that. That was just what where I lived looked like. The world was very technicolour for me at the time, and in a lot of ways. I wore my background very lightly. I went to London. I went to drama school, and somewhere in the back of my mind, I must have been thinking, there must have been some sense of inferiority, there must have been something like that, but by the time I got there, I was like, 'I'm better than everybody else here,' a similarity in that sense of the attitude of a band who sing, 'You love us.' That was the attitude I had going to drama school. It wasn't, 'Oh, I come from South Wales. I come from a working-class place and please accept me.' It was like, 'I'm fucking better than all of you put together! I am Wales, hear me roar,' was the kind of attitude.

Nicky Wire: I think we were unique in Wales in terms of a total desire for fucking eviscerating competition or people, things, anything in our way. I think that can be identified a bit in our upbringings, really fucking hard-working. Not brutal at home at all, but a brutal view of work in terms of our fathers, just work–work–work, and really lovely mothers.

James Dean Bradfield: We were serious about it, saying, 'No, this is going to happen,' and then going a bit further forward and suddenly, poof, people start going, 'Oh, you're from fucking Wales, are you?' Or, 'Oh, only shit bands come from Wales: you must be shit, then.' Or somebody saying, 'Oh, God, you're not going to sound like 68 Guns?' and we're thinking, '68 Guns? That's a good song, actually, shut up.' People would say, 'Whoa, come on, boyo, a bit of Tom Jones.' We'd be going forward more and more, and think 'Fuck! People actually don't expect anything of us at all, do they?' That was the overriding thing, the snidiness of the remarks was unrelenting. It was wherever we went, whether it would be the Fleece and Firkin in Bristol, whether it would be the Wheatsheaf in Stoke or whether it would be the Venue in Edinburgh or the Bull and Gate in London, you would get it: 'Fucking bunch of Taffs.'

Nicky Wire: I always remember this hideous article in the *Independent*, by somebody called Brown. It was verging on racism and he used all these clichés about Wales, how no one can pronounce Ebbw Vale. I've still got my little black book.

James Dean Bradfield: There was a story in the *NME*, I can't remember what record shop it was in Edinburgh, but they said, 'We won't be stocking Motown Junk. Number one, we don't stock records from bands that wear eyeliner, and two, we definitely don't stock shit bands that wear eyeliner that are from Wales.' It was startling, to get slapped by a comment, by a review, or by phrases like Sexy Merthyrfuckers. I remember thinking, 'They actually don't know what to write about us. We're talking about Guy Debord. We're not even talking about Dylan Thomas, Idris Davies, or R. S. Thomas or fucking Saunders Lewis, we're talking about Guy Debord at the moment. We're not taking on any Welsh literature at the moment; we're talking about something else. We're talking about post-situationism, if there is such a thing as post-situationism.' 'Why do you keep doing Welsh puns to everything we do?' It was really uncalled-for. If a band from Stoke was written about, would you be talking about potting all the time, in the Potteries? No, you wouldn't. They didn't know what to write about us. They'd reach for one cliché and get stuck in every time. And at so many venues, in Bristol, in Edinburgh, in Coventry, the local crew would start talking about 'fucking Taffs' the moment we turned up.

Nicky Wire: It wouldn't be allowed today. You Sexy Merthyrfuckers, Guns and Daffodils, Meek Leek Manifesto – I could go on forever. It was harsh. You'd come across all these people, senior music journalists at *Melody Maker*, people like Chris Roberts or Alan Jones, and none of them would ever admit to being Welsh. Never.

James Dean Bradfield: Lots of people would come and challenge me, especially, for fights after gigs, and I would stand there and say, 'OK, go for it, then,' and look at them, and not one of them ever did. 'If you think you're going to scare us off, we're not being cowed.' I think that was my main obsession, not being cowed by anyone.

As in much of the United Kingdom, the effects of ecstasy and rave culture were felt in Wales during the early 1990s. Rural areas of the country had always proved a popular destination for free festivals during the preceding decades and remoter parts of the countryside proved a suitable location for small, locally organised raves. Urban South Wales was also a location for free parties, where unspoken social divisions, such as those between Welsh and non-Welsh-speakers, were, in the after-effects of ecstasy, often quietly examined then put aside.

David Wrench: When I was still living in Wales, up until 1990, there'd be one rave night a month at the Octagon in Bangor, where they'd play Hacienda-type stuff, and it was packed and there'd be small parties, in barns or whatever. I had a friend who had a couple of decks and we'd have some parties in his barn, but it was local people. It wasn't anything: it was kids; it wasn't massive.

Guto Pryce: There were a lot of crusties in North Wales, and they put on good parties. We would go to Bangor a lot. We'd tie it in with recording at Gorwel's.

Cian Ciarán: Bangor Football Club was the place to be. They let people put serious parties on there with sound systems. There were a few old heads in there every weekend, and I was underage, trying to sneak in every week. Everything was shut by eleven, but usually people would go on if there was a party in the quarry: it was a starting point. But that was one of the first places I remember where they played that type of music, loud: 'OK, I've found my crew!'

David Wrench: I think basically what happened in North Wales was, it's where magic mushrooms grew, so people came to pick them, took them and stayed. Hence you have this mix of people who've been there for years, the locals, and then the people who've turned up and either never quite got it together or have really got it together and become very self-sufficient and integrated really well.

Cian Ciarán: I missed the very first outdoor parties, then there were a few in North Wales, Anglesey had Penmon and Parys Mountain, which was a copper mine. The Dinorwig zig-zags; there was some by Britannia Bridge. You'd always get convoys at three in the morning appearing in the middle of nowhere. It was like, 'What the hell's this?' with no warning. They'd come from Liverpool or Manchester to enjoy the countryside and some fresh air and relax. Then we went to those raves in quarries and up in the mountains.

Kirsti Bohata: There was a location just north of Tal-y-bont, which held some iconic and enormous raves. I don't know who was behind it, but it was very well organised. There were multiple dance tents, light displays projected onto the steep valley walls, it was an amazing place. It was eventually shut down, but I think that was only when it started to attract large numbers from England. But often the police facilitated things. We went to one rave, around Brechfa or Lampeter, where we were stopped by police who helpfully told us that we needed to look out for ribbons to find the venue. It might have helped that we spoke to them in Welsh.

Gruff Rhys: I remember the raves in out of the way places. The DIY crew had a couple of people running Bangor and Bethesda. I knew this guy Stuart who got his PA confiscated at the North Wales raves; he was a Bristolian in Bangor. I think that's the connection with how the West Country DIY crew put on raves in the quarries in Llanberis. Michael Mann had used the same quarry hole to shoot his film *The Keep* in the early eighties. It was meant to resemble Transylvania at the time of Nazi occupation which gives you a sense of the atmosphere there.

David Wrench: The raves at Llanberis were beautiful. You'd have to climb up, in the dark, and it would be loads of people with blankets round them, and either a rucksack full of beer or those big things of cider. Everyone would hang out, getting stoned, and then there'd be, somehow, the sound system. They'd lug all the generators up there and lighting, right at the top in the old quarry houses. It was quite amazing. It would be loud. It would be blasting. There'd be constant rumours: 'The police are on their way. The police are on their way.' There was always this constant edginess to it, and occasionally they would turn up.

Up near Penmon it would be literally four sound systems down there in the quarry. There would be some weird elements there. I remember coming to raves in Cardiff and it was a totally different vibe, much more multicultural. It wasn't important where you were from or what your skin colour was.

Guto Pryce: We went on the South Wales party scene a lot, where it wasn't really so much of a hippie thing, but ex-football hooligans, people that had seen the light and were chilling out. It is a cliché but it's very true that a lot of people who were a bit naughty got into that scene and were essentially nice people afterwards – probably still a bit naughty, there was probably a bit of supplying going on and they probably saw a profit, but it was quite a unifying experience. It was attractive to a lot of different types of people. We used to go to a couple in Glynneath and there was a sound system called Freebass from Swansea. We didn't mix with people from Swansea at all. That football hangover was still there. You didn't go clubbing in Swansea unless you were either really hard or you went with girls; if you went with a group of lads to Swansea, you'd have to run to the station.

Rhys Mwyn: By the early nineties, certainly Ffa Coffi Pawb and Y Cyrff, the people who would go on to form Super Furry Animals and Catatonia, had reached a plateau on the Welsh-language scene where there was nowhere to go. We were lucky as Anhrefn, because in the nineties we were abroad more than we were playing in Wales. We'd peaked in Wales. I think there was one year that we did about fifty shows in England and about four in Wales; we literally flew home, having played in front of 5,000 people in Bilbao, and played a pub in Caernarfon called the Ship and Castle, and there were three people there. It's incredible how quickly we went from being popular to playing in front of three people in Wales. Y Cyrff and Ffa Coffi Pawb got to a similar point but got out on a high, and then Mark and Cerys were doing demos as Catatonia and Gruff, Rhys Ifans and Dafydd Ieuan were experimenting with a techno proto-Super Furry Animals. They all very quietly shifted gear and started singing in English.

Siôn Jobbins: I remember by '93 Ffa Coffi Pawb and people started turning to English. I felt I could understand why because I'd written books in English: I can't tell someone then not to sing a song in English, so I understand, but it had been a great thing. We'd had something really precious, really exciting. The only good thing for the Welsh language in the 1980s was that Welsh-language music scene, and I remember thinking, 'That's been taken away from us.' Then you'd have groups from Caernarfon singing in English, and in a way that helped the argument for devolution. It was the same time as the Manics and I think it opened a curtain for a broader, non-Welsh-speaking part of Wales to say, 'OK, you can be contemporary in Welshness, it's not twee revivalist stuff being forced on you. This is a part of your culture as well.'

Rhys Mwyn: In the context of that debate, I was usually there going, 'Singing in English, shouldn't be doing that,' but I also understood you left people with no choice. It's horrible to even discuss it, because I've always said, with the Welsh-speakers you can never fully, fully trust them. Never fully trust them. And I'm one of them. You can come and go quickly. The tendency with that certain strain of Welsh nationalism is they protest when it's gone, but they don't support it when it's there. As a band, we spent so much energy, so much time, so much passion, trying to link up with places like Newport, because the message was quite simple: we're a punk band, we're singing in Welsh, but we're all part of the same thing. There's no copyright on Welshness. A Somali family in Butetown, whatever Welshness is in that particular circumstance, is as valid as someone living in Pwllheli. Welshness is whatever you want it to be.

It always saddened me that the elite element of the Welsh-language brigade kept it to themselves and never realised what they were doing. If you're in Gwynedd and Dyfed, that's an easy mistake to make, because you're surrounded by the language. If you're in the pub in Nefyn, everybody speaks Welsh. It's all great; things are happening. You don't realise what it's like to be in Newport. I totally get it, why people would have felt there was a Welsh-language-speaking elite.

Gruff Rhys: I was party to Rhys' thoughts because Dafydd Ieuan was filling in on drums for Anhrefn, and he used to bring me on tour. He'd tell me, 'You can come on tour. You can set up the gear and stuff.' I'm not sure if he'd tell Rhys and Siôn, and I'd turn up in good faith and come with them in the van and then they were, 'Oh, OK.' And then there were a couple of tours: we did the Ffa Coffi set on one tour and Super Furry Animals, which then was me, Guto, Daf doing electronic music. In '94, we did a tour of France, playing a mixture of squats on the punk rock squat circuit and Celtic gigs, places like Brittany that had a cultural, linguistical undercurrent.

Guto Pryce: Anhrefn were going into Europe and getting out of Wales and we did a few tours with them around some pretty grubby Czechoslovakian squats, but it was a very exciting scene for a teenager, all the little minority language scenes that you had. It was hilarious, going with Anhrefn to Fest Noz in Brittany, essentially everything they battled against: professional Celts in waistcoats and weird bagpipes. One of the early incarnations of Super Furry Animals was a synth techno trance set-up and they took that to piss off the punks and to piss off the Celts, to shake things up, and that was a huge moment of realisation – nothing is sacred at the end of the day; everything needs to be challenged.

Gruff Rhys: There were no phones and no Internet. You'd play a cassette for ninety minutes, but you'd have maybe a seven-hour journey in a van, which would be mostly Rhys Mwyn ranting, so that was my political education in a way. Between '92 and '95, myself, Daf and I think Cian did some gigs with Anhrefn. Guto was with us, we'd all have been party to Rhys' manifesto at length, so we were pretty fired up. And musically, we were a different generation. We were often making introverted, hazy music that wasn't from the punk rock generation. We'd internalised a manifesto that was the antithesis of Britpop but retaining the melodic pop element.

Guto Pryce: I think in the band when we were watching the Britpop scene developing, we thought, 'It's shit, this is really quite regressive.' The lack of inclusivity was quite offensive at times. It suited us to be a Welsh-language band that went to London, and thankfully we were successful. We could have gone to London and not played to anyone, but things happened for the band because of timing and the decision to sing in English was crucial to that. The Welsh language was intimidating and excluding to people who didn't speak it, so you were branded a Welsh nationalist. I guess that's where the Welsh music scene was most healthy in breaking down those barriers and being more inclusive. It gradually got better throughout the nineties.

Alun Llwyd: We put out the first two Super Furry Animals singles on Ankst, which was started by my friend Gruff and myself in Aberystwyth University. Gruff had been writing his own fanzines in Porthmadog; I'd been writing my own fanzines and putting on gigs in Wrexham, but fanzine culture at that point of time came from Anhrefn. Gruff's fanzine wasn't as political as mine; his was better than mine. Mine was really bad, and I got away with it simply because it was tagged as a Cymdeithas yr Iaith fanzine. We'd worked closely with Gruff and Daf on Ffa Coffi Pawb, and then when Ffa Coffi Pawb split up what became then the Super Furry Animals was a logical progression of being in that culture for a while, but suddenly realising there's a big, wide world out there and at the same time wanting to make a living. Ankst then managed Super Furry Animals and Gorky's.

Guto Pryce: We happened to be that band at the right time, but we were cynical of Welsh ghettoism. We were also the generation that got hit by rave and we were pretty open-minded. There was a lot of hugging, a lot of happiness; we had love for everybody in us and we knew we were pissing off some people when we were singing in English, but we knew we were right, or at least, we could justify why we were doing it.

Gorwel Owen: I think Super Furry Animals were very clever in the way they responded to the language. I wouldn't want to speak for them, but they worked out how to respect the language and the rule, but also how to sing in English.

Cian Ciarán: I went to film school in Newport in '94 and lived in Cardiff. I started going to TJ's and so I met 60 Ft. Dolls and the Manics in rehearsal rooms and the English-language Welsh scene was new to me as an eighteen-, nineteen-year-old. I don't remember having that sit-down conversation on the pub table, talking about the alienation of not being a Welsh-speaker, but I've had it from others, not necessarily musicians, the sense of being an outsider, that there's a clique and you're all in it together and you look after each other.

Richard Parfitt: My real experience of the Welsh language was when we met people like the Super Furry Animals, Gorky's and we played with them and Catatonia and we loved them. It was really simple, we started to play with all those bands, and they were really nice to us and they were great, and that was basically it. It was that simple.

Gruff Rhys: In Super Furry Animals we felt an incredible warmth from areas of Wales we'd never been able to tour as Ffa Coffi Pawb, and I think it was a period of consensus. I was enjoying writing in English as a language; having grown up obsessed with Anglo-American pop culture. It wasn't alien, but hopefully not in any sense of being dismissive of my first language. But it was a glasnost, I think, of the old chauvinisms on both linguistical sides. They seemed to be melting away in that period and I think there was a political consensus, as well, building up to the referendum.

Contemporary Welsh music reached the apotheosis of its popularity in the 1996 single 'Design for Life' by Manic Street Preachers. The song entered the UK Top Forty at number 2, its opening line, 'Libraries gave us power', was inspired by a phrase engraved above the entrance to the former library in the docks area of Pill, Newport. The commercial achievement of the single and Everything Must Go, *the album from which it was taken, was reflected in the band's subsequent success at the following year's Brit Awards. The band, who had been vilified for being Welsh at the start of their career, won in the Best British Group and Best British Album of the Year categories, having also been nominated for the Best Single and Best Video. These accomplishments were all the more remarkable given the fact that one of the tightly knit group's founding members and lyricists, Richey Edwards, a totemic presence on stage and in the media, had disappeared on 1 February 1995. The band had taken the difficult decision to continue without him and drawn on their resolve to produce the most immediate and commercially successful work of their career. They had done so without compromising the standards agreed upon during their Valleys adolescence; their performance of 'Design for Life' at the Brit Awards was duly accompanied by footage of fox hunting and the Poll Tax riots.*

1996 was also the year in which Super Furry Animals, a band who regularly sang in Cymraeg as well as English, released their debut album Fuzzy Logic, *which entered the Top Forty at number 23. Within four years the group would release* Mwng, *an album entirely sung in Cymraeg that narrowly missed a top-10 chart placing on its release, an achievement that provided a remarkable instance of equal status for the Welsh language.*

Nicky Wire: Undoubtedly there are communities in Wales who have felt as Welsh, or more Welsh than I have done. There are people in Ceredigion or the Llŷn Peninsula who have obviously always felt completely Welsh. They've never been talked to, or they've never really had much of a platform. The English language obviously gave us a bigger platform. There's nothing political behind that: it's just a fact of life. But I think there was undoubtedly more of a general feeling developing about being Welsh and, let's face it, less of an embarrassment at being Welsh.

Mari James: The Manics were on a Jools Holland programme, I seem to remember it as one of his Hootenanny ones, so it must have been the New Year before the devolution referendum and they had on screen a huge Draig Goch flag, and that was a big wow factor, the Manics were willing to admit that they were Welsh, and did so not under duress – 'But you're Welsh really,' that kind of interview. They were the opposite; they were up there and proud. Moments like that were really important and a lot of that then became embedded.

Eluned Morgan: That was the beginning of a release of confidence for the Welsh nation that totally blossomed afterwards. You saw all those awakenings, which had started before the devolution vote, with the Manics and all of the pop culture. Identity politics was starting to develop then. There was always an assumption before that that it was about economics, and identity politics really started to make an impact.

Nicky Wire: By that point, even if people didn't like us, there was a begrudging sense of 'They have taken a lot of shit and flack, this lot, just for being from Wales.' I think some of the Welsh-language bands were slightly narky that I had a Welsh flag on my amp, I think maybe it was Gorky's. We took the Super Furry Animals on tour and the first date was in Amsterdam and it just happened. Gruff walked into the dressing room and James was going through a massive Badfinger obsession at the time, and Gruff said, 'Ah, Baby Blue, Badfinger,' in that amazing voice of his, and straight away, there was a really lovely bond. I was a big fan of them by that point, I think everyone was because of the music they made. And then we had Catatonia play with us, we had Stereophonics play with us. I'm very cynical of these things, 'Here's a really good band on the up; we want to have them on the bill as well,' I wouldn't say there was ever any deep, philosophical talk.

Guto Pryce: We never went, 'Oh, fuck the Welsh language. I can't be arsed anymore.' We would never do something that we thought would be bad for the Welsh language. We wouldn't want to ever be associated with the royal family or the Conservative Party, for example. Having Alun there was a reassurance, because he came from a protesting background as did Daf and Gruff. We used to do an awful lot of press in the band and we'd be doing it all over the world, and that's probably where we did a lot of our discussing. We wouldn't have such deep conversations on the bus, but we would have eight interviews in a row in Amsterdam, where the European press really wanted to hear about where we were from, and probably make a connection with their own situations. Thinking back, I probably learnt a lot sitting next to Gruff in interviews, because him and Daf had a lot more knowledge of the background and a lot more personal connection to the language movement.

Huw Stephens: So many conversations at home between my mum and dad and their friends were about matters of Wales. I'd go on Welsh Language Society marches with my sisters around the centre of Cardiff; my mum worked for Plaid Cymru for a number of years, so I would end up going and sitting in the car while she was out canvassing, it was completely normal to us. It was never an issue and I was always allowed to make up my own mind about everything.

Gruff is my cousin, albeit ten years older, so I didn't know him much. By the time I was getting into music, he'd been studying and he'd been in bands and split up bands and he was in the Super Furry Animals, which was amazing. But what was fascinating about the Furries was they were from all parts of Wales – North, Gruff, Daf, Cian, Cardiff, Guto, Bunf. They were modern: I got so many cultural references from all the interviews, about Brazilian music or about Japan or about Pete Fowler or about Welsh bands like Datblygu, or about Wales, or about drugs or Howard Marks. The list goes on of the family tree of Super Furry Animals. And musically it was wonderful. You'd see them on *Top of the Pops* and on the cover of the *NME*, and then you'd see them in the pub on Friday and walking around town on a Tuesday afternoon, and you'd see Gorky's going into a rehearsal space and then you'd hear them on John Peel. The most exciting bands, who happened to live on my doorstep.

Gwenno Saunders: I was on tour constantly from when I was sixteen as an Irish dancer, without Internet. I thought, 'Oh, God, I'm from somewhere where nothing ever happens, and particularly my culture, my language, it belongs to old people and in school, and actually things that are a bit shit.' I love it and I'll speak to my mother in it, but I never thought about doing anything in the Welsh language, because I didn't find inspiration there. Then I heard about what was happening at home. I wouldn't have conceived of making music without what happened then with Gorky's, Catatonia and Super Furry Animals, I wouldn't have imagined it was possible to be creative in that way and have a career in my language.

During the eighties and nineties, every comedy show would have a sketch with someone taking the piss out of someone Welsh; it just was common, it was an absolutely common thing to do. And it still seeps in there sometimes, but it was normal for stand-ups to do that. And then, all of a sudden, here were people not apologising for being like that. Gruff speaking in a Gwynedd accent, it had an enormous impact.

Rhys Ifans: I think the Super Furry Animals more than anyone have played a huge part in allowing Welsh people to realise that even if you don't speak Welsh, it's your language. It's still your language. You don't have to speak it for it to be your language. And I think that's something we've all played a huge part in and these were discussions that we were having at the age of twelve, thirteen and fourteen, as a group of people. This is what had to happen.

Guto Pryce: You see drystone walling that has been patched up for centuries, it's fallen down and sheep from the same age-old stock are grazing against it. I know that that's a big part of a lot of people's history. My mum and dad are both from hill sheep-farming backgrounds. But maybe you could say the same about the slag heaps of the Valleys and that landscape and of the slates near Bethesda. It starts getting really . . . heavy, that's the word. You can see the poverty left in the wake of the slate industry, this great industry with its beautiful, beautiful product. You still see these great big slabs that people will pay a fortune for but has hardly any jobs in it. That is as evocative to me of Wales as the sheep and the pastoral, simple life.

Patrick Jones: I was working in an old-school library: an older generation would use it, it was very quiet, 'Shhh,' that sort of thing. I was working there '93, '94, '95. And of course Richey had gone missing in '95, and then people would come to Blackwood almost like a pilgrimage, and then say, 'Nicky Wire's brother's up there,' and journalists would come in. Big pieces were written about the Valleys and how they were a cauldron of despair. We had this slight nudge of Cool Cymru, and I was thinking, 'This isn't cool here.' Blackwood High Street was like the Wild West, in 1995, '96: drug-addled, pissed up, souped-up cars and violence, male testosterone and unemployment, unemployment which felt different perhaps to the eighties. I wrote my first play then, *Everything Must Go*, I started hearing all the voices, and that was trying to capture this sense of Uncool Cymru, and saying, 'We're living in some fragmented reality.'

James Dean Bradfield: 'Design for Life' was a bittersweet moment, but one that felt like it came from a position of innate strength that I knew that we all had, that stemmed from overcoming adversity, because it was adversity.

Nicky Wire: I think I had suppressed any idea of Welshness a little. *The Holy Bible* was about everything but very internal. Richey's words were so amazing. I'd already had my R. S. Thomas re-awakening by this point and Dylan Thomas, who I'd been much more into when I was young, but somehow, having the two Thomases together made me feel better: you had the two opposing versions of Welshness. There's a bit of sentimentality in things like 'Fern Hill'. R. S. Thomas and Dylan Thomas, the two of them taken together made more sense, and 'Design for Life', I don't think the music or the words could have been made anywhere else other than the South Wales Valleys. It's one of my shortest lyrics: we'd come from Richey – 'ifwhiteamericatoldthetruthforoneday' – and arrived at something really succinct. It's compact, it's clean, it's tidy, it's neat, really organised, like a Valleys house.

I think everyone who heard 'Design for Life', even people who didn't like us, were like, 'Fuck'. Sometimes, it needs that touch paper. It needs a try by a rugby player or a goal or something. It's not all about policy, as we fucking know; sometimes you need the other things that bind people together.

In 1996 we had had the success and the Brits is always the year after. When we played the Brits there were twelve million people watching. I did this rambling speech about Jo Calzaghe and comprehensive schools. There was a massive Welsh flag tied round myself and we played 'Design for Life'. I think there was a bit of 'Oh, they're alright, those Taffs.' I remember going up and Colin Jackson giving us a prize – we'd insisted on someone Welsh at least being part of it. The ambition was there, we'd experienced that. Then I got obsessed with that ambition turning into massive fucking self-destruction, with Burton, with Rachel Roberts and our own situation. The amount of Welsh people who get success, who then turn in on themselves at a really early age; it's something really ingrained when people get to a certain level. I then went back to the hyper-realism of R. S. Thomas. We're not a romantic nation like the Irish or the Scots, we have our myths but there's always a really harsh realism.

It does have a kind of choir, brass band, choral element to it, 'Design for Life', but really, it's the sound of marching unions.

SIXTEEN

PA BRIS NAWR AM FYMRYN O URDDAS? / WHAT PRICE NOW FOR A SHALLOW PIECE OF DIGNITY?

Voices

Kirsti Bohata	Kim Howells	Adam Price
James Dean Bradfield	Rhys Ifans	Guto Pryce
Carl Iwan Clowes	Dafydd Iwan	Gruff Rhys
Cynog Dafis	Mari James	Gwenno Saunders
Jane Davidson	Siôn Jobbins	Michael Sheen
Andrew Davies	Tecwyn Vaughan	Huw Stephens
Ron Davies	Jones	Bedwyr Williams
Steve Eaves	Neil Kinnock	Charlotte Williams
Ffred Ffransis	Ben Lake	Rowan Williams
Peter Hain	Eluned Morgan	Nicky Wire
Edwina Hart	Kevin Morgan	Leanne Wood

———

After defeat in the 1992 General Election the Labour Party was led by John Smith. In Smith's native Scotland devolution was becoming increasingly popular and the subject of extensive analysis and debate. The energy and discussion around Scottish devolution was led by the Scottish Constitutional Convention, established in 1989. Members of the convention included the Labour Party, Scottish Liberal Democrats, Scottish Democratic Left, Orkney and Shetland Movement, and more than ten other significant organisations (though not the SNP, because the convention didn't consider the possibility of independence). At

its first meeting the convention published the authoritatively titled
'Claim of Right for Scotland', a document that demanded a Scottish
assembly or parliament, with law-making powers. The convention's
final report – 'Scotland's Parliament, Scotland's Right' – was published
in 1995. The document contained detailed proposals for a devolution
arrangement.

In Wales, where memories of the 1979 campaign remained strong
across the political parties, the idea of revisiting devolution was
regularly met with lingering scepticism. Instead of a constitutional
convention the Labour Party in Wales had established the Wales
Commission, a body that was considered by many in favour of Welsh
self-governance to be non-committal, at best, towards the idea of
Welsh devolution. Among many in Labour there was an added
mistrust in introducing any new political body that might in its
constitution support proportional representation, an electoral system
that would undermine the party's hegemony in South Wales.

Andrew Davies: When Labour had lost the election in '92, John Smith,
who was a very committed devolutionist, took over and the Shadow
Secretary of State for Wales at the time was Ron Davies, and John
Smith asked Ron to basically make the case for devolution in Wales.

Ron Davies: We were marooned in sand in Wales in terms of the drive
towards devolution; in Scotland, they were roaring ahead, largely
because of the poll tax in 1988 when they were the experiment. I can
remember speaking to a good mate of mine, John Home Robertson,
who was on the front bench with me – he was a bit of a Scottish lord
but a very nice guy. 'You haven't seen anything yet,' he said. 'People in
their droves are coming out. It's a huge mistake: you wait till the Poll
Tax hits you in England and Wales.' Everybody exaggerates in politics,
but that storm came about.

John Smith was industry spokesman, Donald Dewar was Scottish
spokesman at the time; they were very close friends, and devolution

was motoring. They had taken the decision way back that they were going to have a more inclusive approach, so they had set up the Scottish Constitutional Convention, which was bringing in other political parties, the SDP and the churches. The important thing was that it was an inclusive process and there was a lot of publicity and everybody was in favour of it and the Scottish Labour Conference was in favour of it. They knew what they wanted, and the UK Labour Party was endorsing it. In Wales it wasn't a public issue in 1992 and Neil Kinnock was a big issue.

Andrew Davies: Learned helplessness is a well-known concept in psychology. Researchers first studied it in dogs, which were trained to associate a noise with electric shock and other stimuli and, as a result, their behaviour was changed fundamentally. They learned that they weren't able to do anything and they consequently stopped doing things that were beneficial, because they associated that with a punishment, and I wonder if reduced, or declining, confidence goes a long way to explaining that sense in Wales at the time of 'Well, there's nothing we can do.'

Ron Davies: So off Neil Kinnock shuffled and John Smith became leader and by that time Smithy was the UK's darling: everybody liked him, a cheery man, good presentation, obviously skilled, excellent parliamentarian. We used to love John on the front bench. He had everything and he was acerbic. I saw him tear strips off the opposition, whoever the opposition were, but it was always with a smile on his face. You'd have people laughing at themselves, because he was so clever at doing it. I was in a pretty good position: I stood and won the seat on the Shadow Cabinet as Shadow Secretary of State for Wales quite easily, and I thought, 'I wonder what happens now.' Shortly afterwards, I had a message, 'The leader wants to see you up in his office,' so up I went, and there was John in his study. Before the conversation had gone much further, he stopped and said, 'You are in favour of devolution,

Ron, aren't you?' Because by that time I'd been to Damascus and back, I said, 'Yes,' and he said, 'That's good, because what I want you to do is make sure that we have a proper parliament in Wales with the same legislative powers that we've got in Scotland.' And I thought, 'Right, OK, thank you very much, suits me down to the ground,' because I knew it was going to be tough, but I don't mind a tough scrap. The structure of the party was such that if you've got the backing of the leader, you can do pretty much anything, but I knew that there were strong forces in Wales, among a lot of parliamentarians, Neil Kinnock, a lot of local government and the grass roots who were anything but pro-devolution. There was still, at a party level, resentment about the Welsh language, as Plaid had risen as a force in local elections. They were getting more vituperation from Labour, they were the 'bloody Welshies' again, it was getting like that.

Peter Hain: I came from a very different political stance to devolution than Neil, who was a close friend of mine, but we disagreed fundamentally on it at the time. In the nineties, he was quite awkward about it, and he was persuaded to keep quiet and that's the best we could do in the '97 referendum. There was that antagonism: rather than a kind of old-fashioned, Ulster Unionist type of vision for Wales, I think it was an antagonism towards division. The argument people like Neil made is that a worker, a miner in Ebbw Vale, is the same as a miner in Durham, as a miner in the Scottish coalfields, or the Kent coalfields, or the old Somerset coalfields or wherever it was. It's a class thing rather than a colonial UK heritage unionism. I think it was the wrong approach and I think it held Labour back and it held the cause of Wales and devolution back, but then I hadn't lived the history of it as people like Neil had.

Neil Kinnock: The confines of fiscal control, which are pretty dreadful within devolution, ensured no Welsh government would ever have enough money. Always, in my view, Wales deserved to have more money to tackle the nature of the challenges, demographically, geographically and locationally we faced. And any sensible national UK government would understand that and realise there are huge returns to be made by reducing that bill through success. But the problem with devolution, and I warned about this back in the seventies, is all it required for the break-up of the United Kingdom was a government in Scotland that despised Whitehall and Westminster and a government in Whitehall and Westminster that didn't give a damn about Scotland, which would put Wales at even greater bloody disadvantage because of the weakening of the union.

Ben Lake: The raison d'être for Plaid Cymru was to have more self-government for Wales, and self-government increasingly, certainly after Gwynfor, and with the two presidencies of Dafydd Iwan and Dafydd Wigley, was what defined Plaid. But then as we looked towards the '97 referendum, self-government meant devolution. And there were certainly elements of the party and the membership who aspired to use it as a stepping stone for something greater.

Dafydd Iwan: In Plaid we had mixed feelings about devolution, because from our point of view, we looked from the other direction: it's not devolution we wanted, it's recognition of Wales as a national entity. The whole concept of devolution is dangerous, in the sense that London has decided to give you certain powers.

Kevin Morgan: Neil was trapped in a certain persona crafted by British Labour, where he was the representative of British Labour in Wales and therefore against everything that Welsh Labour and Plaid Cymru stood for, which was 'Let's make our own decisions ourselves and let's take a leaf out of Gandhi's book, in which bad government, if it's self-government, is better than good government. Let's make our own decisions, and yes, let's make our own mistakes, because that's how we learn, that's how we mature as a democracy.' And that's the only way to develop. You can't develop if you are not the agent of your own transformation. Neil was a different kettle of fish. While I got on with him personally, he was the embodiment of British Labour and one of my best friends, Kim Howells, who I grew up with, was also an embodiment of British Labour. Kim was very critical of devolution.

Ron Davies: I had two big issues: first of all, developing policies about what the assembly would look like, and, secondly, trying to frame the political organisation of it in order to win this potential referendum. At the time I was continually told, 'Referendum? No, we don't need a referendum,' and the Wales Commission was charged with doing work on what the assembly would look like, and the commission was run by two men, Ken Hopkins and Terry Thomas, and to say that they were less than cooperative would be an understatement.

I was Shadow Wales Secretary. I knew what I wanted politically and I knew what the leader was after, so I thought, 'Well, we've got to do this,' and I was creating all sorts of policy papers on organisational matters that the assembly would follow, about regeneration and about the environment and was feeding all that in. That's where the phrase 'Bonfire of the Quangos' came from, Peter Hain used it when we were looking at the structures of what we were going to do about all the quangos, because that was part of our campaign at the time. All of these quangos had been set up by English secretaries of state, getting their Tory mates to run Wales. That was the broad narrative, get rid of the quangos, and Bonfire of the Quangos became quite a popular phrase at the time, although Smithy wasn't happy, because that wasn't the policy in Scotland and it wasn't the policy in England. But there we are. I said, 'Look, we've got to do things differently in Wales, that's what devolution's about.'

Peter Hain: I know there was a lot of grumpiness, and I think Ron particularly was on the receiving end. I was working closely with Ron and supporting him as his campaigner and then I was part of his shadow team, and he had a lot of opposition, a lot of personal as well as political opposition, in the Welsh Labour Party, from the anti-devolutionists and from the right of the party and a lot of personal antagonism amongst MPs.

Ron Davies: I was getting all sorts of grief. But then I was thinking, 'What am I going to do now about building up a broad coalition in favour of devolution?' and that's when I was starting to make speeches about inclusiveness and making sure that we became the first government institution ever to have the word in its founding constitution, which is in the Government of Wales Act, a commitment to inclusiveness and non-discrimination, equality of opportunity as well as a commitment to environmental sustainability.

Andrew Davies: There was all sorts of stuff going on. Ron could see that, unless you had a form of PR, then the assembly was going to be seen as a South Wales Labour fiefdom, the phrase at the time was 'Mid-Glamorgan on stilts'. It would be full of superannuated Labour councillors from the Valleys; it would be very conservative with a small c and not inclusive, which is why there was a lot of talk of inclusive politics. Ron made sure that there was some form of proportional representation, which I know in the Labour group was hated, absolutely hated. It was quite extraordinary, really, this idea that Labour was Wales and Wales was Labour and it was said in an unconscious way, but I think it was very revealing, almost a sense of entitlement, or at least of expectation.

Ron Davies: The Labour Party were saying, 'What's he talking about? Why's he talking about inclusiveness? We don't need more black people, it's more women that we want!' And I started then, talking to Dafydd Wigley, who would be by himself in the Commons. Plaid Cymru would sit on a table by themselves: it was an unwritten rule, you wouldn't go and join a Labour table or a Tory table. It wasn't long before I started going out not infrequently with Dafydd and briefing him on where we were with the devolution project, and the same thing with Richard Livesey of the Liberals, love him, to try and establish a personal rapport and take a sounding about where they might be.

Cynog Dafis: I was the fourth Plaid MP. Plaid had settled in by then and was an accepted presence and I think respected, because of the quality of its contribution to Parliament. We didn't just bang on about Wales and bang on about the parliament in Wales, Dafydd Wigley had been involved from the beginning in a whole range of issues, and this meant that people were respected, and people would say, 'Oh, the Welsh Nationalists, not a bad bunch. They do a lot of very good work.' Oliver Letwin, an amiable fellow Oliver Letwin, and very, very clever of course, said in one of the debates on the Devolution Bill: 'Well, when I came to Parliament, people told me that among the nicest people you could possibly find in Parliament are the Welsh Nationalists,' and he didn't believe them until he got there, and then he found out that we were quite nice people. And then he said, 'But you understand what they're doing: they'll do more and more and more of this kind of thing. They won't be satisfied with what has been offered; they'll want more and more and more and more, all the time.' Which was the whole point.

Andrew Davies: Then John Smith sadly died, and Blair took over, and it was obvious that Blair was not a devolutionist, and that's one of the ultimate ironies of devolution, that the two most influential politicians who helped create devolution were Margaret Thatcher and Tony Blair, neither of whom actually believed in it.

Ron Davies: The issue that remained for me then was this Wales Commission that we had set up in Labour and the real sticking point was proportional representation and legislation – because I wanted legislative powers. Not easy, because in London John Smith had been replaced by Tony Blair; Tony Blair made it pretty clear to me that he'd rather we didn't have devolution at all, but it was on the agenda, there was nothing much he could do about it, so get on and do it, and he recognised the same thing in Scotland. In 1996, it was at the time of the Dunblane shooting, George Robertson, who by this time was Shadow Secretary of State for Scotland, was in an office next to me. Tony Blair had gone to see George Robertson and they chatted about Dunblane and so on, and eventually they got round to devolution, and they both agreed that there would have to be a referendum in Scotland. At this moment in time there was no agreement to have a referendum anywhere. But there would have to be a referendum in Scotland, because Scotland had tax-raising powers, and you couldn't have taxation without representation. George was telling me all this on a Monday morning, and he said, 'Big announcement tomorrow, there's going to be a referendum in Scotland.' There was no talk about a referendum in Wales at all.

I think I must have been up for a Welsh Group meeting, but that evening I received a message, 'Can you go and see the leader?' I knew what it was going to be about; by this time I'd thought through what I wanted. Went to see the leader: 'Ron, right, referendum, we're having a referendum in Scotland. What about Wales?' And I think he expected me to say, 'We're not going to have a referendum.' And I somewhat wrong-footed him by saying, 'Well, if we've got to have an elected assembly, we've got to have a referendum, but we won't win the referendum, Tony, and this is a matter of principle for me, unless we make some concession on legislative powers and on proportional representation.' And he was a bit flummoxed by that. He didn't like it, because Jack Straw was then nominally in charge of constitutional change, and Jack Straw didn't want anything at all to do with it. English nationalist, Jack. But he was prepared to sacrifice that. And on proportional representation, you could see him thinking, 'Well, this might not be a bad thing if we throw a little straw in the wind towards the SDP.' Everybody was talking to Blair, I know Kinnock would have been talking to him, 'Devolution. Ron's bloody nuts, you can't have that!' The Wales Commission were telling him, 'You can't have proportional representation.'

Andrew Davies: The one area where there was accord was between Ron Davies and Dafydd Wigley at parliamentary level, but I think it was very personal. Most Labour MPs were vitriolic about Plaid, and vice versa.

Ron Davies: Things were on a complete knife-edge. There was stuff that I was prepared to accept and not prepared to accept: I had my own red lines, although they were shifting as needs must. Tony Blair said, 'The Labour Party won't have it.' I said, 'They will, Tony. If you come down and say you want us to look at it. I don't want you to come down to Wales and tell them what they've got to do; I want you to come down and say, "I want you, please, to have another look at it."' And he agreed. And so fairly shortly afterwards, he came down to meet the Welsh Executive, and it was a big discussion and it focused on proportional representation. I think it was March 1996. We'd had the Labour Party Conference and it voted unanimously against pro-portional representation. So that was the backdrop. I'd done a deal with Donald Dewar, who was Chief Whip at the time. I'd had a discussion with him and basically was, 'I want a commitment to Henry VIII powers to break the log-jam, and I want a commitment to proportional representation,' and by that time he could see the attraction to that, and the deal was, 'Ron: thus far and no further. I will deliver this, if you don't cause any trouble,' and we shook hands on it and that was the deal.

Cynog Dafis: Even though there were Labour MPs who really hated what we stood for, I could get on very well with them. I used to have breakfast regularly at the Welsh Table with Ted Rowlands, and he was very Welsh, and he was warm. His wife particularly was a supporter

PA BRIS NAWR AM FYMRYN O URDDAS?

of campaigns for Welsh-medium education, but Ted was really anti-devolution, quite strongly, and he did what he could to sabotage Ron Davies' attempts. But I never fell out with Ted. Denzil Davies was the other one, I did have a bit of a tiff with Denzil Davies. He had been a supporter of devolution in 1979, but when it came to 1997, he did everything to make things difficult for Ron particularly, and it was personal. Also, during the campaign itself, he issued press statements that were intended to ensure a No vote. Welsh Labour in Westminster is a phenomenon. I think things have changed now.

Dafydd Iwan: There were people who said we shouldn't have anything to do with this, and we're not about devolution, anyway, we're about, not revolution, but self-government and independence, although we didn't use the word independence then. I think the Labour Party has to be commended, and Tony Blair is to be commended, but he and others really believed that devolution would stop the growth of nationalism in Scotland and Wales: that's what they really believed: 'If we give them this, it will stop them in their tracks,' and it didn't quite work out like that.

Peter Hain: Back in 1994 I had attended a Parliament for Wales Conference in Llandrindod Wells. I spoke, as a Welsh Labour MP, so did John Owen Jones from Cardiff and Paul Flynn from Newport and we were all censured and hauled before the Welsh Executive. There was no prospect of the Wales Labour Party embracing a devolution campaign. The hatred, the antagonism, the sectarianism towards Plaid was very deep: they were the 'daffodil Tories' and all these kinds of epithets. I had organised a Valleys Conference in Neath Town Hall, after the general election in September 1992, and invited Adam Price to come to it and speak, and he did most of the work on a report that Kevin Morgan and I organised for the conference. And there was a lot of criticism of me for inviting him, having him involved.

Adam Price: I worked with Kevin Morgan on Rebuilding our Communities, which was a report we were commissioned to produce by Peter Hain as a key document that was going to be published as part of a conference that was held in Neath. It was looking at the whole history of the economic situation in the former coalfield, and we'd had two Valleys Initiatives already by then. I think the sign-off of the report was something like, 'What unites us is far more important and far more enduring than anything that divides us.' Kevin was a member of the Labour Party; I was a member of Plaid. We worked together and he gave me my first job. But the experience of the conference was a slightly bitter one for me, because even though I was the co-author of the report, and even though Kevin is a fantastically humble man and even though I was fresh out of university and I was twenty-two, and he insisted that I was the co-author and should be treated as such, I was no-platformed at the conference, wasn't even given an opportunity to speak, because I was a member of Plaid Cymru.

Peter Hain: So that was the context we were operating in, with no prospect of building, in other words, the consensus that existed in Scotland on a cross-party basis.

Adam Price: Peter Hain did ask me, when he was setting up the pre-1997 group, which was a kind of precursor of Yes for Wales, whether I would join to informally represent Plaid Cymru, and I refused, because I had been so alienated by that experience throughout the 1990s of – it wasn't even non-cooperation, it was worse than that. I also felt that in 1997 probably the best thing that Plaid Cymru could do was to make sure that this was Labour's policy and that Labour sold it. Because that was the mistake in 1979: we ended up delivering their leaflets.

Cynog Dafis: There were people in Plaid Cymru who didn't want to touch the campaign with a bargepole: 'We're not going to do that again. We're not going to let ourselves fall into the 1979 trap again,' the Plaid

MPs' response was, 'It's not 1979. This is different; the atmosphere is different; the opportunity is different.' I remember arguing, 'There's a Yes vote to be gained out there, and we need to do everything necessary in order to get the Yes vote,' and we did.

Eluned Morgan: There was still huge mistrust within the Labour Party towards devolution and Plaid and I think that probably made life quite difficult for some of us in the party, because that mistrust then rubbed off on those of us who'd been campaigning alongside them. What was clear was that Plaid understood that, in most places, it would be better for Labour to be leading the campaign, and they in turn were clear about what they wanted to achieve, which was devolution, and they knew that their best bet was to partner up with us. In some places, it was clear that the Labour Party should be leading the campaign; in other places it should be the Yes for Wales banner leading it.

Cynog Dafis: I was given the job of contacting Peter Hain, to tell him from the Plaid Group that there was hesitancy, not only within Plaid, but within the Plaid Parliamentary Group about coming out unequivocally in favour of the Yes vote. Anyway, I went to see Peter Hain, and I told him what the quandary was that we were in. I wanted him to assure me that Labour was actually seriously going to campaign, and he said, 'Certainly,' and I took him at his word. And Labour did. Hain himself did campaign even though he told me that they were going to produce a series of leaflets during August and early September, but they never appeared.

Ffred Ffransis: The position of Cymdeithas was we would openly come out in favour of political power here in Wales, and we organised a march from Bala down to Cardiff to vote Yes for a National Assembly. We said that, because of the work of the last fifty years, including our contribution in Cymdeithas yr Iaith, we could confidently now say that the language will survive. The question was, what sort of survival?

Was it going to be placed in certain classrooms in Wales, and respected by everybody, or is it going to be a language which is going to be in constant community use and which you can use in every part of everyday life?

Steve Eaves: Everybody had been aware of this pitfall: we might get a free Wales, but then the language goes down the pan because majoritarianism doesn't favour minority languages. I saw the assembly as a potential process of decolonisation. I see Britain's internal colonies as the UK's first colonies. The later colonies took on a more vicious, overtly racist form, but still the prototypes were here with the so-called unionist way.

Cynog Dafis: It's unquestionably the case that the radicalisation and the awareness, the energy that was released by the language movement played a huge part, a huge part, in the political transformation that occurred. And then, on the other hand, people will tell you – and there's truth in it – that the problem with Plaid Cymru is that it's identified with the Welsh language.

Ron Davies: I got turned over by the commission in a meeting where they wheeled in Kim Howells for some reason – he was European spokesman. They got all of the anti-devolution side in and presented me with a draft document which was to go up to Blair's office, and it ruled out everything: it was basically a Wales Council of Labour type of document, so I wasn't having that, and I put out my own blueprint to make sure that I kept Plaid and the Lib Dems on board. It said, right at the end, it was an afterthought, 'Remember that devolution is a process; it's not an event.' And my selling point was once the assembly was there, it would develop its own momentum.

Andrew Davies: I was approached by Ron Davies and Peter Hain in the summer of 1996 to head up the Labour Party's referendum campaign, but the party establishment in Wales tried to block my appointment, so I didn't actually start until 1 April 1997, just as the general election was in full swing. Virtually no organisational preparation for devolution had been carried out. It now seems obvious that Labour would win the '97 general election but at the time, even Blair would say, 'I'm not counting my chickens.' We went up to London as a team and made the pitch and said, 'Look, in 1979, 80 per cent of the people voted against devolution: this is not a foregone conclusion.' And there had been little or no debate within the Labour Party since 1979, because Wales was seen as Neil Kinnock's back yard, his fiefdom. You couldn't talk about it or debate it. There had been no preparatory work whatsoever.

Mari James: I was a vice-chair of the Yes for Wales campaign. The chair was Kevin Morgan, who was the male, big leader of the campaign, who was Labour but not a big Labour activist. My first couple of degrees were in the LSE, doing politics and economics. There was one seminar in which my topic was Marxist theory of surplus value, and my paper was on that, and I used the example of the Davies family art collection that was in the National Museum in Wales. I loved the Blue Lady painting: she was one of my friends when I was little, and one of the things I was taken to see. I was always told that we had a right to own this collection, that it was partly ours, because the work that my grandfathers had done as miners had provided the money to buy these lovely paintings from France, so I used that as an example of surplus value. I'd been working in London and came back to Wales a couple of years before '97. I was quite horrified at the state of the public sector and the state of the machinery of government then in Wales; there were so many lost opportunities. It hadn't moved forward in all sorts of ways.

Kevin Morgan: I felt Labour was not a homogeneous political entity. I was engaging with these new, emerging elements of Welsh Labour, which were younger – there was more of a balance. There were lots more women in this Welsh Labour current; there was a stronger Welsh-speaking element. So in microcosm for me, this was the new Wales in the making. We had good relationships with Plaid Cymru, whereas British Labour was none of those things. I worked closely with Peter Hain, who worked closely with Ron: they were the two key Labour figures in Welsh Labour and they asked me to be the chair of the Yes for Wales campaign in 1997, which was a civic movement rather than a political party.

Mari James: Yes for Wales only got together in the run-up to the general election. Our mantra was 'Devolution's too important to be left to the politicians.' What we actually meant was it's too important to be left to the Labour Party. But we also meant it was too important to be left to the politicians. We set up the campaign during a Tory government, but with the aim of holding the feet to the fire of the Labour Party with their commitment to a referendum. Initially, it was about saying, 'The people of Wales must decide this,' the big buzzword at the time wasn't sovereignty, it was inclusivity: everybody must be included. But what was happening was that, although there was huge enthusiasm, opinion polls tested on how important it was for people to actually go and vote, and on that score we were very low. When asked about devolution, people replied, 'Yeah, yeah, great. We want Welsh power. We want to make decisions for ourselves!' But they weren't actually going to go out to vote.

Kevin Morgan: I was hugely aware of the opposition from the old guard in local government, many of them totally opposed to devolution, because they saw it as a threat, as a disruption of the status quo, which they were quite happy with. It was absolutely shocking to me how small they thought. I had many a debate with those guys – and they were all guys, of course, at that time – and I was very aware of other oppositional forces. We had to fight like hell to get devolution on the agenda and, compared to Scotland, we couldn't have been more different, because we were trying to smuggle in a new parliament, in effect.

Eluned Morgan: Peter Hain approached me and asked me to become involved in it. I'm very aware I ticked lots of boxes. I was young; I was a woman; I represented Mid- and West Wales in the European Parliament; so you kind of ticked off three-quarters of Wales just by having me on any committee and obviously I spoke Welsh. All of those things were helpful, and I was also passionately pro-devolution. I worked out I made about fifty-five speeches to promote devolution across Wales during that time.

Peter Hain: I don't know that the Welsh language was a dividing issue. I think independence was, and certainly in the referendum campaign, devolution being a stalking horse to independence was very damaging for us. There was no question that the fear of nationalism was very real. It was nationalism in the sense of separatism, not nationalism in the sense of patriotism or pride in your own nation and your own culture, because I think that's common between people who are in Plaid and people who are not. People in Neath who would be solid Labour voters and from mining stock would regard themselves as the fiercest Welsh patriots, but they would be fiercely opposed to separatism. In other words, I don't think the language was the dividing issue in the 1997 referendum; I think it was separatism and independence.

Cynog Dafis: I'm a huge admirer of Ron Davies. I think he's a heroic figure, the painstaking incremental process by which he moved Labour in the direction of supporting devolution, that was no joke, bearing in mind that they were clever people who did everything they could to undermine him. I think his assiduousness and persistence in doing that, his patience and political skills in doing that were astounding. He wasn't averse to making threats, in a nice voice; I think he's a key figure, and the fact then that eventually Labour did lead the devolution campaign, that's down to him.

Dafydd Iwan: We liked Ron Davies and I remember marching with him on a peace march in Cardiff. There were so many things in common, and we knew he believed in a government for Wales and it was often said it doesn't really matter which party delivers as long as we get the instruments of government in our own hands in Wales. If we had to thank the Labour Party for it in the end, it doesn't make any difference. But, of course, the Labour Party had a knack of disappointing us, quite regularly. It's the old story of Lloyd George; once you get into the realm of British politics, self-government for Wales is always a secondary issue and always gets pushed to the side, and the only way to get out of that is to have a definite split between the Labour Party in Wales and the Labour Party in London.

Andrew Davies: Originally, the policy was that if Labour won the general election under Blair, they would automatically legislate for devolution, but Blair started to change his mind – I'm never quite sure why; it's probably more to do with what was happening in Scotland, because Wales never figures. The UK parties couldn't give a toss about Wales; it's seen as a backwater, not really influential. Ever since I was involved with politics as a regional official, I always used to say, in Wales we tended to knock on the door, whereas in Scotland they usually tried to knock the door down. The difference in political cultures in Scotland and Wales was stark and reflected in what I've always described as the difference between Billy Connolly and Max Boyce.

Peter Hain: For Tony Blair, constitutional reform was always secondary, whether that was devolution or whether it was House of Lords reform. His focus was economic success and social reform and social justice; that was his focus. Tony thought that's where the votes

467

were, and he was right about that. There are not many votes in getting rid of hereditary peers or in Freedom of Information Acts.

In May 1997 New Labour won a historic landslide victory gaining a 179-seat majority, the biggest held by any government since 1935. The election was also notable for the success of the Liberal Democrats, who won 46 seats. In its manifesto Labour had included a commitment to hold two separate referendums to address the subject of devolution in Scotland and Wales. It stated:

> *The United Kingdom is a partnership enriched by distinct national identities and traditions. Scotland has its own systems of education, law and local government. Wales has its language and cultural traditions. We will meet the demand for decentralisation of power to Scotland and Wales, once established in referendums.*
>
> *As soon as possible after the election, we will enact legislation to allow the people of Scotland and Wales to vote in separate referendums on our proposals, which will be set out in White Papers. These referendums will take place not later than the autumn of 1997. A simple majority of those voting in each referendum will be the majority required. Popular endorsement will strengthen the legitimacy of our proposals and speed their passage through parliament.*

In July of that year, having entered government three months earlier in the Labour landslide victory, the Secretary of State for Wales, Ron Davies, published the government's devolution proposals in the White Paper 'A Voice for Wales'. Davies then acted as one of the figureheads of the 'Yes for Wales' campaign, which would continually encounter opposition from within the Labour Party.

Peter Hain: I felt very much when I got to Parliament that in Wales, we were being absolutely hammered by the Tories and John Redwood epitomised it. And [the response to that] was manifested in the 1997 election when not a single Tory was elected in Wales.

Andrew Davies: There had been a significant number of Tory MPs. In '79 and '83 the Tories had had quite a considerable vote and a number of MPs, but by '97 they didn't have any.

Jane Davidson: I think the conventional wisdom is that Thatcherism moved a section of the Labour Party in Wales, between the two referendums, between 1979 and 1997, to be more in favour of devolution because they began to see it as a bulwark against more Thatcherism.

Eluned Morgan: If you look at what happened between '79 and '97, what happened was Thatcherism. And for the eleven years before '97, every single Secretary of State for Wales had represented an English constituency. There was a sense that we were almost being reigned over by a foreign power; it was almost like the gift that kept giving, things like John Redwood giving a hundred million pounds of Welsh funding back to England. It was those kind of things that made people think, 'Look, we've got nothing to lose here, because these people are not standing up for us and not representing us.' It was that sense of hopelessness and that anything might be better than this.

Jane Davidson: I think the difference between 1979 and 1997 was the increasing prevalence of poverty in Wales, driven by the actions of the Conservative governments, which meant the appetite for devolution, or for more powers to Wales, and more appetite for people to represent Wales who understood the issues of Wales in a context where they could do something about it, was slowly climbing up. Then of course when people want to portray the other side of the argument negatively, they use slogans and that's where the phrase 'Jobs for the Boys' came in. Certainly, you could legitimately say that in Wales at that point in time, it would be jobs for the boys, because if there were any women, they weren't really allowed in. Until 1997 there had only ever been four women MPs in the history of Wales. Four.

Eluned Morgan: Women were acceptable, but women in positions of power were almost unheard of. I was the fifth woman in the history of Wales to be elected to a full-time political position, as Member of the European Parliament for Mid- and West Wales, that was in 1994. I mean, this is very late in terms of societal changes. We were a long way behind what was going on elsewhere in terms of gender politics and continued to be a long way behind until we got devolution onto a platform.

Mari James: We were able to take advantage of the fact the referendum was at the beginning of a change of government, because the '79 referendum was at the tired end of the Callaghan government, and whatever the question had been then, whatever the background, you turned against it. You needed to move on and you needed to change.

Peter Hain: When we arrived in government, on our first day, there was a thick briefing note on the draft for a devolution bill, so the civil servants had done their preparatory work on the basis of what the Labour Party's policy was, quite diligently and I think quite enthusiastically. I think the problem always is that Wales came second-best to Scotland in Whitehall. In terms of all the Whitehall departments, the way the Cabinet worked, from the leadership down, Scotland came first and Wales came second and I felt that all the way through on everything, and continuously tried to resist it. The original John Smith vision of devolution was not something that registered in the Welsh Office. I think it was more that we were in second draw, second position; Scotland was always in pole position.

Andrew Davies: In Scotland, they had devised the Constitutional Convention, there was a vibrancy to that debate about all these issues, whereas in Wales there was no debate.

Mari James: For quite some time there was not an official Plaid vote to support the Yes campaign, because there was still a reluctance within Plaid to trust Labour, and also a slight concern that we might be in the Labour Party's pocket. There were individuals in Plaid who were working with us, who were delivering leaflets for us, who were going out on the streets with us but that was their own decision, and then at a Plaid conference in Aberystwyth there was a vote there on whether they should support the Yes campaign. That vote was lost, and that was quite a substantial step back. I think that was quite important for Plaid because they weren't being a pushover. A White Paper was being put together so that the vote was on an actual package of measures; it wasn't just saying, 'Yeah, we want some kind of parliament.' And a lot of that was being done at Westminster level.

Ron Davies: For me, the odds were shortening all the time. All I had to do was get this legislation for an assembly across the line. We had a referendum to fight on a far less ambitious plan than I had wanted but the opposition was a handful of Labour dissidents and a pretty disorganised Tory Party.

Andrew Davies: After the general election we made the case to the UK Labour Party for help. The party had thrown virtually the kitchen sink at winning in '97, so there wasn't much money in the bank. What they did commit to was to conduct some focus groups, and those were done by Philip Gould, Blair's polling guru. I was asked, and this shows the level of paranoia in the party, by one of my Millbank Party HQ colleagues to keep a close eye on Philip Gould, to make sure that the feedback he gave was accurate, because he was considered to be too close to Blair and not Millbank. The people in the focus groups were recruited on the basis that they were Labour voters. That came back to the landslide victory in the election, and that was the strategy: if you could get all those who voted Labour in the general election to vote 'Yes', you're home: 'Well, you voted for Tony in the general election, vote for this.' There were two focus groups. There was a male and female group in Maesteg one evening and two the following day in Wrexham. There were ten people roughly, ten men and ten women divided into separate groups in Maesteg, and at the end of the two sessions Philip Gould was deeply depressed. He was saying, 'They don't want it.' He was going round and round the room, saying, 'They don't want it; they just don't want it.'

Philip stayed that night in the Marriott hotel in Swansea – and given what had happened in Maesteg there should be a plaque in the Marriott in Swansea for him! I picked him up from the hotel the next day to drive him up to Wrexham, where the same process was to happen. And he said, 'Do you know what? What I picked up last night was this incredible lack of confidence of people in themselves, their communities and the future.' He said, 'What do you think about this as a campaign slogan: "Wales deserves a voice?"' I said, 'I think that's really powerful,' and it was a variation on that that was ultimately used, both for the 1997 devolution White Paper 'A Voice for Wales' and the 1997 referendum campaign.

Kim Howells: Of course, we had to go round the country and convince people this was now all a good idea. My wife Eirlys even now says to me, if I start fulminating about something that's coming out of the Assembly, 'Don't come out with that stuff! At least I voted against it, unlike you: even in the privacy of a bloody voting booth, you didn't vote against it!'

Peter Hain: I don't think I was really aware how big a change of opinion was needed until I was knocking on doors in the Valleys. I think where the opinion had swung was the Thatcher government, the closure of the mines, the feeling that Wales had been absolutely screwed by the Tories, and that that opened up traditional Labour anti-devolution, anti-national, anti-independence, which was all seen in the same box, to saying, 'Well, hang on, we need to have some control over our own lives, because the Tories are otherwise going to destroy us.' There was a swing, but if you're asking me, frankly, did I realise how steep the mountain was, no, I didn't, until I started knocking on doors. And no criticism of Ron, but he wasn't knocking on doors in the way that I was.

Kim Howells: I don't remember knocking on any doors; I remember going to address public meetings and speaking to branches, when the hell would anybody have had time to go knocking doors for that?

Siôn Jobbins: I remember thinking it was very lucky that there was peace in Northern Ireland and the final vote was so close that every little thing made a difference. Also, the idea of Wales as a small nation in Europe made sense then, because Europe was popular, people were starting to travel beyond Spain and small countries like Latvia came into people's awareness. I don't think your average voter in Ebbw Vale or Wrexham thought this, but I think subconsciously it made sense that Wales was part of this continent with lots of other similar countries, and that made a big difference. In 1979 we still had the Cold War, and there was an argument for being part of a big military bloc against the Communists, and you can understand how that percolates down and why would you want to undermine that? That's gone by '97, and I think the fall of the Berlin Wall and Europe are factors in devolution which we don't appreciate. It made it safer to vote Yes.

Kirsti Bohata: I spent quite a few weeks in the month leading up to the vote persuading our carers, of which there were probably five or six or seven individuals, saying to them, 'So, what are you going to vote? What are you going to vote?' and they often replied, 'Oh, I don't know if it's up to us,' and I think I did actually manage to persuade a few of them to vote Yes. There was a real lack of self-confidence: 'Do we want this? Can we do this?' At the time, I felt that using Scotland as an example was almost a negative, because it was like, 'Well, Scotland are over there and they can do it, but we can't,' and it almost worked against Wales saying Yes. My main memory is of persuading everybody I thought could possibly vote Yes to do so. I wasn't campaigning; I wasn't out canvassing, it was just people I came into contact with. I was surprised at how uncertain people who I thought were very Welsh, were mostly Welsh-speakers, working-class in the sense that they were care workers, were really, really not convinced that it was for them.

Dafydd Iwan: Plaid and the SNP came together at certain conferences and I went up there a few times and there was always a speaker from the SNP in our conferences, and a speaker from Plaid in their conferences. I first met Nicola Sturgeon at a demonstration near the nuclear submarine base at Faslane. Gwynfor Evans had started a very strong relationship with Winifred Ewing so there have always been cases of discussing issues together. Historically they've been far more grown-up about it in Scotland. They had been thinking of the constitution in great detail and getting unions and churches together in a forum to discuss it.

Mari James: Ron Davies was determined that this should be all-party, that was the only way in which it could be won, but that there was still opposition within the Labour Party, and they needed to counter that with Plaid coming on board, Plaid telling its voters to vote Yes also. It's strange to think about it now, but the Welsh Liberals were very pro-devolution and thought that the Labour Party were a wash-out and couldn't be trusted, and they had quite a lot of votes to deliver in key parts of the country, the Powys area in particular. It really was every vote would count. We needed all the Welsh Liberal votes to counter some of the Labour No votes.

Kevin Morgan: In Scotland they had think-tanks commissioned, but above all, they had the Constitutional Convention which brought everybody together, and they framed the Scottish Parliament in the terms that I wanted us to frame ours in Wales: they called it a Claim of Right from the Scottish Nation, which was a fittingly grand and capacious way to frame a new democratic order.

Eluned Morgan: We hadn't done any of that groundwork, we were scrabbling around without that support base, which had been built up and that intellectual, robust approach to devolution that had been developed over years and years in Scotland.

Andrew Davies: There was a wide engagement across civil society about what a Scottish Parliament could do, what powers it should have. There was nothing like that at all in Wales, for partly political, partly institutional reasons. There was no preparation, no widespread debate. Nothing.

Leanne Wood: Labour had just won the election in the May, and then we were having the referendum by the September of the same year, so we'd only had that window from July to mid-September. And I can't remember when Ron Davies produced the white paper, but it was so weak, it was so disappointing. There was a conference in Cardiff, that would have been in the July, called Socialists Say Yes, and it was an attempt to bring people on the Welsh wing of Labour with Plaid and the Communists and the Socialist Workers Party and Socialist Party and Arthur Scargill's outfit, whatever they were called at the time, I think the Socialist Labour Party, together.

There were lots of different sects in the room, probably about 200 people there, but we managed to pull together a motion of what we wanted to see our new assembly look like, and it included things like guaranteed gender balance, about this assembly being able to decide its own powers, so it was the self-determination principle. There were a few things included to try and ensure that it was properly representative, that wages should be the median worker's wage, that kind of thing. It was a good contribution to the overall campaign, because what we wanted to avoid was some of those old left sects going off and running a campaign against the assembly campaign, so the purpose of it was trying to say, 'The Left position is this,' and it worked. But they were so far ahead of us in Scotland.

Kevin Morgan: We argued that devolution was essential to maintain the fabric of the United Kingdom as well as promote a democratic Wales: they were two sides of the same coin. Critics would use the slippery slope argument, that devolution will lead to independence. And I personally would always say – because I didn't have to speak for a party – that may be true. But if it works, we will have the kind of devolution we want, and we shouldn't be fearful of novelty; we should embrace it and have the self-confidence to make it work.

Mari James: We tried to make the campaign look like what we wanted Wales to look like afterwards, and instead of pursuing this national gift we have for setting up committees we decided that this was going to be a single-issue, task-and-finish group, and task-and-finish groups have gone forward into the way in which the new polity in Wales works.

Eluned Morgan: I don't think any of us knew which way the vote was going to go. You can get wrapped up in your own campaign and your own propaganda and get carried away with the enthusiasm of the people around you. I don't know to what extent that was being felt on the streets of Ely, that buzz wasn't there. In West Wales, certainly there was a slightly different atmosphere, but all of that was very predictable. In the areas where there was a high proportion of Welsh-speakers, there was a direct correlation between Welsh-speakers and people who supported devolution.

Cynog Dafis: In Plaid we played what I think was a canny game. We held off publicly from supporting Labour's proposals until the end of July and said at that time that Labour's proposals were inadequate, that we wanted legislative powers – we wanted the Scottish model, basically. We did do all of that. But all the time, I was absolutely sure that we needed to move ourselves into a position where we would support a Yes vote, and the mechanism that Dafydd Wigley employed for that was to get a joint statement from the Lib Dems and the Greens and Plaid coming out in favour of the Yes vote, and that was at the end of July. Even before that we had set about the task of setting up a telephone canvassing system by Plaid. But I must tell you, the Yes campaign was pathetic. It was really ineffective. I remember tearing my hair out, trying to get them to publish some leaflets, and they kept on saying, 'We'll do it by next week. We'll do it by next week,' and in the end Plaid Cymru produced its own literature, branding it as Yes Campaign literature. There could have been a bigger Yes vote, had there been a better campaign.

Peter Hain: During the campaign on the ground, I decided to launch a tour of the Valleys. Our first port of call was Pontypridd market, and I was bloody horrified by what I met there. It was really heavy lifting. It was then that I realised that we could lose this. First of all, you had hostility from Plaid members to the model of devolution, and even amongst radicals it was very difficult. I remember talking to Nicky Wire of Manic Street Preachers, and I couldn't get them on board to back the Yes campaign because it was a watered-down version. Now, he's Labour stock, he was not Plaid, but he felt that it was a sell-out and was not the real thing. And there was quite a lot of feeling amongst radical opinion that the model was not good enough, it was not a proper parliament and so forth. And that's fair. But my point was, this is what we've got and we've got to get to base one, and we had the 1979 referendum result, very different from Scotland, a four to one defeat.

Nicky Wire: I remember Peter Hain approaching me backstage after a gig, it was one of those nights that I was so far gone, James had been giving me the eye on stage, so I don't know how much sense I would have made to Peter. We liked him; we just thought the proposals didn't go far enough. But as a band we never wanted to directly support, or be associated with anything at an institutional level, for the same reasons we didn't want to play at the Olympics in the presence of the Queen.

On 31 August 1997 Diana, Princess of Wales, died in a car crash in Paris. The days after her death were characterised by a marked change in the emotional register of much of the population. This took the form of a shared, if not collective grief and a public exhibition of mourning that contradicted Britain's reputation for suppressed emotions. The funeral of Diana was held on 6 September. The viewing figures for its television coverage were estimated to be over thirty million, among the highest audiences ever recorded and a number that in 1997 included over half the population.

Ron Davies: The death of Princess Diana had a palpable impact. Up until then the campaign had been on track and proceeding according to plan, if not spectacularly, or with much enthusiasm for either side. On the Saturday, prior to her death, there was a genuine sense felt by campaigners all over Wales that the momentum was ours. I felt it, too, chatting to the dyed-in-the-wool Labour voters on the street in Bedwas, in my constituency, that we were on course for a good win.

Mari James: I got a call at five o'clock in the morning from the BBC, and I thought, 'Why are they ringing this early for an interview?' and Diana had been killed in the car. We had to be shown to be supportive. Nobody knew how mad the whole country was going to go, but we had to call off the campaign. And the take-over of the country with that peculiar feeling then lost us momentum at a crucial time.

Ron Davies: With the tragedy of her death campaigning came to an immediate halt. Then Britain was in mourning, up until her funeral on 6 September, and whichever way you turned there was the Union flag, the royal family and the outpourings of a bereaved people somehow coming together. Democracy, identity and self-determination, all those themes that were our message, didn't exactly chime. There was that dark shadow of grief, introspection, guilt, uncertainty and of a people huddling together for comfort. On the doorsteps, when campaigning recommenced, it was Diana people wanted to talk about, not devolution. It wasn't possible to measure the impact, but I'd been knocking on these doors for nearly thirty years and I didn't need people to tell me the tide wasn't with us.

Eluned Morgan: Princess Diana died and it was staggering the impact that that had on the campaign. It absolutely came to a halt. I brought somebody over from Catalonia to help us to campaign – we were trying to bring in an international dimension, to demonstrate small nations going it alone – and it was really shocking to try to explain to her what was going on, because the streets were totally deserted.

Cynog Dafis: I thought that there was a Yes vote out there, and then, of course, there was the Lady Di incident and that certainly sabotaged things. There's a long story to be told there, that came as the campaign was beginning to pick up some kind of momentum, and of course it all had to be put on ice, for a week, and this strong sense of identification with Britain and royalty and that kind of thing, that fed into the process, and it didn't help. Bearing that in mind I think we did well to get out the Yes vote that we did.

Tecwyn Vaughan Jones: I remember doing a television interview and I'd been asked what I thought, and I said, 'Well, this is a great opportunity for the country to unite now. We've had a great discussion; we've discussed a lot of relevant things; people are a lot more informed, and I think we can get together and unite.' And then Princess Diana was killed, and that took all the attention away from it.

Peter Hain: Ron's great idea was that he would have an assembly of what he called all the talents. They would come from all walks of life. When I used to have to do this debating schedule with the No campaign, they would always say, 'Look, it'll be jobs for the boys.'

Kevin Morgan: The No campaign was led by Nick Bourne. He was a Conservative and, perhaps ironically, eventually became a Conservative Assembly Member himself, but there was a bunch of them, David Davies the MP from Monmouthshire, I used to debate often with him. They used to say that it'll be jobs for the boys. And this was one of their most powerful arguments, and I used to say what Ron said: 'We are opening this process up to people from the worlds of business, the world of art and entertainment, of public services,' and we did. And all those people came forward. And many of them got on the list of possible AMs. So that part of Ron's vision worked.

Ron Davies: Victory was far from assured. I knew that very well. The opinion polls had shown a constant but not very impressive lead for a Yes vote but I always thought there was a likelihood of the No vote turning out in greater numbers. We hadn't run a very inspiring campaign and the fair balance requirement on the broadcasters meant that however hard we tried to make the running, the No campaign was always given equal air time with their Just Say No! message. The Diana factor also played heavily.

Nicky Wire: For years you had the negative form of nationalism, where you hate something so much it makes you feel that you're right. We'd had that with Thatcher and the Miners' Strike. Then the history of Wales seemed to come into focus at that point in the nineties, everything seemed to connect, through the arts, through the amazing politicians we'd had. Someone like Aneurin Bevan, I'd always been aware of him, my dad had always talked about him, how Nye would have eaten everyone alive. It seemed to be a lot easier all of a sudden, to build a national story around our past.

Michael Sheen: The fact that Nye Bevan, who is hailed as such a hero and is an almost Jungian symbol of energy and renewal and life for the Welsh, was so against anything nationalistic, or devolution, or an independent Wales – I think that's a very difficult thing to get your head round for a lot of people; our id, our life-force, as a Welsh nation, is very split. You can be really into Bevan because of what he did around the NHS, but then if you are interested in independence or more self-government, then Bevan becomes an enemy, an anti-figure. Kinnock was against devolution, but it was put back in the manifesto in '92.

You've got the energy and the connection to the past that lives in the language, but the language itself was sacrificed in order to have some sense of Britishness and to enjoy the fruits of empire, and that deal that was done was the same deal that was done back in the sixteenth century, when, to have representation in Parliament for Wales, we had to give up the language and take on English to be the language of administration. That deal is not that different to the nineteenth-century deal that was, 'Right, again, give up the language, speak English and you can come and be part of Britain and take all that on board.'

That deal has fractured the Welsh, not just as a nation, but in terms of our energy and our flow of energy, to be able to move forward, to be able to gain momentum and make things happen. It's so split off; it's so dissipated. Look at our actual infrastructure – the rail network is such a perfect symbol: the infrastructure was put in to get stuff out of Wales during the Industrial Revolution. Take all your raw materials and get it out, get stuff out to the ports and away, so when we want to move from South Wales to North Wales, even now, you have to go into England to come back. It's madness. That's only one element of how disconnected and fractured we are. If you think of our energies, our natural energies, the same thing was happening.

If I'm part of the natural energy of Wales, then I left Wales. I went out. My pathway didn't lead within Wales; it led me out, and yes, there was a pathway for me and it did lead to success, but it doesn't for everyone necessarily, but for all kinds of reasons it did for me, but it didn't lead to success back in Wales, it led to success out there. In the same way as the coal and coke was taken out, the talent does the same thing as well. All the energy comes out of Wales. It's very difficult, you look at any one element of Welsh history, that kind of life force, and it can't gather the right kind of momentum. At a certain point you go, 'Oh, that's where it falls down, Wales doesn't benefit, someone else benefits from it.'

Kirsti Bohata: Wales is often reactive. Wales defines itself against things that are done to it or said about it; there's always a sense in which Wales is second-best, and it's responding to somebody else. There's that Catatonia song about 'coming second-best is close to ideal', and I'm not sure what they meant by it, but I tended to think of it as a representation of Wales. The fact that England went round the world being bastards, and yes, the Welsh were involved in this as colonialists, but on the other hand, you can like Wales for the fact that it is the underdog, you can rally around it. Devolution in a sense becomes a bit scary, because you'll have to take control and do something about it.

Rhys Ifans: I think something like *Twin Town* really had a part in tipping the vote. It was the first film in many, many decades that in some ways represented and celebrated joyously, with recalcitrance, a working-class community in South Wales. And it had a sense of it being our film. Anything then that felt culturally that Welsh people could gather around and feel was theirs was really crucially important, because there was fuck-all else. There was rugby, of course, but that's it. There was nothing. It was a wasteland; it was a cultural wasteland in terms of places where the different Welsh tribes could gather. I remember screening *Twin Town* at the Aberystwyth Film Festival and hearing several members of the S4C hierarchy being absolutely fucking outraged that Wales was being represented in this way, to the point of being violent, which was music to my ears.

Bedwyr Williams: I was always baffled by the people that found it easier to believe that a resurgent Welsh nationalism, or at least Welsh self-governance, would be worse for them than what a Conservative government gave them. There were intelligent people who thought that.

Kirsti Bohata: There was an energy. Ed Thomas' play *House of America* was first performed in 1988 and is born of the Miners' Strike and of Wales being in the doldrums. The film adaptation came out in 1996 or '97. It's a really grim film, a really grim play, about this inward-looking environment, Wales having nothing to offer, the only way to survive is to get out, and if you stay in, it's a literally incestuous awful space. The film soundtrack has got the energy of that Welsh music scene in the nineties that lifts it and it's an actual half-decent film from Wales. You've got a sense of, 'Oh, look, we might be edging into something credible, something that you don't cringe about,' the awful associated cringiness of Wales being a bit crap, but this wasn't, it was plausible and a bit cool. I do think that that cultural confidence that came with the music, certainly amongst the younger generation, would have been important for winning the devolution vote.

Mari James: In 1997 there was an atmosphere and a culture of change across the board, of which Welsh devolution was one part. The referendum was really about embedding this particular change in a way that you couldn't unpack it if another party came in. And that was very important. The Rubicon was crossed in '97, absolutely no question.

Charlotte Williams: That was certainly true. There was a growing sense of pride, and from beyond language activism, a much more general sense of 'We've got to invest in this country, all of us, and it will have returns.' I certainly thought that, in terms of the articulation of race and racism, if we have more devolved government, then we're going to have more of a say, and we're going to be able to put this much more on the agenda so there was momentum building up from people of colour. A politics of race in Wales was emerging, suggesting an interrogation of what Welshness is and it was timely to think about that if we were going to have greater self-government. But also recognising an attachment to place and the reworking of the history of Wales to demonstrate that Wales has always been multicultural and global.

Kevin Morgan: Without a shadow of a doubt the Yes for Wales campaign was one of the finest things I've ever been involved with. It was open, pluralistic; it was culturally led; it was non-partisan, non-tribal; it was fun to be in. You felt you were part of something bigger than yourself; you felt part of the future rather than the past and that's what was so exciting about it all for me.

Mari James: We had a way of utilising leafleting flash mobs. They used to descend on wherever the nearest shopping centre was. All the cast of *Pobol y Cwm* at the time decided they were going to do something to support the campaign. At the beginning of their rehearsal sessions they would say, 'Right, how many are up for helping the campaign at the end of this?' They'd give us a ring, they'd say, 'OK, we're coming down with fifteen people, or twenty people.' Having that kind of really recognisable media presence was crucial, and I don't know if they ever realised it.

James Dean Bradfield: I was busy trying to reconnect myself with Wales. I was living in London and really wanted to come back, getting fed up of living on that Paddington to Newport train, so I was coming back to Cardiff, seeing friends in Cardiff, spending a lot more time with my mum and dad, going to see Cardiff Blues, sometimes going to Newbridge to see rugby there as well, and realising that I was very, very much more comfortable back in the Valleys and back in Cardiff than I was anywhere else.

It was quite an enthralling campaign in its own way, because the first part of the devolution campaign was quite calm until about a week out, and then it got really feverish and really taut. Up until then there had been some good debates. I remember on the night itself, the vote itself was amazing. It was actually genuinely exciting. You had Glamorgan winning the county cricket championship that year; lots of things coalesced around this period. And Cool Cymru did not bother me a jot. I was quite happy with it. I was like, 'Oh, wow, fucking hell, I'm hearing "Patio Song" by Gorky's all over the fucking radio, how cool is that?' Catatonia, all over the radio. It was great, the 'Phonics, 'Fucking hell, they're going to be big.' It felt like, 'We're living in different times,' and seeing something like Gruff astride a tank in the national papers, it was like, 'God, we're here.' I loved hearing a disc jockey saying: 'We can't play the music from the Super Furry Animals' new single, because it's got an f-word all the way through it.' It was brilliant.

Guto Pryce: 'This is great; it doesn't go far enough.' I can remember us as a band having that conversation about the referendum, but in the end coming to the point that it was better than nothing, and we definitely had to support it. Gruff was on *Newsnight* from City Hall in Cardiff just before the referendum.

Gruff Rhys: I was on *Newsnight* or something similar on the BBC, Huw Edwards was hosting. I think Dafydd Wigley was on the panel as well, with some Tory guy from North Wales and maybe Ron Davies as well. SFA were recording a track called 'Smokin' at Grassroots Studio around the corner. So Gorwel Owen was in town as well.

Ron Davies: On polling day, reports came back that the turnout wasn't going to be great and I sensed from going round my own constituency that we were in front, but without any huge enthusiasm. I went across to the College of Music and Drama after the polls closed where the count was to take place. The mood was fairly subdued and tense. The early results were not encouraging. They came mainly from the smaller authorities, mainly from the most anglicised eastern boundary: Newport, Wrexham, Flintshire, Torfaen. They all voted No and got us off to a bad start, to be followed later by Monmouthshire, Vale of Glamorgan and, much to our disappointment, by Cardiff itself. The mood was sombre to say the least but one of my private office staff had done some rapid number crunching and gave us some hope. Despite the loss in those authorities, the Yes vote was very much greater in those No voting areas than 1979 – and the swing, if uniform across Wales, could get us home. There were more than enough votes from some of the larger councils still to be counted to make up the difference.

Mari James: We knew that the first few results were going to be No votes. There were some crucial ones in the middle of the night, and there were some that we didn't know the exact timing of them coming in. We didn't know Carmarthen was going to be last. During the night, it looked as if it would be a No vote. Some of the London press that were there got bored and said, 'OK, it's a No vote, so it's not a story,' and left. There were also people from Downing Street who were there and who left, because they'd spoken to their boss and said, 'Don't come down tomorrow. Change the plans. They've let us down; don't come over tomorrow; they're going to vote against; it's going to be a No vote; they're voting against Labour.'

I was sitting on the next table when they were having some of this conversation, and I said, 'No, you can't say that at this stage.' There were some votes that were still coming in: we knew Carmarthen would be a massive vote whenever it came in, we knew the Valleys would be massive votes whenever they came in, but they were much bigger than we expected. The majorities in the Valleys were enormous; it was going back to the old days of weighing the votes, but they were weighing the voting on a Welsh parliament. They were 20,000 majorities when we thought, on a good day, it would be ten. The other place that was crucial, and to me the place that told us we were probably going to win, was Powys. Because we'd done these estimates before, and there were 4,000 more Yes votes in Powys than we expected: and that was down to the Liberals.

Eluned Morgan: It was unbelievable; it was an absolute roller-coaster. I remember going over to the Royal College of Music and Drama, and it was very subdued, very quiet, and I guess we all thought that it wasn't going to happen. Then I went over to the Park Hotel, where everyone was getting drunk, people were effectively drowning their sorrows. I think people were not very confident at that point. Then, when the results came through, I remember making calculations the whole time: how much do we need, how much do we need? There was always a possibility that the Carmarthenshire vote could bring in the result that we needed. I remember making the calculation how much we needed, and they called the amount and I just roared. It was quite strange. It took a while for everybody else to make the calculation and understand, and then the whole place erupted – erupted – in a way that I've never seen the like of it before. It was definitely the greatest political moment of my life, from absolute despair to absolute jubilation. You don't often get those moments in politics.

Ron Davies: The last result which came to us was Powys. Events moved quickly, the Returning Officer went through the formalities and delivered the final overall result that we had won by 6,721 votes. It was too close for comfort – but a win was a win. We were on our way to establishing the first ever directly elected assembly, soon to be parliament, of the people of Wales.

For the first time I had the inclination, and the opportunity, to look at the draft victory speech. I was musing to myself that the speech didn't seem very inspirational, but before I really knew it I was on the podium, under the lights, with great cheers, the waving of flags, in front of people who had gone through years of campaigning, and the agonising hours of waiting on this night, for this moment. It was a bit surreal and very emotional. I knew my speech started off, 'Good morning!' I managed to get that out, then a further surge of emotion which I could only hold back by saying, unscripted 'and it IS a very good morning in Wales!' Fortunately, it seemed to catch the moment and became a bit of a byword for the referendum result and much of what followed.

Mari James: I was in the college for most of the night, and I was in the college when the result came through, with all that gang of men holding their arms out and saying, 'It's a good morning in Wales.' The expectation was that Wales would vote Yes, but by a very tiny majority. And actually, that was what happened.

Dafydd Iwan: It was a tremendous night. I was on television for most of it, and then I went down to the Park Hotel and the party was in full swing there: it was a glorious night. And there were people from the Labour Party there as well. For those who believed in Welsh self-government, it was a great night. We realised we had to grab that chance and start the process, and that victory, slim as it was, was the night we will never forget, because we realised we were starting on the journey to freedom.

Andrew Davies: The count was a real roller-coaster of an evening and given I had left a secure job to work in the campaign, on several occasions that evening I assumed I would be unemployed in the morning. For me it was a mixture of relief and elation when the final result was announced. A post-count party had been organised by the

Yes campaign in the Park Hotel in the middle of Cardiff, which was a great contrast from the count, with an almost exultant atmosphere. As a socialist, I always saw devolution as being about the democratisation of decision-making in Wales, not about nation building. Maybe it was the coming down to earth after the count, but I confess I had mixed feelings on hearing the singing in the party. I had never experienced such overt nationalism before, the singing at the Arms Park was very different, and it left me feeling rather uneasy at what emotions we might have released.

Gruff Rhys: We all stayed up all night at my house for the referendum result, after leaving some live TV media party with free booze when the result seemed in the balance. The euphoria at the end of the night was like winning the pools. It was very emotional, I was phoning around all my family at 6 a.m.

Cynog Dafis: I was in the Marine Hotel in Aberystwyth. A group of us had arranged to be together there following the results as they came out, and the same thing happened to us as happened to everybody else: we were down in the depths. But I remember saying to myself, 'Well, what are we going to do next?' I remember I'd got over the disappointment and was beginning to gird my loins for the next stage. I had things to do the next morning, I couldn't get drunk and couldn't really celebrate because I had surgery arranged for nine o'clock the next morning in Tregaron.

Edwina Hart: A lot of alliances were built up in that referendum campaign, like our local group within Swansea. We had Plaid, we had Liberals, Rob Humphreys of the Open University was very active in it and money was put in by the trade unions. And it was those type of things that made us get through without a Constitutional Convention: it was all those people that forgot about their politics. I remember the night we won, I was in Rob Humphreys' house; there were some people celebrating in Cardiff who'd done a damn sight less work than Rob Humphreys or I had done. It was really all those little groups that helped achieve the victory.

Tecwyn Vaughan Jones: I drank half a bottle of whisky, and I remember phoning up people at four o'clock in the morning who were in bed, waking them up to announce what had happened, which didn't make me very popular. I hoped very, very much that the referendum result would change people, people in Cardiff, people in Swansea, to think of themselves more as Welsh, and then we could have a united front. I don't think the referendum was a uniting force, because I think the majority was far too small. If there was a majority of about 70 per cent, it would have felt different, or if Cardiff had voted Yes, if Newport had voted Yes – these are critical cities in Wales.

Mari James: It was a tragedy that Cardiff voted No. Some of the political leadership in Cardiff had always been against devolution and of course the national capital is often slightly out of kilter. We knew that Cardiff was a tussle and we knew that some of the Labour constituency parties in Cardiff weren't actively campaigning. It was a huge disappointment, and it would have been fabulous if Cardiff had voted Yes. But they were wrong, weren't they? They didn't represent the voice of the nation.

Gruff Rhys: I was elated the next day – though Daf was in a foul mood when we all met in the pub near the studio at lunchtime. We sat outside; it was a sunny day but Daf was in a mood because the result was so close and Cardiff had voted No. I've still got the papers from the day – the *Daily Mirror*, who briefly had a Welsh edition, had a full-page dragon on the front cover with a 'Vote YES for Wales' headline on it. The state did pull out all the stops. It felt like a rare window of opportunity.

Eluned Morgan: It was deeply depressing, because Cardiff was obviously going to benefit more than anywhere else. I think probably the language was still a dividing point, even up till '97, and there's a possibility people considered identity an issue. How Welsh are you? Are you more Welsh if you're a Welsh-speaker and from West Wales? You didn't sense any feeling of Welshness on non-rugby days in a place like Ely.

Gwenno Saunders: I was an Irish dancer in *Lord of the Dance* in Las Vegas, I was seventeen. It was like 6 a.m. or something and I was in an apartment, and then the phone goes in the living room and my mother is on the other end shouting 'WAAAAAAHHHHH'. I was like, 'Oh, OK, this is exciting; what's this all about?' It felt like Wales was the centre of the universe for a minute. And that had never happened before in my life; it had been this huge struggle. My childhood memories are about struggle, struggle, marching, campaigning, rain, trying to push for things to change, nothing changing, ever.

On 18 September 1997 Wales voted in favour of the creation of a National Assembly Government for Wales. The winning margin was 6,721 votes, or less than 1 per cent of the overall turnout recorded in an election that had been called, then delivered, in a remarkably short space of time and had reversed the considerable four to one majority against devolution recorded at the 1979 referendum.

The following year the Government of Wales Bill passed through Parliament, and on 31 July 1998 the Government of Wales Act reached the statute book, putting in place the legislation to set up the first ever National Assembly for Wales. That September, Ron Davies defeated Rhodri Morgan to become Labour's candidate for First Secretary of the Assembly.

By the end of the following month Davies had resigned both as Secretary of State for Wales and First Secretary of the Assembly. His decision to step down was made in response to 'an error of judgement' that took place on Clapham Common, London, and had led to him being mugged at knifepoint. At the press conference called to tender his resignation the word 'sorry' could be discerned written in block capitals on Davies' hand. The man who had created the political means by which Wales might achieve a degree of home rule and who had engineered a narrow victory in its favour, one unthinkable a decade or less earlier, would no longer lead the first Welsh Parliament.

Andrew Davies: What struck me was how quickly everything was done. The general election in May, referendum in September, the Government of Wales Act, 1998, and then first elections in May '99. It was extraordinary. Following the referendum victory I was asked by Tom Sawyer, the General Secretary of the UK Labour Party, to design an inclusive candidate-selection process for the Wales Labour Party which would help counter the accusation of 'Jobs for the Boys' or 'Mid Glamorgan on Stilts' and deliver Ron Davies' commitment to an assembly of all the talents. I used equal opportunity processes to design an open and transparent candidate-selection process which we hoped would attract a wide cross-section of talents and help exclude 'the usual suspects'. While not as successful as we had hoped, combined with 'Twinning' to try and ensure gender balance, it nevertheless did represent a big step forward and resulted in an assembly that became the first legislature in the world to achieve equal gender balance.

Mari James: It was very difficult after the victory, there was so much to do, Ron needed to have a break and Ron didn't have a break. He not only got the referendum through, he got the bill through as well and he got the legislation through, and I think that's often overlooked in the history of it. It's said he got the referendum through, but he wasn't the First Minister. But he got the legislation through. I remember doing a BBC interview and it started by saying, 'Now Ron Davies has gone, there won't be a Welsh Assembly any more, nothing will happen now.

Does this mean it's been a waste of time for the last however many years?' This was in the conversation on the phone beforehand. I said, 'What are you talking about? The legislation's all gone through; there is an Act of Parliament in Westminster to set up a Welsh Parliament.' I think people forget how much Ron actually had to deal with, and that he was battling all the way. It would have been fabulous if he'd have stayed on.

Andrew Davies: That's one of the great counterfactuals, isn't it? It would have been very different. It's a tragedy really, because I think devolution would have turned out very differently if Ron had remained leader. I do.

Peter Hain: It was a tragedy, an absolute tragedy, not just for him, but for Wales, actually.

Ron Davies: For me, a strong defence against cynicism and negativity, which I am occasionally prone to, is to reflect that, from a General Election on 1 May 1997, our democracy, served by an independent and professional Civil Service, could put on the Statute Book, by July 1998, an Act of Parliament which revolutionised the way Wales is governed. And it placed in the hands of the Welsh people their own future governance.

Kevin Morgan: We were damn lucky to win the '97 referendum and I really didn't think we would do it in all honesty. Ron wanted to bridge those different traditions in Wales. I always said to him, he reminded me of something out of the *Mabinogion*, because the definition of a leader in the *Mabinogion* is someone who builds bridges, not creates walls, and Ron was a bridge-builder. And so, for all those reasons, he was held in very, very high esteem in the nationalist movement, but not in the British Labour movement. It was a tragedy he had to resign and didn't get to lead the first Assembly. Ron wasn't cynical at all; he was very, very optimistic that creating a new institution was the dawn of a new era, and this could be a more pluralistic Wales.

Eluned Morgan: I don't think devolution would have happened without Ron, the margin was so tight; but more than that, he managed to keep the Valleys MPs on board and walked a tightrope. There was still a lot of scepticism about devolution in a lot of them, and as a Valleys MP himself he managed to keep them on board. I think that his role in history should be recognised.

Huw Stephens: Some of the parents who fought for devolution and who fought for stronger Welsh political infrastructure, saw their children be part of that explosion. For someone like Dr Carl Iwan Clowes, it must have been so thrilling to see on the front page of the *Western Mail*, 'Welsh Assembly opens. Ron Davies to lead' and second page 'Super Furry Animals No 1 in the album charts'. It's not a coincidence.

Carl Iwan Clowes: I was very pleased, in a personal way, when Cian once quoted something that I'd said to the kids as children when they were playing with the fire – we always had a wood fire, and it wasn't the best at going into flames: 'Leave it, leave it, the molecules are agitating and it'll burst into flame shortly,' and sure enough, a flame suddenly comes and it's away. I said, 'That's what's happening in Wales at the moment.' Not a genuine fire, I hope it never comes to that, but I see the molecules agitating in every corner.

Leanne Wood: It was always going to be a big tank to turn around, wasn't it? And we haven't done it yet: we're a long way off. There are problems I still see in the Valleys today when I walk around my communities, and there's little pockets where people have worked together to try and overturn some of that, despite the fact there are also pockets where things have got considerably worse for people.

Adam Price: I think we've struggled with pan-Welshness, and it's pan, it's not a monolith. It's not creating some false unity; Pan is a god that celebrates diversity. Pan-Welshness is about recognising a connection in each other, and also seeing a version of Wales which is a bit like you but three degrees slightly off, and that's wonderful.

Kirsti Bohata: One aspect of what devolution achieved, partly because there were so few powers for it to do anything much else if you look at it cynically, was it gave Wales the power to do work in culture. Things like the 'Library of Wales' and improving support for publishing and the arts. And devolution made Wales visible. Suddenly in these books – 'A Companion to . . .', 'A Guide to . . .', these Cambridge and Oxford histories, Welsh literature in English is now a thing, and it's almost tied exactly to devolution. As soon as you make Wales an actual politically recognisable entity, suddenly, there was a need to take account of it. Devolution has changed how Wales was perceived and how therefore Welsh culture was recognised as actually existing, beyond the Welsh language. Devolution had a massive effect on the identity of Wales through its culture.

Rowan Williams: A definition of Wales, or Welsh identity, frankly, is the language, or rather, what I'd call the language and its echoes. In that *Cambridge History of Welsh Literature*, which is a good collection, they describe R. S. Thomas and Emyr Humphreys as representing the echo of Welsh at several levels. It's not as if Anglophone Wales, whether you're talking about Cardiff or Swansea or Newport, is merely an extension of Gloucestershire. There is an echo, cultural and linguistic, attitudinal, that carries to these places from within the rest of Wales. Thinking back to teenage years in Swansea and regular spells up in the valley with family, I wasn't conscious of the language issue being the great divide. I think the language is very important, and one of the things that happens with the dissolution of communities and solidarities is that type of echo is weaker. And that means also that part of the identity of Wales has to be what it is not to be English, not to be the invading power, not to be the hegemonic power, and while it's never a good idea to say: 'My identity is that I'm not them,' with all kinds of subaltern communities, colonial communities, that is inexorably part of what you have to negotiate through.

Michael Sheen: We are haunted by our past. We live in a Wales that is haunted by itself, the line in the Thomas poem about 'sham ghosts', that's it exactly. This idea of being tied to the past, or not having a present or a future, that kind of stasis, that stuck thing. That idea of being tied to the past is not just one to do with nostalgia, or that sentimental idea of hiraeth; I think it's more concrete than that. We are literally held back by our past, and so there is a need to look at the past, but then to act upon it. There's a theory that a ghost has something that has to be laid to rest for them to be freed, and I think that's very true. The past is not past in Wales, and there's that beautiful line in the Thomas poem about 'The soft consonants, Strange to the ear' and in that he describes that the language itself, the Welsh language, carries something that is alien and familiar at the same time to the Welsh. For him as it is for all us Anglo-Welsh, there was particularly something that calls to you in that language and it speaks of something that is not worked out yet, that is still unresolved, and must be laid to rest, but it can only happen if we act upon it.

EPILOGUE

The National Assembly for Wales was established at great speed with little preparation. Despite the narrowness of the Yes vote victory, the losing side accepted the outcome with good grace, to such an extent that leading members of the No campaign were happy to stand for election and duly took up positions as Assembly Members.

In 1999 the inaugural Assembly administration was a Labour-led minority government which focused its energies on greater accountability of the delivery of public services; in 2000 the Labour Party entered coalition with the Liberal Democrats. For any unreformed devolution sceptic, the argument that the Assembly would be little more than an enhanced version of a managerialist Mid-Glamorgan Labour council seemed irrefutable. The Assembly was a form of government that struggled to assert itself in the popular consciousness.

Despite such perceptions, the Assembly demonstrated a willingness to assert a bold vision of Wales. It was an outlook that befitted an administration that was taking power on the cusp of a new millennium; in 2000 the Assembly passed a policy into statute entitled 'Learning to Live Differently'. It was a radical piece of legislation.

It stated:

> The Assembly takes the view that our current way of living is unsustainable, and that real progress can no longer be gauged by standard measures of economic growth alone.
>
> We believe that economic growth can and must be pursued in ways that are conducive to a sustainable Wales . . . to fulfil its

legal obligations, the principles of sustainable development
must be mainstreamed into the way the Assembly operates.

The new Cardiff government had created an opportunity, to say
nothing of the challenge, to formally embed environmentalism and
community resilience into Welsh society.

The means by which this legislation could be transposed from the
statute book into people's everyday lives remained unclear. Most of the
country's population regrettably remained unaware of the Assembly's
aspirations. The prospect of Wales 'learning to live differently', beyond
its new, Richard Rogers-designed Assembly buildings in Cardiff Bay,
was remote. The Assembly's failure to communicate these principles
was an early example of the institution's inability to explain its function
or to engage with its constituency. It was a failure that inevitably bred
cynicism and disaffection.

The National Assembly for Wales was inaugurated at a time of
substantial investment at the hands of the New Labour government,
now in its second term, during which the public sector witnessed a
rapid growth in job creation. As a result, within five years of being
operational, the Assembly could point to an unemployment rate in
Wales that was lower than the national UK average.

In 2004, two decades after the start of the Miners' Strike, Wales
had finally staged a form of economic recovery, although levels of
economic inactivity in parts of its former coalfields remained high.
These areas received substantial expenditure from European Union
funds. That their benefits, such as new building and road programmes,
skills development and support for business, were rarely appreciated
was further evidence of communication failures by the Assembly and
its civil service, which was regularly accused of taking too piecemeal an
approach to distributing funding that might tangibly impact people's
lives.

The Government of Wales Act of 2006 granted the Assembly law-
making powers and oversight of the foundational policies of economic

development, health and education. It also strengthened the Assembly as an administration, with statutory control of local government, culture, highways, town and country planning and other essential functions of a legislature. These were issues that had to compete with the twin policy responses that followed the financial crisis of 2008 enacted by the Conservative-led government that took office in 2010: austerity and quantitative easing.

At the time of the crisis, Wales's economy had grown reliant on public spending and the cuts administered from Westminster were felt deeply in communities that had experienced intergenerational poverty. One of the principal functions of austerity was the lowering of expectations about what was achievable in society and of normalising the use of emergency measures such as food banks. Throughout the ensuing decade, numerous reports estimated that up to 30 per cent of children in Wales were living in poverty, the highest levels in Britain.

The growing reputation of Wales as a country with a dynamic and rigorous commitment to environmentalism needed to be reconciled with its continuing, endemic poverty and the speculative, property-led economy of South Wales and Cardiff in particular, a city that saw its position in the film and television production industries flourish internationally, even as its relative wealth led to a sense of the capital city decoupling from the rest of Wales. Although property prices in the country remained lower than the national average, the asset inflation that followed the Great Recession as elsewhere further accelerated inequality within Wales. The country became an increasingly popular destination for retirees and for second homes. As the century's second decade was under way, the tourism industry was, for the first time in Wales's history, of greater value than agriculture to its economy. The sector relied on a precarious local workforce employed to clean and prepare rental properties on an ad hoc basis for often absent property owners. These were workers who were mostly unable to purchase homes of their own, in the place of their birth and of their family and communities. Such problems were not unique to Wales, but the enduring impression of a language and culture under threat from aggressive market forces continued to obtain.

By 2015 Labour had been in power for a decade and a half in a series of coalition administrations, a situation that ensured less continuity in government than the party's apparent grip on power suggested. Even as its ability to drive through policy was constantly questioned, the Assembly continued to create bold and imaginative proposals. That year it published the Wellbeing of Future Generations Act, a law that set out to 'improve social, economic, environmental and cultural wellbeing' in Wales. The Act was designated the lead legislative guide to which Welsh ministers and local authorities were accountable for delivery across the country's public sphere, including local health boards. Its statutes proposed seven wellbeing goals: A Prosperous Wales, A Resilient Wales, A More Equal Wales, A Healthier Wales, A Wales of Cohesive Communities, A Wales of Vibrant Culture & Thriving Welsh Language and A Globally Responsible Wales. 'The past', Eric Hobsbawm said, 'is the raw material for nationalism.' In an increasingly ageing society, one in which substantial assets are held mostly by people over sixty-five, to govern in the name of future generations represented a radical idea.

The Wellbeing of Future Generations Act provided (and provides) Wales with a unique means of constructing a unitary sense of belonging. The ultimate idealised version of Wales, the community of communities that had once existed both in the South Wales Coalfield and Y Fro Gymraeg, was now legislated for as a desirable political destiny. The question of how such a policy might be delivered and such a transformation effected remained unanswered and in practice appeared to be circumvented, or ignored, by many organisations bound by the legislation.

An unexpected opportunity for Wales and the Welsh Government, led since 2018 by First Minister Mark Drakeford, to assert itself and act with a renewed sense of purpose arrived during the global pandemic of 2020. The crisis was the first occasion when many in Wales, and certainly many outside the country, including, it was rumoured, members of the recently elected Westminster government, realised that health and education were devolved matters that fell outside the jurisdiction of London. That Wales could operate independently of Westminster was noted both by its own population and a London government animated by patriotism and the attendant manufacturing of divisive grievances. In the Senedd election held in 2021 Labour, whose manifesto included a commitment to radical federalism, were returned to power with their joint largest vote share.

Wales is a nation that continually discovers ways in which to assimilate its own language into its identity. Today it is common to hear Cymraeg spoken when walking through Cardiff, the capital city that previous generations had to travel across in order to receive a Welsh-medium education. In January 2020 the Assembly became officially known as 'Senedd Cymru' or the 'Welsh Parliament'. Its guidance states that the institution will be commonly known as the Senedd in both languages. A Welsh government now has a Welsh name.

For the generations under the age of forty, the battles over Cymraeg that raged in Wales at the end of the twentieth century are largely irrelevant, especially as Welsh history is a subject that features only rarely on any curriculum. A romantic, possibly even sentimental strand of Welsh identity is readily invoked by listing the radical nineteenth-century epiphanies of the Chartist Uprising, the Rebecca Riots and the Merthyr Rising. These moments of social insurrection feel more familiar than the Miners' Strike, the Aberfan disaster, the drowning of Tryweryn or the campaign attributed to Meibion Glyndŵr, though it was in the shadows of these disputes and crises of the recent past that our future as a nation was decided.

The growth in confidence in the language includes an increased popularity in the use of Cymraeg words that cannot be accurately translated into English. It is a vocabulary that provides a sense of national identity, a quality that has proved to be one of the defining, if accidental features of the Senedd's first twenty years of existence.

One of the most popular Cymraeg words is the near-ubiquitous 'hiraeth'. Its over-familiarity has weakened the charm of its approximate meaning, that of a love of place, or an emotional attachment to a location that defies articulation. It is a word now defined in the *Collins English Dictionary* and suitable for appropriation by the many indigenous food and drink companies that have been a hallmark of Welsh success and Welsh confidence in the twenty-first century.

Another word in this untranslatable lexicon is 'hwyl'. A prosaic definition would locate the word as a Cymraeg equivalent to the Irish '*craic*', or the French '*joie de vivre*'. A richer interpretation might include words such as 'passion', 'fervour' or 'spirit'. Certainly, the cadences of many Nonconformist preachers and those whose oratorial style they influenced, such as Nye Bevan, could be described as communicating with great hwyl.

The origins of the word lie in a much older sense: 'hwyl' is the sail of a ship, the means of steering a course. Even in the face of objections to devolution from Westminster, Wales has rarely been better placed to chart a route through any turbulence that threatens the country's stability. It remains, however, a nation that appears continually to require a renewed sense of self-confidence and self-knowledge from the representatives charged with its governance, to say nothing of the need for a deeper sense of empathy for the population in whose name those elected seek to govern. The ideal of a community of communities is more simply expressed in one word: 'people'. And it is the people of Wales who not only understand but define the true meaning of the word 'hwyl'.

DIOLCHIADAU /
ACKNOWLEDGEMENTS

I am indebted to the individuals whose voices are present within these pages. This is their history.

*

My enduring and heartfelt thanks to my editor, Alexa von Hirschberg and to my agent, Jonny Geller.

And my deep gratitude to Jesse Ingham, Liz Dexter, Robin Turner, John Cale, Risé Cale, Eden Myfanwy Cale, Jack Levinson, Theodore Cale Levinson, Nita Scott, Ben Thompson, Paul Hawkins, Matt Jarrett, Rhian Jones, Rob Jones, Harriet Hand, Jon Heslop, Bec Goss, James Lynch, Sian Tucker, Dai Crab, Rebecca Spooner, Gavin Johnson, Richard Thomas, Simon Wright, Maryann Wright, Dai Davies, Jeremy Deller, Jon Savage, Emma Warren, Owen Hatherley, Terence Dimmick, Emyr Williams, Steve Humphries, Garmon Gruffudd, David Price, Anywyn Price, Donald Sommerville, Anne Owen, Catryn Ramasut, Mo Hafeez, Jo Ward, Andrew Walters, Cate Timothy, Huw Evans, John Grindrod, Lauren Nicoll, Gruffud ab Arwel, and Dan Papps.

Extract from 'Welsh Landscape', by R. S. Thomas from *Collected Poems (1945–1990)*, first published in Great Britain in 1993 by J. M. Dent, The Orion Publishing Group. Copyright © 1993 R. S. Thomas; printed by kind permission.

Extract from *Prison Letters*, by John Jenkins, published by Y Lolfa, printed by kind permission.

Quotes by Mansel Aylward, Marilyn Brown, Jeff Edwards, Bob Griffiths, Len Haggett, Calvin Hodgkinson, Hettie Taylor, Alan Thomas, Bernard Thomas and Karen Thomas are from *Surviving Aberfan: The People's Story* by Sue Elliott, Steve Humphries and Bevan Jones, published by Grosvenor House, printed by kind permission.

Extract from and translation of 'Cân i Gymry', by David R. Edwards and Rhiannon Matthews, © Cyhoeddiadau Ankst, printed by kind permission.

In Memoriam:

Jan Morris (1926–2020)
Hywel Francis (1946–2021)
David R. Edwards (1964–2021)
Dawn Foster (1986–2021)

✻

MYNEGAI / INDEX

Names of Voices in the book are shown in **bold**. The page numbers on which each Voice is quoted are listed under the subheading 'Voice'; where the page numbers are numerous, the subheading 'Voice (chapters)' directs you to the first page of each chapter in which the Voice is quoted.

Labour Party in 120, 122, 408–9, 411–12, 422; local government reorganisation by the Conservatives 422–3
Lower Swansea Valley Project 115, 118–19
lung conditions 15, 86–7, 100, 144

Mabinogion (Welsh myths and legends) 153, 493
MacGregor, Ian 264, 287
Machynlleth, Powys 171, 172–3 *see also* Centre for Alternative Technology (CAT)
Maerdy Colliery: amenities 85; chairpersons 88–9; disaster (1885) 371; Miners' Strike (1984) 289, 316, 321, 322–3, 328–9; working conditions 87
Maerdy, Rhondda 259–60, 371, 385–6
Maesteg, Bridgend 260, 281; St John's Colliery 125–6, 263, 267, 280, 288–9, 302, 313, 321
Man (band) 222–3
Manic Street Preachers (band): Brit Awards success 443–4, 449; celebrate being Welsh 444–5, 448–9; continue after Richey Edwards' disappearance 444; English language use 444; gigs and tours 433, 434–5, 436, 445, 478; identity and sound 432–3, 434; influence of 432, 444–5; influences 396–7, 432–3; recordings 443, 448–9; Welsh clichés about 434–6 *see also* Bradfield, James Dean; Edwards, Richard James 'Richey' (Richey Manic); Moore, Sean; Wire, Nicky
Manpower Services Commission 381, 390; Youth Training Scheme (YTS) 381, 383–5
manufacturing industries, loss to foreign markets 258, 418–19 *see also* factories
Margam Steel Works 288–9, 299–301, 314, 375 *see also* Port Talbot Steel Works
Marston, Tom: in Aberfan disaster rescue effort 108; attends WEA classes 98–9; management style 92–3; works in steel industry 264; Voice 92–3, 98–9, 108, 116–17, 264, 269, 310–11
McGahey, Mick 273–4
medical care *see* health and medical care

Meibion Glyndŵr (Sons of Glyndŵr): arson of empty properties 209–10, 211–12, 214, 215, 217, 219–20, 221–2, 231, 233; attacks on other properties 222, 223–4; Colour Party 227–8; end of campaign 230–1; members 211, 212, 213, 217, 223–4, 228, 233; public attitudes towards 213, 214, 218, 222, 231; satirised by *Not the Nine O'Clock News* 231; slogan and symbol 213, 214
mental health: asylums 21, 387; suicide 388
Mental Health Act 1983 381
Merthyr Tydfil 40, 89, 99; Hoover factory 120, 373
Merthyr Vale Colliery 101 *see also* Aberfan disaster
metal workers 380
Methodism 17, 19–20 *see also* Chapel and Chapel tradition(s)
Mettoy factory, Swansea 120
Militant (group) 269, 270
Militant (magazine) 270
military appropriation of rural Wales 9–10
milk quotas 297
Millington, Mary: arrest and prison sentence 409–10; in Côr Cochion 409–10; at Greenham Common 245–6, 249, 251, 409; learns Welsh and moves to Wales 251; Voice 245–6, 249, 251, 409–10
Millward, Tedi 31, 32, 50
Miners' Federation 6
Miners' Strike (1984): Army involvement 302, 322; attacks on lorries 318; Cymdeithas yr Iaith support 293–4, 296–7, 330, 335–6, 339; end of strike 315, 316–17, 320–3, 328–9; fatalities 318, 319; Flying Pickets concert 316; government response 278, 281, 287, 312, 316, 317–18, 322; holidays for miners' children 294, 296, 297; impact on mining communities 322, 324, 325, 372; impact on wider communities 331, 333; lack of Labour support 278–9, 281, 282, 283, 296; lack of national ballot 272, 277–8, 279–80, 281, 282; lack of TUC support 278–9, 283–4; media narrative